CLASSICS AND CONTEMPORARY THOUGHT

Edited by Thomas Habinek

Horace and the
Gift Economy
of Patronage

*The publisher gratefully acknowledges
the generous contribution to this book
provided by Joan Palevsky.*

Horace and the Gift Economy of Patronage

Phebe Lowell Bowditch

UNIVERSITY OF CALIFORNIA PRESS
Berkeley   Los Angeles   London

University of California Press
Berkeley and Los Angeles, California

University of California Press, Ltd.
London, England

Library of Congress Cataloging-in-Publication Data

Bowditch, Phebe Lowell, 1961–
Horace and the gift economy of patronage / by Phebe Lowell Bowditch.
    p.   cm. — (Classics and contemporary thought ; 7)
Includes bibliographical references and index.
ISBN 0-520-22601-1 (cloth : alk. paper).—ISBN 0-520-22603-8 (pbk. : alk. paper).
1. Horace—Knowledge—Economics.   2. Authors and patrons—Rome—History.   3.
Authors and patrons in literature.   4. Rome—Social life and customs.   5. Rome—
Economic conditions.   6. Patron and client—Rome.   7. Gifts in literature.   8. Gifts
(Roman law).   I . Title. II. Series.
PA6411.B66   2001
874'.01—dc21   00-024673
                                                                                    CIP

Manufactured in the United States of America
9 8 7 6 5 4 3 2 1 0

10 9 8 7 6 5 4 3 2 1

The paper used in this publication meets the minimum requirements of ANSI / NISO Z39
0.48-1992(R 1997) (Permanence of Paper). ∞

For Andrew

CONTENTS

ACKNOWLEDGMENTS

I have many people to thank for their support during the evolution of this book, whose ideas saw their initial and rudimentary development as a Ph.D. thesis. The members of my Ph.D. committee, Albert Cook, Michael Putnam, and Martha Nussbaum, gave me valuable critical response at different stages of that work, bringing a coolheaded sobriety and intellectual rigor to the various drafts they read. I am very grateful to them—feeling *gratia* in all its most positive ways. I regret that Albert Cook's death in 1998 prevents his seeing the final results of his unstinting encouragement, which continued long after the completion of my thesis in 1992. Florence Verducci, as my professor during undergraduate years at Berkeley, inspired my great respect for and continuing fascination with Horace.

At the University of Oregon, Mary Jaeger went above and beyond the call of collegial duty by reading through the entire book manuscript with an eye for error, contradiction, and inconsistency that was greatly appreciated. Very many thanks are owed to Thomas Habinek for his initial interest in and support throughout the project. The shrewd observations of the three readers for the University of California Press have greatly improved the final form of the book. The criticisms of Peter White, who revealed his identity as a reader, were much appreciated, particularly given my divergent approach to patronage. Kate Toll, acquisitions editor, provided consistently cheerful and responsive support throughout the entire review process, and I benefited from Seth Schein's generous comments at the end. Cindy Fulton, Jacqueline Volin, and Alice Falk, who copyedited the manuscript, were very helpful during the final phase of production. I would also like to thank those who read individual chapters at various stages: Helen Deutsch, John Nicols, Karen Ford, and Steven Shankman have all given me valuable commentary. I am similarly grateful to the

Oregon Humanities Center for providing me with a quarter off in which I was able to make substantive headway on the thorough transformation of my dissertation into the present book. Dieter Manderscheid and Jason Herman were indefatigable research assistants.

Sections of an article, "The Horatian Poetics of Ezra Pound and Robert Pinsky," *Classical World* 89.6 (1996): 451–77, are reprinted with the permission of Matthew Santirocco, the journal's editor, whose support of the book project has always been forthright.

The patience and caring of my friends and family throughout this work's production is of course what saw me through it, in particular Patricia Stewart, Meredith Sibley, Phebe Bowditch, and Andrew Bourne Sibley, my husband, who has borne with all the tribulations of the writing process right there along with me. To him I dedicate this book.

NOTE ON TRANSLATION

My policy on translation throughout the book is as follows: If I translate
fairly literally, I put quotation marks around the English and then usually
give the Latin either in the body of my text or in a footnote. If I paraphrase
or adduce the Latin as evidence for a statement that is not an exact trans-
lation but rather a conclusion drawn from the implications of the Latin,
then I simply include the Latin in parentheses and do not place my state-
ment in quotation marks.

All translations of poetry are my own: where necessary, grace has been
sacrificed to accuracy. As a Latin text for Horace, I use the Teubner edition,
Shackleton Bailey 1985, unless otherwise noted. I use the Oxford Classical
Texts for citations of Vergil and Lucretius. For the prose works of Cicero,
Seneca, and Suetonius, I generally use the translations of the Loeb editions
unless otherwise noted.

Introduction

GLADIATORIAL IMAGERY:
THE RHETORIC OF EXPENDITURE

"The gladiator: crude, loathsome, doomed, lost (*importunus, obscaenus, damnatus, perditus*) was, throughout the Roman tradition, a man utterly debased by fortune, a slave, a man altogether without worth and dignity (*dignitas*), almost without humanity" (Barton 1993, 12). No wonder that so many scholars of Horace, confronted with his image as a retired gladiator at the beginning of *Epistles* 1.1, either make little comment or smile wryly at the irony of the speaker's rhetoric and dismiss the trope as humorously extreme in its depiction of patronal relations as well as public performance.[1] Tired of beseeching the crowd, already presented with the wooden foil symbolizing discharge, the speaker complains that Maecenas, his patron, wishes to confine him again to his old school and sport (*quaeris / . . . antiquo me includere ludo*).[2] Such highly figurative language has been read—and rightly, to a degree—as ironic metaphor: in complying with a patron, Horace was certainly no slave; and though perhaps his odes were not as well received as he might have wished, he never presumed to please the Roman masses. Thus, the opening of the poem is generally considered an elaborate conceit to justify the poet's decision

---

1. Cf. Kiessling and Heinze 1960, ad loc., on the technical aspects of the image; G. Williams 1968, 4: "humor and parody"; Kilpatrick 1986, 2: "ironic comparisons." Acknowledging the darker side of the image, Johnson (1993, 12) pinpoints the problem: "Horace is not like the gladiator Veianius, and writing poetry is not like being condemned to hack one's way out of the theater of death."

2. For a full quotation of the passage, see chapter 4.

to abandon lyric and embark instead on the new genre of the verse epistle.[3]

But what if this figurative image of a *ludus* (gladiatorial school) and the shows (*munera*) for which such training prepared, compounded by the gladiatorial reference at the end of *Epistles* 1.19, were given a more "literal" reading—one that privileges the terms of the metaphor rather than its referent—and were placed within the context of a larger cultural practice?[4] What if these images were understood not only as ironic figures for Horace's compromised freedom but also within the context of imperial patronage as a form of public expenditure dependent on spectacle? As Paul Veyne remarks, "'Giving gladiators' became the best way to make oneself popular," so that although the practice began as a funeral *largesse,* during the late Republic and early Empire it turned into *euergesia* "pure and simple," a form of electoral corruption (1990, 222).[5] Both Suetonius and Augustus himself record the emperor's lavish spending on such gladiatorial games, mock sea battles (*naumachiae*), athletic competitions, beast hunts, and theatrical performances (Augustus, *Res Gestae* 22–23; Suet. *Aug.* 43). Although originally brokered through Maecenas as a middleman, might not the regime's expenditure on Horace as a public poet be reflected in this image of a *munus,* "gladiatorial display," ultimately directed at a public, however difficult to define, whose loyalty and adherence the emperor desired? That is, perhaps we should view the poetic rhetoric of Horace's vision of patronal relations here as embedded in a greater cultural practice of expenditure that also functions rhetorically in its aim to control and to persuade.[6]

Over the past few decades it has become increasingly clear in literary studies that a text can be interpreted as neither an isolated document nor a simple reflection of its historical backdrop. Socioeconomic practices account for the conditions of any work's production as well as for many of the "symbol systems" by which a text communicates meaning to an audience. This is particularly true for Augustan literary patronage: social relations of exchange provided more than a context for the production of

---

3. Becker (1963, 38) makes no comment on the the gladiatorial imagery and merely claims that in contrast to philosophy, "das Dichten . . . als bloßes Spiel und Getändel erscheint." This figurative reading is eased by the play on *ludus,* a word also used to connote poetry. Hence, even critics who emphasize the seriousness beneath the irony subordinate the metaphor—the gladiatorial imagery—to its referent, Horace's generic choice. See Macleod 1983, 286, and Hirth 1985, 114–15. I discuss this image further in chapter 4.

4. On such a "literal" reading, see de Man 1979a, 3–19; Dunn 1995, 165–69; Hinds 1998, 10–16. This reading involves taking the rhetorical figure seriously so that, in the case of metaphor, the terms of the vehicle as a mode of persuasion are privileged over the tenor or referent.

5. On gladiators, see too chapter 4, nn. 24 and 25.

6. See Dunn 1995, 171, for such an approach to the pronouns of lyric.

verse; they also informed a shared system of rhetorical figures through which poets negotiated both their own interests and those of their varied audiences. My study of Horace explores these rhetorical negotiations but argues that they are embedded within, and partly determined by, material and discursive practices outside of the literary text. The triangular relationship of poet, patron, and "public" audience must be interpreted in the social context of ancient Rome, where the exchange of goods and services provided for the ideological cohesion of a community. Poetry, as one such good exchanged, not only distinguishes a benefactor, providing the important boons of status and immortality, but it also speaks to a wider audience and, as Horace's gladiatorial image suggests, constitutes a form of gift or public *munus* to the community at large. The language of *munera*—"gifts," "games," "funereal offerings," or "political office," to name the major definitions—along with related socioeconomic diction, appears in several contexts in Horace's poems. Focusing on the trajectory of Horace's work during the early years of the Augustan Principate (31–12 B.C.E.), I argue that the cultural practices behind such contexts—social benefaction, political euergetism, and religious sacrifice—inform the relationship between a discourse of sacrificial expiation in Horace's *Odes* and the rhetorical gestures of autonomy displayed by the speaker of the *Epistles*.

Drawing on scholarship in cultural anthropology on gift economies, I interrogate in several Horatian poems the rhetoric that suggests the following related concepts. First, the public service (or *munus*) that the poet performs by writing his political poems constitutes a form of sacrificial expenditure, and ultimately a sacrifice of self, that the philosophically oriented first book of *Epistles* reclaims: as a priest of the Muses, or *sacerdos Musarum,* Horace's political poems provide the "gift" of purification for a people corrupted by the civil wars. Second, though many of the poems serve to reinforce a certain ideology of voluntarism in Augustan literary patronage, they also expose its contradictions. Just as gift-exchange societies conceal economic interests behind the concept of the disinterested gift, so the rhetorical language concerned with benefaction similarly occludes but may also reveal calculation in regard to the return gift of verse. Horace deploys different registers of imagery to expose the conflict between the "philosophy" of voluntary benefaction and the often-distorted reciprocity ethic by which the practice in fact operated in the upper echelons of Roman society. And third, Horatian poetic rhetoric often draws on larger cultural practices of expenditure in a way that produces an ideological effect sympathetic to his patrons even as it simultaneously provides the ground for the poet's gestures of autonomy. At the risk of simplification, my inquiry may be summed up by this question: if the gifts of patronage symbolically expropriate the poet's self, obligating him to make the return gift of poetry as the embodied or "reified" form of his labor, then in what ways and to what degree does the figurative language concerned with this exchange permit resistance to that same patronal discourse?

During the 20s B.C.E. the Augustan regime solidified its power by transforming political structures and by communicating a coherent—if negotiable and evolving—ideological vision.[7] Although no mere propaganda, Horace's political poems contribute to, and arguably constitute, aspects of that vision: in particular, the sequence of poems called the Roman Odes presents a construction of history that both accounts for civil decline and lays the moral foundations for social and spiritual renewal. Recent criticism has tended to downplay the propagandistic character of these poems and, perhaps as a consequence, resists viewing them in a socioeconomic context of exchange relations.[8] However, any discussion of Horace's political poems must not only acknowledge a context of patronal benefaction but must also consider the degree to which that context intersects with other discourses of exchange and expenditure. Not much prior to 32–31 B.C.E., the literary evidence suggests that Maecenas, perhaps the figure then closest to Augustus (still called Octavian), gave Horace his celebrated "Sabine farm."[9] The political poetry of Horace's *Odes* 1–3 was written over the course of the next decade and published in 23 B.C.E., the very same years that decisively established Augustus in power. Rather than view the gift of land as an isolated act in the Horatian biography, or even as simply an example of the gifts presented by the elite to their friends, we should consider it both in the context of the massive land expropriation and redistribution that marked the 40s and 30s and in relation to sacrificial practices implied by the Horatian posture of the *sacerdos Musarum,* or "priest of the Muses."

Land grants, since the time of Sulla and even before, were both an incentive held out to prospective soldiers and, arguably, a means of securing loyalty—a political strategy that enabled a general to maintain relations with his veterans, once released from service, and thus to move from the sphere of military to political power. In the context of literary patronage,

7. See Syme 1960 [1939], 387–475; Raaflaub and Toher 1990 for a reevaluation of Syme and more current views of the Augustan Principate. Zanker (1988) addresses the evolution of "ideology" in the plastic arts; see, too, Galinsky (1996) and the essays in Powell (1992). Critics of the past decade no longer see Augustus in the Orwellian terms of Syme, but increasingly take the position of Feeney (1992, 3) that ideologies of the period were a "product of contestation and dialogue" and that "'Augustanism' was not a dogma conceived by a small band and handed down to a receptive, passive audience." On the "politics" of the terms "Augustan" and "anti-Augustan" in criticism of the period, see D. Kennedy 1992.

8. See chapter 2, n. 67, and my discussion later in the introduction.

9. Fraenkel (1957, 15) gives 31 B.C.E. as the *terminus ante quem* for the gift of the Sabine farm. The evidence for both gift and date derives from the comments of Porphyrio and Pseudo-Acro on *Epodes* 1.31 and *Odes* 2.18.12–14, and the implications of *Satires* 2.6. See chapter 3, n. 6, for further and more recent bibliography on Horace's estate.

the gift of land by figures close to the center of political power must similarly be considered as a strategy to aid the benefactors. In Horace's case, I argue that the probable grant of his estate in the early 30s puts into circulation a form of capital that is further circulated in terms of a symbolic discourse of sacrificial expenditure in his poems. For example, the appearance of the estate in a discourse of Epicurean quietude in the first Roman Ode has often led critics to find the "public" nature of these poems problematic, since the call to public service found in many of the odes' gnomic statements sits oddly with the poet's foregrounding of his own withdrawal from the sphere of political action (e.g., Lyne 1995, 158–63). However, I suggest that the estate figures here partly as an indication of the *munus,* or gift, that leads to the assumption of the role of priest, or *sacerdos,* whose poetry constitutes an act of expiatory sacrifice for the sake of a "public" audience. Sacrificial practice in ancient Rome, as Richard Gordon has recently analyzed, "could be made into aesthetic action, action for itself, free of self interest"; and "formulaic religious action represented the pure accumulation of 'symbolic capital[,]' . . . the most durable form of wealth" (1990a, 193–94). As I discuss at greater length in chapter 1, "symbolic capital" exercises power in the form of gratitude and obligation, and it is precisely this form of capital or wealth that the regime initially creates with grants of land—and that Horace perpetuates through his invocation of a sacerdotal motif. Not only does the priestly role accord with these odes' ideological production of Roman imperialism in terms of destiny, piety, and proper religious observance, but it also serves to "veil" the exchange of land for poetry by presenting them as voluntary expenditures on the part of both benefactor and poet.[10]

Though the evidence for the benefaction of the estate is admittedly tenuous, deriving from the poems themselves with reinforcement from the scholiasts and Suetonius, scholarly literature has fostered a vision of Maecenas's gift as both indisputable fact and canonical myth. Whereas the mythic stature of the estate quietly reinforces the assumption of fact regarding its provenance, the illusion of empiricism in turn reifies the poet's relationship with his patron as one indissolubly linked with this act of benefaction. Rather than get caught in this circle of assumptions regarding historical events that elude empirical recovery, I choose to view Horace's estate as a symbol of benefaction that is variously constructed in his poetry and multiply implicated in cultural discourses and practices of the Augustan period: in addition to sacerdotal practice and hierarchical patronage, we see land expropriation and redistribution, Epicurean withdrawal from

10. I borrow the term "ideological veil" from Gordon (1990a, 192), who, himself quoting from Merquior (1979, 24–34), writes that "ideology acts as an 'unconscious veil distorting the image of social reality within [a] class and sublimating its interest basis.' "

public life, upper-class "friendship," and the intellectual pursuits of villa society, as well as market economics, slavery, and the material production of a livelihood. Indeed, I believe that the very ubiquity of the farm's implied presence in so many poems, coupled with the frequent absence of extended reference, lends the implicit image its discursive power.

In keeping with the excessively stratified nature of Roman society, and the biography of "freedman's son" that Horace presents for himself in his verse, representations of the estate reveal it particularly as a source of anxiety concerning the poet's status: Does the gift convert the freeborn poet too completely into a client, entailing too many obligations to those clearly superior in terms of political as well as socioeconomic status; or does it constitute a symbol of the poet's elite landholding rank, a gift in the spirit of voluntary and affective friendship? And, if the latter, do the estate's associations with aristocratic *otium* belie or create fissures in the poet's creed of modest living and rustic simplicity—an attitude at once propagandistic or "Augustan" and self-interested? The answer to all these questions is, of course, affirmative, but which affirmative dominates is always determined in relation to the identity of the particular audience whose interests the speaker has in mind (and frequently identifies with).

To determine the actual lineaments of Horace's audience and the literate population in ancient Rome under the Principate is by no means easy, or even possible; the effort has occupied much recent scholarship.[11] The difficulty is compounded by the numerous ways in which literature might be experienced—at a "public" performance, at a private recitation for a small circle, listening to a slave employed as reader, or, finally, reading—though probably vocalizing aloud—to oneself. Hence, there may very well have been those who "heard" poetry in the most public of contexts but who were not in fact literate themselves. Superimposed on this issue of the actual audience, as determined by the specific context in which a work was either heard or read, is the variety of audiences notionally implicated in the text itself. Thus, a single ode or epistle of Horace's has at least four different levels of audience, to whom it speaks regardless of the actual site of consumption: the addressee or the pronominal "you" of the lyric or epistolary form, Horace's patrons—Maecenas and Augustus—to whom individual poems or whole collections are addressed, the greater readership of Rome (for example, the public to whom Horace's epistolary collection

---

11. For discussions of the multiple audiences of Horatian verse, see Oliensis 1998, 6, and Gold 1992, 162–63. For levels of audience in relation to public readings or performance in particular, see Quinn 1982, 140–64. See Harris 1989, 222–29, for a quick overview of literacy and "book production" in the late Republic and early Empire. Both Quinn and Harris emphasize that literature was most often an aural experience, citing the common use of readers by the upper classes.

is "set free" in *Epistles* 1.20), and posterity.[12] In spite of the frequency with which these several audiences may overlap, the generic transition from the *Odes* to the *Epistles* accentuates the distinction between "public" and "private" and actively reconfigures the relations between poet, patron, and audience, as Horace retreats from the public position of lyric priest, offering a gift of symbolic sacrifice, into the didactic role of the philosopher in his epistolary garden.

The concept of the "gift," I suggest, brings into focus this particular dynamic by which the social relations defining Horace's experience of literary patronage at once determine and are reflexively modified by his poems. The idea of a gift economy as a hermeneutic lens or methodological tool for interpreting this reciprocal dynamic is by no means unprecedented. In his monumental exploration of imperial *euergetism* in the Greco-Roman world, *Bread and Circuses* (1990), Veyne shows the strong influence of Marcel Mauss's essay *The Gift* (1990 [1950]) and the subsequent work in cultural anthropology that it promoted. Moreover, scholars of personal or "social" patronage, such as Richard Saller (1982) and Suzanne Dixon (1993), as well as of the Roman economy, such as Keith Hopkins (1983b), also offer interpretations informed by anthropological studies of the gift. Only Dixon's study, however, draws explicit parallels between the character of "primitive" economies and the meaning of gifts and debt in the Roman elite. Moreover, although the work of scholars such as Leslie Kurke (1991), among others, has demonstrated the relevance of anthropology to the interpretation of Greek literature, such scholarship has not, for the most part, been undertaken in Roman literary studies. Because anthropological studies have been invoked in discussions of the Roman economy and social relations, but rarely examined in detail as comparative paradigms and then not in the context of interpreting Latin literature, my first chapter attempts to be as explicit as possible about the relevant areas of comparison and the usefulness of anthropology as a hermeneutic point of departure.

Indeed, as Mauss's speculations suggest, the early history of Roman contract law may have reflected social attitudes toward material transactions that resemble those of the gift economies of Polynesia, Melanesia, and the native peoples of the Pacific Northwest—the societies on which he based his case studies (1990 [1950], 47–53). In his analysis of the rituals and language of Roman legal transactions Mauss, followed by Emile Benveniste and Pierre Bourdieu, observed that the ideas of "gift" and "contract" were originally compressed into a single vocabulary that later split into two (Benveniste 1973, 66–82; Bourdieu 1977, 172). In line with Mauss's observations, we find that the *Epistles* present a vision of Horace's "past" lyric self

---

12. Oliensis (1998, 6–7) places Maecenas and Augustus, when not the addressees, in the category of "overreaders"—an audience implicated in, but not directly addressed by, a poem.

that evokes the idea of the *nexum,* a form of debt-bondage in archaic Rome incurred when a loan was paid off through the recipient's physical labor:[13] the body of the debtor was quite literally owned by the lender until the loan was made good. In his discussion of the archaic economy, Mauss views the *nexum* as a kind of transitional state between primitive gift exchange and Roman contract law (1990 [1950], 49). Though patronage was not legally a contractual relationship, Horace's literary treatment of benefaction—particularly in the seventh epistle—evokes the trace of contract law's "prehistory."

In addition, the mytho-historical past that Rome constructed for itself— the hybrid world of the Homeric era—displays social gift exchange in the rituals attending *xenia,* or guest-host friendship. Horace's own reference to *xenia* and the aristocratic gift exchange by which it functioned, again in *Epistles* 1.7, points up the degree to which such former social stages, whether mythical or historical, could provide a way of conceptualizing the obligations and expectations entailed in patronage. Traces of older economic systems inhabit the culture of the late first century B.C.E. as the "ideological fallout" of previous periods.[14] To what effect does Horace invoke these older systems and figure patronage in terms of a specifically *contractual* reciprocity? And what effect does such figuration have on the maintenance or reappropriation of poetic autonomy? That is, though Horace may present his debt as "paid off," in what ways does he still need to reclaim authority? It is questions such as these that the chapters on *Epistles* 1 treat.

Insofar as I introduce the conclusions drawn by cultural anthropologists about strictly "primitive" nonmonetary cultures, my paradigm of a gift economy may appear an inexact fit for Roman literary patronage in some particulars. However, as Charles Martindale has pointed out in his book on hermeneutics and classical scholarship, *Redeeming the Text,* a particular hermeneutic lens or methodology enables us to "perceive" phenomena that otherwise we might not see (1993, 2). Because critical access to the institution of patronage is mediated, for the most part, through textual sources, it is never free of the ideology inherent in language.[15] This problem of getting behind the language that a society uses to describe its own functions is of course compounded when so much of the documentary evidence avail-

---

13. For discussions of the *nexum* and problems with the evidence, see Watson 1975, 111–24. See too the bibliography of Mauss 1990 [1950], 137 n. 5.

14. Turner (1974, 14) claims: "The culture of any society at any moment is more like the debris, or 'fall-out,' of past ideological systems." Cf. Kurke 1991, 88, for the relevance of this idea to archaic and classical Greece.

15. See D. Kennedy 1992 on the problem of language and ideology for the critic of the Augustan period.

able is literature. Hence, the gap between the interpretive lens—the paradigm of a "gift economy"—and its object of study allows me "to take [a] stand outside the Roman value system in order to understand it" (Wallace-Hadrill 1989, 4). Such a stance would seem inevitable for the twenty-first-century American critic, but the spirit of historical empiricism in which much philological study has been conducted assumes not only the complete objectivity of the critic but also a corollary: that a society's self-conception accurately describes the way that society functions. The task of the empiricist is thus to gather together the evidence and let it "speak for itself," a procedure that assumes a one-to-one correspondence between language and reality or takes language to be, in Simon Goldhill's phrase, "a transparent illustration of thought" (1986, 111).[16] However, anthropologists have long noted the discrepancies between the claims that a society makes and "the unrecognized system of ideas and organization of attitudes giving rise to the express statements of significance" (Goldhill 1986, 112). And though the dangers of distortion afflict any act of interpretation, a hermeneutic lens focused on the possible distortions and ideological veils in a society's own self-conception may in fact clarify rather than obscure.

Nonetheless, I emphasize that my reading of Horace in the following chapters is an interpretation, and all interpretations are, for better or worse, translations into meaning: that is, by rendering the inaccessibility and opacity and refractoriness of a foreign culture into terms that are meaningfully productive for us, an interpretive reading necessarily performs a kind of translation. As Peter Rose points out in his defense of the relevance of a Marxist approach to classical antiquity, the intelligibility of our answers depends on the terms in which they are cast.[17] The type of reading practices that fall under the rubric "Marxist" in fact share a certain ground with anthropological approaches. Both note the presence of ideological distortions in a culture's self-conceptions; but whereas anthropology tends to emphasize the functional element of ideology and symbolic systems, Marxism focuses more on the potential antagonism between interest groups lying beneath an ideology that serves to maintain the position of those with economic power.[18] My interpretations of the social relations of patronage are informed overall by the writings of Mauss, Marshall Sahlins, Karl Polanyi, and Bourdieu, but I have eschewed a dogmatic or fundamentalist application of any single theoretical paradigm, preferring

16. See Habinek 1998, 8, for reading practices that challenge the notion of the transparency of the linguistic sign. On "historical empiricism" as a philological method that denies its hermeneutic status, see Galinsky 1992b, 1–40, and Peradotto 1983, 22.

17. Rose 1992, 22 n. 39: "for any answers about a different society to be intelligible to us, they must at least be cast in terms that are analytically productive for us."

18. See Saller 1982, 37–38, on these two views regarding patronage.

rather to make use of a range of insights drawn from different disciplines or schools of thought when the literary rhetoric of the poems is profitably addressed by such means. Hence, my discussion of the gaps or fissures in the patronal system's "ideology of voluntarism," particularly in regard to poems that figure Horace's estate, owes much to reading practices that fall loosely under the critical aegis of "Marxist aesthetics." This approach usefully highlights, for example, how the contrary figurings of patronal experience that seem to intersect at the site of the estate derive from more than the essential anxiety about status that benefaction, as a practice, often mobilizes. Such representations reinforce the ideology or interests of the elite even as they reveal the exploitation that the system of benefaction might enable. In addition to insights informed by anthropological and Marxist approaches, readers will also encounter concepts drawn from linguistics, the writings of Michel Foucault, and deconstruction. Though some will no doubt question this apparent theoretical eclecticism, my varied recourse to different writers is always taken to illuminate the text and make it possible for us to "perceive" phenomena that otherwise we might not see.

RECENT STUDIES OF HORACE AND LITERARY PATRONAGE

The need for critical distance is all the more imperative in the case of Horace. Even a half century after the lessons of the New Critics have taught the reader to beware the postures of autobiographical personae, to distinguish between the historical self and the artifice it assumes on the page, the Horatian speaker continues to project a seductive believability. Two of the most recent full-length books on Horace (Johnson 1993; Lyne 1995), for all their authors' negotiations between irrecoverable history and the mimetic illusions of poetry, clearly (and willingly) rest their interpretations on reconstructed versions of a "historical" Horace.[19] This recourse to historical background is a literary approach more characteristic of "conventional" than of "new" historicism, insofar as it attempts to reconstruct the thoughts and intentions of the poet. However, it also indicates the overall critical trend away from the purely formalist concerns of New Criticism and a renewed interest in the context—social, historical, economic, and political—of any literary work's production. In some ways, the change of orientation is more noticeable in studies of genres or periods in which the literary texts are not as apparently suffused in the momentous political changes of the time as are the works of Augustan Rome. The subject matter,

---

19. While Johnson is conversant with the innovations introduced by poststructuralist theory to classical criticism over the past twenty years, his "psycho-biographical" (and fascinating) reading of the *Epistles* betrays a willingness to fall under the spell of Horace's seeming accessibility if not candor. My own argument is, no doubt, similarly vulnerable.

explicit or otherwise, of much Augustan literature—empire and its discontents—makes a dismissal of context nearly impossible.

Thus, it may be precisely because Horace the "propagandist" has always been an issue in Augustan criticism that there have been few, if any, full-length New Historical treatments of his poems. The "return" to history for which such an approach calls may seem not new enough, too dangerously capable of collapsing the cultural discourses shaping poetic rhetoric into the biographical referentiality of the "old" historicism.[20] Ellen Oliensis (1998), for example, reads Horace's poems as gestures of deference and authority, appealing to and manipulating a variety of historical audiences; yet her interest focuses more on the poems as performative speech acts than on their embeddedness in culture.[21] Other theoretical approaches to Horace tend to limit the context of inquiry to the verse itself, either exploring modes of rhetorical persuasion (Davis 1991), uncovering the constructions of gender implicit in such rhetoric (Ancona 1994), or, finally, analyzing the ultimately deconstructive tendencies of figurative language (Fowler 1995; Lowrie 1997). Ironically, these recent deconstructionist approaches to Horace point up the degree to which certain critical issues will always be at stake in his poems. On the one hand, as Don Fowler remarks, the debate over whether Horace or Ovid was "pro-" or "anti-" Augustan has yielded to such question as "What is the relation that we construct between Horatian or Ovidian discourse and that of other contemporary systems?" (1995, 250). On the other hand, despite the terms of Fowler's argument, which examines whether the rhetoric of Epicureanism, allied with Callimachean aesthetics, could even permit valid or "authentic" panegyric, his conclusion—that such poetic emperor worship unravels as a result of contradictions and tensions in the lyric discourse—ultimately rescues the poet from sycophancy. In other words, the claim of failed unity and the desire to shift the inquiry from the level of sincerity to that of the discursive strands of the lyric fabric itself may in fact conceal a romantic desire to safeguard Horace from the charge of compliant toadyism and thus protect a form of "agency" external to the text.

In whatever terms the issue of panegyric is posed, it suggests that the socioeconomic practice of imperial patronage looms as the inescapable

---

20. For the distinction between "new" and traditional or positivist historicism, see Preminger and Brogan 1993, s.v. "historicism." See too the collection of essays in Veeser 1989. Greenblatt 1980 is the seminal text for New Historicism. Goff (1995b, 1–37) provides a very lucid discussion of the status and history of literary theory, and New Historicism in particular, in relation to classics as a discipline.

21. Because Ellen Oliensis's book came out at the time that my manuscript was under review, I was unable to profit as much as I would have liked from her insights into Horace's poems. As I acknowledge in chapter 3, n. 58, her work on Horace's *Satires* is an exception to this.

backdrop to Horatian poetic discourse. Scholarship on literary patronage has evolved considerably since the early views of Sir Ronald Syme, which held that Augustus, via Maecenas, orchestrated a unified program of poetic propaganda to influence public opinion (1960 [1939], 459–75). On one end of the spectrum are the literary critics such as James Zetzel (1982), Matthew Santirocco (1986, 1995), or R. O. A. M. Lyne (1995), whose attention (variously directed) to the conventions and rhetorical representation of patronage either disassociates the text from historical causality, reveals the poet as creating his own agenda, or problematizes any full-fledged endorsement of the regime. At the other extreme are historians such as Peter White (1993), whose meticulous and valuable examination of the historical evidence leads him to conclude that poets celebrated Augustus out of a spontaneous attraction to, and fascination with, the emperor's potent image and the social changes that he effected. Writing from a perspective both historical and literary-critical, Barbara Gold (1987) essentially sees patronage for the Augustan writers as "subject matter in itself" and a "literary phenomenon" in which the "desires of patrons seem to have influenced the writers . . . only in indirect and nonspecific ways" (1987, 66).[22] Similar assumptions also underlie the work of Michael Putnam (1986), whose readings of Horace's fourth book of *Odes*—poetry notoriously "requested" by Augustus—encourage a rejection of toadyism in order to preserve the poet's aesthetic integrity. By no means ignoring and often emphasizing Horatian irony and its subversive potential, scholars of Horace (with some exceptions, of course) tend to endorse a view of the poet's *libertas* that accords with what I have dubbed "an ideology of voluntarism" in the literature on benefaction.[23] To be sure, this endorsement of the poet's creative independence fully acknowledges the practice of reciprocity in Roman social relations; but it tends to downplay the psychology of debt in a gift economy—how the persuasive coercions of *gratia,* or gratitude toward a patron, may affect the ideological content of the poetry itself.

I believe that this investment in Horatian "agency" issues from two basic sources. On the one hand, Horace's situation involves the plight of human liberty, and though the historical modalities of this concept clearly change over time, the desire for freedom—whether from social roles or government interference, whether circumscribed or infinite—remains with us. On the other hand, as Ernst Doblhofer (1966) early acknowledged, critics often respond to the political climate of their own countries, displaying biases that reflect their own historical situation.[24] And thus, just as Syme's dark

22. See, too, Gold's statement that "men like Virgil and Horace . . . were independent and free to choose when they wrote and what they wrote, or even if they wrote" (1987, 14).

23. Notable exceptions to this tendency include G. Williams (1990) and Horsfall (1981).

24. For discussion of Doblhofer, see Fowler 1995, 248–66.

view expressed in his *Roman Revolution* must be seen in the light of Nazi totalitarianism, so critics who adhere to a vision of the unconstrained autonomy of the artist in their assessment of Horace may reflect the premium that they, often tenured scholars of the ivory tower and citizens of liberal democracies, place on their own academic freedom and political liberties.

As I have outlined, my discussion of Horatian verse seeks to frame the issue of patronal pressure in new terms, employing the concept of a gift economy as a hermeneutic lens that brings into focus the contradictions inherent in literary patronage and in the rhetorical language by which it is figured. For example, those who argue for the voluntary nature of poetry in support of Augustus sometimes give a material justification, claiming that all the Augustan poets were *equites* before any imperial benefactions were made and thus had no actual need of material support. This statistic appears to support the poets' "uncompromised" position: not in need of the regime's help, they offer a voluntary celebration, neither the obliged response to specific requests nor the return issuing from actual debt.[25] Peter White, who makes this argument, acknowledges that poets derived substantial benefits—"Gifts of cash, estates, emoluments, and dowries"—from their powerful "friends," but he insists that such gifts, "once conferred . . . were valuable also in the sense that they left the recipient relatively independent of the giver" and that "support was not directly keyed to literary output" (1993, 17). White's treatment of the evidence is both impressive and persuasive on many counts, but I nonetheless believe that an examination of the poetic rhetoric by which Horace figured his experience of patronage, when considered in relation to Rome's cultural practices of exchange and expenditure, suggests a greater degree of debt and obligation than the phrase "relatively independent" would imply.

For as I discuss at length in chapter 1, the gift economy operates by displacing the economics of debt into the sphere of courtesy, so that obligation is concealed beneath the decorum of disinterested giving. This decorum, an ideology of voluntarism, appears in such Horatian rhetorical motifs as the *cornucopia*, the spontaneous fertility of the golden age, or the posture of the *sacerdos* sacrificing for the public at large. These poetic figures suggest the dynamics of what the cultural anthropologist Pierre Bourdieu identifies as the social misrecognition of the economics of gift

25. On the equestrian status of many Republican and Augustan writers, see Nicolet 1966, 441–56; Taylor 1968; P. White 1993.5–14, 211–22. In addition to an appendix on the financial, and hence social, status of the major writers of the period, White includes one on the contexts in which the verb *iubeo* appears in relation to requests for poetry. The apparent lack of any real exercise of power in the situations he cites leads him to ascribe use of the verb to mere convention, further support for his case for voluntarism in the Augustan poets. For an interpretation that acknowledges the implications of actual power in such language, see Santirocco 1995, 236.

exchange—in this case, a reconstrual of calculated transactions in terms of friendship, generosity, or imperial euergetism (expenditure for the public good) (Bourdieu 1977, 171; Harker, Mahar, and Wilkes 1990, 19). However, in Horace these rhetorical motifs are often undercut by their context or by allusive echoes in later poems that unmask such images as complicitous with the ideology of voluntarism. Horace's epistolary poems to Maecenas, for example, look back to the sacrificial rhetoric of the Roman Odes from the perspective of contractual exchange.

By going to social and cultural anthropology, I am by no means ignoring the extensive writing by the ancients on the theory or philosophy of benefaction, liberality, and social exchange. Rather, as chapter 1 demonstrates, I wish to illuminate this material from an anthropological angle, and I analyze the Horatian representation of patronage from both perspectives. Such an approach owes much to the field of "cultural studies." On the one hand, like other contemporary critics, I aim to bring the insights of other disciplines to bear on the study of antiquity. Thus, to take a clearly interdisciplinary example, recent work on Catullus makes use of feminist film theory and the concept of the "gaze" as a means of understanding the sensual relationship between the reader and the visual pleasures offered by Ariadne, and the golden age, in Catullus 64 (Fitzgerald 1995, 140–68). On the other hand, those engaged in cultural studies acknowledge the tenuous and even artificial boundary between "literary" and "nonliterary" texts and seek to understand the reciprocal relations between the two, recognizing that cultural practices often constitute discursive or semiotic systems in their own right. As Dennis Feeney remarks in his discussion of the interpenetration of literary and religious discourse in ancient Rome, "Rather than asking how religion is transmuted into literature, . . . we should instead be thinking in terms of a range of cultural practices, interacting, competing, and defining each other in the process" (1998, 1).[26] Similarly, in addition to employing the insights of anthropology, I wish to view the literary representation of patronage in relation to a range of discursive and material practices involving exchange and expenditure—one of which is social benefaction itself.

AUTONOMY AND THE DISCURSIVE CONVENTIONS OF PATRONAGE

For a study that interrogates the poetic rhetoric of literary patronage, the "nonliterary" texts of Aristotle's *Nicomachean Ethics,* Cicero's *On Duties,* and

---

26. Feeney also quotes the relevant observation of Conte that "'real life' is itself 'the locus of cultural images and models, symbolic choices, communicative and perceptual codes'" (1998, 1).

Seneca's *On Benefits* all contain material pertinent to the practice and psychology of ancient social relations considered in "economic" terms. But to restrict an inquiry to just these sources as a conceptual lens through which to view the Horatian poetic subject in his relation to patronal discourse poses a few problems. First, these ancient texts, particularly Cicero and Seneca, deal with the broader social phenomenon of liberality or benefaction, of which literary patronage is really a subset with its own unique characteristics. Second, these works are prescriptive rather than descriptive, presenting the ideology of benefactions analyzed by those in the society itself, who have no critical distance on their own historical context. Third, as many have noted, philosophers and poets alike avoid the language of patronage, and the corresponding diction of *clientela* or "clientship," when describing relations between those of elite social status.[27] Literary patronage, as I discuss in more detail below, was referred to almost exclusively in terms of *amicitia* or friendship.

Nonetheless, these social discourses of benefaction clarify the problem of Horatian autonomy or agency in relation to discursive conventions. As Seneca and Cicero so repeatedly display, codes and conventions governed the behavior of those giving and receiving benefactions; the ideal prescriptions contained in *On Duties* (*De officiis*) and *On Benefits* (*De beneficiis*) suggest the degree to which patronage, friendship, and the practice of benefaction were discursive practices in the Foucauldian sense—social modes of interaction that could achieve greater or lesser degrees of ideal stylization in their own right. Given this discursive element within the actual practice of patronage, the stylized treatment of its conventions in verse would be simply a higher order of representation: poetry and philosophical treatise are drawing on, and reciprocally informing, many of the same cultural codes. From this point of view, the problem of Horatian autonomy becomes the issue of the freedom of the Horatian subject. If, as I discuss further in chapter 4, the Horatian subject is an effect of language, a composite of social discourses invoked and activated by the speaking "I" of lyric and epistolary forms, then autonomy becomes a matter for language as well. On the one hand, the production of poetry as a gift involved in the exchanges of poet and patron takes place within the conventions of actual patronage; on the other hand, the invocation of the discourse of *amicitia* (friendship, patronage among the elite), together with all the related concepts of *gratia* (gratitude, favor, influence), *beneficium* (benefit, favor, kindness), *officium* (duty, favor), *munus* (gift, favor, duty, public show), and so

---

27. Moreover, Nicols (1995, 11) stresses that the Romans, in fact, made a distinction between formal "patronage" and "benefaction": "That is, to the modern 'patronage' is indeed created by a benefaction, while to the Roman formal *patrocinium* may not have been."

on, as a "culture pattern" that informs the rhetorical figures of poetry, puts the issue of the poet's autonomy on that same level—that is, the level of poetic representation.

The problem of autonomy in relation to subjectivity regularly besets New Historical interpretations: where is a freely choosing self if linguistic consciousness is simply a culturally determined effect of social discourses?[28] For Horace, I argue, the question of liberty should be posed in terms not so much of freedom from the patron as of freedom within the overlapping discourses of patronage, friendship, and "literary benefaction." In this regard, the discursive or semiotic aspect of actual material practices should be kept somewhat distinct from the ideological lens or prescriptive discourse through which they were conducted. Taking as my starting point that literary patronage as a material practice operates as a system of gift exchange or gift economy, I argue that Horace experienced all the constraint and obligation—the sense of debt, gratitude, and compulsion to return—that such an economy would impose on him. The "context" of a gift economy, then, inevitably informs the text beyond conventions such as the dedication to a patron or the *recusatio*—the "refusal" poem in which a poet declines to write political panegyric even as the gesture toward praise is duly made. The poems themselves, in addition, constitute objects in which the labor and subjecthood of the poet have been reified. As we shall see in the discussion of the *Epistles* as they look back to, and comment on, the lyric poems, Horace's epistolary self draws attention to such "reification" of the self as a potential consequence of the patronal system. Ultimately, however, these references constitute one of many discursive systems or registers of imagery on the level of poetic representation; once he has revealed literary patronage as potentially exploitative, the poet renegotiates his relations by rhetorically inscribing himself in the ranks of the elite.

Reified selves occur as a result of systems of exchange, when the "subject" status of a person becomes implicated in the exchanges of objects and has a value determined by such exchangeability. Though we are accustomed to think of reification as the result of capitalism, Sahlins points out that in primitive reciprocity there is a "mystic alienation of the donor" in the gift that parallels Marx's notion of alienated human social labor in commodity

---

28. For the problem of the autonomous subject in New Historicism, see Lentricchia 1989, 241: "The central commitment of historicists, old and new, is to the self as product of forces over which we exercise no control—the self as effect, not origin. . . . The central, unacknowledged, and perhaps unacknowledgeable desire of historicism—it is not part of their officially stated position on the self—is to avoid the consequences of that central commitment, to find a space of freedom and so free us from a world in which we are forced to become what we do not wish to become."

production (1972, 181).[29] This mystic presence of the donor in the gift is what ensures reciprocity, causing the one who receives an object to be given over to, or temporarily bought by, the one who gives it, until a compensatory return has been made (Mauss 1990 [1950], 50). Though not "primitive," the system of Roman patronage operates by such reciprocity; and the seemingly voluntary gift may be said to reify or alienate its donor and its recipient when the context foregrounds the various values, the economic or symbolic capital, into which the benefaction may be translated. For example, if the context reveals calculation on the part of the giver regarding some kind of return, or if the recipient perceives or represents his "gratitude" in the reified terms of an obligatory "payback" in which the emphasis on commensuration outweighs the libidinal feeling of thankfulness, then a form of reification, however loosely defined, has entered the process.

But though such calculation with its open expectation of reciprocity is sometimes visible in the letters of Cicero and Pliny, members of the elite who publicly advertised their own participation in the practice of benefaction, it is clearly presented as problematic in the philosophical literature on the topic. When Seneca, for example, distinguishes between a voluntary return of gratitude (*referre gratiam*) and repayment in a monetary context (where the verb *reddere* would be employed), he points up an ideological discomfort with the calculation or manipulation of benefits and services to which the system potentially was inclined.[30] Indeed, as I discuss in more depth in the next chapter, one of the most distinctive features of the discourse of benefaction is the libidinal or emotive language in which the practice of gift giving was conducted. And so when we examine the discourse of patronage and friendship in Cicero's letters, the reciprocity ethic—though taken for granted—is generally couched in terms of the emotions of friendship and esteem. Thus, in a letter of Plancus to Cicero, Plancus concludes by professing both his strong affection and his desire, through the performance of reciprocating services, to make Cicero's previous favors or benefactions "more pleasing" (*iucundiora*) to him as benefactor (*Fam.* 10.23.7).[31] And in a recommendation letter that Cicero writes to Caesar, seeking to attach the young Trebatius Testa to Caesar's retinue on his Gallic campaign, Cicero invokes the language of friendship

---

29. See Appadurai 1986, 11–16, for a more expanded notion of the "commodity" that applies, in certain instances, to primitive gift exchange.

30. Sen. *Ep.* 81.9: *Sic certe solemus loqui: "ille illi gratiam rettulit." Referre est ultro, quod debeas, adferre. Non dicimus "gratiam reddidit," reddunt enim et qui reposcuntur et qui inviti et qui ubilibet et qui per alium.*

31. All translations of Cic. *Fam.* are from the Loeb edition, W. Williams 1929, unless otherwise noted.

as a preface to his request: "Observe how I take it for granted that I have in you a second self (*te me esse alterum*), not only in what concerns me personally, but also in what concerns my friends. . . . I am beginning to wish that whatever Trebatius had hoped for from me, he should expect to get from you" (*Fam.* 7.5.1).[32]

And yet, as also appears in the literature, the libidinal and affective context of the transactions may yield to a pure emphasis on reciprocal obligation, revealing the bonds of friendship as a more contractual relationship. Not surprisingly, this emphasis is most evident when a relationship other than that between the letter writer and the recipient is being discussed. In a letter rebuking Trebatius for his formerly mercenary attitude toward his post in Caesar's retinue in Gaul, Cicero writes: "For you were in a hurry to snatch the money and return home, just as if what you had brought the commander-in-chief was not a letter of recommendation, but a bill of exchange [*syngrapham*]" (*Fam.* 7.17.1).[33] Here, we may note that Trebatius is figured as attempting to convert Cicero's "influence" or *gratia* with Caesar into its cash equivalent. Such conversion of "symbolic" into "material" capital, as chapter 1 demonstrates, is a characteristic operation of the gift economy. This very attempt to profit from the debt imposed by benefactions reveals an economic interestedness that belies the libidinal language of friendship. Thus Caelius in a letter to Cicero complains that Appius, having refused a loan of money, "is beginning to hate me, because he is indebted to me for great kindnesses; and miser that he is, being unable to enforce upon himself the discharge of that debt, he has declared a secret war against me" (*Fam.* 8.12.1). Resentment of this kind constitutes the negative extreme to which the sense of debt could lead, but it is important to register such emotion as a response to the benefactor's open efforts to call in the debts created by his benefactions.

For all their tact, affection, and humor, Horace's two epistolary refusal poems, 1.1 and 1.7 to Maecenas, suggest the background scenario of a benefactor wishing to call in old debts. However, as I argue, even as the poet reveals his relationship with the regime as having an underlying contractual component, he also manipulates the discourse of libidinal voluntarism as a means of reconfiguring his social relationships. To fully understand such manipulation, we must review briefly the two major questions besetting discussions of Augustan literary patronage. First, does the language of *amicitia* allow us to speak of patronage? And second, to what de-

---

32. For the language of friendship in terms of "another self," see Cic. *Amic.* 6.22–24. For critical commentary on this series of letters, see Shackleton Bailey 1977, vol. 1, letters 26–39.

33. Shackleton Bailey 1977, ad loc., defines *syngrapham* as "A recognition of debt in the form of a contract signed by both parties."

gree does the relationship resemble its social counterpart, and in what ways does it constitute a unique phenomenon?

LITERARY *AMICITIA*

One of the difficulties with making assertions about literary patronage in the Augustan period, and about Horace's experience in particular, is that so much of the evidence (with the exception of Suetonius's biographies) comes from the poetry itself. Another related problem is the ambiguous nature of the language used to describe the relationship. As I mention above, the terms *patronus* and *cliens* were rarely used to refer to the relations between a benefactor and his protégé, whether social or literary, in the aristocratic elite.[34] As a passage from Cicero's *De officiis* claims, Romans of some social standing thought it "like death to be called clients or to benefit from patronage" (*patrocinio vero se usos aut clientes appellari mortis instar putant,* 2.69).[35] Consequently, the more circumspect if possibly misleading terms *amicitia* and *amici,* most straightforwardly translated as "friendship" and "friends," were used to describe relations of a frequently utilitarian— if not an economically dependent—nature between those whose status is clearly different.[36] Such terms are confusing for the modern scholar because we are accustomed to associate a certain nonutilitarian parity with the concept of friendship.[37] To add to the confusion, the intimacy of shared interests and values that such parity implies did characterize the more

34. By the time of the late Republic, the term *patronus* appears in three specific contexts: it can refer to an orator defending someone in court, to a person who takes an interest in the welfare of a community or a civic or corporate body, or, finally, to a master who has freed his slave. See Saller 1982, 9; P. White 1993, 30. Significantly, Horace uses both *patronus* and *cliens* to describe the disastrous patronal relationship initiated by the lawyer Philippus in *Epistles* 1.7, a striking example of usage that fits none of the above three contexts (the client, Volteius Mena, is not a beneficiary of Philippus in the courtroom).

35. My translation. Saller (1989, 52) adduces Sen. *Ben.* 2.23 and *Brev. vitae* 19.3 as evidence that this attitude continued into the Empire.

36. Saller 1982, 15. Saller (1989) clarifies that the social behavior and conventions required of an aspiring junior aristocrat—or *amicus inferior*—in regard to his *potens amicus* were those typical of the more humble and openly labeled *cliens:* e.g., the morning *salutatio* by which a client pays his respects to a patron. Horsfall (1981) inclines to Saller's view that the language of *amicitia* encompasses patron-dependent relations among the elite. I will generally refer to Maecenas as Horace's benefactor or "patron," although, as I argue in chapter 4, the poet discursively refashions his relationship with him into a more egalitarian relation that merits the translation "friendship." I refer to Horace as "protégé," "dependent," or "client," depending on my reading of the connotations of the context.

37. P. White (1993, 13–14) claims that it is the sympathy of cultural interests and pursuits that creates parity between figures like Maecenas and Horace, despite the evident difference in their social status.

philosophical conceptions of *amicitia* in Roman intellectual thought.[38] Moreover, in the case of Horace and Maecenas, as the numerous allusions to the high regard and affection between them testify, personal feelings of real friendship transcended their initial social or economic disparities.[39] Finally, in addition to the wide range of meanings covered by *amicitia*, Horace's own poetic exploitation of the connotative ambiguities of the term contributes to the difficulty of determining its sense in any particular context. His frequently adopted Epicurean attitudes, for example, often complicate his exploration of *amicitia* understood in patronal terms.[40]

It is precisely this language of friendship that contributes to White's view that "literary patronage" is a misnomer when applied to the relationship that the Augustan poets had with their benefactors. For not only does the term "literary patronage" imply regular material support, it also suggests "a more or less deliberate policy of encouraging literature and art" (P. White 1978, 79). A scrupulous and judicious examination of the primary historical and poetic texts provides no evidence, for White, of either consistent material benefits or of a conscious will, by either the government or simply powerful friends, to shape the literary output of poets in their orbit (1993, 110–55). Consequently, White interprets *amicitia* as an example of "the affect-laden language" that marks the discourse of friendship among the Roman elite and suggests that it "is probably to be interpreted as an effort by both parties to neutralize those status differences which do still stand between them" (14).[41] Finally, although he argues that the literary rela-

---

38. Cicero's *De amicitia* is just one example of the Roman adoption and synthesis of Greek theories of friendship, which furnished part of the cultural backdrop of the late Republic. Parity is an important component of Aristotle's view of friendship in books 8 and 9 of the *Nicomachean Ethics*. For an overview of friendship in the classical world that argues against the functionalist view held by many critics, in particular those influenced by anthropology, see Konstan 1997. See Brunt 1965 for a discussion of *amicitia* that separates it from an easy equation with party politics and restores its philosophical nuances even in the public and social contexts of the late Republic.

39. Cf. the claim of Suet. *Poet. Vita Horati*, that Maecenas in his will requested Augustus to be as mindful of Horace as of himself: *Horati Flacci ut mei esto memor*. For a good overview of the trajectory of Horace's relationship with Maecenas, see Gold 1987, 115–41. For the aesthetic development of the relationship over the course of *Odes* 1–3, see Santirocco 1986, 150–68, which charts an evolution from the poet's initial dependency on Maecenas to his creative independence from, and even spiritual patronage of, his benefactor.

40. *Epistles* 1.18 provides a good example of the tension between the philosophical and the sociopolitical connotations of Roman *amicitia*.

41. P. White adds: "In any society the category of 'friend' often functions in opposition to ascriptive categories, contrasting self-selected relationships with those given by kinship or other institutional identities" (1993, 14). Konstan (1997, 21; 1995, 329) essentially agrees with White's position and argues that when the language of *amicitia* is used by poets to refer to their benefactors, the diction was intended to mean what it said. In an earlier article on poets

tionship is embedded in Roman social practices, he downplays the signifi-
cance of even sporadic material benefactions in comparison to other
"goods and services" that a more powerful *amicus* could give his depend-
ent.[42] In particular, as I have already noted, he emphasizes that the Augus-
tan poets all enjoyed the status of *equites,* and thus the economic
wherewithal of such standing, before any material benefactions were made
by their powerful friends. Hence, White claims that the connotation of
economic dependency implied by the term "patronage" is misleading. This
argument clearly aims to restore historical particularity to the language of
amicitia, and to reconstruct the milieu in which poets, their friends and
benefactors, and the larger public interacted, but I believe it does not suf-
ficiently acknowledge the psychology of debt, created in the form of *gratia,*
that drives a gift economy.

In Horace's case we find the most evidence of what the modern critic
would call "literary patronage": not only do the poetry and the biography
point to concrete, material benefactions—the grant of the Sabine estate,
in particular—but the panegyric and patriotic content of the fourth book
of *Odes* and the *Carmen saeculare* corroborate Suetonius's information that
Augustus requested the one and commissioned the other.[43] Although my
focus is not on the openly encomiastic verse of Horace's later period, my
analysis nonetheless tends to justify the use of the term: for insofar as I view
Horace as needing to recover, or poetically negotiate for himself, a com-
promised autonomy, I incline to the opinion that Horace received bene-
factions from a regime more than a little interested in his poetic support.
As I argue in chapter 4, Horace's epistles to Maecenas suggest as much and
coyly flirt with demystifying their past relationship as one of patron-client
exchange rather than friendship.

On one level, the debate over whether "patronage" is an appropriate

---

in early Imperial Rome, White (1978, 81) cites the common practice of distinguishing persons
of higher status with such titles as *potens amicus, magnus amicus,* or *dives amicus,* not as polite
and euphemistic references to a "patronal" relationship, but rather as examples of the partic-
ularly Roman consciousness of nuances of status. Perhaps this position can be reconciled with
his later claim that the language of *amicitia* was intended to neutralize status differences by
saying that phrases like *potens amicus* functioned as compromise formations or negotiations
that both acknowledged the distinction in status *and* attempted to soften it.

42. P. White 1993, 18: "Important as material goods were, however, they did not outweigh
the more intangible but everyday rewards which the leaders of society were in a position to
bestow."

43. P. White nonetheless concludes that "It would be perverse to read the *Secular Hymn* as
a composition written to glorify Augustus, to articulate his ideology, or to summarize his ad-
ministrative program" (1993, 127). This statement strikes me as too extreme in its wish to
deny encomiastic intent. I agree, however, that "ideology" is not a prepackaged set of beliefs
able to be summed up in a poem.

term for Horace is a matter of translation and reflects the cultural baggage that inevitably attends the particular scholar setting the level and perspective of inquiry. As Andrew Wallace-Hadrill writes concerning patronage in general: "Is it a pattern of relationships that exists objectively in certain societies whether or not the participants themselves acknowledge or approve it, or is it a way in which the actors perceive and formulate the relationships in which they are engaged? That is to say, are we talking about a structure or an ideology?" (1989, 65). His answer to this question—that both structure and ideology are involved in our inquiry—suggests additional reasons for the connotative ambiguities of the term *amicitia:* not only does it protect the self-image of the person of lower status, as Cicero's comment implies, but its philosophical implications of ideal parity and genuine affection for another make ideologically palatable the objective constituents of the actual structure as one in which each party profits. That is, a desire to maintain the appearance of disinterested giving—to establish a certain distance from a crude expectation or exploitation of the reciprocity ethic—by espousing an ideology of voluntarism may partially determine this preference for the language of emotive relationship.[44]

In his frequently invoked definition of personal patronage, or social *amicitia,* Saller lists three necessary criteria and emphasizes the role of exchange as paramount in the relationship: "First, it involves the reciprocal exchange of goods and services. Secondly, to distinguish it from a commercial transaction in the marketplace, the relationship must be a personal one of some duration. Thirdly, it must be asymmetrical, in the sense that the two parties are of unequal status and offer different kinds of goods and services in the exchange—a quality which sets patronage off from friendship between equals" (1982, 1). Cicero's discussion of such ideal friendship recognizes the component of utility in the relationship, but sees it as the *result* of a spiritual feeling of fellowship.[45] In contrast, patronage may be said to dominate as the meaning of *amicitia* when the relationship is defined primarily by the exchange of goods and services otherwise unavailable— that is, when utility precedes sentiment. If one accepts Saller's criteria, examples of the language of friendship applied to utilitarian fellowship are ready to hand. The letters of Cicero, Pliny, and Fronto all display this "affect-laden" terminology when referring to relationships both useful and

44. For example, when Porphyry comments that Horace should use the terms *patronus* or *cliens* rather than *amicus* in *Epode* 1, his objection points to the difficulty of conceiving Horace's relationship with Maecenas, at this early stage, as a "friendship"—particularly when the poem emphasizes Horace's gratitude for the benefactions he has received: *satis superque me benignitas tua/ ditavit* (31).

45. Cic. *Amic.* 8.26–9.32, esp. 9.30: *Sed quamquam utilitates multae et magnae consecutae sunt, non sunt tamen ab earum spe causae diligendi profectae.* See Brunt 1965, 1–2, for further discussion.

hierarchically differentiated.[46] Horace's own *Epistles* offer several instances: in his letter to Iccius, for example, the poet presents an aristocrat, or man of "some social standing," living on and enjoying the fruits of Marcus Agrippa's estate in Sicily. The ostensible occasion for the letter is to encourage Iccius to "make use" (*utere*) of Grosphus, a wealthy landowner also in Sicily, whose friendship may be acquired "inexpensively" through the provision of modest services: "If he will ask for anything, oblige him willingly; Grosphus will seek nothing but what is just and fair. The going rate of friends is cheap (*vilis amicorum est annona*) when good men are in need" (1.12.22–24). Here, despite the obvious difference in status between Iccius and Grosphus (Cicero reminds us that landownership was the paramount indication of social standing),[47] their prospective relationship is called one of *amici*. To be sure, Horace's emphasis on the more utilitarian nuances of *amicitia* verges on ironic exaggeration, and he perhaps pointedly invokes such praxis only to oppose Cicero's ideal views.[48] Nonetheless, we should recognize that exchange, inequality of station, and the implicit projection of their "friendship" into the future—Saller's three criteria for patronage—are all here.

My own recourse to a scholar of social—and personal—patronage to identify the problems posed by the Latin terminology points up the second question with which we began: to what degree was the literary relationship unique and to what degree was it merely another form of *amicitia* in which one of the parties happened to be a poet? Certainly Saller's three criteria are present in literary *amicitia* if we consider "inequality" of station as reflecting not exclusively differences in wealth or the social status of *eques* or senator that such money conferred but also proximity to political power. For example, several months after Horace first meets Maecenas, he is said to be included *in numero amicorum* ("in his group of friends" or "in the category of those called friends"; *Sat.* 1.6.62), a phrase that at face value points simply to a distinction between those who are "in" and those who are "out," and inadvertently suggests what Dixon calls the "ideology of internal egalitarianism" within the elite (1993, 453).[49] However, this

46. Wallace-Hadrill (1989, 77) refers to Cotton (1981) for documentary examples.

47. Cic. *Off.* 1.151. See the discussion in d'Arms 1981, 6, and Finley 1973, 42–44.

48. Dilke 1965, ad loc., and others refer Horace's statement to a saying of Socrates, the ironist par excellence: "Economists say one should buy when something of great value is going cheap: as business is now, good friends are for sale very cheap" (Xen. *Mem.* 2.10.4).

49. On the phrase *in amicorum numero*, Horsfall (1981, 5) speculates: "by the late second century B.C. there were even, in the manner of the Ptolemaic court, classes of 'friends' at the *salutatio* (Gelzer, 104f.); the existence of a written register of clients cannot, I think, be proved, but the work of the *nomenclator*, or, worse still, of the imperial *officium admissionis*, will have been unimaginable without some semi-formalised register. Horace was now on the *numerus*, and should have had no problems with the *nomenclator*."

inclusion is simultaneously seen in terms of gradations of power, of proximity to the ultimate source of benefactions: Horace is now closer to the "gods" than is the average man on the street. This phrase is uttered by a passerby whom the poet encounters in *Satires* 2.6 as he hurries off to pay his morning call to Maecenas. While the passerby inquires about the place of settlement for veteran soldiers—information to which the poet is presumed to have access because he is now "close" to power—the main thrust of the poem concerns a different "resource" from which the poet's *amicitia* with Maecenas has profited: the grant of land that has given Horace his escape from the irritations of city living. It is significant that the satire connects these two resources—land and information—in an almost overdetermined way: even as the poet is presumed to have *knowledge about* land grants because he is close to the gods, the beginning of the poem shows the poet *actually having* land because he enjoys such divine proximity.[50] One might go further and say that he is now presumed to have knowledge because gifts from the powerful have distinguished him as one in the know. Thus, as the street encounter emphasizes, Horace's status is relational; previously no different, perhaps, from the veteran soldiers who receive land as a means of ensuring their continuing loyalty, he is then ranked somewhere between his *potens amicus* ("powerful friend" or "patron" among the elite) whom he visits and the man seeking information.

Finally, we should also note that although Horace shrewdly avoids displaying himself as "in attendance" on his patron,[51] the morning *salutatio* as a client's obligation—and the public visibility of such an *officium*, or duty—points up the degree to which the reciprocity ethic that marked both friendship and patronage was more "visible" and publicly "revealed" as exchange in an openly patron-client relationship.[52] The tension between such open exchange and the moral and affective discourse of friendship is what earns Trebatius Testa a reproof from Cicero for his mercenary attitude toward Caesar: in that case, the relationship between the young man and the general to whose retinue he attaches himself is marked as an example of elite patronage not only by the discrepancy of power between the two but also by the openness with which Trebatius views it as an opportunity to profit.

When we turn from questions concerning the ambiguity of the term *amicitia* to those actual goods and services exchanged between a poet and his benefactor, the relationship displays characteristics that are decidedly

50. The concentric structure of knowledge and resources in relation to a central locus of power, staged by this encounter, conforms to Wallace-Hadrill's understanding of patronage in terms of social integration (1989, 63–87).

51. On the motives for Horace's exclusion of this scene, see Oliensis 1998, 48.

52. See too chapter 4, n. 60.

sui generis. Because this material has been so well covered by critics such as Gold and White, I offer only the briefest summary here. To be sure, as the poems of Horace, Juvenal, and Martial evidence, poets often perform the duties expected in the purely social context of *amicitia* or patronage among the elite—greeting their patron in the morning *salutatio*, providing companionship on a journey or at a dinner, or listening to the literary efforts of their superiors. In return, the greater *amicus* of a poet may provide the services of social visibility, literary endorsement, and often a concrete place or venue for reciting works (P. White 1978, 85; 1993, 14–27; Gold 1987, 1–2). A benefactor might give lump sums of cash and, as in the case of Vergil and Horace, the important boon of land. While endorsements and the like clearly distinguish this relationship as one specifically pertaining to literature and its audience, it is qualitatively set off from social or personal *amicitia* by the poetry itself, as the most significant "good" exchanged. The nature and circumstances of literary production in antiquity even encouraged the objectification of poetry as a concrete good. The use of papyrus rolled up into a scroll made a collection of poems a tangible gift; and the elegists present images of their poems—histrionic missives of self-representation—sent to their mistresses through the streets of Rome, etched on tablets.[53] As I discuss in chapter 5, Horace's thirteenth epistle conceives of *Odes* 1–3 in just such terms: an object of "reified labor" exchanged in his relationship with Augustus.

But embedded in the poems as concrete offerings are the varied conventions, topoi, and generic categories that literary patronage structures as a form of gift: the dedication, the *recusatio*, the invitation poem, the literary epistle of advice or recommendation, and the full-blown panegyric all display the socioeconomic roots of the relationship as a potentially motivating force for the verse.[54] In particular, it is the status conferred on their recipient by political panegyric or dedications that constitutes a substantive gift in the exchanges of literary *amicitia*. Moreover, the public acknowledgment implied in this status is complex: on the one hand, it refers to the standing of the recipient in the eyes of his contemporaries—an issue that, as we shall see in chapter 1, gets into questions of ideology; on the other, good poetry also confers the even more prestigious status of immortality—public recognition that transcends temporal boundaries.

53. Catull. 1.1, *Cui dono lepidum novum libellum,* conflates the "abstract" gift of the dedication with the materiality of the scroll itself. See Gold 1987, 2–3, on the objectification of poetry; Habinek 1998, 112–13, on the uses of papyrus as a sign of elite prestige and hegemonic control.

54. Generic conventions thus are to be distinguished from the theme of patronage in verse: conventions, rather than "themes," display the "material trace" of the socioeconomic world. For the invitation poem as a form of gift, see Pavlock 1982. Also see Edmunds 1982, 184–88.

Here, it is important to note with Joseph Hellegouarc'h (1963, 203) that the Latin word for "gratitude," *gratia,* originally meant a form of "praise" (*laus*), so that the "return" implied in phrases such as *referre gratiam*—"to render thanks"—consisted quite simply in the praise of a patron's generosity. Indeed, we see the similar phrase *gratus referam camena,* "I gratefully celebrate in song," employed by Horace in *Odes* 1.12.39, where the sacrifices of distinguished Romans of the past—Regulus, the Scauri, and L. Aemilius Paullus—have earned Horace's gratitude. As a poem that begins with the speaker's rhetorical query as to whose praises he should sing, "what man, or hero . . . what god," and whose prominent parade of figures from these three categories ends with Caesar second only to Jove, this rather stiff encomium alludes to the dynamics of imperial patronage and the gratitude of praise through their displacement onto the figures of the past.

Using a different form of metonymic displacement, Horace simultaneously accords with the demands of gratitude and creates a discursive site that resists obligations. For if patronal *munera* have created debts that require various expressions of acknowledgment in the form of dedications, encomia, and ideological endorsement of the Augustan regime, then one can display gratitude by showing the pleasure that these gifts have occasioned. By representing his Sabine estate in its "pleasing" aspect, as the passive sense of *gratus* denotes, Horace may express his gratitude at the same time that he removes his *res,* or property, from the discourse of implicit exchange by valuing it for its aesthetic character.[55] That is, rather than remain in perpetual debt to his patrons, a debt symbolized by allusions to the "exchange value" of gifts from the regime, the poet endows the ultimate symbol of that beneficence—the representation of his Sabine "farm"—with properties that stress its character as a *locus amoenus,* thus making it a symbol of aesthetic production. Although it is a *munus* that requires reciprocation, the farm is conceived as *a-moenus,* as something outside the realm of political office, profit, and negotiation. This conception involves simultaneously appropriating the discourse of libidinal voluntarism (the affective language of friendship) and displacing it onto the estate. By discursively fashioning the farm as a place of pleasure—property, or *res,* valued for its aesthetic sensuousness—the poet aligns himself with the values of elite *otium* rather than with the material dependency and debt of a subordinate "client," and he thereby lays rhetorical claim to the aristocratic status of the landholding elite.

Whether his poetry is understood as public ritual or as private epistles, then, Horace's literary "gifts" target and implicate an audience beyond his

---

55. See Benveniste 1973, 161, and Moussy 1966, 161–80, for the semantic range of *gratus* as "pleasing" or bringing pleasure.

immediate patrons. To understand fully the role of this third party in the patronal gift economy, we must turn to the writings of anthropology and their relevance to Horace. This is the subject of chapter 1, which follows a brief synopsis of the book.

· · ·

After a discussion of the economic diction in Horace's letter to Augustus, chapter 1 makes explicit in what ways cultural anthropology illuminates contradictions in the Roman discourse of benefaction and its relevance to Augustan literary patronage. Drawing on the work of Moses Finley (1973, 1974), Keith Hopkins (1983a), Veyne (1990), and Dixon (1993), authors who have made use of the anthropological literature on the gift, I first discuss the view of the ancient economy as embedded. Acknowledging the presence of coin and cash transactions in ancient Rome, I explore the degree to which the views of Cicero and Seneca on benefaction resemble the "functionalist" ideas about exchange held by Mauss (1990 [1950]), Sahlins (1972), Bronislaw Malinowski (1961 [1922]), and Lewis Hyde (1979). I then discuss benefaction in light of Bourdieu's (1977) ideas of "symbolic capital": here, gift exchange conceals economic self-interest and serves to reproduce social relations of domination. Finally, I consider certain key events in the received "biography" of Horace in light of this conflict between the ideology of voluntarism (and its model of social cohesion) and the presence of economic interest, symbolic capital, and exploitation.

In keeping with the functionalist view of a gift economy, chapter 2 explores odes in which I perceive the public *munus* of Horatian verse as a "voluntary" sacrificial expenditure that is intended to promote social cohesion. Drawing on René Girard (1977), a literary critic much influenced by anthropology, I contend that both the Pollio ode and *Odes* 3.1–6, as lyric invocations of tragedy, perform a symbolic sacrifice—and gift—of expiation for the crimes of the civil wars. From one perspective, tragedy serves as a mimesis of the public ritual of sacrifice and, in Girard's view, as a genre that reestablishes cultural differentiation. Assuming the role of *sacerdos Musarum*, Horace performs a metaphorical sacrifice for the Roman public by offering political lyric that, like tragedy, seeks to restore distinctions and the capacity to make them in a society where civil war has threatened to erase all difference. This gift of sacrifice, moreover, is embedded in political and social forms of exchange. By assuming the role of public priest, Horace deflects attention from the regime as the political source for his sacrificial expenditure on behalf of the people: although appearing "voluntary," Horace's *munus* of expiation is in part a reciprocating gift that responds to his own debt for receiving patronage from the state.

In the anthropological terms of a gift economy, the acceptance of gifts or property, *res*, symbolically expropriates the spirit and labor of the recipient. Rhetorical imagery that runs throughout the Horatian corpus suggests that if the Roman Odes constitute the embodiment of the poet's sacrificial labor, then it is the gift of the Sabine estate that lays a claim to such expenditure of self. Chapter 3 therefore examines representations of land or property in light of a rhetorical tension between an ideology of voluntarism and the contractual connotations of the gift. Drawing on concepts of Marxist aesthetics that address the ideological work of literature, I first discuss Vergil's *Eclogues* in regard to its historical backdrop of land expropriation and redistribution during the civil wars, and then the function of Vergilian allusions in Horace's depictions of the Sabine farm in the *Satires* and *Odes*. The *Eclogues*, I argue, assimilate a discourse of benefaction—as exemplified by land grants—to the conventions of the pastoral landscape. Horace, in turn, appropriates topoi associated with the golden age, or pastoral more generally, in a way that both confirms the model of social cohesion to which patronage aspires and reveals a certain calculated self-interest behind such aspirations. Such a "double hermeneutic" appears in different guises in *Satires* 2.6 and *Odes* 1.17. Moreover, it is in these two poems, particularly in the image of the *cornucopia* of 1.17, that we perceive the rhetorical strategies that later govern the epistolary speaker's treatment of patronage in his verse letters. By converting his estate into a *locus amoenus*, he simultaneously creates a *locus* of signifying excess that enables the aesthetic subversion of the patronal discourse, which expects his *gratia* to be expressed in particular forms.

Chapter 4 argues that Horace exploits this signifying multiplicity of the Sabine farm to refashion his relationship with Maecenas over the course of *Epistles* 1. Though the estate incurs an ongoing obligation in the discourse—or cultural practice—of patronage, it simultaneously provides the ground of independence from which the poet speaks in an egalitarian relationship of *amicitia:* the farm constitutes both the benefaction that the poet promises to return in *Epistles* 1.7, should it continue to oblige him, *and* the symbolic *rus* (country) from which he makes this gesture. What I emphasize in this chapter is how Horace dramatizes this ambiguity, incorporating gestures of refusal and independence into a poetics of socioeconomic exchange. Images of currency and exchange suggest that the "coin" of the speaker's language has value depending on his audience. By employing two types of *ainoi*, or illustrative stories, that appeal to different levels of status in his simultaneously public and private audiences, the speaker both reveals the economic self-interest that drives the implicit, if distorted, contract behind patronage and reinscribes himself in a relationship of aristocratic and egalitarian *amicitia* distinguished by an ideology of decorous and voluntary giving.

Chapter 5 focuses on the epistolary representations of Horace's estate in regard to the "contractual" understanding of patronage and the symbolic implication that the speaker's self has been expended as "reified labor" in the poetry of the *Satires* and the *Odes*. As a preface to my discussion of the Horatian poems, I analyze the dynamic of privation, song, and plenitude in Vergil's second eclogue. I then provide close readings of *Epistles* 1.14 and 1.16, letters to Horace's bailiff and to Quinctius, arguing that the poet represents his self as "reappropriated" through the epistolary process and the construction of the estate as a *locus amoenus*. By invoking details from either a golden age *topos* or the more inclusive generic frame of pastoral, the speaker identifies with an Epicurean vision of plenitude. Such plenitude and the capacity of the farm to render aesthetic and philosophical returns derive from what I call an "economy of *otium*," a concept introduced in chapter 3.

By making a distinction between the farm's role in producing real goods in a market economy and its role as source of aesthetics and Epicurean *ataraxia, Epistles* 1.14 and 1.16 reveal the poet's social anxiety and ambivalent claims to the aristocratic elite. Thus, despite taking an egalitarian tone, the speaker rhetorically exploits his bailiff by setting him up to compete in a philosophical agon concerning the problem of desire. By displaying the bailiff as an "enslaved" soul, the speaker naturalizes what are in fact social and economic disparities, confirming his own entitlement to the philosophical pursuits enabled by *otium* and shoring up the boundaries of elite affiliation and aristocratic status.

In the conclusion, I discuss the epistolary speaker's "gift relations" with his reader: by invoking the textual image of a *locus amoenus* the speaker not only restores himself through the philosophical praxis of writing these letters; he simultaneously emits, or gives, a pleasurable icon of himself that appeals to his readers in a way consonant with Bernard Frischer's (1982) understanding of Epicurean motivation and conversion.

This reading explores the rhetoric of Horace's poems as both shaped by, and participating within, the cultural discourses of religious expenditure (sacrifice), imperial expenditure (the *munera* of games, public buildings, etc.), and the social expenditure of private liberality or benefaction. Such a hermeneutic lens enables me to understand the particular relationship between the discourse of religious expiation informing the Roman Odes and the socioeconomic rhetoric of refusal informing the speaker's posture to his patron in the *Epistles*. These gestures of independence are revealed as participating within a larger patronal discourse of debt and expenditure that informs the speaker's representations of self, "public" and private audience, time, his Sabine property, and the verse itself as reified object of exchange.

CHAPTER ONE

The Gift Economy of Patronage

POETRY AND THE MARKETPLACE

Horace's Epistle to Augustus, 2.1, a survey of Roman literary history set within the frame of a *recusatio,* or "refusal poem," ends with a striking conceit.[1] After the conventional demurral that he is inadequate to the task of encomium but others are present to perform the duty, the speaker displaces the *princeps* and imaginatively identifies with the hazards faced by a ruler wishing for the precious boon of immortality.[2] In characteristic Horatian fashion, the speaker drives his point home through the rhetorical ploy of negation: he himself would blush with shame to be the recipient of disfiguring panegyric, fearing to be borne out into the street—the funereal echoes are unmistakable—as crumbling papyrus that has become the temporary wrapping of such goods as incense, spices, pepper, or the short-lived perishables of the vegetable market. By evoking a worst-case scenario in which the speaker, as subject of poor encomium, is destined to perish with his poet, Horace effectively demonstrates the importance of securing the talents of good writers:

---

1. Written in response to Augustus's request for a *sermo* addressed to him, *Epistles* 2.1 has naturally been viewed as somewhat strained in its flattery of the *princeps:* e.g., see Griffin 1984, 204; Brink 1982, 495, 561, 563. By contrast, Fraenkel (1957, 383) views Horace as "perfectly at ease," while Kilpatrick (1990, 14) and G. Williams (1968, 71–77) remark the poet's tact and fair-mindedness. For discussion of Horace's evocation of the tension between verbal (written) and visual (performed) communication in *Epistles* 2.1, see Habinek 1998, 98–102. See Rudd 1989, 1–12, for an overview of the circumstances of the poem's composition.

2. Horace's assumption of Augustus's role as subject of encomium here is an ironic version of what Zetzel (1982, 96) calls the "paradigm of the displaced patron."

>   sed neque parvum
> carmen maiestas recipit tua nec meus audet
> rem temptare pudor quam vires ferre recusent.
> sedulitas autem, stulte quem diligit, urget,   60
> praecipue cum se numeris commendat et arte;
> discit enim citius meminitque libentius illud
> quod quis deridet quam quod probat et veneratur.
> nil moror officium quod me gravat, ac neque ficto
> in peius vultu proponi cereus usquam   65
> nec prave factis decorari versibus opto,
> ne rubeam pingui donatus munere et una
> cum scriptore meo, capsa porrectus operta
> deferar in vicum vendentem tus et odores
> et piper et quidquid chartis amicitur ineptis.   70

But neither is your majesty suited to song of the small style nor does my modesty venture to try subjects that my strength refuses to bear. Zeal, moreover, foolishly annoys those whom it cherishes, especially when it recommends itself with measure and art; for one learns more quickly and remembers more easily that which one derides, than what one approves and respects. I have no patience for the service that burdens me, and I desire neither to be laid out anywhere in wax, with distorted features, nor to be celebrated in ill-formed poems, lest I blush presented with the boorish gift, and together with my poet, stretched out in a covered box, am borne into the street where they sell incense, perfume, pepper, and whatever else is wrapped in wastepaper. (2.1.257–70)

On the surface, the displacement of the emperor here serves as an ironic means of rhetorically justifying the refusals, and authenticating or "owning" the conventional inadequacies, expressed by the *recusatio:* if Horace were Augustus, he would be chary of the misshapen distortions of bad poetry; the same "modesty" or "sense of shame" (*pudor*) that prevents the poet from attempting the high style causes him to blush should he himself be presented with a "boorish gift" (*pingui . . . munere*). The obvious irony lies in the artistry with which Horace leaves us with a striking image by which we remember him, suffusing his visage with the red flush of life, even as he is borne out in a casket of commodities to be sold on the street.

But beneath the rhetorical manipulation of the addressee, the persuasive claim of "I can imagine your situation in a way that justifies mine" has an even more significant implication concerning poetic value and the tropes by which it is expressed. The phrase *pingui donatus munere* not only alludes to the Callimachean aesthetic by casting celebratory poetry—presumably epic—in the metaphorical terms of "fat sacrifice"; it also looks back to an earlier passage in the epistle, where the word *munus* refers not to verse but to the patronal benefactions or gifts that might elicit it.[3] After referring to the poor encomium that Choerilus produced for Alexander in exchange for actual money, the speaker assures Augustus that "Vergil and Varius, poets cherished by you, dishonor neither your judgment about them nor your gifts that, to the great glory of the giver, they have borne away" (*At neque dedecorant tua de se iudicia atque / munera, quae multa dantis cum laude tulerunt/ dilecti tibi Vergilius Variusque poetae*, 245–47). These poets do not "dishonor" their patron insofar as their poems do not—the subtext implies—"disfigure" (*dedecorant*) him. All these references to poetic production and value suggest a spectrum of economic systems by which poetry is both produced and rhetorically figured. On one end of the spectrum is a form of "market economics," where goods have an exact exchange value, and on the other is a gift economy, where the decorous gift of poetry presumably grows in value even as it ensures immortality.[4]

Taking the *Epistle to Augustus* as a point of departure and frame for my discussion, this chapter lays out the principles of a gift economy that I perceive as relevant to the cultural practice of benefaction in ancient Rome. Ultimately, my aim in subsequent chapters is not to read Horace's poems as exemplifying a blueprint for the social principles underlying the ancient economy; rather, I wish to use anthropological theory in conjunction with the moral philosophy of Cicero and Seneca to shed light on what I see as an interrelated symbolic system in which Horace poetically figured some of the exchanges comprising his experience of patronage. The Epistle to Augustus is a good place to begin because it explicitly discusses the various goods, both material and abstract, that were exchanged in a relationship of literary patronage. As I suggest, the speaker takes pains to distinguish between poetry produced in direct exchange for cash and poetry that reciprocates more vaguely defined "gifts" (*munera*). In the latter case, as Vergil and Varius witness, Augustus's *munera* yield in return not only decorous poetry but also the *laus* or public glory of the giver's generosity: Indeed, the glory of reputation depends, to a degree, on its celebration in verse. Such celebration, whether implicit or explicit in poetry, constitutes a "good" in an exchange relationship; but it becomes problematic in a "market" situation where money directly purchases verse:[5] generosity, in particular, has no place in a financial contract.

3. In its connotation of "fat sacrificial offering," *pingue munus* alludes specifically to Apollo's warning at the beginning of Callim. *Aet.* 1.23: "poet, feed the sacrificial victim to be as fat as possible, but keep the Muse slender."

4. Cf. the organic metaphor for the afterlife of verse in *Odes* 3.30.7–8, *usque ego postera / crescam laude recens*. As another poem in which Horace displaces Augustus and calls himself *princeps*, 3.30 presents the inverse of *Epistles* 2.1, where the poet imagines extinction.

5. Though a manuscript of the eighth–ninth century claims that Varius received 1,000,000 sesterces for his tragedy *Thyestes*, this was in the context of theatrical production to accompany

The story of Choerilus as a paid hack in the service of Alexander provides the negative exemplum in this regard. As the scholiasts point out, Horace has somewhat altered the traditional story: according to Porphyry, Alexander claimed that he would rather have been Homer's Thersites than Choerilus's Achilles; and according to Pseudo-Acro, the king had arranged to give a gold coin for every good line and a blow for every bad one, with the result that Choerilus was flogged to death (see Rudd 1989, 114). But in Horace's version, Alexander, entirely devoid of literary judgment, is pleased with Choerilus's verses and pays him handsomely. By thus altering the received narrative details, Horace wishes not only to praise Augustus's discernment in regard to Vergil and Varius but also to make a statement about the negative effects of commodifying poetry. As Choerilus's ill-fashioned and misbegotten poems reveal, such verse more easily turns unseemly and distorts the image of a ruler:

> gratus Alexandro, regi magno, fuit ille
> Choerilus, incultis qui versibus et male natis
> rettulit acceptos, regale nomisma, Philippos.
> sed veluti tractata notam labemque remittunt
> atramenta, fere scriptores carmine foedo
> splendida facta linunt.

He was pleasing to the great king Alexander, that Choerilus who carried away royal coin, philippi, which he received for badly formed and ill-conceived verse; but just as black ink, when handled, leaves a mark and blot, so generally writers blemish bright deeds by their unseemly poems. (2.1.232–37)[6]

No doubt Choerilus produced bad poetry because he lacked talent, but Horace also implies that the openly venal exchange of verse for money is more likely to yield such flawed results than is the gift economy in which poets such as Varius and Vergil participate. The claim that were one "to summon [Alexander's] judgment to assess books and these gifts of the Muses" (*iudicium . . . / ad libros et ad haec Musarum dona vocares*, 242–43), one "would swear it was born in the thick and heavy climate of the Boeotians" (*Boeotum in crasso iurares aere natum*, 244) further supports this subtext that literary patronage should operate as a gift economy in order to be effective. "Gifts of the Muses" denotes the poetry contained in *libros*, but

---

public games. See Jocelyn 1980, 387–400, for a discussion of the evidence. As P. White (1993, 147) points out, "drama had an institutional function which set it apart from other kinds of poetry." Brink (1982, 252) pointedly remarks on line 246 that the *munera* are "unlike the *Philippi*" of 234, 238.

6. In these lines about a poet's disfiguring his subject, there may be a trace of the story that Alexander would rather be Homer's Thersites than Choerilus's distorted Achilles.

the phrase also connotes the talent and inspiration that issues from the Muse; thus, had Alexander responded to literary talent as a gift to be discerned and then cultivated with gifts and benefactions (*munera*) of his own, he presumably would not have been lauded in such poor verse. The phrase *crasso . . . aere*, though clearly signifying the "thick and foggy air" of Boeotia, responsible for the dim-wittedness of its inhabitants, at the same time echoes the word for bronze coinage and money more generally, *aes, aeris*, whose ablative form, *aere*, differs from that for "air," only in the pronunciation of its vowels as a diphthong: the bad judgment denotatively produced by this thick-aired climate is connotatively rooted in the use of "crude money." Moreover, as Kiessling and Heinze point out (1960, ad loc.), the verb *vocares* personalizes Alexander's "judgment" (*iudicium*) and encourages reading *natum* or "born" as referring to Alexander himself: here we have a subtext that connects Alexander, "born from thick, crude money," to the gold philippus, a coin struck in the image of his father, with which the son paid Choerilus. From the Roman perspective, this negative, cautionary exemplum, implying the dangers of commodifying poetry, may also suggest more specifically *aes . . . grave*, the bronze *as* or one-pound "heavy" coin that began to be cast after the fashion of Greek coins sometime in the fourth century B.C.E. Although the "easily counterfeited, singularly ugly," and clumsy *aes grave* was no longer in circulation after 200 B.C.E. (Harl 1996, 24, 31), *aere . . . crasso* may very well hint at this early form of coinage whose crude, thick images constitute a "distortion" much as, this subtext suggests, poems created for cash payment "deface" their subject.

We see a similar wish on the speaker's part to dissociate the "good" poet from a venal relationship in lines 118–20: fashioning verses may constitute "deviant behavior" (*error*), but this form of mild lunacy (*levis haec insania*) has its merits (*virtutes*). For the mind of the authentic poet—whom the language of madness validates—is scarcely greedy (*vatis avarus / non temere est animus*, 119–20); and when self-serving thoughts do motivate him, he runs the risk of finding himself in Choerilus's situation. The speaker implies as much when he humorously recounts the various ways in which poets damage their reputation, ending with hopes for early discovery and immediate imperial patronage. In this fantasy, as soon as Augustus hears of poets composing verse, "you obligingly send for us, forbid our poverty, and compel us to write" (*commodus ultro / arcessas et egere vetes et scribere cogas*, 227–28). These lines, in turn, prompt the reflection that it is worth a ruler's effort to be informed of the literary talents of those who would write encomia or, more metaphorically, about "those whom Merit, proved in both peace and war, would have as keepers of her temple" (*qualis / aedituos habeat belli spectata domique / Virtus*), for she is not "to be entrusted to an unworthy poet" (*indigno non committenda poetae*, 229–31). Alexander's poor judgment regarding Choerilus is then adduced as a case in point. What we may notice here is how the negative portrayal of a market economy in regard to verse is effected largely through the metonymic associations of the speaker's thought. It is when poets begin to write specifically for compensation, with a view to profit, that the patronal experience approaches the open exchange of verse for money and its negative consequences. The speaker does not explicitly condemn such an exchange, but the evolution of his discussion and the juxtaposition of Alexander's cash payment with Augustus's gifts implies a condemnation. Similarly, the negative judgment in the final image of the poem is effected through metonymic association. Here, the gift economy collapses into a market system and the gift of bad poetry—*pingui munere*—becomes (and what could be a closer metonymic relationship than that between a wrapper and its good?) no better than what "you can buy on the street."

Thus, in contrast to the material perishables of the street market, destined to disappear in the act of consumption, good poetry lives on, acquiring an organic life of its own. But in addition to securing cultural immortality, poems produced in an effective gift economy also create powerful ideology. Indeed, here we encounter perhaps the strongest case for eliciting poetry through gifts and benefactions rather than an immediate cash compensation. As I discuss in more detail below, the concept of the gift is associated ideally with voluntarism and spontaneity. The true gift, insofar as it does not look for a return, should stir an equally spontaneous, voluntary, and unconstrained gratitude. In the context of Augustan Rome, where poetry supportive of the contemporary regime could provide a valuable form of persuasion as it communicated the desirability of political arrangements, a seemingly spontaneous—that is, voluntary—inclination to celebrate the emperor or merely to give an endorsement, however qualified, would be a mark of authenticity and credibility. It is finally "the public" who would be most impressed by the appearance of spontaneity that a gift economy effects. For the public—whether an aristocratic readership or "listening audience" of *nobiles,* or a more general audience of the type that would have attended theatrical performances (such as the *Eclogues* apparently enjoyed)—ultimately vested Augustus with his authority. In many ways, the senatorial elite whose own pretensions to power first made them targets of the proscriptions would later become the audience whose endorsement Augustus would be most interested in acquiring and confirming. The appearance of voluntarism in the production of ideology—which functions to naturalize social and political arrangements—would only further its credibility.

Chapter 3 explores the relationship between the gift economy and ideology in greater depth, but it is worth noting here how the speaker's *recusatio* suggests their interconnection. After the speaker praises Vergil and

Varius in phrases employing a gift lexicon, he relates panegyric to the vision of stable empire:

> nec magis expressi vultus per aenea signa
> quam per vatis opus mores animique virorum
> clarorum apparent. nec sermones ego mallem
> repentis per humum quam res componere gestas
> terrarumque situs et flumina dicere et arces
> montibus impositas et barbara regna tuisque
> auspiciis totum confecta duella per orbem
> claustraque custodem pacis cohibentia Ianum
> et formidatam Parthis te principe Romam,
> si quantum cuperem possem quoque.

[A]nd the features of illustrious men stand out no more clearly, rendered in statues of bronze, than do their character and spirit, presented in poets' work. And I would not choose to compose my poetic chatter, moving close to the ground, rather than verse on great deeds—singing about the lay of distant lands, and rivers, and citadels set on mountain peaks, and strange kingdoms, and the wars completed throughout the entire world under your auspices, and the bolts restraining Janus, custodian of peace, and Rome so feared by the Parthian, since you are our leader, if my ability were also as great as my desire. (2.1.248–57)

As Matthew Santirocco points out in his discussion of this epistle, the Augustan *recusatio* depends on a pretext of patronal pressure that poets, by employing the topos, advance on their own. By presenting the poet as capable of refusal, the *recusatio* thus places him "at some psychic and artistic distance" from the patron. Indeed, this epistle shows Horace appropriating Augustus to his own poetic agenda, a rhetorical strategy that allows the poet to maintain aesthetic independence even as it proves that he had a hand in the creation of political ideology (Santirocco 1995, 231, 243). I would add to his analysis the following points: First, the posture of refusal is possible only in a gift economy, in which poets respond to gifts (*munera*) but do not have to write poetry to order. Second, the brief description of the stability of the Roman Empire under Augustus's rule, the content of the poems the speaker would write if he could, takes on a paradoxical force and persuasiveness because he forgoes further elaboration. Finally, that the poems *do* serve the interests of the patron, however obliquely, indicates a psychic compulsion inscribed within the dynamic of a gift economy.

One might object that the persuasions of ideology would be a moot point by 12 B.C.E., the date assigned to the epistle, when Augustus's power had been relatively secure for almost two decades. However, as Richard Gordon has argued in his analysis of the iconographic representations of the emperor as both priest and sacrificer during the early Empire, the gifts, or *munera,* of public euergetism were a significant strategy by which both Augustus and the aristocratic elite cast an "ideological veil" over their material base of power and thus successfully perpetuated it (Gordon 1990a, 192–94). That the tropes and conventions associated with literary patronage employ this same economic language suggests the degree to which poetry as a form of public expenditure similarly served the interests of ideology. In this regard, the reference to the "temple worthy of Apollo" (*munus Apolline dignum,* 216) echoes, as an example of public euergetism, the *munera* of literary patronage and the civic function that they fulfill. And although Horace mentions the Palatine library in reference to patronage of written texts, pointedly contrasting them to the spectacles and public theater decried earlier in the epistle, he nonetheless presents his poems as aspiring to reach a wide—that is, public—audience.

This epistle clearly demonstrates that the diction of *munera, dona,* and *officia*—the language of gifts and of services reciprocating benefactions, rather than a lexicon associated with coinage, buying, and selling—characterizes the exchanges of Augustan patronage. It also shows that the value of such gifts partially lies in an aesthetic of decorum, where the tasteful judgment of the giver, appropriately matching gift to recipient, is confirmed by the decorousness of the return. Moreover, as Horace's own stylized *recusatio* makes clear, the discourse of gift exchange, as opposed to the commodification of verse through open purchase, allows the poet to "give" what he can—he would give more if he could (*si quantum cuperem possem quoque):* in Horace's case, this "ideology of voluntarism" translates into the conventional Callimachean gesture of praise in the very negation of such intent. The speaker respects the principle of decorum in this manner, writing finely spun poems (*tenui deducta poemata filo,* 225) in accord with his own talent, rather than offering the "insipid gift" or *pingue munus* that dooms poet and ruler alike to the short-lived products of the street, destined to disappear in smoke. Finally, such a posture of voluntarism ironically serves the interests of political ideology—the stability of Roman imperium guaranteed by the figure of Augustus—by presenting it as a given, a political arrangement so "natural" that the speaker can choose (in the interests of writing good or "authentic" poetry) not to celebrate it. That is, by focusing on his inadequacy to the task of panegyric, the speaker appears to take for granted the vision of empire that he in fact has just constructed.

When we return to this epistle to examine the chronology of Horace's generic transitions in relation to the regime and its "requests" or benefactions, we shall see that the gift economy in fact imposed a degree of constraint, obligation, and debt on the poet that belies the ideology of voluntarism. These are the tensions of *amicitia,* of patronage among the elite, that the poems of *Epistles* 1, always making reference to the poet's lyric past, coyly explore and attempt to resolve. To fully understand how the poet renegotiates his debts, relying on rhetorical manipulation of goods both material and symbolic, we must first look at the "embedded" character of the ancient economy.

THE EMBEDDED ECONOMY OF ROME

In his essay "Aristotle Discovers the Economy," Karl Polanyi distinguishes between capitalist societies that possess "an institutionally separate and motivationally distinct economic sphere of exchange" and those in which "the elements of the economy are . . . embedded in non-economic institutions." In the latter type, no transaction has a purely economic value; rather, the "economic process itself . . . [is] . . . instituted through kinship, marriage, age-groups, secret societies, totemic associations, and public solemnities" (Polanyi 1968, 84). Premonetary societies most clearly display this social dimension of exchange in their many ritual forms of interaction. And though much of the work of cultural and economic anthropology focuses on societies that can be, or have been, studied as active systems, the literature of the ancient world provides abundant evidence of both premonetary gift exchange and its continued influence on social interaction even after coin was introduced. For example, the gifts that a host lavishes on a visitor in the Homeric poems are the material embodiment of the bond of *xenia* or "guest-host friendship." The exchange of such goods serves the additional end of both social cohesion—*oikoi* or homes in different regions are linked together—*and* differentiation: that is, a certain gift or good might serve to distinguish its recipient as belonging to a particular rank.[7] To be sure, the Homeric world presents a fictional hybrid of different periods of early Greek history, and care must be taken in drawing firm conclusions about the reality of the economic practices depicted in the poems. All the same, their ideology of aristocratic gift exchange may be said to represent an early stage of the "status-based" or "embedded" ancient economy.[8]

Moses Finley, in particular, has developed this "primitivist" view of the classical economy, arguing that the idea of "profit" in a capitalist sense is

7. For a thorough reading of various types of exchange in Homer based on the models of reciprocity employed by Sahlins (1968, 1972), who modifies Polanyi, see Donlan 1993. In Sahlins's categories, Homeric gift exchange constitutes "balanced reciprocity," a direct quid pro quo. Nonetheless, as Donlan observes, "the quasi-kinship quality of guest-friendship . . . imposes obligations of 'generalized' reciprocity, of the kind due from kin and friends, which go beyond the formal duties of hospitality and gift-giving"—i.e., balanced reciprocity (150).

8. Donlan (1993, 137 n. 1) discusses the various problems associated with reading the Homeric poems for information about an actual social reality of the Greek world before the Archaic age. See Finley 1982 [1955] for such a reading.

foreign to the ancient world.[9] As Keith Hopkins points out in a summary of Finley's conclusions, "classical man did not behave like economic man. There was in ancient society no moral reinforcement for productive investment, nor for profit maximization; no heavenly salvation was promised to the puritanical saver. Instead, high status involved competitive and ostentatious expenditure, whether in the service of the state, or in the local community, or in the pursuit of purely personal political glory" (Garnsey, Hopkins, and Whittaker 1983, xiii–xiv). But even though classical man may not have behaved like Max Weber's conventional economic man, Pierre Bourdieu suggests that the economic motive of acquiring "symbolic capital" drives the gift-giving impulse in primitive man and thus, for Finley, in classical man as well. "Symbolic capital" refers here to both the status that the giver accrues and the debt or obligation that donation imposes on another.[10] I shall discuss this term later in more detail, but the point here is that a form of economic calculation was very much present in classical man: the desire for symbolic returns, or "capital," constitutes a wish for economic profit on one's expenditures. It is this relationship between debt, status, and expenditure that has led economists and historians alike to remark the gift-exchange ideology in both public and private benefactions in the Greco-Roman world: the posture of voluntary, decorous giving in fact serves to veil or mystify the economics of such exchange.

It is important all the same to acknowledge that after the introduction of coinage, monetary transactions and modified markets were a distinct feature of ancient society.[11] For Rome, in particular, scholars have emphasized that the second and first centuries B.C.E. saw a dramatic increase in the monetization of the economy.[12] As Kenneth Harl notes, administrative and military costs of the Republic, and the imperial expansion of the years 200–90 B.C.E., demanded payrolls in coin; Hopkins, arguing for the "thickened network of Roman trade" in the first two centuries C.E., remarks that even in Egyptian villages labor contracts were often expressed in terms of money (Harl 1996, 38; Hopkins 1983a, xx). The work of these scholars is in keeping with Polanyi's claim that "the development from embedded to

9. See Finley 1973 for an overview of his ideas about the ancient economy; Finley's chapter "Aristotle and Economic Analysis" (1974) similarly concludes that the economy was not a separate sphere of activity in the ancient world—i.e., that it was not "disembedded," to use Polanyi's term. For a view that challenges Finley's conclusions and the orientation of the Cambridge "primitivists," see Cohen 1992 on Athenian banking.

10. On "symbolic capital," see Bourdieu 1977, 171–83; Harker, Mahar, and Wilkes 1990, 5, 13–14.

11. See Harl 1996 for the argument that Roman coinage was in use for both fiscal and commercial purposes more than scholars have previously acknowledged.

12. Harl 1996, 38–72; Hopkins (1983b, xx) notes that between 157 and 80 B.C.E., "the volume of roman silver coins in circulation increased tenfold (Hopkins (1980) 109)."

disembedded economies is a matter of degree" and that the latter comes into being with the widespread use of coinage, or money more generally, as a means of exchange. Polanyi ascribed the "empirical discovery" of the distinction between these two types of economy to Sir Henry Sumner Maine, the historian of Roman law who, in the 1860s, argued that forms of *contractus*, "rights and duties derived from bilateral arrangements," were the cornerstone of modern society. In contrast, the *status* of birth and kin relations defined a person's rights in ancient society (Polanyi 1968, 82–84). It is sometimes claimed that the precursors of Roman contract law were *nexum*, an ancient form of debt-bondage, and *mancipatio*, the transfer of ownership of *res mancipi*.[13] Both of these were transactions conducted *per aes et libram*, an act that involved the weighing out of a fixed amount of bronze as a measure of value. Though *nexum* became obsolete in the late fourth century B.C.E., *mancipatio* continued into postclassical times. That these early forms of Roman *contractus* are roughly simultaneous with the advent of coinage underscores the relationship between money and contract as the beginnings of what eventually evolves into disembedded, motivationally distinct market systems.[14]

And yet it is precisely the formulas involved in these exchanges, and the etymology of many of the terms referring to early forms of Roman contract, that led Marcel Mauss to perceive in them the older characteristics of primitive gift exchange (1990 [1950], 48–53). In light of Mauss's perception that early Roman law displays the "traces" of gift exchange, and that "the Semitic, Greek and Roman civilizations were the first to draw a strong distinction between obligations and services that are not given free, on the one hand, and gifts, on the other," Bourdieu has commented: "It is no accident that the vocabulary of the archaic economy should be entirely composed of double-sided notions that are condemned to disintegrate in the course of the history of the economy, since, owing to their duality, the social relations they designate represent unstable structures." (Mauss 1990 [1950], 48; Bourdieu 1977, 172).[15] If the institution of *nexum*, or debt-bondage, suggests the initial ideological fallout or historical debris—one side of the earlier double-sided notion—then the Roman ideology of ben-

13. Varro, *Ling.* 7.105 is a major source for interpretations of *nexum*. On both *nexum* and *mancipatio*, see Watson 1975, 111–49, esp. 135: "*Mancipatio* as contract is revealed by the weighing of bronze and the reference to it in the transferee's declaration, both of which are integral parts of the ceremony."

14. Watson 1975, 137: "The business with bronze and scales involved an actual weighing out of the price and is not an indication of formalism in early Roman law. Not until around 280 B.C. did the Romans coin money[;] . . . the ceremony of *mancipatio* itself indicates unambiguously both that bronze had become the standard medium of exchange and that a fixed weight of bronze, such as a pound, had become a measure of value."

15. See also Benveniste 1973, 53–162.

efactions, both public euergetism and private liberality, constitutes a later continuation of the gift exchange that characterizes a society based solely on *status*. That is, although Rome possessed coin and engaged in monetary trade and transactions, the highly stratified system of social and political patronage, or benefaction, still functioned as an embedded economy.[16]

Paul Veyne's monumental book on euergetism in the ancient world (1990) takes the concept of the gift as its organizing principle. As Oswyn Murray points out in his introduction to the English edition, Veyne's study in fact implies a distinction between the concepts of gift economy and gift exchange. A gift economy presumes the absence of real reciprocity—that is, the goods and services exchanged are incommensurable and cannot be acquired in any other way. Veyne's book deals with private expenditure for the public good, a subject somewhat different than personal patronage in the upper classes, but we should nonetheless recognize in the above distinction elements of Richard Saller's definition: it is the asymmetry of the relationship—the difference in status and public position—that results in each person offering something to which the other does not have access. In contrast to such a "gift economy," gift exchange implies a "society halfway to becoming 'rational' in our sense, since people could count the values in this exchange, and establish a market in the gift" (Murray 1990, xiv.).[17] In some ways, we could argue that this objection to the terminology of "exchange" retrojects the nineteenth-century application of the term in the analysis of market and commodity relations back onto the alien, "primitivist" economy. Moreover, as I shall discuss further, it is precisely the interconvertibility—or exchanges—of material and symbolic capital that distinguishes the economics of a gift economy. In any case, Veyne himself avoids the concept of exchange for other reasons as well: in keeping with the emphasis on voluntarism in the philosophical literature on benefactions, he stresses that the ancient world perceived public giving as a kind of duty and privilege reserved for the wealthy upper classes.

This public or civic function of the private individual both subsumed the ideology of aristocratic gift exchange in the Greek polis and (more

---

16. Eisenstadt and Roniger (1984, 166–85) discuss the mixture of clientelism (or patronage) and free market economy in terms of an "ascriptive-hierarchical" society in which clients have some access to markets, but still exchange goods and services with their patrons. Nicols (1995, 1–9) places Republican and Imperial Rome in this category.

17. Indeed, this is precisely what Tchernia (1983, 101) argues to have occurred in the trade between the Gallic peoples and Italians in the first century B.C.E.: in return for a steady supply of Gallic slaves, Italian merchants traded wine; while the Gauls themselves distributed wine as a prestigious gift after the fashion of a potlatch, the Italian merchants, "By multiplying the occasions for the giving of gifts and counter-gifts between the Gallic peoples and the Romans, . . . conferred an exchange value upon commodities which had until then above all had a use value."

relevant to our purposes) is reflected in the monetary criteria of the Roman orders of senators and *equites*.[18] Indeed, the financial demands on the politically ambitious in the late Republic and early Empire were so great that the nobility, though rich in land, had to resort to borrowing huge sums of cash (Finley 1973, 56). But the spending of such vast amounts of money on public games, dinners, or distributions to the *plebs* was expected of the powerful and, ideally, was supposed to be voluntary and free of self-interest. Discussing Aristotle's distinction between the liberal and the magnificent man (*Nic. Eth.* 4.4), Veyne emphasizes that "Euergetism is the manifestation of an 'ethical virtue,' of a quality of character, namely magnificence," and he goes on to comment that the magnificent man "gives without receiving presents in exchange. He devotes his fortune to higher values, civic or religious, and does not introduce his bounty into the system of exchange of favours that characterizes the more modest virtue of liberality" (1990, 14). In keeping with Aristotle's definition, Suetonius records Augustus as unstintingly generous to all classes, but willing to withhold distributions in order "to show that he did all this not to win popularity but to improve public welfare" (*Aug.* 42). And yet, as Tacitus so memorably acknowledges, Augustus maintained power by having "charmed all with the sweetness of leisure,"[19] a phrase that implies the effects of—or the "symbolic capital" garnered by—the emperor's considerable expenditures on "bread and circuses."

The Roman philosophical writers, too, analyzed the art of giving as a quality of character, and both Cicero's *De officiis* and Seneca's *De beneficiis* provide a kind of handbook for the proper behavior of a Roman aristocrat. However, even in the case of private benefaction, where the more modest virtue of liberality is exercised, an emphasis on voluntarism in these writers conflicts with and sometimes conceals the actual code of reciprocity. Seneca, for example, patently claims that "In benefits the book-keeping is simple—so much is paid out; if anything comes back, it is gain, if nothing comes back, there is no loss. I made the gift for the sake of giving. . . . The good man never thinks of [benefits] unless he is reminded of them by having them returned. . . . To regard a benefit as an amount advanced is putting it out at shameful interest." On the other hand, in problematic contrast with the injunction to the giver to forget the benefit once conferred is the prescription "to surpass in deed and spirit those who have

18. See Kurke 1991, 89, for the transition from aristocratic gift exchange to euergetism in the Greek polis; for the financial criteria of *equites* and senators, which changed under Augustus, and the need for conspicuous consumption to establish status and ensure political loyalty—the mark of an embedded economy—see Suet. *Aug.* 41; Finley 1973, 46, 53, 56; Duncan-Jones 1974, 17–32; Hopkins 1983, 168.

19. Tac. *Ann.* 1.2: *cunctos dulcedine otii pellexit.*

placed us under obligation, for he who has a debt of gratitude to pay never catches up with the favor unless he outstrips it" (*Ben.* 1.2.3, 1.4.3).[20] One might say that by placing the burden of gratitude on the recipient, the giver is free to forget in the secure, if repressed, knowledge of delayed return.

Cicero acknowledges more explicitly the conflict between a prescriptive ideology of honorable giving and the self-interested exploitation of the system: "In granting favours, on the other hand, and in requiting gratitude, the most important function of duty (if all else is equal) is to enrich above all the person who is most in need of riches. But people generally do exactly the opposite; for they defer above all to him from whom they expect the most, even though he does not need them" (*Off.* 1.49).[21] Despite this acknowledgment, Cicero himself enacts a form of the conflict, insofar as the publication of his letters is a deliberate attempt to reap the symbolic capital of overt generosity (see Dixon 1993, 452). Discussing these paradoxes, the social historian Suzanne Dixon claims that they are more acute in the upper classes, where the "ideology of internal egalitarianism" leads to a certain "notional reticence about the essential reciprocity of all giving" (453, 454).

As I have suggested, the economic transactions of literary patronage are embedded, to a certain degree, in these social practices of personal—as well as imperial—expenditure. However, the tensions in the prescriptive literature on benefaction are precisely what renders its explanatory power less than sufficient for my analysis of the relationship between the public poetry of *Odes* 1–3 as a form of "expenditure" and the more private poetry of *Epistles* 1. Thus, in keeping with historians such as Veyne and Dixon, I turn to the writings of cultural anthropology to provide a hermeneutic lens for the rhetoric of benefaction in Horatian verse, considering attributes of a gift economy from the perspectives of both anthropological functionalism and social domination.

Expenditure

In his seminal work on the nature of the gift, *Essai sur le don,* Marcel Mauss analyzes the phenomenon of expenditure in terms of the potlatch: the ritual giving, destruction, and consumption of goods practiced by native tribes and peoples of the American Northwest (Tlingit and Haïda) and British Columbia (Haïda, Tsimshian, and Kwakiutl). For these tribes, public ceremonies of gift giving, and sometimes pure destruction of goods, serve

---

20. See also Sen. *Ben.* 2.17.7: "The best man is he who gives readily, never demands any return, rejoices if a return is made, who in all sincerity forgets what he has bestowed, and accepts a return in the spirit of one accepting a benefit." All translations of *De beneficiis* are from the Loeb edition (Basore 1935), unless otherwise noted.

21. Unless otherwise noted, translations of *De officiis* are by M. Atkins from the edition of M. T. Griffin and E. M. Atkins (1991).

to establish the prestige and honor of the donor. Moreover, the act of giving is rivalrous, each individual competing in order "to transform into persons having an obligation those that have placed you yourself under a similar obligation" (Mauss 1990 [1950], 37). The public and theatrical character of the potlatch both ensures the accountability of those put under obligation by the gift and provides the "third party" or audience in whose eyes the political status of the donor is increased. However, as in the other cultures Mauss studies, such expenditures are represented as "apparently free and disinterested but nevertheless constrained and self-interested. Almost always such services have taken the form of the gift, the present generously given even when, in the gesture accompanying the transaction, there is only a polite fiction, formalism, and social deceit, and when really there is obligation and economic self-interest" (3). We see several characteristic features of ancient patronage here—the public display of generosity, the tacit obligation to reciprocate, and the accumulation of status through expenditure.

Status here is best understood in terms of symbolic capital—both the reputation in the eyes of the community and the credit in relation to the recipient, which the giver accrues by giving away goods. By exercising the capacity to give away material worth, the giver converts material capital into the symbolic capital of honorable generosity. In keeping with Bourdieu's extension of this term, we may also consider it as the prestige value that material objects may possess, often in excess of their actual worth, or that less tangible "goods"—such as a poem's praise, a dedication, or the favor of a social introduction—confer on their recipient in the Roman context.[22] Moreover, as Bourdieu claims, social and economic values are entirely interconvertible: if certain material goods or "gifts" have a social or "prestige" value that confers symbolic capital on both the donor and the recipient, then this credit can be converted back into a narrowly conceived economic value. Again extending this idea to the Roman economy of patronal benefactions, we perceive that despite the incommensurability of the goods exchanged, it is their inaccessibility except through exchange that contributes to the economic value of symbolic goods and vice versa. Thus, we may consider again the example of Cicero's recommendation of Trebatius to Caesar, discussed in the introduction: when Cicero rebukes his young

22. Bourdieu 1977, 177–78: "The only way to escape from the ethnocentric naiveties of economism, without falling into populist exaltation of the generous naivety of earlier forms of society, is to carry out in full what economism does only partially, and to extend economic calculation to *all* the goods, material and symbolic, without distinction, that present themselves as rare and worthy of being sought after in a particular social formation—which may be 'fair words' or smiles, handshakes or shrugs, compliments or attention, challenges or insults, honour or honours, powers or pleasures, gossip or scientific information, distinction or distinctions, etc."

friend for attempting to cash in on his letter of recommendation, treating it as a bill of exchange with which he may lay claim to the material advantages to be had on Caesar's campaign in Gaul, we witness the conversion of symbolic capital or *gratia* (in this case Cicero's influence with Caesar) into the straightforward economic value of material wealth. And yet Trebatius can really only get this material wealth through the favor of the introduction that Cicero has given him, and Caesar can only reap the symbolic capital of having done a favor for Cicero by assisting in the enrichment of Trebatius in Gaul. Finally, this traffic in the symbolic and material may often combine the two kinds of capital in one expenditure: in crude terms, Maecenas's gift of land to Horace—an economic or material value— had the far more important symbolic value of lending the poet the status of a landholder, a man of independent means; expenditure such as this, in turn, creates the symbolic capital that encourages Horace to celebrate his patron, creating the ultimate cultural value of Maecenas's immortality.

This loan of status, by which the gift reflects both on the recipient and back on the giver, is apparent in Horace's frequent use of the word *decus* to describe Maecenas in relation to himself: "glory," "ornament," "honor"— the range of meanings suggests the honor that Maecenas confers on the poet through association with him and by his benefactions to him, as well as the glory that the poet reciprocates by honoring his patron in his poems.[23] But this reciprocal exchange of status, in which giver and receiver are both distinguished by the gift, depends, as Mauss suggests, on a third party to witness the transaction. It is in the eyes of the community that the giver accrues status by giving away wealth; conversely, wealth confers status on the recipient by virtue of its desirability in the eyes of others. Status depends, to some degree, on the envy of those who possess less, and the public display by which this envy is incited underscores the word's etymological root in the Latin *videre* (to see). What we understand as a "status symbol" is ineffective unless it can both be read by a large audience that is literate in a particular cultural code and, at the same time, be accessible only to a fraction of that public. As Peter White points out, the gifts made by a *potens amicus* to a poet in the late Republic and early Empire might be of greater symbolic than material value, serving to distinguish the status of the beneficiary in connection to the donor (1993, 88). The complexity of this triangular relationship, and the necessity of the witness to exchanges of status, is concisely summed up in Andrew Wallace-Hadrill's comment about the delicate balances of political patronage: "The people below you estimate your standing in the eyes of those above you; and those above

---

23. *Odes* 1.1.2, 2.17.4, 3.16.20. P. White 1993, 18: "The loan of status was especially important for anyone who hoped to mix with the elite." See Gold 1987, 121, on the phrase *praesidium et dulce decus meum.*

estimate your support from below. . . . Much of the value of *clientela* lay not in a solid and dependable block of votes, but in its contribution to appearances, by which the majority of voters themselves had to judge" (1989, 83). Indeed, claiming that the vote of the urban poor was most effectively courted by "bread and circuses," Wallace-Hadrill points up a similarity between a patron's "consumption" of *clientela* and expenditure on the public games: the impulse behind the giving—whether to clients or to the public at large—arises from the wish to accumulate symbolic capital, the appearance of generous magnanimity.

Social Cohesion

The gift-exchange psychology underlying Roman patronage involves more than a competition for status. Though the rivalrous consumption and giving away of goods constitute a "war of property," the obligation to receive gifts ensures the opposite—the creation of social bonds. Three related features of the process of gift exchange contribute to this creation of community or social interrelatedness: first, the tendency of the gift to pass to a third party in place of pure reciprocation; second, the tendency of the gift to increase in value—that is, the reciprocal gift is often larger than the initial one that elicited it; and third, the frequent "intermingling" of souls and objects, as Mauss would characterize it, that occurs when a person perceives the object given away as an extension of the self. Before exploring these features in relation to the Roman world and the Horatian experience of patronage, we should look more closely at the anthropological writings that best exhibit them.

In his analysis of the Maori, a hunting people of Polynesia, Mauss isolates a quality called the *hau*, or the spirit of the gift, which causes the receiver to reciprocate and give a present in return to the original donor.[24] Though Mauss has been criticized for falsely perceiving a mystical force in the concept of *hau*, his study nonetheless points up both the essential movement of the gift—its tendency to be passed on—and the frequent presence of a third party that turns the simple exchange into a process of circulation.[25] For example, in Marshall Sahlins's revisionary treatment of Mauss's analysis, the *hau* is translated as an "excess"—that is, a "return on" or "product of" the original gift—that must be given back to its source. Sahlins cites the custom of Maori hunters who, when they have killed birds in the forest,

---

24. On the notion of the *hau*, see Mauss 1990 [1950], 10–13; Sahlins 1972, 150–83.

25. Lévi-Strauss (1987, 47) writes, "But instead, in *The Gift*, Mauss strives to reconstruct a whole out of parts; and as that is manifestly not possible, he has to add to the mixture a supplemental quantity which gives him the illusion of squaring his account. This quantity is *hau*." See Derrida 1992, 76–77, for further discussion of Lévi-Strauss's critique of Mauss and Mauss's invention of the *hau* as an explanatory force.

invariably return a portion to the priests who are thought to make the woods fertile with such game and who give a portion of what has been given them back to the forest so that it might abound with birds. In this scheme, there is a perpetual circulation of a "gift" for which no original donor can be specified. The priests' gift to the forest is called *mauri*—the embodiment of *hau,* the power of increase. The forest, in turn, gives its game to the hunters, and they give back a portion of their kill to the priests. Rather than interpret the *hau* as a spiritual force, Sahlins claims that it represents "yield," making the point that for the Maori, "one man's gift should not be another man's capital, and therefore the fruits of a gift ought to be passed back to the original holder." A third party thus becomes necessary in order to "show a *turnover:* the gift has had issue; the recipient has used it to advantage" (1972, 160). Reciprocation here is a matter of giving back the increase on a gift to the person who made such increase possible.

Sahlins here prefers a purely economic understanding of the concept of *hau,* but a more recent interpretation of this Maori term inclines once again to the spiritual understanding of Mauss. Lewis Hyde's *The Gift: Imagination and the Erotic Life of Property* opens with chapters that explore the anthropological literature on gift exchange as a way of understanding characteristics of the gift that apply to art. Hyde's analysis of the Maori ritual particularly emphasizes the ceremony—called *whangai hau,* or "nourishing the spirit"—by which the priests return a portion of the birds to the forest. As Hyde points out, the etymological root of "generosity" is the word *genus, generis,* "offspring" or "stock"—a noun related to the verb *gignere,* "to beget" or "to produce" (1979, 35). In the animistic world of the Maori, the spirit of the forest is made generous, is encouraged to become abundant, by the ceremonial gifts of the priests. When Hyde generalizes this particular scenario into a paradigm that contrasts gift circulation with commodity exchange, he asserts that the spirit of increase or generosity has the effect of establishing social bonds between the parties involved (18–19, 35–39). Because *hau* can also mean "excess," or the power of increase, it could suggest the libidinal element of emotion—the emotional excess that accompanies a gift. Hyde implies as much when he appropriates an essentially psychoanalytic language to discuss the communal ego created by gift circulation (17–18). Viewing the ego as an elastic concept, a libidinal pool of emotional energy that may widen to constitute a social entity, Hyde thus extends Mauss's observation that gift exchange causes souls and objects to intermingle. Understood psychoanalytically, such intermingling results from the libidinal cathexis, or emotional attachment, to the object given to another. It is this emotional valuation of the object exchanged that Hyde captures in the phrase "the erotic life of property."

Hence, contrary to the exchange of commodities in a fully disembedded economy, where the precise monetary value of an object allows for the liquidation of the relationship between the contracting parties, gift exchange (ideally) serves to create social bonds. As C. A. Gregory succinctly writes, "commodity exchange establishes a relationship between the objects exchanged, whereas gift exchange establishes a relationship between the subjects" (1982, 19). To take another example, in the Trobriand Islands the practice of *kula*—"ring" or "circle"—essentially connects a vast network of people through inter- and intratribal trade. One of the most significant rituals is the trade of decorative bracelets and necklaces, ornamental objects invested with high prestige value.[26] These decorative goods are not simply traded between two individuals but rather are passed from one person to another in arcs extending over considerable geographical territory. Moreover, while the receiver of an object does acquire a form of "ownership" over it, the relation is, as Mauss remarks, far more complex, entailing "ownership and possession, a pledge and something hired out, a thing sold and bought, and at the same time deposited, mandated, and bequeathed in order to be passed on to another. For it is only given you on condition that you make use of it for another or pass it on to a third person, the 'distant partner,' the *murimuri*" (1990 [1950], 24). It is this tendency of a gift to pass on to a third person and not necessarily back to the original giver that helps create social bonds: for, as Sahlins notes, when two partners trade, "balanced exchange may tend toward self-liquidation."[27]

The circulation of decorative objects among the "primitive" tribes of the islands off New Guinea may seem a far cry from the exchanges of Roman patronal relations, but, as will become clear, the point of the comparison lies in the cohesion that results from an ongoing passage of gifts. Such cohesion may be seen to be of two kinds, both integrating different social strata and solidifying bonds among those at the top of that hierarchy. Although persons of lower rank participate in many of the peripheral gift exchanges that take place beside and in conjunction with the trade of the *kula*, the giving and receiving of the bracelets and necklaces as high "prestige" objects is generally reserved for the "chiefs" alone (Mauss 1990 [1950], 27–29). Such objects serve to distinguish their recipient as belonging to a particular social stratum even as, by marking that rank, they underscore the recipient's obligation to give generously in keeping with the

---

26. For descriptions and analysis of the *kula*, see Malinowski 1961 [1922], 81–104, 350–65; Mauss 1990 [1950], 21–31; Hyde 1979, 12–18.

27. It is worth quoting Sahlins (1965, 178), in full here: "The casual received view of reciprocity supposes some fairly direct one-for-one exchange, balanced reciprocity, or a near approximation of balance. It may not be inappropriate, then, to footnote this discussion with a respectful demur: that in the main run of primitive societies, taking into account directly utilitarian as well as instrumental transactions, balanced reciprocity is not the prevalent form of exchange. A question might even be raised about the stability of balanced reciprocity. Balanced exchange may tend toward self-liquidation."

material basis of the acknowledged status. Thus, not only does a Trobriand chief have the obligation to pass on the symbolic bracelet or necklace, but his very possession of it marks his rank and wealth, which he is similarly obliged to give away in the form of feasts or other tribal festivities (Malinowski 1961 [1922], 62–65, 97).

It is the "symbolic capital" or prestige value of the ornamental jewelry that makes the analogy to the Roman world illuminating. Such objects fulfill a social function suggestively similar to that of such diverse symbolic goods in the Roman world as a book's dedication or the Roman office of the priesthood. Thus, when Horace calls Maecenas his *decus,* both "glory" and "ornament," he not only displays the status that his patron's association and wealth have conferred on him, as discussed earlier, but also circulates this symbolic capital to those included as addressees in his poems. To be sure, Augustus, Vergil, Agrippa, and Pollio all possess their own resources, both material and symbolic. Nonetheless, the prestige of the dedication, as an ornament, casts its reflection on others: it creates a "ring" or network of status that reinforces the self-conception and interaffiliation of the elite. In contrast to such circulation among the upper echelons of society, we might consider the distinction or honor of a "symbolic good" such as the priesthood, a civic office generally filled by the elite—one that, as the next chapter argues, has particular relevance for Horace's public posture as "priest of the Muses." Though many sacerdotal positions were electoral, under the Principate they were increasingly used as instruments of patronage (Gordon 1990c, 221). And as Gordon has claimed, the prestigious appointment to such an office brought with it the reciprocal duty of vast expenditure on real goods, a form of public prestation whose end was the creation of symbolic capital or the loyalty and gratitude of the masses (194). Thus *munus,* in its sense of "public office" or responsibility, evinces the double-sidedness of the vocabulary of the ancient economy and reveals its etymological origins in the Indo-European root **mei,* meaning "exchange" (Benveniste 1973, 79). And yet these examples demonstrate not "balanced exchange [that] may tend toward self-liquidation," but rather the circulation and transmutation of capital, both symbolic and material. It is in this regard—the socially motivated expenditure and interconvertibility of forms of wealth—that we remark the "gift economy" of patronage.

Disequilibrium and the Perpetuation of Debt

Though the circulation of many goods in primitive societies operates according to "spheres of exchange," or social tiers, the stratification of Roman society was such that the "goods and services" exchanged in the patronal system often crossed lines of status and could not be acquired through other means.[28] Quoting Sahlins's view concerning the potential liquidation of balanced trade, Saller specifies that "a precise one-for-one exchange—that is, a complete and conscious absolution of debt—leaves both parties free to break off the relationship without moral recriminations" (1982, 15–16). Saller points here to the mutually reinforcing character of the criteria he uses to define patronage: because the unequal status of the two parties implies an incommensurability of the goods and favors exchanged, indebtedness is perpetual and ambiguous.[29] Saller addresses patronage in the upper classes, but one of the most conventional of such exchanges in formal *patrocinium* has traditionally been conceived in terms of the political support that a *cliens* gave to his patron in return for legal protection and material benefits (Saller 1982, 29; Wallace-Hadrill 1989, 68–69). The nature of such favors or duties precludes precise determinations of value, because in an embedded economy they have no exact "exchange value"—they are outside a monetary system that could provide them with a common denominating term. Moreover, even if a good did have an exchange value, such as the legacies that clients often left their patrons as a final gesture of honor,[30] it was offered as a gift and hence carried an emotional value that eludes quantification. Such impossibility of determining precise values leads each party to feel potentially still in debt to the other, thereby ensuring that the relationship continues.

Ambiguity of debt arises from other sources as well. For example, the rivalrous desire to outdo the other—as in the competitive potlatch—consistently produces a gift in excess of the first, thus maintaining and reconfiguring the disequilibrium of debt initiated by the initial expenditure.[31] Moreover, in a highly stratified culture in which "gifts" are exchanged as *beneficia* and *officia* across the invisible lines of status, the recipient of a benefaction remains, in a sense, forever indebted to a benefactor of a higher order. In contrast to actual monetary debt, Seneca claims that "to the [creditor for a benefit] I must make an additional payment, and even after I have paid my debt of gratitude, the bond between us still holds; for, just when I have finished paying it, I am obliged to begin again, and friendship endures" (*Ben.* 2.18.5). A person unable to repay his benefactor in full instead disseminates similar benefactions to those of lower status. In place

28. See Gregory 1982, 49, on spheres of exchange.

29. As Seneca (*Ben.* 3.9.3) comments, "Since benefits may be given in one form and repaid in another, it is difficult to establish their equality."

30. Saller 1982, 29, 71–73. Significantly, Horace left all his property to Augustus, a gesture that points up the emperor's stature as a patron and that became common practice after his reign.

31. For such ambiguity, though not rivalrous on the surface, see Cic. *Fam.* 2.6.1–2 and the discussion of the passage in Saller 1982, 17.

of a pure reciprocity, a passage of goods and services down a hierarchical network of similar relations pays off the debt to society at large and provides for social cohesion.

In a telling passage of *De officiis,* Cicero himself distinguishes between monetary exchange (or debt absolved) and the duties and benefactions that characterize patronage: "As someone has happily said, A man has not repaid money, if he still has it; if he has repaid it, he has ceased to have it. But a man still has the sense of favour, if he has returned the favour; and if he has the sense of the favour, he has repaid it."[32] Cicero quotes this dictum to point out that patronage of the poor who are unable to repay the service in kind leads to a lasting emotional gratitude that cultivation of the rich may not yield. Notwithstanding the problematic politics of his comment, his example underscores the contrast between the closure of a relationship based on monetary exchange and the sense of ongoing emotional indebtedness in response to a favor. Moreover, the paradox of still retaining the favor, despite having returned it, points up the social implications of the connotative range of the word *gratia:* on the one hand, *gratia* refers to a favor done by one person for another, and thus reflects a concrete action or service; on the other hand, the word suggests the feeling of gratitude—"the sense of the favor," as the translation would have it—that the recipient of such a service experiences.[33] Hence, a person could both return a favor and yet still have it; most important, this double valency of the word, a kind of connotative elasticity, suggests the social function of cohesion that patronage serves.[34] Though repaid, a favor leaves behind a sense of thankfulness that binds the receiver to the giver.

Finally, we should note here a point to which we shall return in chapter 3. Couched in the comparative terms of monetary debt, Cicero's dictum illuminates the apparent paradox behind the exchange of favors ("apparent" because the connotations of *gratia* become paradoxical only in a monetary context): though repaid, *gratia* leaves behind an excess or residue, a trace of itself—something that, in fact, causes the favor to increase in value. Cicero refers to increase even more specifically when, quoting Hesiod, he claims: "But if, as Hesiod bids, one is to repay with interest, if possible, what one has borrowed in time of need, what, pray, ought we to do when chal-

32. Cic. *Off.* 2.69: *Commode autem, quicumque dixit, "pecuniam qui habeat, non reddidisse, qui reddiderit, non habere, gratiam autem et, qui rettulerit, habere et, qui habeat, rettulisse."* I translate here from the Loeb edition (W. Miller 1913).

33. This latter meaning also reflects the sense of *gratia* as "influence" exercised by the benefactor over the recipient. Hellegouarc'h (1963, 202–8) provides the fullest lexical discussion of the term.

34. See Saller 1982, 69–78. Wallace-Hadrill (1989, 71–78) discusses patronage more in the context of social integration—the capacity of the system to incorporate "outsiders," either those newly arrived in the city of Rome or people living on the city's periphery.

lenged by an unsought kindness? Shall we not imitate the fruitful fields, which return more than they receive?" (*Off.* 1.48).[35]

From the viewpoint of anthropological "functionalism," this increase suggests both the Maori's concept of the *hau* and Hyde's idea of "libidinal excess"—the tendency of the gift to accrue value in its passage and to provide the social glue for community.[36] For it is precisely because a person can never truly pay back a benefit to the original donor—making *gratia* an ongoing emotion (or sense of obligation)—that the gift is passed down to a third party.[37] Hence, community arises both from the emotions stirred by the gift and from the movement of reciprocating benefactions down a hierarchical network of relations. Discussing this functionalist or integrative view, Wallace-Hadrill writes that "what justifies describing the network as a whole as a patronage network is that it involves exchanges between those closer to the centre of power and those more distant from it, and has the effect of mediating state resources through personal relationships" (1989, 77). While the functionalist view of patronage recognizes reciprocity as necessary to integration, it emphasizes the social rather than the economic dimension of exchange: that is, functionalism ultimately sees the exchange of goods and services as emanating from the need and desire for social cohesion rather than from a desire for profit. Cicero, again, suggests such a patronal ideology when he claims that people "are 'bound' together in strong fellowship, by the giving and receiving of benefactions [or favors], so long as they are mutual and pleasing" (*ex beneficiis ultro et citro datis acceptis, quae et mutua et grata dum sunt . . . firma devinciuntur societate; Off.* 1.56).[38]

Delay and the Mystifications of Time

But the same qualities that provide for social cohesion may also be seen as exploitative. As Bourdieu points out, the temporal delay between a first gift and its reciprocation may symbolically bind the recipient to the donor, but it also serves to mystify the economic aspect of this type of exchange:

35. Trans. W. Miller 1913, Loeb edition: *Quodsi ea, quae utenda acceperis, maiore mensura, si modo possis, iubet reddere Hesiodus, quidnam beneficio provocati facere debemus? An imitari agros fertiles, qui multo plus efferunt quam acceperunt?*

36. See Saller 1982, 37–38, for the conflict between Marxism and anthropological functionalism as opposing hermeneutic lenses for examining ancient patronage. The functionalist view suggests that "in societies with great differences of wealth and prestige, patron-client bonds, cemented in accordance with the reciprocity ethic, provide cohesion between different class and status groups" (37).

37. Seneca (*Ben.* 2.25.1) asserts: "For what so much proves a grateful heart as the impossibility of ever satisfying oneself, or of even attaining the hope of ever being able to make adequate return for a benefit."

38. This is my own translation.

staggered and separated over time, the initial gift and its return appear spontaneous, voluntary, and unmotivated by the expectation of profit or the sense of obligation (1977, 171). By concealing economic self-interest in this way, a donor more effectively accrues the symbolic capital of credit from which he may draw at a later time of need. As I discuss above, Seneca inadvertently suggests the enabling ideology behind this contradiction between the ideal of voluntary and disinterested benefaction and the very real practice of reciprocal exchange: because the burden of return is placed on the recipient, the giver is free to represent his benefactions in the light of disinterested generosity. This enabling ideology, understood in the sense of a "legitimating discourse," serves to reproduce the relations of domination implicit in patronage by deflecting the necessity for return into the social sphere of *gratia,* with all its connotations of kindness, favor, and gratitude.[39] Indeed, Seneca makes a point of distinguishing between the verb *reddere,* employed in the context of monetary repayment, and *referre gratiam,* "requiting a favor" in the economy of *beneficia:*

> We are, as you know, wont to speak thus: "A. has made a return *(gratiam rettulit)* for the favour bestowed by B." Making a return means handing over of your own accord that which you owe. We do not say, "He has paid back the favour" *(gratiam reddidit);* for "pay back" is used of a man upon whom a demand for payment is made, of those who pay against their will. . . . Making a return means offering something to him from whom you have received something. The phrase implies a voluntary return; he who has made such a return has served the writ upon himself. *(Ep.* 81.9)[40]

Yet the consistent use of analogies drawn from a monetary context in Seneca's and Cicero's examples reveals the "socially maintained discrepancy between the misrecognized or, one might say, socially repressed, objective truth of economic activity, and the social representation of production and exchange" (Bourdieu 1977, 172). Although such analogies are invoked to demonstrate the differences between the functioning of debt and credit in a coin or "disembedded" economy and their operation in a gift economy, the recourse to such models nonetheless points to the very real potential for economic calculation in the distribution of benefits.[41] Such potential is underscored not only in verbs that elsewhere do refer to "returning" *beneficia* as a specifically economic activity but also in the metaphor of "buried treasure" or "investment" used to characterize *beneficia*

39. See Bourdieu 1977, 188, on the reproduction of systems of domination.
40. Trans. Gummere 1920, Loeb edition.
41. The use of economic metaphors to discuss interpersonal relations that were not specifically contractual is certainly not new in the Roman writers and was common among the Greeks; Aristotle considers certain categories of friendship in such terms. See the discussion in Konstan 1997, 78–82.

from the donor's view.[42] When Seneca compares a *beneficium* to a *thesaurus alte obrutus* to be dug up only in need, his language quite literally "reveals" the concealing (*obrutus*) of an investment for the future. And the presence of a third party may contribute to the delay that conceals the economic interest in these transactions, further deflecting attention from the desire for profit.[43]

When Bourdieu analyzes the "labor" devoted to the social repression of the "objective truth of economic activity" (1977, 172, 194), he is concerned specifically with economies in which there are no markets, not the "ascriptive-hierarchical" society of Rome in which patronage coexisted with a modified market system. Yet as the discussion earlier in this chapter makes clear, Bourdieu's comments apply to benefaction as retaining an element of "double-sided notions that are condemned to disintegrate . . . since . . . the social relations they designate represent unstable structures which are condemned to split in two" (172). In this scheme, given that the two resulting types of relations originated in "one" set of social relations, it is reasonable that the social sphere should retain traces of the economic and vice versa: thus, just as the status system of patronage and benefactions contains elements of the economic calculation that Bourdieu perceives as the "repressed economic truth" of gift economies, so Mauss's analysis of early Roman contracts speculatively attributes a mystical or primitive attitude to a specific *res*, a thing or service, that is always part of the transaction.

Such an attitude, of course, is precisely one strategy of the mystification to which Bourdieu alludes. Thus the power inherent in the "thing," or the *hau* of the Maori, which Mauss in essence generalized as the gift's power to compel reciprocation or circulation, serves to disguise the economic interest behind exchange by enchanting certain goods—"personalizing" them so that as gifts, they are extensions of the giver rather than embodiments of economic value. Again, we may note that the system of benefaction suggests just such social, even libidinal, enchantment or misrecognition in the multivalency of *gratia* as a "social" concept that expresses the gratitude, the concrete favor, or the influence and obligation generated by gifts. Alternately, the conventions that accompany the transfer in Roman contract may be traced back to the "power" of the thing in its social aspect (the "other side" of the double-sided originary notion). The etymology of

---

42. For the metaphor of buried treasure, see Sen. *Dial.* 7.24.2; Saller (1982, 25) discusses the image. For the use of verbs that connote monetary activity, and that contradict Seneca's distinction between *reddere* and *referre*, cf. Sen. *Ben.* 3.9.3: *Cum aliter beneficium detur, aliter reddatur, paria facere difficile est.*

43. Dixon (1993, 458) quotes Cicero writing to Atticus that when he praises Varro to Atticus, he wishes Atticus to tell Varro so that the latter might "give cause for satisfaction" (*Att.* 2.25.1).

res, as connected to the Sanskrit *rah, ratih*, "gift, present, . . . something that gives pleasure to another person," and the concept of the Roman *familia* as including both people and *res*—the things of the household—explain some of the juridical formalism of Roman legal transfer. The presence of five witnesses to a *mancipatio*, the ceremony *per aes et libram* by which *res mancipi* were transferred to a new owner, suggests to Mauss a "public trial" and the position of the contracting party as *reus:* placed under moral obligation or "guilty," "linked" by the *res* received to the "spirit" or *familia* of the original contractor (1990 [1950], 50–51). Here, the mystic, "enchanted" power of the thing in its etymological origin as pleasurable gift is visible in the traces of spiritual bonds, created through *mancipatio* or *traditio*, between the original contractor and the recipient (51).[44] *Nexum*, or debtbondage, as an early and extreme form of contract *per aes et libram*, thus implies (ironically, given the absence of "pleasure" here) that the "legal 'lien' springs from things as much as from men" (48).

If the *nexum*, as I claimed above, constitutes the initial ideological fallout of an economy in the process of becoming disembedded, the concomitant idea of "social bonds" may be visible in the frequent language of "binding" that appears in the prescriptive and epistolary material on social relations.[45] That is, the contractual nature of debt-bondage and the libidinal bonds between persons, whether in a patronal relationship or in a more elite relation of *amicitia* between those of high status, may reflect the two directions into which the archaic economy, as Bourdieu would have it, "split in two."[46] Indeed, as a condition in which a debtor "pays off" his obligation through labor over time, the *nexum* may even be said to express in disembedded form the element of temporal delay that serves to mystify the economic aspect of gift exchange.

44. See Watson 1975, 134–49, for the distinction between *mancipatio* and *traditio: mancipatio*, which constituted the transfer of *res mancipi*, or "land, rustic praedial servitudes, slaves, oxen, horses, mules, and asses," included a ceremony *per aes et libram*, "with a scale and a fixed weight of bronze" (136). *Traditio* referred to the physical transfer or delivery of property that was *res non mancipi*, or those things that were excluded from the category of *res mancipi* (145). See nn. 13 and 14, above.

45. See Cicero's use of the word *devinciunter* in *Off.* 1.56 (quoted above). Note, too, Cic. *Fam.* 15.11.2, in which Cicero discusses his indebtedness to Gaius Marcellus for both his private favors and public services to the Republic, and refers to such debt as a binding *vinculum*. Cicero refers to M. Aemilius as "bound by favors" (*meis beneficiis devinctus*) to him (*Fam.* 13.27.2).

46. Significantly, when Cicero recommends Trebatius to Caesar, he writes that he "hands him over to you from my hand to yours, as they say" (*hominem tibi ita trado de manu (ut aiunt) in manum tuam istam, Fam.* 7.5.3). As Shackleton Bailey (1977, ad loc.) suggests, the phrase *de manu . . . in manum* "may derive from grasping by the hand in token of acquired ownership." That is, it may signify *mancipatio*, or the "taking in the hand" of certain *res*.

GIFT AND DELAY IN THE HORATIAN CHRONOLOGY

Although the individual chapters of this book all explore the concept of a gift economy as a poetics informing Horatian verse—particularly the relationship between the *Odes* 1–3 and *Epistles* 1—it is nonetheless important to set the sequence of these two collections in a broader temporal context. As I suggest in the introduction, attempts to reconstruct the historical backdrop to Horace's relationship with Maecenas, and to the regime at large, necessarily involve some assumptions regarding irrecoverable facts. However, such a reconstructed scenario clearly exhibits the temporal delay by which the reciprocity ethic is represented as voluntary benefactions or favors. The evidence on which we may build our speculation can be broken down into three main categories: the external bits of biographical information that can be gleaned from Suetonius, the internal evidence of the poems themselves, and the relationship between the dates of publication of the poems as collections and the progress of the regime in establishing its authority. As has been recently argued, Horace may well have received up to five pieces of property from either Maecenas or Augustus himself, in addition to the sporadic gifts of actual money that the emperor may have made.[47] Most significantly, what appears to be the first grant of land—the Sabine farm—is made at a time just preceding, if not virtually simultaneous with, the victory at Actium. The political odes of books 1–3 are then written over the next decade; their decisive shift in genre, from satire to lyric, coincides with the period during which Octavian, later Augustus, secured the foundations of his political power. Though the so-called Roman Odes evolved into a sequence after their initial composition, they nonetheless all date to the years 29–26 B.C.E., just around the time when Octavian (in 27 B.C.E.) acquired significant proconsular authority and changed his name to Augustus, even as he made a show of yielding all his power to the Senate and people. Moreover, the second of the two major redistributions of governmental authority that ceded powers to Augustus while appearing to restore the Republic occurred in 23 B.C.E., the very same year as the *Odes* 1–3 were published as a collection.[48] As already noted in the introduction, when Horace then publishes his *Epistles* 1 in 19 B.C.E., his opening poem makes a literal "show"—in this case, the metaphor of a gladiatorial show—of declining to write more lyric.

What is striking about this chronological sequence is the staggered, yet almost choreographed, timing of the gift-reciprocated-by-a-countergift

---

47. See P. White 1993, 147–48; Lyne 1995, 9–11, and the sources cited therein; and see my introduction, n. 9.

48. See Eder 1990, 103–11, for a full discussion of the restructuring of government during the 20s.

exchanges between the poet and his benefactors. Moreover, to place this sequence in a larger temporal frame, we should note that the Sabine estate itself was a benefaction constituting an expression of *gratia* for Horace's dedication of *Satires* 1 to Maecenas, and plausibly for the "propaganda" value of those poems (Du Quesnay 1984). Thus, as both a reciprocating benefaction for past services and a gift that continued to lay a claim on Horace, the estate symbolizes that very ambiguity and disequilibrium of debt so characteristic of a gift economy. The "excess" associated with a reciprocating gift, the "little bit more" that Hesiod mentions and that re-configures the debt, often appears in the phrases by which Horace referred to benefactions he received. As the speaker claims in *Satires* 2.6.4, the tra-ditional "thank-you" letter for the estate, the gods have done even more and better for him (*auctius atque di melius fecere*) than he wished. And though the dedication poem of *Epode* 1 presumably addresses the initial gifts of Maecenas, we nonetheless remark the emphasis on "more" in the conven-tional locution that his generosity has enriched the poet "sufficiently and then some" or "more than enough" (*satis superque me benignitas tua ditavit,* 31). However, for all that such gifts serve to create and continually renew Horace's sense of debt, the trope of a retired gladiator, as I discuss further in chapter 4, suggests a form of public expenditure that not only responds to but also releases the poet from the continuous demand for reciprocity. The public *munus* of the political odes in fact makes good the debt created by the *munus* of Horace's estate.

Significantly, after the publication of *Epistles* 1 in 19 B.C.E, Maecenas appears only once more in Horace's poems, in *Ode* 4.11. Human nature abhors a vacuum, and scholars have been quick to give voice to the poet's silence: Maecenas's absence from Horace's later works has been variously interpreted as indicating a fall from power caused by some indiscretion, a power struggle with Agrippa, and a withdrawal from imperial literary pa-tronage intentionally planned by the regime.[49] Much of the evidence for a cooling of relations between the emperor and Maecenas stems from Sue-tonius, and more than one source points to the contrary. Whatever the causes of this change in Horace's texts, the poems do suggest that Maecenas no longer plays the role of a patron who brokers Horace's relationship with the regime at large and that Augustus has become more actively involved. One of the clearest documented examples of an actual request comes from Suetonius's biography of Horace. After narrating the *princeps*'s commission of the *Carmen saeculare* and the fourth book of *Odes*, Suetonius quotes a fragment of a letter in which Augustus chides Horace for failing to address a *sermo* or "conversational poem" to himself. Since Suetonius's diction and

---

49. See G. Williams 1990, 258–75, for a lucid discussion of the evidence and the idea that Maecenas's withdrawal from the scene was preconceived.

the tone of the letter have often inclined critics either to perceive patronal pressure or to assert fundamental Horatian autonomy, the relevant passage is worth examining in full:

> As to his writings, Augustus rated them so high, and was so convinced that they would be immortal, that he not only appointed (*iniunxerit*) him to write the Secular Hymn, but also bade him celebrate the victory of his stepsons Tiberius and Drusus over the Vindelici, and so compelled (*coegerit*) him to add a fourth to his three books of lyrics after a long silence. Furthermore, after reading several of his "Talks," the Emperor thus expressed his pique that no mention was made of him: "you must know that I am not pleased with you, that in your numerous writings of this kind you do not talk with me, rather than with others. Are you afraid that your reputation with posterity will suffer because it appears that you were my friend?" In this way he forced (*expressit*) from Horace the selection which begins with these words[.][50]

Suetonius goes on to quote the beginning of the Epistle to Augustus, 2.1. Although the verbs that Suetonius employs here—*iniunxerit, coegerit, expressit*—suggest a strong degree of compulsion, scholars have often attempted to soften their force.[51] Moreover, as some would argue, the teasing tone of the emperor may also be understood as undermining the initial impression of patronal demand.[52] Finally, the epistle can even be cited by those who claim that the reference to patronal pressure reflects the highly stylized convention of the *recusatio,* fabricated by the poets as part of their own posture of refusal. For though, as already noted, the epistle ends with Horace's admission of talents inadequate to the task of epic, we know from Suetonius that Augustus did not ask for such verse; rather he wished to be the addressee of "conversational" poems or *sermones,* a category many understand as inclusive of either the *Epistles* or the *Satires.*[53] To introduce the

---

50. Suet. *Poet., Vita Horati,* trans. Rolfe 1924 [1914], Loeb edition.

51. Fraenkel (1957, 364) understands these verbs to reflect Suetonius's own context, post-Domitian Rome. However, as G. Williams (1990, 269–70) points out, Horace himself uses the verb *cogere* in the Epistle to Augustus: *cum speramus eo rem venturam ut . . . arcessas et egere vetes et scribere cogas* (2.1.226–28). Williams, Santirocco (1995, 236–37), and Griffin (1984, 189–91) acknowledge the power relations implicit in these verbs even as they admit actual compulsion to be absurd; P. White (1993, 114–15) claims that such language was typical of the way poets and their *amici* discussed "suggestions" about poetry they might write. I believe White goes too far in emptying these verbs of any coercive implications; see my introduction, n. 25.

52. E.g., Putnam 1986, 22–23; for the contrasting view, see Griffin 1984, 191, who quotes Macrobius's observation that "power does compel, not only if it invites but even if it beseeches."

53. Suetonius's use of *sermones* is generally interpreted as referring either to satires or epistles, understood as Horace's more "conversational" poems (those of his "pedestrian" Muse). However, Habinek (1998, 100) reads *sermones* as strictly the conversations represented in Horatian satire: by responding to Augustus's request with an epistle rather than a satire, Horace reinforces the poem's thematic emphasis on privileging written communication over visual spectacle.

motif of refusal in a context in which the addressee gets what he asked for might underscore the conventionality of the trope.

Yet from the point of view of gift exchange, Suetonius's diction of compulsion may not be so far off the mark. For by referring to Horace as potentially *familiaris*, Augustus invokes the discourse of *amicitia* or elite patronage, whose language and conventions presume an intimacy or "proximity" that disguises the more economic interests of the relationship. As Bourdieu points out,

> The general law of exchanges means that the closer the individuals or groups are in the genealogy, the easier it is to make agreements, the more frequent they are, and the more completely they are entrusted to good faith. Conversely, as the relationship becomes more impersonal, i.e. as one moves out from the relationship between brothers to that between virtual strangers . . . , so a transaction is less likely to occur at all, but it can become and increasingly does become purely "economic" in character, i.e. closer to its economic reality, and the interested calculation which is never absent even from the most generous exchange (in which both parties account—i.e. count— themselves satisfied) can be more and more openly revealed. (1977, 173)

Augustus, by suggesting that Horace (with an eye to posterity) is potentially *embarrassed* by an intimate—*familiaris*—relationship with the emperor, ironically plays on the muddy distinction between patronage and friendship. In a sense, the emperor taunts the poet with the economic reality beneath the fiction of voluntary benefaction: because Horace did not include Augustus in the circle of *amici* addressed either in *Epistles* 1 or *Satires* 2, the poet must see their relationship as only contractual. In other words, Augustus does more than jokingly suggest that Horace might be embarrassed by being seen as *liking* power and thus uneasy about being associated, albeit indirectly, with the less savory aspects of the emperor's rise to prominence—perhaps the most overt implication of his humor; the emperor also, as a superior, challenges the poet not to experience *gratia* and to feel a justified independence based on the satisfactory fulfillment of a mere exchange.[54] In this sense, patronal compulsion may exercise itself by self-consciously drawing attention to the affective component of the relationship and thus, covertly, to the continuing indebtedness that Horace *ought* to feel.

Such an analysis puts the diction of the speaker's *recusatio* in the Epistle to Augustus in a different light. As we recall, the issue of immortality is there cast in terms of aesthetic refinement and decorum—the poetic gift that lacks discrimination, *pingui munere*, dooming poet and subject alike to

---

54. Saller (1982, 21), challenging Hellegouarc'h, asserts the importance of *gratia* regardless of the status differential between beneficiary and donor.

mortal oblivion. The speaker responds, clearly, to Augustus's taunt that Horace is concerned with his own reputation and thus his own "immortality," but he deflects the focus from posthumous embarrassment concerning political compromise to misgivings about aesthetic shortcomings. On the one hand, this move is the typical deflection of the *recusatio* in which generic allegiances provide a polite excuse for lack of compliance with a patron's request. On the other hand, our knowledge—that Augustus's actual complaint concerned a failure to be addressed in a *sermo* or "talk"— leads us to consider the *recusatio* not in terms of the demurral it contains but rather as a trope whose entire function is to ensure that we not attend to the poet's modified compliance and the pressure of the reciprocity ethic. For Augustus in fact gets a form of the genre he requested, along with the status of an addressee as well as posthumous fame. Horace, for his part, invokes the conventional *recusatio* as a means of underscoring the voluntary nature of the poem.

But beneath the ideological veil of voluntarism we can detect traces of the discourse of reciprocity or debt made good, a discursive web of images that I analyze in greater depth in chapters 4 and 5. Here, in the Epistle to Augustus, we may note that the language with which the speaker characterizes the poetic gift "that burdens" him (*quod me gravat*)—an attention for which he "has no patience" (*nil moror officium*, 264), a "zeal foolishly oppressing the one whom it cherishes" (*sedulitas autem stulte quem diligit urget*, 260)—recalls that of *Epistles* 1.13, the poem traditionally understood as a playful if fictive evocation of a cover letter to accompany a copy of *Odes* 1–3 presented to Augustus. In this epistle, the speaker instructs Vinius Asina not "to incite dislike for the poems [he] delivers through the zealous performance of duty" (*ne ... odiumque libellis / sedulus importes opera vehemente minister*, 4–5) and urges him to toss away the poems if the "heavy" pack begins to chafe rather than throwing them down unceremoniously at Augustus's feet (*si te forte meae gravis uret sarcina chartae, / abicito potius quam quo perferre iuberis / clitellas ferus impingas*, 6–7). The ironic *gravis ... sarcina chartae*, "heavy pack of papers," may very well be alluded to in the later poem when the speaker, identifying with Augustus, claims *nil moror officium quod me gravat*. That is, not only does the refusal justify itself on Callimachean grounds, but it also refers to a previous delivery of poems—poems similarly neoteric in their aesthetic affiliation (and thus the ironic opposite of *gravis*) but nonetheless possessing a significant *pondus*, or authoritative weight, in their ideological contribution to Augustus's interests. Finally, the speaker of 1.13 refers to his poems as verses that may "delay" the eyes and ears of Caesar (*carmina quae possint oculos aurisque morari / Caesaris*, 17–18), diction similar to that at the beginning of *Epistles* 2.1. While the language of unduly "delaying" or "catching the attention of" an addressee or recipient of verse is somewhat conventional in Horace's poems to his patrons (see *Sat.* 1.1.14 and *Ep.* 1.7.83), the other images shared by these two epistles imply a more pointed allusion. By embedding echoes of *Epistles* 1.13 in the *recusatio* motif of the Epistle to Augustus, the poet hints at the economic calculation behind the *munera* of the emperor and claims that the *Odes* have already reciprocated his gifts.[55] The *recusatio* in this instance refers to a past debt made good even as it asserts an ideology of voluntary giving.

By returning to Horace's letter to Augustus after examining the characteristic features of a gift economy, we may now perceive more clearly some of the contradictions in Augustan literary patronage. The spectrum of systems—poems at one end purchased for money, at the other end produced voluntarily as gifts—appears less polarized: once temporal delay and the posture of decorous giving are understood as social strategies for veiling the calculated exchanges of material and symbolic capital, the economic interest behind literary benefaction is revealed. At the same time, anthropological functionalism suggests that the symbolic capital of loyalty and gratitude elicited by gifts produces social cohesion. Indeed, Wallace-Hadrill's claim, discussed in the introduction, that any critical analysis of patronage must speak in terms of *both* structure and ideology sums up this imbrication of economically interested exchange and the language of libidinal voluntarism—of friendship, affection, goodwill, and gratitude—through which those exchanges were conducted.

Social cohesion, we noted, results particularly when the gift passes to a third person, a feature of "primitive" gift circulation (such as the *kula*) that, mutatis mutandis, also marks the basic triangulation or "network" of patronal relations in Roman society. Our theoretical paradigm suggests that literary patronage displays not the ongoing circulation of a prestige object but the transmutation of forms of "capital": a material boon such as land produces the symbolic capital of gratitude or obligation, which, in turn, becomes poetry that reaches an audience beyond the patron alone.

As the speaker claims in the letter to Augustus, a poet's gifts not only immortalize Rome's leading men but also serve the public state by educating the young—the poet's civic function: "although reluctant in battle, ill-

---

55. By these specific allusions, not just *Odes* 1–3 but also *Odes* 4, if dated before the epistle, would certainly be included in the dynamic of reciprocal *munera*. See Brink 1982, 552–54, on the dating. Indeed, an alternative reading of *nil moror officium quod me gravat* might subtly imply that Horace, still speaking as writer rather than recipient of verse, wishes to have nothing to do with the *officium* of composing panegyric, a service that he finds oppressive and has already executed with *Odes* 4. From this point of view, the embarrassment regarding posthumous reputation that is both an issue in Augustus's own letter, as narrated by Suetonius, and an image informing the funereal metaphor at the end of the Epistle to Augustus turned out to be remarkably on target: *Odes* 4 has not fared well with critics of Horace, many of whom consider its encomiastic pieces hollow, insincere, and aesthetically inferior. See further references cited in Putnam 1986, 21 n. 5.

suited to fighting, he is useful to the city, if you believe that great matters are assisted by small things; the poet fashions the tender and lisping mouths of children" (*Ep.* 2.1.124–26).[56] Though these lines denote the use of poetic texts as a means of shaping the speech patterns of the young, the poet helps shape moral character as well with precepts and noble exempla (126–30), a civic function clearly visible in the Roman Odes. As scholars have long pointed out, the quintessential expression of the poet's role as the didactic spokesman for civic values is Aristophanes' depiction of Aeschylus in the *Frogs,* and Horace's vision of poetic service here recalls the comic poet's view of Greek tragedy. In this regard, as we shall see in the next chapter, Horace's *munus* of poetry invokes a discourse of euergetism— private expenditure for the public good—even as it suggests a form of political or civic office. Reciprocating the regime's gifts with the production of ideology, the speaker—in the metaphoric posture of a priest, the public office of *sacerdos*—converts the symbolic capital of benefactions received into cultural capital of poems for the people. Let us then turn to an analysis of exemplary poems of *Odes* 1–3 in which discourses of religious, political, and social exchange combine to present Horatian lyric as a form of expiation for the crimes of the civil wars.

56. We also see traces of the Callimachean aesthetic in the emphasis on *parvis . . . rebus* (small things).

CHAPTER TWO

Tragic History, Lyric Expiation, and the Gift of Sacrifice

The assassination of Julius Caesar in 44 B.C.E. ushered in a new wave of civil warfare in a Roman state still reeling from the turbulent clashes of the first triumvirate, the perilous and shifting alliances of Pompey, Caesar, and Crassus. The next thirteen years witnessed acts of singular brutality as the *puer vindex,* "the avenging boy" Octavian, Caesar's great-nephew and adopted heir, set about to avenge his "father" and consolidate his power. For those who doubted the nervy resolve of the freshly bearded adolescent, the ruthless murders of the proscriptions spoke with determined if bloody authority. The hit list created by the second triumvirate, Antony, Lepidus, and Octavian, made examples of their enemies by terror, as they freely employed the extremes of visual symbolism. The fate of Cicero, prominent statesman and orator, sent a persuasive message: apprehended as he made his escape to the sea, Cicero adorned the forum, his decapitated head framed by severed hands. Perhaps, as Plutarch suggests, this eminent victim of the proscriptions owed the final touches of his gruesome end to a vindictive Antony, himself the victim of Cicero's *Philippics* (*Cic.* 48–49); but Octavian later displayed his own capacity for unassisted cruelty. When, after the dissolution of the second triumvirate, the forces of the Antonine faction had abandoned the city of Perusia to the besieging Caesarians in 41 B.C.E., Octavian had the entire town council of the renegade city systematically executed (see Syme 1960 [1939], 212, with sources).

It is no coincidence, then, that Horace's famous ode to Pollio, the first poem of the second book of *Odes,* has been construed as a warning to a man who, having sided with the Antonians at the time of Perusia, later undertook a history of the civil wars.[1] Indeed, Horace's ode sheds light on

---

1. See André 1949 for a full discussion of Pollio's biography.

the quip with which Pollio apparently answered Octavian's pointed taunts in obscene rhymes during the siege of Perusia—"but I keep quiet: for it's not easy to write (*scribere*) against one who is able to proscribe (*proscribere*)."[2] Though Pollio lived out his life in easy neutrality after the decisive defeat of Antony at Actium in 31 B.C.E., Horace nonetheless poetically associates his person with the hazard of writing about the past, manifest in the poem as the potential for explosive repercussions—whether emotional or actual—inherent in addressing topics of political delicacy. But the nature of violence as vindictive, demanding reciprocity, goes deeper and lies at the very heart of the civil wars—at the heart, at least, of Augustan writers' own conception of the turmoil of the late Republic. It is partly in response to this idea of unceasing violence that Horace assumes the sacred office of lyric priest in many of his political odes.

In this chapter I suggest that Horace's adoption of the role of *sacerdos* (civic priest) in the Roman Odes is implied in the motif of expiation that governs the ode to Pollio. I see *Odes* 2.1 as establishing a generic paradigm for understanding the persuasive force of the religious rhetoric of the Roman Odes. By constructing the civil wars in ways that invoke the genre of tragedy, Horace draws on the connotations of drama as a mimesis of sacrificial ritual; such generic associations combine with his own lyric as a ritual offering and effect a symbolic purification through tragic catharsis. For a Roman audience familiar with generic conventions, these poems construct history in a way that simultaneously implicates the present generation in a tragic cycle of violence even as it offers citizens the possibility of expiation. At the same time, the *revocatio* (calling back) at the end of *Odes* 2.1 signals a deferral of the treatment of political themes, and the civil wars in particular, until the beginning of the third book (Lowrie 1997, 186). However, the political and historical dimension is always woven into Horatian personal narrative: I therefore also discuss *Odes* 2.13 as a poem whose invocation of ritual *devotio* ("military self-sacrifice" or "formal curse") sheds further light on this discourse of tragedy and purification. Finally, given the nature of sacrifice as a form of gift, I consider this symbolic transaction in the context of the exchanges of literary and political patronage. Ultimately, the trope of lyric sacrifice has sociopolitical connotations: though a gift directed at the gods on behalf of the people, the poet's sacrificial expenditure also reciprocates the regime's benefactions through the creation of ideology sympathetic to Augustus.

A persona often adopted by the Augustan poets, the *vates* is a figure generally conflated with the Horatian *sacerdos* and understood to combine the

---

2. Macrobius 2.4.21: "*at ego taceo: non est enim facile in eum scribere qui potest proscribere.*"

visionary inspiration of the ego-figure of Greek choral poetry with the Callimachean motif of the poem as sacrifice.[3] Though the two terms are necessarily connected, particularly as metaphorical postures assumed by poets, there is a clear distinction between the social roles to which these concepts refer (Lyne 1995, 184–85): a *vates* constitutes a visionary or prophet, but not in a necessarily official capacity; *sacerdotes,* on the other hand, are specifically priests, public "high-status" officials of the state whose function was to advise on religious matters and to oversee rituals.[4] This is an important distinction, and one to which we shall return in the analysis of *Odes* 3.1–6; nonetheless, as my reading of 2.1 and other related poems suggests, Horace's posture as a "visionary" in many ways anticipates his public office of the priesthood. Moreover, though it is clear that the Horatian role of *sacerdos Musarum* (priest of the Muses) fits the larger context of Augustus's renewal of religion and the restoration of temples, critics have not pursued the full implications of this social and religious discourse of ritual in their interpretations of Horace's political poems—most notably the Roman Odes and their relation to other poems of the corpus.[5] Indeed, the preoccupation with locating the aesthetic precedents of the Augustan persona of the lyric visionary or sacerdotal priest reflects what Dennis Feeney has identified as the critical tendency, until recently, to separate the discourses of religion from those of literature. Such a bifurcation is compounded by "the traditional disregard for the cultural power of Roman religion," which, together with "the long-engrained aestheticising tendency in the study of Roman literature" (Feeney 1998, 7), resists acknowledging the full religious, social, or political impact that the literary invocation of ritual language may in fact have had on the elite readership of Rome.

---

3. The fullest treatment of this persona is Newman 1967. Callimachus, in the preface to *Aet.* 23–24, famously compares writing to sacrifices when Apollo admonishes him to fatten calves but keep his lines slender. In his discussion of Propertius 4.6, Cairns (1984, 140–41) understands the poet-priest figure in the context of choral hymn and the ritual setting in which choruses would function. For the topos of writing as sacrifice, see also Menander Rhetor 437.20–52; Falter 1934, 77–78; Wimmel 1960, 299. On priests and their political and ideological function in ancient Rome, see Beard 1990 and Gordon 1990a, 1990b, 1990c.

4. See Beard and Crawford 1985, 30–31; Beard and North 1990, 47. For a full discussion of Roman priests, see Wissowa 1902, 410–30.

5. For example, Witke (1983) makes excellent observations about the "sacred space" that the Horatian speaker clears for himself in the first ode but does not comment on the implications of this space for sacrifice and the related ideas of purification or expiation. Lyne (1995), despite his focus on the tension between the public and private in Horace, and his astute appendix on the nature of the *sacerdos* (184–85), similarly does not discuss the Roman Odes as participating in a discourse of sacrifice. Cf. Syndikus 1973, 14–15, on Horace's ritual language and use of a priestly persona to attain for his poems the sacred dignity that these poetic conventions signified in Pindar and Greek choral lyric. See nn. 66 and 67 below for further bibliography on the Roman Odes.

Recent studies of Augustan literature and art have begun to reverse this trend, arguing for the capacity of representations of ritual to invoke experiences or produce effects similar to those elicited by actual participation in religious rites. Andrew Feldherr, for example, analyzes how Livy's use of narrative strategies to reconstruct sacrificial spectacle reveals his text as performing a state-building function (1998, 156). This analysis of Livy's reproduction of the visual elements of sacrificial acts, leading a reader to respond to a representation as he or she might to the performance of an actual rite, draws on John Elsner's "viewer"-oriented interpretation of the Ara Pacis (153). Elsner argues that the reliefs on the Ara Pacis situate viewers in the same position as a participant of sacrifice: bringing all their cultural associations of previous ritual experiences to an altar whose explicit function was for sacrifice, they in fact temporarily fulfilled the incomplete sacrificial process whose setting was the Ara Pacis (1991, 51–52). Elsner might himself take issue with the "state-building" function of Livy's text, for he rejects the interpretation of the strictly ideological effect of Augustan iconography as "too totalizing," emphasizing instead the viewers' possible subversive and conflictive responses to art as they construct meaning. Nonetheless, such a model, which locates the construction of meaning in the dialogic interaction between an audience's associations and the work of art, allows for the greater impact and cultural power that the literary invocation of religious discourse may have had on a Roman audience. Sacrifice was arguably the most pervasive ancient religious discourse; and, as historical narrative, sculpture, and numismatic evidence affirms, it invariably drew attention to priests as the performers of the ritual killing.[6] We must consider, then, this larger cultural practice as a system that the metaphor of the Horatian "priest" invokes in order to produce a particular effect on his readers.

One of the most common and important rituals during the Republic was the expiation of prodigies: strange or portentous phenomena such as talking chickens and rain showers of blood, or the more mundane event of statues struck by lightning, would be understood as signs of divine displeasure, a disturbance of the *pax deorum* ("peace of the gods" or "equilibrium between the human and the divine level") that must be addressed.[7] The consuls were ultimately responsible for deciding which prodigies required expiation, but the sacrifices that were part of that process were performed by priests. Such sacrificial rituals aimed to purify the people, to

---

6. Beard 1990, 11; Gordon 1990c, 204. For a comprehensive discussion of sacrificial ritual in the Roman world, see Wissowa 1902, 344–65.

7. See Händel 1959, 2290–95; Liebeschuetz 1979, 9–11; MacBain 1982; Beard and Crawford 1985, 30, 34; Livy 22.1.8–20. I borrow the phrase "equilibrium between the human and the divine level" from Thome (1992, 86).

compensate the gods for whatever injury they had suffered, and to avert the future calamity signified by the prodigy.[8] As expiatory offerings that placated or appeased the anger of the gods, *piacula* are generally considered as a form of payment in a transaction that releases (*luere*) the people from their debt (Thome 1992, 86–87). Nonetheless, as several passages in Livy demonstrate, during the process of expiation both actual sacrifices as well as other offerings made to the gods—money, statues, or sculptures such as a "thunderbolt of gold"—would be referred to in the language of gifts, *dona*—the term associated with "ostensibly free will offerings."[9] Public feasts, too, might be held in honor of the gods, a practice in keeping with other forms of civic euergetism, emphasizing that expiation would involve not only "gifts" to the gods but also expenditure that directly benefited the people.[10]

During the civil wars the practice of expiation was gradually abandoned—fewer prodigies were reported and when they were, expiation was often not carried out (Liebeschuetz 1979, 57–58; MacBain 1982, 103–4). The last prodigy for which the ancients record official expiation during the first century B.C.E. occurs in 37.[11] And yet, as the powerful second ode of Horace's first book gives witness, the discourse of prodigies and ritual expiation continued to provide a way of structuring experience: the flooding of the Tiber in 27 B.C.E., reported by Dio as a prodigy, signifies divine anger over the civil wars and leads the Horatian speaker to the question, "to whom will Jupiter assign the role of expiation of our crime?" (*cui dabit partis scelus expiandi / Iuppiter*, 29–30). The poem then launches into a roll call of Olympian deities, invoking Apollo, Venus, Mars, and finally Mercury, whose secular incarnation in the form of Augustus Caesar makes him the only

---

8. Expiation could thus be both compensation for *damnum* inflicted in the past and a way of buying off disaster in the future. See Scullard 1981, 23.

9. On *dona*, see Pascal 1982, 16; Benveniste 1973, 80, notes that *donum*, as the expression of a "gift" that does not (ostensibly) call for a return, differs from *munus*, whose etymological origin in the Indo-European root **mei* implies exchange. For the language of *piacula*, see Livy 22.9.7; for the language of the *dona* of money, statues, and a "golden thunderbolt" for Jove, see Livy 22.1.17–20, 21.62.8. For *dona* with regard to actual sacrifices, see Livy 22.10.3, where the pontifex maximus advises the Roman people to offer up to Jove the animals of the spring: *ratum donum duit populus Romanus Quiritium, quod ver attulerit ex suillo ovillo caprino bovillo grege . . . Iovi fieri.*

10. On the feast added, originally in connection with expiation, to the ceremony of the Saturnalia, see Livy 22.1.20. Beard, North, and Price (1998, 1:38) note that the *remedia* of expiatory offerings "might offer an opportunity for holding elaborate ceremonies, sometimes including new festivals or new entertainments, so boosting public morale by civic display."

11. I follow the appendix in MacBain (1982)—based on the prodigy lists of Luterbacher (1967 [1904]), which I have also consulted—and Wülker (1903). Liebeschuetz (1979, 58 n. 2), however, cites later lists according to the prodigies noted in Dio 50.8.1–6; 50.10.2–6; 53.20.

candidate for answering "present."[12] The speaker encourages Caesar, as *primus inter pares,* to take up the role of expiation, but the poet's own implicit role as a priest here—he observes and interprets the prodigy—suggests that he too will do his part, in keeping with the Roman symbiosis of religion and politics. As the *vates* who, at the end of *Odes* 1.1, strikes his head against the stars and then ushers in the lofty tone of 1.2, the Horatian lyric speaker anticipates his later role as priest of the Muses, in which he offers his poems as symbolic acts of expiatory sacrifice.

Such expiation, however, takes place in the context of a tragic view of history and the "purifying" potential of catharsis. I do not intend this interpretation to seamlessly conflate Aristotle's concept of purgation of the emotions with the religious purification implied by expiation; rather, as we shall see, Horace's invocation of tragic motifs, in a religious context of expiation, implicitly assumes the ritual "purifying" sense of catharsis that was included in the complex semantic range of the word in its pre-Aristotelian usage (Halliwell 1986, 186).To be sure, I believe that certain Aristotelian tenets about drama do inform Horace's tragic vision transposed to lyric: in addition to the importance of catharsis, albeit within a specifically religious context, we encounter a form of *prohairesis,* or tragic "choice," as well as Aristotelian unity of action. But from a social perspective, the ritual, performative effects of Horace's lyric invocation of drama fulfill the same function as sacrifice—not only purification but also the reinforcement of social cohesion and stratification.[13] Thus, before turning to a close analysis of the tragic rhetoric of *Odes* 2.1, 2.13, and 3.1–6, I briefly review some concepts of René Girard, whose understanding of the social and ritual function of tragedy, as a mimesis of sacrifice, has bearing on my argument.

Girard is no stranger to critics of the classics. His notion of the scapegoat and the origins of ritual violence has not only furthered the understanding of Greek tragedy but also provides a compelling lens through which to view narratives of formative periods of Roman *imperium,* as well as the Romans' sense of their own demise. Livy's accounts of the fall of Alba, for example, or the rape of Lucretia and her subsequent suicide, have both been read

12. The final injunction, that Caesar not let the Medes ride unavenged, draws foreign policy into this discourse of ritual purification and, according to G. Williams (1980, 13, 118, 160), makes Parthian blood the sacrifice that will expiate Roman guilt for the civil wars.

13. As Habinek (1990a, 213), notes, "In Roman religion, as in Greek and other religions organized around the institution of sacrifice, sacrifice not only defines membership within a group (those who eat of the same sacrifice are bound to one another physically and psychologically) but establishes hierarchy as well, with the most important (Roman *princeps*) receiving the first and sometimes largest portion of the flesh."

in terms of Girard's understanding of the social function of sacrifice.[14] In this view, ritual sacrifice constitutes a means of checking the inherently self-propagating and vindictive nature of violence. As a form of deflection it depends on a series of substitutions: the "surrogate victim" provides an initial scapegoat for the violent inclinations of a community, while the victim of a sacrificial rite further substitutes for the human surrogate.[15] As an example from later Roman history, we may consider Carlin Barton's analysis of the ambivalent attitudes toward violence that help constitute the Roman identity under the early Empire. Discussing the monstrous figure of the *stupidus* as a "sacrificial decoy" required to shore up "Roman" identity, Barton writes: "The perception of the civil wars and the monarchy as permanently transgressing the *discrimina ordinum* [distinctions of rank] brought into play a 'physics' corresponding to René Girard's 'Sacrificial Crisis': a collapse of the *sensus communis,* a shared system of categorizing and ordering. It was a loss of a sense of common identity, and a sort of permanent civil war" (1993, 146). Though Girard's view of the dynamics of violence does not answer to all its manifestations in the Horatian *corpus,* his conception certainly illuminates Horace's treatment of the civil wars. The dissolution of a cultural system of differences and distinctions perfectly describes the state of affairs to which the Horatian speaker claims Rome has fallen.[16] Whether through the symbol of crumbling temples, the soldier who mistakes war for peace, or the adulterous wife who, already engaged in the violation of boundaries, bestows even her illicit favors indiscriminately (*Odes* 3.6.2–3, 3.5.37–38, 3.6.17–32), Horace presents a society in which images of disintegration and confusion suggest the cultural breakdown that marks Girard's crisis. At the root of this bankruptcy is the insidious nature of the civil wars, a form of mimetic rivalry in which internal

14. On the role of sacrifice in the fall of Alba, see Feldherr 1998, 112–64 (144–49 for the specific relevance of Girard, and 145 n. 93 for important qualifications). For Girardian readings of the Lucretia episode, see Joplin 1990; Calhoon 1997.

15. Girard 1977, 4–6, 8–10. An important component of Girard's understanding of sacrificial practice and its efficacy is the *similarity* of the substitute victim to the original object of violence. However, should the substitute resemble the object it replaces too much, then it stimulates the call for reciprocity and vengeance that it was meant to thwart.

16. Girard 1977, 49: "The sacrificial crisis can be defined, therefore, as a crisis of distinctions—that is, a crisis affecting the cultural order. This cultural order is nothing more than a regulated system of distinctions in which the differences among individuals are used to establish their 'identity' and their mutual relationships." Such a crisis is illustrated by the myth of Oedipus: having killed his father, he becomes king and husband to his mother, and father to his sisters and brothers. The distinctions between the cultural roles of the family structure have been completely erased. Civil war, often envisioned in terms of fraternal strife (e.g., the rivalry between Eteocles and Polyneices), is the quintessential example of the sacrificial crisis: its reciprocal violence threatens to spread and destroy all cultural differentiation unless a scapegoat can redirect the internal violence outward.

competition has ultimately led to what Girard defines as "bad" violence, the phenomenon whose call for reciprocity entails an escalating cycle of destruction. Only sacrifice, as a "good" act of violence, can forestall this process.

As we shall see, the invocation of tragedy both reenacts the sacrificial crisis and constitutes a mimesis of the sacrifice as antidote.[17] For the origins of tragedy in sacrificial ritual, though certainly disputed and speculative at best, suggest that the fall of the tragic protagonist reenacts on a mimetic level the slaying of a victim.[18] In addition to this "symbolic" fall—sometimes quite literal, as in the case of Agamemnon or Pentheus—are the numerous sacrifices integral to tragic plots that do not entail the protagonist's demise. In Girard's view, tragedy fulfills a function similar to that of ritual sacrifice (itself a substitute for an originary act of mob violence), but on a level that has evolved from actual killing. Combining mythic narrative with the mimesis of ritual, tragedy serves to purge a community of its own impulses toward reciprocal violence. To be sure, we cannot ascribe Girardian theory to Horatian intention; all the same, I see Horace's construction of Roman history in terms of a "tragic fall" that draws on the genre's associations with ritual sacrifice as a means of both thwarting the impulse to vengeance and purifying those stained with past bloodshed.

Horace's creative amalgam of the motifs of Greek tragedy and Roman religious ritual causes the discourse of sacrifice to shape the rhetoric of the Roman Odes in different ways. On the one hand, constructing the fall of the Republic as the demise of a tragic protagonist invokes the trope of *mimesis*, insofar as tragedy constitutes an imitation (evolved into mythic form) of the ritual of sacrifice. On the other hand, the posture of the *sacerdos*, or lyric priest, invokes the trope of *metaphor*, insofar as the activity of the poet-priest turns or "tropes" his poems into metaphorical sacrifices. These two intersecting sacrificial discourses, as tropes expressive of tragedy and lyric respectively, further intersect in their "ideal" effects: just as tragedy produces catharsis in its audience, so sacrifice constitutes an act of expiation or "purification"—the original sense of "catharsis"—in a religious context. And so, though poets may not have been "concerned to elucidate the meaning of sacrifice exactly, but to put it to work in a system of meanings

17. See Girard 1977, 64–66, 292–93, for the role of tragedy as a mimesis of the sacrificial crisis. Though Girard believes in the ritualistic origins of tragedy, he does not return to the views of the Cambridge Ritualists (95–96).

18. The tragic fall as an extended "trope" or figure that represents and substitutes for sacrifice arguably reflects the origins of tragedy in sacrificial ritual. See Frye 1957, 213; Girard 1977, 291–91, 95–118; Seaford 1994, 340. Burkert (1966, 87–121) reviews the evidence for such origins in the sacrifice of a goat. The representation of actual human sacrifice in tragedy has been taken up more recently by several scholars; see Pucci 1992, 513 nn. 1–2, for further bibliography.

of another kind" (Feeney 1998, 117–18), I argue that through this imbrication of religious and literary systems of meaning, Horace does intend his poems to have a performative effect on his audience.

Ultimately, it is the restoration of a system of differences, the stratified hierarchy of the *discrimina ordinum* and the social cohesion such hierarchy grounds, that the Roman Odes seek to effect by invoking a discourse of sacrifice. Let us then turn to the ode to Pollio as our paradigm, a poem that dramatizes the danger of contamination, and thus the propagatory nature of bad violence, even as it provides the ritual framework for symbolic sacrifice, or Girard's notion of "good violence."

POLLIO'S HISTORY AND THE PURIFICATION OF RITUAL VIOLENCE: *ODES* 2.1

Motum ex Metello consule civicum
bellique causas et vitia et modos
   ludumque Fortunae gravisque
    principum amicitias et arma

nondum expiatis uncta cruoribus,   5
periculosae plenum opus aleae,
   tractas et incedis per ignis
    suppositos cineri doloso.

paulum severae Musa tragoediae
desit theatris: mox, ubi publicas   10
   res ordinaris, grande munus
    Cecropio repetes cothurno,

insigne maestis praesidium reis
et consulenti, Pollio, Curiae,
   cui laurus aeternos honores   15
    Delmatico peperit triumpho.

iam nunc minaci murmure cornuum
perstringis auris, iam litui strepunt,
   iam fulgor armorum fugacis
    terret equos equitumque vultus.   20

audire magnos iam videor duces[19]
non indecoro pulvere sordidos,
   et cuncta terrarum subacta
    praeter atrocem animum Catonis.

19. With the Oxford Classical Text I read *audire . . . videor* in line 21 rather than Shackleton Bailey's *videre . . . videor.*

Iuno et deorum quisquis amicior   25
Afris inulta cesserat impotens
   tellure victorum nepotes
     rettulit inferias Iugurthae.

quis non Latino sanguine pinguior
campus sepulcris impia proelia   30
   testatur auditumque Medis
     Hesperiae sonitum ruinae?

qui gurges aut quae flumina lugubris
ignara belli? quod mare Dauniae
   non decoloravere caedes?   35
     quae caret ora cruore nostro?

sed ne relictis, Musa procax, iocis
Ceae retractes munera neniae,
   mecum Dionaeo sub antro
quaere modos leviore plectro.   40

You handle the civil conflict that began with Metellus's consulship, the causes of war, its evils, and its patterns, Fortune's game and the grievous alliances of leaders, and arms stained with blood still to be expiated, a work full of perilous hazard, and you advance through fires concealed beneath treacherous ash. For a brief time may your Muse of grim tragedy be absent from the stage; soon, when you have set in order affairs of state, you will resume your lofty calling in the Cecropian buskin, Pollio, distinguished defense for worried clients and the Senate taking counsel, you, for whom, too, the laurel gave birth to lasting glory in your Dalmatian triumph. Already, now, you strike my ear with the threatening roar of horns, now the trumpets sound, now the flash of weapons terrifies the horses and the faces of the horsemen. Now I seem to hear the great commanders, soiled with no dishonorable dust, and the whole world overcome except Cato's fierce soul. Juno and whoever of the gods more friendly to Africa had withdrawn, powerless, from the unavenged land have borne back as sacrificial offerings to Jugurtha the grandsons of his conquerors. What plain, made fertile with Latin blood, does not give witness with its tombs to our sacrilegious wars and to the sound of Hesperia's crashing fall, heard even by the Medes? What pool or what river is unaware of our mournful war? What sea has Italian slaughter not discolored? What shore lacks our gore? But lest, wanton Muse, you set aside light themes and handle anew the office of the Cean dirge, seek with me measures of a lighter strain deep within the Dionaean grove.

A poem that characterizes the project of writing about the civil wars as a "work full of perilous hazard," the ode to Pollio addresses the difficulties faced by an author who takes recent history as a subject. Richard Heinze, among others, understood this hazard in political terms, as a personal danger of reprisal that Pollio, a staunch supporter of Republican *libertas*, courts by writing of topics sensitive to Octavian.[20] As I observed above, the danger of reprisal certainly shaped the quip with which Pollio supposedly answered Octavian's taunts at the time of Perusia; but it is quite possible that Pollio's wit, as recorded by Macrobius, has encouraged earlier scholars to interpret the hazard to which Horace refers in exclusively political terms. For if one dates the ode to the years immediately following Actium, a reference to the dangers of partisanship would be indelicate on Horace's part.[21] The terrors of the recent past were ones that Octavian, soon to cast aside the role of avenger to become Augustus the merciful, wished to put behind him.

Indeed, that Pollio remained neutral after Actium leads other scholars to interpret the grave tone of the beginning, and the reference to danger, as a comment on the difficulty of historiography and thus as a decorous compliment to Pollio's literary talents.[22] Though such a reading certainly accords with the conventions of a dedication poem and offers a connotation of "perilous hazard" that should not be excluded, it ignores how the more concrete images of the stanza govern the rhetorical development of the poem: the fire still smoldering under a layer of ashes (*ignis / suppositos cineri doloso*) and the arms smeared with yet unexpiated gore (*arma / nondum expiatis uncta cruoribus*) suggest both a danger in the still fresh and ensnaring memories that could be inflamed in an audience and the criminality of civil war, a sacrilegious condition that continues to contaminate the present state. The idea of writing as potentially hazardous—the civil wars as a topic perhaps too hot to handle—contributes to the poem's thematic and imagistic coherence.

At first, the opening lines of this ode present the subject of Pollio's history in a stately, distanced, and analytical tone. The objective tone, coupled with the deferral of the verb until the seventh line, tends to deflect attention from Pollio as the author of this history. Not until the verbs *tractas* (you handle) and *incedis* (you proceed, you advance) do we understand that if the civil wars are the subject of Pollio's work, then the treatment of those wars and the political and emotional risks of writing about contemporary history are Horace's main concern here. Indeed, the poem acknowl-

---

20. See Kiessling and Heinze 1960, ad *Odes* 2.1, and Sallman 1987, 82 n. 48, for further literature that inclines to the interpretation that Pollio courts a specifically *political* hazard. See, too, the characterization of Pollio as fiercely Republican in Syme 1960 [1939], 291, 320.

21. Nisbet and Hubbard 1991 [1978] (hereafter referred to as N-H), 9–10, 14–15. N-H interprets the reference to danger in political terms, as the smoldering animosities of Republican *principes*, with the qualification that Horace's lines, exaggerating the peril, must have echoed Pollio's own *captatio benevolentiae*.

22. See Syndikus 1972, 347. Fraenkel (1957, 235) understands the danger as the hazard attendant on great undertakings of divine inspiration, a motif he charts throughout the *Odes*.

edges head-on that the civil wars were considered delicate material, and it indirectly suggests how they suffered distortion, suppression, or misrepresentation by the Augustan writers (Bowditch 1994, 419, with passages cited in n. 27). As Tacitus himself claims at the beginning of his *Histories,* the concept of *libertas,* both as a specific right to freedom of speech and as a more general right to participation in government, began to suffer erosion under the Principate (*Hist.* 1.1).[23] While I do not believe that Pollio courted any actual danger of reprisal from Octavian by writing of the civil wars, and such a political risk is not meant as the primary "perilous hazard," the theme of *libertas* is nonetheless suggested by a series of topographical images. Pollio as a figure walking upright through the buried fires looks ahead to the image of Cato fiercely unvanquished while the rest of the world has been overcome (*et cuncta terrarum subacta / praeter atrocem animum Catonis*). The prefix *sub-* (under, beneath) here recalls the earlier *ignis suppositos* (fires beneath the ash) and suggests at least a rhetoric of suppression that these figures defy. Like Cato's spirit, Pollio's undertaking symbolizes a courageous assertion of *libertas.* The risk, however, does not derive from Pollio's specific subject, the conflicts of the first triumvirate or the war between Pompey and Caesar. Rather, the poem's rhetorical development demonstrates that the topic is dangerous because of the recent conflicts of the second triumvirate and the insidiously contaminatory nature of civil war in general.

What makes the topic particularly inflammatory is the potential response from a contemporary audience—that is, the context in which a work is read or performed. For the image of embers smoldering beneath ash suggests suppressed material that could easily erupt again. The ode develops this metaphor of fire when the speaker, as Pollio's audience, has the visionary experience of being in the midst of battle. It is with this stanza that the speaker abruptly abandons his advisory and panegyric stance toward Pollio, and the poem evolves into a personal dirge for the blood spilled in the civil wars. The speaker's sentiments are inflamed when he imagines a public reading of the history:[24] as a fire might spread, the explosiveness of the material first arouses the speaker's senses—"Already, now, you strike my ear with the threatening roar of horns, now the trumpets sound"—only to stir the latent fires into a full-blown song of sorrow. In a sense, the poem itself catches on fire, as the objective tone of the first half modulates into passionate threnody.[25] The last stanza points up this shift in the poem's

23. For *libertas* in the Republic, see Brunt 1988, 281–350, and Wirszubski 1968.

24. That Pollio introduced recitations at Rome lends a specific historical backdrop to the poem's dynamic between the speaker as audience and Pollio as an addressee whose performance of his history provokes a song of lamentation.

25. Sallman (1987, 82) stands out among critics of this poem in recognizing that the

emphasis, suggesting even that the speaker's Muse has boldly usurped or appropriated the theme of civil violence from Pollio.

On one level, the adjective *procax* depicts the Muse as a "wanton" or "forward" mistress, impudently stealing Pollio's fire when she should more appropriately retire with the speaker for a tryst in Venus's cave. But her boldness has other implications: like Pollio, who bravely walks through the still-smoldering ashes, Horace's Muse brazenly takes up the office of funereal song, drawing attention to the excessive slaughter of the wars.[26] Again, a topographical register of images comes into play with the implied concealment of *sub antro* (deep within the cave) set against the openness of the Cean dirge. The speaker's Muse, stirred by Pollio's "advance" through the *ignes suppositos,* must be called back *sub antro*. The repetition— *sub-ponere* followed by *sub antro*—underscores that the "high" emotion of the lament, having flared up from the cave, is a response to the fiery material of Pollio's subject. This spatial register extends the affinity between Pollio, walking with stately majesty, and Cato, alone unvanquished while the rest of the world is *subacta* (subdued), to Horace's Muse, boldly singing a dirge before withdrawing to lighter, and thus "lower," themes.

The echo in the verb *retractes* (to handle anew, to refinger) of the form *tractas* in line 7, where Pollio is said "to handle" the subject of the wars, furthers this identification of the speaker's Muse with Pollio.[27] But this verb also reminds the reader of how and why the Muse takes up the dirge. Added to the metaphor of a natural catastrophe whose power spreads unchecked, which the motif of fire brings to the speaker's inflamed sentiments, is another image of contagion and contamination: when Pollio is said to handle a work full of dangerous hazard (*periculosae plenum opus aleae*) the noun summarizes a lengthy series of other objects that are the specific focus of his history. The final element in this series, startling in its abrupt concreteness after a list of abstract nouns, is the "weapons smeared with gore not yet expiated" (*arma / nondum expiatis uncta cruoribus*). This image emphasizes the tactile and sensuous connotation of *tractas,* particularly as the verb *tractare* may refer to the touching and handling of wounds.[28] By treating the topic of the civil wars, Pollio metaphorically handles these weapons and

---

speaker's inflamed passions reveal the *periculosae . . . aleae* of line 6 to be the danger of inciting a strong emotional reaction.

26. Nadeau (1980, 181) comments that the *enargeia* of these stanzas suggests Horace's own involvement in the civil wars.

27. N-H, ad loc., considers the imputation that Pollio also wrote a *nenia* to be uncomplimentary, interpreting *retractes* in terms of the speaker's own vain rhetorical repetition in his dirge.

28. *Oxford Latin Dictionary* (hereafter *OLD*), s.v. "tractare," 2d. Cf. N-H on both *tractas* and *retractes,* ad loc.

old wounds and, the image implies, risks contaminating himself with the impurity of still-criminal blood.

The taboo and impure nature of this blood derives in particular from its having been shed in acts of civil warfare. The murder of kin was an especially heinous crime for the ancients; as the *Oresteia* dramatizes, it initiates cycles of vengeance that do not end until an act of purification takes place. When the speaker claims that he "rehandles" the subject that Pollio "handles," one implication is that the pollution of civil bloodshed has metaphorically spread from the historian to the lyric poet. This poetic enactment of the dangers of pollution by bloodguilt occurs through the trope of a performance, or recitation, in which the focus moves from the objective content of Pollio's history to the subjective pathos of the speaker's lyric lament. That Pollio writes of the blood crimes of the first triumvirate, whereas the speaker presumably evokes the effects of the civil wars of more recent history as well, only underscores the ancient idea that blood pollution spreads in generational cycles of vengeance. This erasure of distinctions, here temporal and generic, suggests the state of cultural dissolution that characterizes Girard's "sacrificial crisis."

In *Violence and the Sacred*, Girard describes such a period as a cultural disorder, when the dissolution of distinctions lends itself to images of infection, contagion, and contamination. At the heart of this crisis is a violence whose force multiplies "like a raging fire that feeds on the very objects intended to smother its flames. The metaphor of fire could well give way to metaphors of tempest, flood, earthquake . . . [and] the plague." It is the spilling of blood that most threatens to erase cultural distinctions: "When violence is unloosed, however, blood appears everywhere—on the ground, underfoot, forming great pools. Its very fluidity gives form to the contagious nature of violence. . . . Its very appearance seems, as the saying goes, to cry out for vengeance" (Girard 1977, 31, 34). Indeed, the ode's motif of fire is related to that of an unchecked bloodletting: the image of blood, still wet and criminal (*nondum expiatis uncta cruoribus*), spreads—in keeping with Horace's metaphor of a fire that might be stirred to life—to dominate the eighth and ninth stanzas (29–36). Slaughter and civil bloodshed (*sanguine, caedes, cruore*) permeate these lines much as they do the geography that the speaker, in his series of rhetorical questions, declares the witness to this indiscriminate violence. The interrogative pronouns and adjectives—*quis, qui, quae, quod*, and *quae*, repeating in polyptoton—evoke a pervasive contamination that erodes even the identity of place. And as the complex assonance and consonance of *decoloravere . . . / . . . ora cruore* suggest, even the distinction between human and nature has dissolved, as human gore mixes with the shore.

It is often argued that when Horace uses the phrase "bloodshed not yet expiated" (*nondum expiatis . . . cruoribus*) he conceives of expiation as possible in the sacrifices of enemy blood. Kiessling and Heinze lend weight to this view (1960, ad loc.), referring to *Odes* 1.35, where an attack on the Parthians is offered as an alternative to civil violence. Other scholars point to the end of *Odes* 1.2; there, in answer to the question posed earlier, "to whom will Jupiter give the role of expiating the crime?" (*cui dabit partis scelus expiandi / Iuppiter*, 29–30), the poet responds with the final image of Caesar not permitting the Medes to ride unavenged.[29] Such an interpretation attends to the literal, denotative suggestions made by *Odes* 1.2 and 1.35; but the failure of the ode to Pollio to make a specific foreign policy proposal encourages a different, self-reflexive reading that involves the public function of Horace's verse.

For even if civil violence is seen as inflaming the speaker's song and causing images of bloodshed to spread, "contaminating" the eighth and ninth stanzas, the lament could also be said to serve the opposite function. In Girard's analysis, only the sacred act of ritual violence can contain the impulse toward vengeance and cycles of retribution.[30] Tragedy, as a mimesis of sacrifice, constitutes a form of "ritual mimicry whose cathartic effects are believed to ward off the impending crisis it imitates so faithfully" (Girard 1977, 4, 63). Because the civil wars present a society already in the throes of what Girard labels a sacrificial crisis, there is no question of "warding" off such a catastrophe. However, as I emphasize later in this chapter in my discussion of the Roman Odes, poems prefigured by the ode to Pollio, Horace as a sacred priest intends his poems to stem the tide of cultural dissolution. And in the poetic frame of this ode, the speaker's emotional vision of the war is conveyed in diction and rhetoric suggesting that purification and an end to generational violence must be sought through the cathartic effects of a tragic view of history.[31]

When Pollio is said to handle (*tractas*) the hazardous subject of history, the verb calls to mind the Cleopatra ode (the last poem of the first book,

29. G. Williams 1980, 117–18; for a similar argument, although not in reference to 2.1, see Thome 1992, 89. Kiessling and Heinze (1960, ad loc.) quote the passage in Tac. *Ann.* 1.49 where Germanicus sends his army against the enemy as a *piaculum* for Roman rage and impiety: *truces etiam tum animos cupido involat eundi in hostem, piaculum furoris, nec aliter posse placari commilitonum manes, quam si pectoribus impiis honesta vulnera accepissent.*

30. As Girard (1977, 58) claims, the slim boundary between pure and impure violence allows the latter to be transformed, given the right conditions, into a form of sacred violence.

31. For Girard (1977, 4), "There is no question of 'expiation'"; the ritual sacrifice that tragedy imitates at a later stage of evolution is intended to direct the violent impulses of a group onto a substitute victim, not to expiate for previous crimes of violence. However, expiation and a conscious sense of criminality are clearly issues in Horace's ode. For the development of a Roman consciousness of personal guilt in the late Republic, a phenomenon that can be linguistically charted, see Thome 1992. See Commager 1962, 160–225, for an overview of the cycle of sin and "redemption" as a theme in Horace's political poems.

excepting the *sphragis*), where the Alexandrian queen bravely takes up the snakes that will kill her (*fortis et asperas / tractare serpentis, Odes* 1.37.26–27).[32] The use of the verb in the Pollio ode and the image of treacherous ash (*cineri doloso*) suggestively evoke this serpentine imagery: a slippery subject, the history of the wars could backfire and undermine Pollio's intention to "order" public affairs (*publicas / res ordinaris*). From one perspective, as we have seen, the way in which the poem catches fire confirms this danger. And yet all the words serving as temporal adverbs in the first five stanzas imply that the violence of the speaker's vision, his inflamed emotions, are the proper response to Pollio's historiography, and thus to a successful "ordering" or disposition of the events of the past.

Taken in isolation, the first adverb of the poem, *nondum* (not yet), connotes the continuation of war, a civil conflict that multiplies and propagates because there has been no expiatory ritual. The adverbs and conjunctions of the next stanza, *paulum, mox,* and *ubi* (a little while; soon; when, after), denote stages in Pollio's career; but, specifying further points of time in a continuum, they also create a context for the moment anticipated by *nondum*—the time of purification. This moment, in turn, depends on the tragic inspiration of Pollio's histories. For a little while only (*paulum*) let the Muse of tragedy be away from the stage (*Musa tragoediae / desit theatris); soon* (*mox*), after (*ubi*) Pollio has put public affairs in order (that is, after he has written his history), he will once again take up the distinguished office of the tragic buskin; in keeping with the verb *incedis* (you proceed, you advance, 7), diction connoting a stately carriage, the stanza implies that Pollio's tragic Muse—no longer in the buskin—is with him and that she, too, absent from Rome, walks through the ashes of history.[33] And though the poem explicitly draws attention to Pollio's temporary leave from writing tragedy, and thus makes a clear distinction between the genres of drama and history, the semantic interplay of the temporal adverbs throughout the poem suggests that his tragic Muse inspires Pollio's present work, that it is she who sets public affairs in order (*publicas res ordinaris*).[34] Just as the speaker's Muse is seen at the end of the poem to have temporarily abandoned her appointed role of light, erotic song, so Pollio's Muse leaves her

32. Syndikus (1972, 349) points out that the abrupt change in *Odes* 2.1 from a dedicatory emphasis at the beginning to the subjective experience of the war resembles the sudden shifts of focus in *Odes* 1.37 and *Odes* 2.13, where the mock curse against the planter of a tree evolves into a vision of the underworld.

33. Ullman (1942, 50) takes these lines to indicate that Pollio writes in the vein of tragic historiography; against his position, see N-H, 9. For discussions of the degree to which Horace's poem imitates Pollio's work, see Seeck 1902; Kornemann 1903; Sonnenburg 1904.

34. Note that Aristotle (*Poet.* 1450b22), when referring to the plot, uses the phrase τὴν σύστασιν . . . τῶν πραγμάτων (the order of things), for which the cognate verb would be συνίστημι. The Greek equivalent of *ordinare*, however, is συντάττειν.

usual post to take care of other business—the task of tragic historiography.[35]

The result, Pollio's history, displays the civil wars of Caesar and Pompey as retributory vengeance exacted for Rome's wars with Carthage and Jugurtha—that is, as violence that displays generational cycles of tragic reciprocity. The idea that the transgressions of a later generation are both violations in their own right and a form of divine punishment for the crimes of forebears underlies much Greek tragedy (Liebeschuetz 1979, 92–95). Thus Juno's wrath, presenting historical events in the mythic light of divine anger, may be understood not only as an epic motif but also as a component of the tragic vision informing Pollio's work. It appears in the central stanza of those describing the speaker's imagined response to Pollio's recitation. As the most "objective" of these five, the stanza seems to divide the speaker's response into the Aristotelian categories of pity and fear: the rhetorical questions of the lament for the dead exhibit an almost redundant pity (29–36), while the first two stanzas (17–24) describe a battle whose startling and fearsome drama appears in the threatening sound of horns (*minaci murmure cornuum*), the horses terrified by armor (*iam fulgor armorum fugaces / terret equos*), or the fierce soul of Cato (*atrocem animum Catonis*).

Although the speaker's vision of this scene suggests a fear more akin to awe than to the apprehension of individual disaster, the latter, more conventional understanding of tragic fear is perhaps implied:[36] a tragic representation of the fall of the Republic conceives of Rome as an individual, and the speaker's choral lament suggests as much. For the speaker's fear soon turns to pity for the fallen hero/victim, and the profusion of blood (*sanguine, caedes, cruore*) in these ornate and austere lines specifically recalls passages of the *Oresteia* and, more generally, invokes the sacrificial falls of many characters of tragedy.[37] But as in tragedy, violence is here represented in a ritual frame. The pity and fear of catharsis, originating in the speaker as an audience, evolve into a lyric dirge similar to the odes of

---

35. Whether or not such a genre was specifically practiced in distinction from other forms of historiography is debated. See Walbank 1960; Feldherr 1998, 166–69; and n. 33 above.

36. See Heath 1987, 11–17, for a cogent discussion of the tragic emotions; on tragic fear, in particular, he writes that "'fear' in the formula 'fear and pity' must be understood to cover a wide range of related emotional responses. It includes the species of fear described rather too narrowly in *Rhet.* 1382a21ff.: the emotional disturbance felt when someone for whom our emotions are closely engaged is threatened by impending harm; also, presumably, our response to tension, suspense and excitement in narrative is to be included. But no less important is the instinctive shuddering recoil from what is made horrific by tabu, superstition, numinous awe, physical grisliness or unpleasantness" (13).

37. One is reminded of the exchange between the Chorus and Cassandra, Aesch. *Ag.* 1072–330, where the seer's visions repeatedly emphasize the slaughter of the past, the present as it is happening, and the future retaliation of the Furies.

a tragic chorus. Indeed, choral lamentation, Walter Burkert reminds us, is a possible link to the sacrificial origins of tragedy (1966, 114–15). Thus when the speaker refers to "rehandling" (*retractas*) the "lamentations" or "funereal office" (*munera*) of the Cean dirge, the phrase echoes not only Pollio's treatment of history (*tractas*) but also his nominally abandoned office of tragic poet, his great civic calling (*grande munus*) that the speaker now fulfills with lyric.

Critics often refer to the tragic vision that informs the Augustan writers' view of the civil wars, but they do not draw the logical conclusion from Horace's lyric enactment of the trope—that the speaker's emotional response to Pollio constitutes a form of cathartic purification.[38] Yet the phrase *publicas res ordinaris* (you will have set public affairs in chronological order) also connotes the arrangement of a subject, the parts of a literary work, and thus suggests the "particular configuration of events" that produces tragic catharsis.[39] It is the structure of a plot, the sequence of actions or external states constituting the vicissitudes of fortune, that evokes emotions in the audience of Aristotelian tragedy. The speaker's response to Pollio's historiography therefore proceeds from the way in which the historian's Muse orders the events of the recent past in a tragic light. Such "ordering," in turn, brings about a form of expiation through the stimulation of tragic catharsis:[40] the juxtaposition of *mox* (soon) and *ubi* (when) in line 10 looks back to the *nondum expiatis* (not yet expiated) of the first stanza, and the two words create a narrative sequence of their own. Pollio, writing a history, handles material that has not been atoned for; not yet, but soon, when those issues have been ordered in writing, expiation will be possible. When? "Now" (*iam . . . iam . . . iam . . . iam*), the fifth and sixth stanzas seem to announce with the urgency of an epiphany. These two stanzas refer literally to the immediacy of the speaker's imagined experience of Pollio's recitation and the powerful *enargeia* of his writing: the historian has brought the battle of Pharsalus and the consequences of Thapsus—Cato's noble suicide and Caesar's ultimate supremacy—vividly to life in the speaker's mind. But the repetition of *iam* four times in these two stanzas cannot but refer as

---

38. Syndikus (1973, 347) claims that in the second half of the ode, "Im Bürgerkrieg sieht Horaz selbst eine ungeheuere Tragödie, die Tragödie Roms"; Lyne (1995, 93) writes of Horace's representation of Rome's "tragic guilt"; Lowrie (1997, 181) notes that "Although history and tragedy are first differentiated as the two sides of Pollio's literary career, they collapse when it comes to Horace's self-definition." See n. 33 above.

39. For definitions of *ordinare*, see *OLD*, s.v., 1c, 1d. On catharsis in relation to plot, see Halliwell 1986, 170–71, 179; Arist. *Poet.* 1449b24–28, 1450b20–36.

40. Since the pollution of bloodguilt is one of the contexts that calls for purification, an element of religious catharsis must be at play in the speaker's emotional—e.g., cathartic—response to Pollio's history. See Halliwell 1986, 186, for the pre-Aristotelian, "religious" connotations of catharsis.

well to an expiation for the crimes of history established by the previous temporal adverbs—*nondum, mox,* and *ubi.*

In addition, the emphasis on the present moment in time (*iam*) as the subjective experience of the speaker when he "seems to hear" (*videor . . . audire*) suggests attributes particular to lyric as a genre.[41] Horace uses this exact phrase in *Odes* 3.4 to evoke the heady enthusiasm of inspiration by the Muses: after calling on Calliope to descend from heaven and make her presence known through voice, lyre, or flute, the speaker addresses his audience: "Do you hear [her], or does a delightful madness deceive me? I seem to hear and to wander through holy groves where pleasant waters and breezes steal" (*Auditis? an me ludit amabilis / insania? Audire et videor pios / errare per lucos, amoenae / quos et aquae subeunt et aurae,* 3.4.5–8). In *Odes* 2.1, it is Pollio's historiography—or the tragic Muse inhabiting Pollio's history— that unleashes this lyric experience. And the complex connotations of *iam,* referring here both to the immediacy of a lyric epiphany and to the time of expiation, establish a relationship between the two.[42]

Such sacrificial connotations of the lyric epiphany conform to the discourse of sacred ritual implicit in the Horatian posture of a "seer" (*vates*) or "priest" (*sacerdos*). For as the language of the fifth and sixth stanzas suggests a visionary experience, so the lament that evolves from such a state corresponds to a sacrificial offering:[43] the "lamentations" or "office of the Cean dirge" (*Ceae . . . munera neniae*) explicitly acknowledge the eighth and ninth stanzas as a form of rite for the dead. In a funerary context *munera* can refer to verbal lamentation as well as to concrete offerings, and often there is no clear distinction between the two (N-H, ad loc.). When Catullus, for example, addresses his brother's grave, his poem becomes the very funereal gift offered to his brother's ashes: "I come, brother, to these wretched last rites, so that I might present you with the final offering paid to death, and address your mute ash in vain" (*advenio has miseras, frater, ad inferias, / ut te postremo donarem munere mortis / et mutam nequiquam alloquerer cinerem,* 101.2–4). In *Odes* 2.1, the similar idea of offering or "gift" in *munera* looks back to the seventh stanza, where Juno is said to bear back Roman

---

41. Frye (1957, 250) addresses this relationship between lyric and vision or dream. For the historical origins of the critical view that lyric is associated with "pure subjectivity," see Arac 1985, 353–55, and his reference to Hegel 1975, 2:1133.

42. In fact, the most immediate reference for *iam* is to the time of its own linguistic context, the time of Horace's lyric verse as a poetic utterance. In Benveniste's essay "The Nature of Pronouns" (1971, 217–22), temporal adverbs such as "now," belonging to a class of what he calls "indicators," share with the first- and second-person pronouns the characteristic of referring before all else to the *present* instance of discourse in which they are uttered.

43. As N-H, ad loc., claim, the language of stanzas 5 and 6 suggests the vision of a seer— for example, the Sibyl's predictions of *bella, horrida bella* in Verg. *Aen.* 6.86.

soldiers as human sacrifices to the spirit of Jugurtha (*victorum nepotes / rettulit inferias Iugurthae,* 27–28). However, in contrast to the cycle of revenge that characterizes Juno's offerings, the "gifts" of the speaker's dirge have the connotations of a pure violence, the implications of a sacrifice whose ritual context serves an expiatory function. Indeed, *pinguior*—literally, "more fat" or "more rich" (29), a common epithet for sacrificial victims and the adjective that refers to the plain enriched with Latin blood—both looks back to the sacrificial sense of *inferias* and looks forward to *munera,* where such violence is transformed within the ritual context of the lament itself.

The idea that the Cean dirge provides ritual purification may, in fact, connect the image of fire with the symbolic sacrifice of the poem. For the emotions unleashed by Pollio's recitation, as we recall, constitute the "fire beneath the ash" of line 8. When this fire spreads and transforms the objective focus of the first four stanzas into the subjective experience of the speaker, we might claim—on the level of metaphor—that the flames contained within the context of sacred ritual, the *munera* of the dirge, symbolize a purification of the very bloodguilt whose potential to contaminate they initially enact. That is, the poem in flames, as a symbol of purification, thwarts the tendency to reciprocal violence that it imitates. Perhaps it is no coincidence that with the phrase *Ceae neniae* Horace invokes Simonides, native of Ceos and the lyric poet whose most famous elegy was written for the dead of Plataea, a battle whose aftermath also witnessed elaborate purification ceremonies relying on fire.[44]

Finally, given the prominent position of this ode, we should consider its implications in the context of patronage. As the dedicatee of *Odes* 2, Pollio here occupies a "patronal" position, following Maecenas as the primary dedicatee of *Odes* 1 and anticipating the addressees in the dedicatory position of 3.1, the young men and women of Rome. For though 2.1 begins as a dedication poem in a context of patronage, focusing on the achievements of Pollio, it evolves into a choral lyric that assumes the civic office of tragedy, the very *munus* from which the historian has turned. Thus, the rhetorical development of the poem dramatizes the way in which "praise" poetry for a "patron"—at least a patron by virtue of poetic position—is not consumed in the act of exchange but becomes a gift passed on to a wider public.

The ode to Pollio offers a paradigm of how certain Horatian poems effect a sacrificial function—with their perlocutionary force, they strive to act

---

44. For an argument that connects the *lustrum,* as a ritual of purification, to the use of fire, see Ogilvie 1961.

upon the audience with all the rhetorical persuasiveness of the symbolism of sacrifice.[45] In this regard, the rhetorical trope of "lyric as sacrifice" maintains the potency of the realm of religious ritual from which it is drawn. I see the Pollio ode as paradigmatic because for all that the speaker appropriates Pollio's role and offers lyric as a substitute for the civic *munus* of tragedy, he initially represents himself as an audience to the tragic construction of history—as though to suggest the effects that he intends to produce in his readers through his own later role of priest, with his lyric sacrifices. Before turning to the Roman Odes to test this paradigm, exploring the implications of those poems in the context of sacrifice and tragic mimesis, let us examine one other overt instance of the lyric impulse as a ritual response to violence.

RITUAL *DEVOTIO* AND THE LYRIC CURSE: *ODES* 2.13

Ille et nefasto te posuit die,
quicumque, primum et sacrilega manu
    produxit, arbos, in nepotum
        perniciem opprobriumque pagi;

illum et parentis crediderim sui   5
fregisse cervicem et penetralia
    sparsisse nocturno cruore
        hospitis; ille venena Colcha

et quidquid usquam concipitur nefas
tractavit, agro qui statuit meo   10
    te, triste lignum, te, caducum
        in domini caput immerentis.

quid quisque vitet numquam homini satis
cautum est in horas. navita Bosphorum
    Poenus perhorrescit neque ultra   15
        caeca timet aliunde fata;

miles sagittas et celerem fugam
Parthi, catenas Parthus et Italum
    robur: sed improvisa leti
        vis rapuit rapietque gentis.   20

quam paene furvae regna Proserpinae
et iudicantem vidimus Aeacum

---

45. For a discussion of the trope of sacrifice as a form of persuasion, see Pucci 1992. Invoking de Man (1979a) and Culler (1978), Pucci (1992, 515) points out that in the *Oresteia,* the "persuasive act imprints on the construct of the sacrifice the undecidability of a trope, and this trope in turn becomes the resource of persuasion."

sedesque descriptas [discretas/discriptas] piorum et
    Aeoliis fidibus querentem

Sappho puellis de popularibus,   25
et te sonantem plenius aureo,
    Alcaee, plectro dura navis,
        dura fugae mala, dura belli!

utrumque sacro digna silentio
mirantur umbrae dicere, sed magis   30
    pugnas et exactos tyrannos
        densum umeris bibit aure vulgus.

quid mirum, ubi illis carminibus stupens
demittit atras belua centiceps
    auris et intorti capillis   35
        Eumenidum recreantur angues?

quin et Prometheus et Pelopis parens
dulci laborem decipitur sono,
    nec curat Orion leones
        aut timidos agitare lyncas.   40

That man, whoever first planted you, did it on an inauspicious day, and
raised you with a sacrilegious hand, O tree, for the destruction of future
generations and the shame of the countryside. I could believe that he
broke the neck of his own parent and scattered the inmost hearth with
the blood of a guest murdered at night; that one has handled Colchian
poisons and whatever crime, anywhere, is conceived, who placed you,
baneful tree, to fall on the head of your innocent master. Never, from
hour to hour, does any man sufficiently beware what he should avoid:
the Punic sailor shudders before the Bosphorus, but does not fear the
unsurmised fates beyond, from elsewhere; the soldier fears the Par-
thian's arrows, loosed in swift flight; the Parthian fears chains and a dun-
geon's death in Italy; but an unforeseen violence has snatched and will
snatch away the races of men to their destruction. How I almost saw the
realms of dark Proserpina, and Aeacus dispensing judgment, and the fa-
bled seats of the pious [or seats reserved for the pious], and Sappho la-
menting, on Aeolian lyre, of girls from her native land, and you, Alcaeus,
with golden plectrum, resounding more fully the sailor's hardships, the
cruel duress of exile, the hard life of war. The shades are amazed at both
as they sing themes worthy of sacred silence; but the crowd, pressed
shoulder to shoulder, is more intoxicated by battles and tyrants driven
out. What wonder, when bewitched by those songs, the hundred-headed
beast relaxes his black ears, and twisting in their hair, the snakes of the
Eumenides are refreshed, born anew? Why, even Prometheus and the fa-
ther of Pelops, enchanted by the sweet sound, forget their trials, nor
does Orion care to provoke the lions or the fearful lynxes.

The unleashing of lyrical energy as a ritualized response to brute force appears in *Odes* 2.13, the poem in which Horace indulges comic imprecations against a tree whose fall almost causes his death. While the speaker's poem testifies to his survival, the near accident sparks a meditation on blind fate, violent chance, and the prospect of the underworld. During the heyday of biographical criticism, scholars predictably focused on this ode as a description of a real event, charmed by the contrast between the poet's "lived" experience and his fanciful imagination of the world of the dead.[46] More recently, the poem has been remarked for its use of autobiographical event as a trope that serves to authenticate the lyric calling of the poet (Davis 1991, 78–89; Lowrie 1997, 202). The descent to the underworld—the poet's version of epic *katabasis*—and the vision of Sappho and Alcaeus charming the dead place Horace in the company of the great lyric poets while suggestively evoking the figure of Orpheus as a mythic prototype (Klingner 1964, 326; Syndikus 1972, 425). For the purposes of my argument, I focus on the ways in which the poem's evolution from the rhetoric of curse to a vision of lyric potency conforms to the ideology of sacrifice. Echoes of diction and recurring imagery establish a relationship between this poem, the ode to Pollio, and the Roman Odes; ultimately, in keeping with my analysis of *Odes* 2.1, I emphasize that this network of associations figures Horace's public poetry as a civic *munus:* a voluntary expenditure that seeks, like sacrifice and its ritual reenactment in tragedy, to bind and thwart the propagation of cycles of civil violence.

On a basic level, the poem arises from the speaker's near extinction, making the scrape with death a source of lyric creation. Such lyric, in turn, retrospectively ascribes the tree's fall to its evil planter, whose actions precipitated the seeming "accident" and its nefarious consequences. The contagion of the tree's violence, spreading from its antisocial origins to its potential effects, resembles the way in which images of blood permeate the ode to Pollio. Such a comparison between the comic exaggeration of the one poem and the tragic motifs of the other may appear far-fetched; however, as we shall see, within its humorous and personal context, *Odes* 2.13 has a serious historical dimension that connects it to the Pollio ode. Whereas 2.1 performs an expiatory function, this poem might be said to transform the explosive violence of the tree's fall into beneficent cultural energy. To be sure, there is no overt ritual here, but the poem as curse enables what Girard describes as the conversion of "bad" violence into "good": "Any phenomenon linked to impure violence is capable of being inverted and rendered beneficent; but this can take place only within the immutable and rigorous framework of ritual practice" (1977, 58).

---

46. Kiessling and Heinze 1960, 209–10; see Klingner 1964b [1952], 325–27, for a good summary of the scholarship.

In a number of ways, the poem suggests a ritual utterance in its own right. To begin with, the first three stanzas comically invert the tradition of a blessing, the *makarismos* that might accompany the planting of a tree.[47] Roman agricultural practices were often marked by these sorts of rituals, which manifested the conservative piety of the rustic farmer. We see such a positive ritual context in *Odes* 3.22, where the poem serves to consecrate a pine tree on Horace's estate to Diana and promises a yearly sacrifice at the informal "shrine" in her honor. In contrast, *Odes* 2.13 begins as a kind of imprecation, suggesting not only an inversion of the *makarismos* but also the poetic genre of *arai,* or "curses." Francis Cairns has suggested that *arai,* originally a Greek genre, were grafted by Roman writers onto the indigenous legal concept of the *flagitatio,* a form of "extra-legal or pro-legal self-help" by which a person could attempt to regain stolen property or force a debtor to pay through incessant demand and verbal insult (1972, 93–95). Cairns proposes similar generic hybridization for *Odes* 1.30, where the poet grafts the Roman institution of the *evocatio,* a military leader's ritual summoning of his enemy's gods to abandon a besieged city, onto the Greek kletic hymn (1971, 446). In keeping with such generic hybrids, the specifically Roman concept of the *devotio* informs the background of the "curse" of *Odes* 2.13.

For the Roman imagination, Livy's description of Decius's ritual "devotion" of himself and his enemies to the infernal gods, followed by the general's active pursuit of death in battle, constitutes the paradigmatic instance of the military *devotio.* But scholars suggest that in this famous instance, the voluntary self-sacrifice of a general who symbolically assumes the impurities of his own people actually combines two related forms of more commonly practiced *devotiones/consecrationes:* on the one hand, *devotio* was a punishment by which criminals were consecrated to the gods of the underworld; on the other, a *devotio* was simply a form of *maleficium,* or curse, that handed over the enemy to the infernal gods as a kind of substitute or "sacrifice," enabling the salvation of the speaker.[48] While *Odes* 2.13 presents no overt consecration of an enemy to the powers below—indeed, it is the poet who imaginatively experiences the realm of Dis even as he eludes it—the informal curse of the beginning suggests a kind of retrospective *devotio* or *maleficium* offered for the very grace of that escape.

---

47. N-H, 202; see Klingner 1964b [1952], 327, for arguments *against* viewing the exaggerated tones of the opening as comic.

48. For the ritual *devotiones* of the Decii, see Livy 8.6.9–11, 8.9.1–13, 8.10.11–14, 8.11.1, 10.28.12–17, and the analysis of Feldherr 1998, 85–92. See Pascal 1990, 258–65, and Thome 1992, 85–87, for a lucid discussion of the evidence of the Roman ritual and the semantic range of the concept. Barton (1993, 42–45) discusses the *devotio* in relation to the figure of the gladiator. I am indebted to her summary of the concept, and to her further references to Bouché-LeClercq 1892, 113–14, and to Macrob. *Sat.* 3.9–13.

There is further and varied support for this generic or conceptual influence. On a strictly linguistic basis, the speaker refers to the tree in *Odes* 3.4.27 as the *devota . . . arbor* (damned tree) that would have destroyed him had the Muses not been his protector. While *devota* here has its more general sense of "accursed," its use nonetheless implies that the more specific references of the *devotio* may be at play in *Odes* 2.13. The poem's own stanzaic progression supports the idea that the *maleficium* directed at the planter serves as a kind of consecration in exchange for the speaker's safety: the curse precedes and appears to evolve into the gnomic reflections of the miraculously "saved" man, which turn to a lyric vision of the underworld, with all its intimations of immortality; thus, not only is the speaker spared in this particular "biographical" incident, but the episode also suggests the only form of salvation or immortality known to the ancient world—a place in cultural memory.

Moreover, the sacrificial substitution that characterizes the *devotio* of an enemy accords with the literary convention of the *katabasis* as requiring that the person wishing to journey to the underworld make some kind of sacrifice. Particularly in epic, the *katabasis* provides the hero with a renewed sense of purpose and destiny: Odysseus gets his sense of direction from Tiresias; Aeneas, having reached the Elysian fields, is given his mission to lay the foundations of Roman *imperium* by his father. But in order to guarantee that these men return from the world of the dead, the narrative convention demands a "sacrifice," a life in exchange for the one who returns to the realm of the living. Elpenor tumbles to his death from Circe's roof before Odysseus sets out to meet Tiresias (Hom. *Od.* 10.552–59); and both Palinurus, who is the famous "one for many" demanded by Neptune at the end of *Aeneid* 5, and Misenus, who is killed for his impiety while Aeneas is visiting the Sibyl, constitute the human sacrifices that the convention demands (Verg. *Aen.* 5.815, 840–71; 6.162–82). To be sure, Horace's poem as lyric cannot function in the same way as epic narrative, but the speaker does arguably acquire a renewed sense of his destiny as a poet of public, civic issues. Hence, I suggest that the informal curse serves symbolically to consecrate the tree's planter in exchange for the speaker's "experience" of the underworld as a living man. As though to represent this consecration, the figures who are punished in the underworld do penance for the same type of crimes as the infamous *ille* (that man) of the opening.

The concept of *devotio* as consecration in the form of legal punishment may also lurk behind the curse. As Nisbet and Hubbard point out, the curse functions as a diatribe against first inventors—those "originators" (like the first shipbuilder) whose discoveries have had some negative consequences for humanity (1991 [1978], ad loc.). And by treating the planter as the ἀρχὴ κακῶν (source of evils), the speaker presents him as a criminal, a moral agent capable of the most heinous of crimes. To some degree a parody, the literary topos nonetheless casts the tree's fall in an ethical light, and this backdrop of criminal behavior lends greater symbolic weight to what would otherwise be a chance event. In fact, the humorous exaggeration employs imagery and invokes crimes reminiscent of Girard's sacrificial crisis—poison, bloodshed, parricide, and a sense of burgeoning disaster: On an impious day (*nefasto . . . die*), with transgressive hand (*sacrilega manu*) that nameless evildoer planted the tree whose fall could precipitate destruction for generations to come (*in nepotum perniciem*). The image suggests contamination spreading forward in time even as it infects the space surrounding Horace's estate (*opprobriumque pagi*). The extreme claims, however, do not stop there, for the jocular exaggeration that marks the speaker's outraged tone extends to conjectures about crimes the planter has committed. The lawless violence in which he indulged, his egregious violation of cultural taboos, initiated a chain of destruction that precipitated the tree's fall. Capable of parricide (*parentis . . . fregisse cervicem*), the murder of a guest (*penetralia / sparsisse nocturno cruore / hospitis*), and the insidious devilry of a Medea (*venena Colcha . . . tractavit*), the planter has a past that leads teleologically to the tree's fall and the speaker's near death. The implied motifs here suggest the cyclicity of tragedy or the chain reaction of Girard's "bad violence." The verb *tractavit* (he has handled) further underscores this sense of contamination, recalling the image of Pollio who "handles" (*tractas*) a dangerous and bloody topic that could flare up on him. The planter's poisonous touch, morally sullied by the *nefas* (wrongdoing, crime) that he has handled, infects the tree whose fall could precipitate a widening circle of destruction.

It is important to register this echo of the ode to Pollio, because it reinforces the overall similarity between the poems as linguistic imitations, or symbolic enactments, of rituals involving forms of sacrifice. Both poems forcefully exhibit an abrupt turn or shift in direction—the violent Horatian *Abbruch* that recalls Pindar. As I have been suggesting, in these poems the violence of this lyric shift of focus or direction invokes the discourse of sacrifice as a ritualistic response to uncontrolled, contaminatory, and vindictive bloodshed.[49] *Odes* 2.13 does not explicitly present such images of transgressive violence in the context of the civil wars; nonetheless, the reminiscence of the ode to Pollio, combined with other patterns of diction, hints at the historical backdrop constituting one frame of reference for the rhetorical treatment of "autobiographical" event in this poem.[50] Indeed,

49. Syndikus (1972, 349) notes that *Odes* 1.37, 2.1, and 2.13 each exhibits a sudden, unexpected shift of direction.

50. Lowrie (1997, 216–17) offers a list of words that figure in "personal narrative" poems

the only other use of *tractare* in the *Odes* besides 2.1 and 2.13 is in 1.37, where Cleopatra handles the poisonous asps—an action whose greater context is the civil battle of Actium, despite the poem's suppression of the figure of Antony. *Cruor* (blood, gore), appearing in 2.13 in the context of the murder of a guest, figures elsewhere in the *Odes* only in 2.1, in the significant phrase "arms smeared with unexpiated blood (*cruoribus*)," and later in the speaker's lament, "what shore lacks our blood (*cruore nostro*)." Moreover, the phrase "destruction for future generations" (*in nepotum / perniciem*, 2.13.3–4) anticipates the figure of Regulus in 3.5.14–16, predicting the blight of ignominy contaminating the future (*perniciem veniens in aevum*) should Rome ransom back her soldiers from the Carthaginians. Once again, by limiting his lyric use of *perniciem* to only these two poems of the *Odes*, Horace asserts a relationship between the two contexts: one private and occasional, the other public and historical. Finally, the entire indefinite relative clause that *tractavit* introduces in 2.13, "whatever crime anywhere is conceived, he has handled" (*et quidquid usquam concipitur nefas, tractavit*), recalls a similar phrase in 1.35, a poem whose ending bluntly addresses the civil wars: "Alas, alas, the shame of our scars, and crime, and brothers [killed]. What have we, a hardened generation, recoiled from? what have we, impious, left untouched?" (*Heu, heu, cicatricum et sceleris pudet / fratrumque: quid nos dura refugimus / aetas? quid intactum nefasti / liquimus*, 33–36). And not only does 1.35 anticipate many of the themes of the Roman Odes, but its ending, a series of rhetorical questions, exhibits the same tone as the speaker's emotional dirge in 2.1.[51] Moreover, it is this language of impiety, with all its implications of contagiousness through touch and guilt down the generations, that characterizes the planter in the speaker's curse in 2.13.

In this light, the hypothetical planter functions as a kind of ritual victim that, in Girard's terms, "draws to itself all the violence infecting the original victim and through its own death transforms this baneful violence into beneficial violence, into harmony and abundance" (1977, 95). Girard is here discussing the function of the *pharmakos,* but such a scapegoat performs much the same function as the consecrated person in a *devotio.*[52] Insofar as the fall of the tree evokes the phenomenon of unpredictable and dangerous violence, it metaphorically calls for the same sacrificial discourse as the brutalities of civil warfare. Given the verbal allusions remarked above,

---

like 2.13 and then reappear in *Odes* 3.4, the ultimate poem of "Personal Myth" that evolves into the Gigantomachia as allegory for the civil war. Scholars often see 2.13 as preparation for the Roman Odes: see Nicoll 1986; Porter 1987, 244; Lowrie 1997, 202–5.

51. See Syndikus 1972, 323, and Witke 1983, 7–18, for the various relationships between 1.35 and the Roman Odes.

52. For the element of a "scapegoat" in ritual *devotio,* see Thome 1992, 87.

we have a metaphor for the fall of the Republic, the subject that *Odes* 2.1 treats in a frame of tragic history and funereal ritual.[53] *Odes* 3.4.25–28 correlates the Horatian theme of danger narrowly averted on both these public and private levels when the speaker ascribes his salvation from the rout at Philippi, as well as from the *devota arbor* (cursed tree), to the protection of the Muses. Moreover, the central stanza of 2.13, where the speaker generalizes the theme of death's unpredictability, also alludes to the poet's involvement with the Republican cause and Brutus's army: the arrows and *celerem fugam* (swift flight) of the Parthian, vainly feared by the soldier who does not in fact know when death will strike, echo the poet's "autobiographical" (and Alcaic) flight when he abandoned his shield at Philippi (*celerem fugam / sensi relicta non bene parmula*, 2.7.9–10) (Nadeau 1980, 205). Finally, the adjective *inmerentis* (innocent), which is applied to the speaker as not deserving to be crushed by a tree, appears in the same genitive form in *Epode* 7, where Horace describes the civil wars as Rome's fate "ever since the blood of innocent Remus flowed across the ground, a curse for generations to come" (*ut immerentis fluxit in terram Remi / sacer nepotibus cruor*, 7.19–20). Thus, if the tree's fall is metaphorical, then Horace can be metaphorically an "original victim" for whom the planter as *pharmakos* is substituted in the speaker's curse in 2.13, consonant with the function of the ritual victim to draw to itself the impulse toward self-propagating civil violence. And so, as a lyric ritual, the poem serves to "devote" or sacrifice the planter, who embodies the threat of civil violence, to the underworld.

Through this *maleficium*—the symbolic *devotio*—the spread of violence is checked, and the speaker transforms the explosive, potentially negative energy of the incident into a procreative, cultural force. The poet's lyric vision stresses its ontological status as a poetic construct—the seats of the pious are characterized as *descriptas*[54]—and this aesthetic realm of the dead reproduces song as Sappho and Alcaeus are found to charm the shades with their own *carmina*. The fall precipitates a chain of culture, sparking the speaker's poetic vision, which in turn contains poets in the act of song.

The ritual effects of the poem in terms of restraint and containment—binding the energy of cyclical violence—are mirrored in this vision of po-

---

53. I am grateful to my colleague Mary Jaeger for emphasizing the fall as a metaphor.

54. N-H, ad loc., citing Tac. *Ann.* 2.19.1, read *descriptas* as "marked out," "assigned," or "allocated." Their interpretation is, however, more in keeping with the manuscript variant *discriptas*, which suggests the "allotted" or "distributed" seats of the dead. The third manuscript variant, *discretas*, "set apart," is favored by Kiessling and Heinze (1960), Quinn (1992 [1980]), and Shackleton Bailey (1985). The variants, as I discuss below, are highly suggestive in the context of the Roman theater and public performance. Scribal errors notwithstanding, I find it plausible that Horace himself may have entertained more than one of these manuscript variants; if poems were shared privately before the author's "final" relinquishing of them in a poetry book, it is possible that different versions entered the manuscript tradition at the start.

etry in the underworld. There, Sappho and Alcaeus command a reverential silence, spell-binding not only the crowd of shades but also the hundred heads of Cerberus (*belua centiceps*) and the snakes in the hair of the Eumenides.[55] The representation of the crowd as densely packed, shoulder to shoulder, metonymically slides into the next image of Cerberus and acquires a suggestion of unpredictable passions subdued.[56] This metonymic identification finds further support in Horace's description of the *vulgus* elsewhere: in *Epistles* 1.1.76 the crowd, or *populus Romanus,* is labeled specifically as a beast of many heads (*belua multorum es capitum*). Thus, Horace's implicit conflation of Cerberus's heads with such a *vulgus* evokes the brutish and inconstant passions of a Roman crowd.[57] Mob violence returns us to the bloodshed of the civil wars, Girard's sacrificial crisis, and the bad violence that initiates a cycle of tragic vengeance.

The mythic monsters populating the speaker's underworld perfectly symbolize this aspect of tragedy: whereas Cerberus represents the monstrous factionalism of the crowd, the Eumenides recall their earlier identity as the Furies, spirits of vengeance for bloodguilt and the curse of the house of Atreus in the *Oresteia.* The reference to Tantalus as the *Pelopis parens* (the father of Pelops) underscores the generational aspect of this tragic cyclicity even as it echoes the characterization of the planter, at the poem's outset, as capable of kin murder. The recurring violence threatened by the tree's fall finds its complement in the images of crowding multiplicity in the underworld—the dense throng, the hundred heads, the nest of snakes all suggest a monstrous fertility, a reproduction of the same.[58] But first the speaker and then his precursors Sappho and Alcaeus contain that violence, stilling and stopping its contagion, transforming it from bad to good, and making it into something new, like the serpentine locks of the Furies affected by song (*Eumenidum recreantur angues*). The reference to these spirits

55. For the relationship between song and charm (as a form of magic) in the Greek poetic tradition, see Walsh 1984.

56. Lowrie (1997, 203) notes the relationship between the charming of Cerberus and the "eagle snoozing on the scepter of Zeus in *Pythian* I [6]," a poem that, as Fraenkel (1957, 273–85) emphasizes, significantly informs *Odes* 3.4, the allegorical Gigantomachia.

57. Nicoll (1986, 608) similarly observes these Horatian echoes in his argument that the crowd, unlike Horace, is still seduced by clichéd slogans represented in *pugnas et exactos tyrannos* (31), phrases that evoke the Republican catchwords of the tyrannicides.

58. Girard (1977, 143–68) discusses the effects of a cycle of reciprocal violence. Rooted in mimetic desire, such violence causes the participants to become mimetic doubles of each other. The erasure of difference and distinction propagates more of the same. This procreation of "doubles" constitutes something monstrous, and Girard contends that "monsters," of some form or other, are always present in texts that reflect "the sacrificial crisis." See Lowrie 1997, 144–64, for a discussion of Cleopatra as the monstrous embodiment of civil war, the divisions of which have been transferred onto her as a form of scapegoat who provides for expiation.

in their beneficent guise is telling: the effects of lyric poetry enact the same transformations as does the ideological remaking of the Furies at the end of the *Oresteia,* a point that looks ahead to the Muses' "re-creation" of Caesar in the Pierian cave (*vos Caesarem altum . . . / Pierio recreatis antro,* 3.4.37–40).[59] This reading of *recreantur,* within an overall interpretation of the social cohesion and beneficence that results from sacrifice (here invoked by the planter as *pharmakos,* or scapegoat), is more compelling than understanding the word as signifying the arousal of the snakes.[60]

Tragedy in a lyric context returns us to the public function of Horace's poems as a civic *munus* (public show, offering). As Nisbet and Hubbard note, the *vulgus* or "mob" of the dead, pressed shoulder to shoulder, suggests the standing-room-only crowd of a Roman *contio,* a public meeting or assembly at which speeches were given. Similarly suggestive of a Roman context of performance are the alternate manuscript readings in line 23: *sedesque discriptas piorum* (assigned) and *discretas* (appointed) seats for the pious. The image calls to mind the *lex Iulia theatralis,* Augustus's legislation decreeing separate areas for different social orders in the theater. Though this particular law may very well have postdated the composition of Horace's ode, the practice of such divisions was firmly in place before its passage: Elizabeth Rawson claims that Augustus's legislation served to tighten the provisions of preexisting laws such as the *lex Roscia* of 67 B.C.E., which established fourteen rows of the theater for the *equites.*[61] Hence, whether or not Augustus's concern with maintaining social stratification in audiences at public events had yet taken the form of law, these Horatian images of performance, with allusions to Roman public venues, lend an Augustan topicality to the figures of Sappho and Alcaeus as poets of orally performed lyric. Because the Greek poets serve not only as models for Horatian meter and themes alternately private and civic but also as emblems of this poem's thematic exploration of the relationship between song and violence, their mastery and command of the underworld "mob" appear similarly analogous to the poet's own dynamic with his Roman audience.

In the Roman Odes, poems prefigured by the figure of Alcaeus here,

---

59. That Horace had Aeschylus specifically in mind may be further suggested by the figure of Prometheus, though here he is placed in Tartarus rather than on the Caucasus.

60. For *recreantur* as "aroused," see N-H, ad loc., followed by Nicoll 1986, 608. Given the general cessation of activity in the still lyricism of the moment—the two hundred ears of Cerberus comically drooping, Orion no longer caring to drive the lions and lynxes through hell in banal and eternal repetition—the passage overall suggests that passions are being tamed, not provoked: the twisting circuitous tangle of serpents—free-floating violence—becomes momentarily fastened in place as the tragic cycle ceases.

61. Rawson (1987) gives 26–17 B.C.E. as the *termini post quem* and *ante quem* for the *lex Iulia theatralis.* See Zanker 1988, 147–56, for the importance of the theater to Roman identity and the *discrimina ordinum.* For the manuscript variants, see n. 54 above.

Horace asserts that he hates the "sacrilegious mob" (*profanum vulgus*) and keeps them at a distance. In what sense, then, does he invoke the rhetoric of performance? To review and evaluate all the evidence concerning performance of poetry in the Augustan age, and Horace's apparent distaste for it beyond the circle of his immediate friends, is beyond the scope of my argument; I tend to agree with Kenneth Quinn that "there is an element of unreality . . . about Horace's claim to be interested only in writing for a few friends" and that "semi-public readings may have been more frequent than he cared to admit" (1982, 152).[62] And while reading practices and literacy rates are difficult to ascertain,[63] there is a general consensus that poetry was regularly performed in the Augustan period and that the literate public became acquainted with new work through some form of recitation rather than by the silent reading of a papyrus scroll. Indeed, the possible allusion to seating division in the theater in *Odes* 2.13 may very well accord with the "distance" at which the poet keeps the *vulgus* in 3.1. But whether or not the more public Horatian odes were performed for audiences larger than the select few of the Augustan circle—and I believe that they must have been—it is the rhetoric of spectacle, ritual, and civic poetry that concerns us here.

As in the Pollio ode, Horace in 2.13 anticipates the Roman Odes as a form of civic *munus,* fulfilling a public function not altogether different, in both its strategic mechanisms and its desired effects, from the role traditionally accorded to tragedy.[64] We have evidence that Varius's *Thyestes* was specifically commissioned for the *ludi* (games) with which Octavian celebrated his victory at Actium; another possibility is that the play was performed at the dedication of the Temple to Apollo on the Palatine in 28 B.C.E.[65] It seems that the educated elite had a heightened awareness of the relevance of tragedy and its emphasis on kin murder, and in particular the

62. More generally, see Quinn 1982, 140–65, for analysis of the evidence concerning public performance during the late Republic and early Empire. Quinn concludes that poetry was heard in three other contexts in addition to the private readings enjoyed by the Augustan circle: in a competitive format before an appointed judge; at a formal *recitatio*—the noncompetitive type of reading, supposedly introduced by Asinius Pollio, to which a wide public was invited; and in performances by professional *cantores* at which mimetic spectacle became a mode of interpretation. See Cairns 1984, 149–54, for speculation about the performance of Propertius 4.6, a poem that, like the Roman Odes, invokes the trope of public ritual.

63. On ancient literacy, see the introduction, n. 11, and the essays in Humphrey 1991.

64. I am not returning to Mommsen's idea that the Roman Odes were conceived as a unit explicitly to celebrate ideas connected with the *princeps* in 27 B.C.E. when he adopted the name Augustus. Essentially I agree with Heinze (1960, 190–204), who argues that the Roman Odes were not initially conceived as a self-contained cycle but that their present order is nonetheless intended to suggest a certain unity.

65. See Jocelyn 1980, 391 n. 24, for sources and the suggestion that the dedication of the Temple to Apollo was the more likely occasion.

relevance of the inherited curse of the house of Atreus, to the civil warfare of the recent past. But whereas Varius's *Thyestes* actually functioned as a dramatic spectacle, Horace presents his lyric—whether "read" in the privacy of the home or heard in the context of a *recitatio*—as able to perform the civic function of the great tragedies of Athens.

THE ROMAN ODES AND TRAGIC SACRIFICE

The symbolic context of ritual clearly informs the rhetorical posture of the speaker in the opening image of the Roman Odes, where the call for silence echoes the *sacrum silentium* of the crowd enthralled by the music of Sappho and Alcaeus:

> Odi profanum vulgus et arceo;
> favete linguis: carmina non prius
> audita Musarum sacerdos
> virginibus puerisque canto.

> I hate the sacrilegious mob and keep it at a distance; hold your tongues
> in pious silence; I, priest of the Muses, sing for youths and pure maidens
> songs previously unheard. (3.1.1–4)

Claiming that he "sings" for the new generation, the speaker appears to disdain the *vulgus* that his lyric predecessors charmed, fearing its sacrilegious interruption. In the sixth Roman ode, however, when the speaker asserts that the present generation of Romans, though "guiltless," will pay for or "expiate" the sins of their fathers until they reform their irreligious ways, the distinctions between the "pure" and the "impure" invoked at the cycle's opening have dissolved and the audience becomes the general *Romanus*. Yet the audience has not radically altered, nor are the youths and maidens of the opening now inexplicably corrupt. Rather, the cycle of poems has dramatized their full implication in the generational decline that the Roman Odes articulate as a social vision. Thus, in this section I argue for reconsidering the ritual context of the opening of the cycle, and the poems that follow, in terms of the implicit metaphor of sacrifice: on the one hand, the trope of "poems as sacrifice" holds out the possibility of purification; on the other, it serves to construct the "Roman subject" as both inevitably contaminated—and therefore in need of "cleansing"—and a necessary participant in the process of his or her own expiation. As in the ode to Pollio, such purification depends on an audience's experience of its own history as a form of tragedy—the genre in which fall and redemption are so intimately connected.[66]

---

66. The bibliography on the Roman Odes is immense. Discussions from which I have

It is sometimes acknowledged that Juno's speech in 3.3, coupled with Regulus's in 3.5 and the gloomy prognostication for the future in 3.6, suggests the tragic motif of the curse inherited from past generations—the cyclic repetition of crime and countercrime that marks the house of Atreus (Liebeschutz 1979, 92–93).Others have observed that the movement of the Roman Odes as a whole, from hope to despair, displays a tragic rhythm (Silk 1973, 136–37; Santirocco 1986, 116). But these have generally been isolated remarks, and scholars have not sufficiently pursued the implications of the tragic vision of history in the poems.[67] To some extent, the dominant critical approaches to the Roman Odes reflect the influence of "source criticism": because Juno's long speech of 3.3 shares many characteristics with the goddess' ultimatums in book 12 and Jupiter's prophetic visions in book 1 of the *Aeneid,* and because the ultimate source for the divine council to discuss Romulus's deification is Ennius, critics have viewed the elevated tone and mythological subject matter in terms of epic rather than tragedy.[68] And yet in the *Poetics* Aristotle imputes a similar structure to the plots of tragedy and Homeric epic, and the *Iliad* is often seen as the prototype for the unity of action that the ancient critic regarded as fundamental to tragic drama (1449b15, 1451a17–35). It is, he insists, plot or the arrangement of incidents that produces tragic catharsis—and, as I argue, the sequence of odes, particularly the movement from 3.3 through 3.6, is intended to evoke just such an effect. By presenting recent history as a consequence of errors made in a mythological past, Horace encourages his audience to experience the tragedy of Rome's fall.

---

benefited include Fraenkel 1957, 260–85; Commager 1962, 194–225; Pöschl 1968, 47–61, esp. 58–61; André 1969, 31–46; Reckford 1969, 70–84; Syndikus 1973, 2:3–6, and his commentary on the individual poems, 7–97; Grimal 1975, 135–56; Witke 1983; Santirocco 1986, 110–22; Lowrie 1997, 224–65. See discussion of individual poems for further references.

67. Previous scholarship has focused either on determining thematic/schematic patterns within the sequence of the Roman Odes as a cycle—e.g., Wili 1948, 201–13, Heinze 1960, 190–204, Santirocco 1986, 112–22, Porter 1987, 152–70—or on tracing the literary tradition of panegyric and its relation to the presence of Augustan "ideology," determining Horace's investment in promulgating such ideology in the poems (the never-quite-exhausted question of sincerity): for believers of Horace's praise of Augustus or his program, see Fraenkel 1957, 260–86; Doblhofer 1966, 122–59; for the less convinced view, see La Penna 1963; Lyne 1995, 158–68. See Commager 1962, 194–225, for a New Critical approach to the aesthetic strategies of these poems. Much recent criticism of the Roman Odes and poems traditionally seen as Horatian panegyric has concentrated on the difficulty of praise as a successful poetic project: see Lowrie 1997, 224–65, on "whether the struggle between lyric and narrative authority fragments the coherence of any possible praise-making" (224); and Fowler 1995, 252, who claims that Horace's union of Callimachean aesthetics with a Stoic and Epicurean philosophical stance undermines the integrity of panegyric.

68. E.g., Syndikus 1973, 35–37; Witke 1983, 38, 41–42; Lowrie 1997, 224–65. Witke's index, for example, has entries for both erotic elegy and pastoral as genres within the Roman Odes, but not tragedy.

Let us first establish the curse. Before laying down the conditions for Romulus's accession to heaven, Juno locates the origin of Troy's demise in Laomedon's betrayal of his promise to pay the gods for building the city. This violation of *fides,* compounded by the judgment of Paris and by Helen's wantonness, doomed Troy and made its destruction the compensatory payment for Laomedon's crime:

> hac Quirinus
> Martis equis Acheronta fugit,   15
>
> gratum elocuta consiliantibus
> Iunone divis: 'Ilion, Ilion
>   fatalis incestusque iudex
>   et mulier peregrina vertit   20
>
> in pulverem, ex quo destituit deos
> mercede pacta Laomedon, mihi
>   castaeque damnatum Minervae
>   cum populo et duce fraudulento.[']

With this [merit] Romulus avoided Acheron on the horses of Mars, when Juno spoke pleasing words to the council of gods: "Ilion, Ilion, the fateful and unchaste judge and foreign woman turned you to dust, from that time when Laomedon cheated the gods of their agreed-upon pay, and damned you to me and chaste Pallas, with your people and deceptive leader." (3.3.15–24)

Juno goes on to claim that should another Troy be attempted, she would initiate another cycle of destruction. Her mythic time frame provides a tragic origin for later generations of history: the sins of the Trojan past both explain the bloody auspices under which Rome was founded and establish a paradigm whose repetition can be averted only if her audience responds properly. Her shrill and emphatic pronouncement that her vengeance will hound even a third attempt to renew the walls of Troy suggests the cyclic violence of a tragedy:

> [']Troiae renascens alite lugubri
> fortuna tristi clade iterabitur,
>   ducente victrices catervas
>   coniuge me Iovis et sorore.
>
> ter si resurgat murus aeneus   65
> auctore Phoebo, ter pereat meis
>   excisus Argivis, ter uxor
>   capta virum puerosque ploret.'

The fate of Troy, should it be reborn, will be repeated with mournful destruction, under doomed auspices, with myself the consort and sister

of Jove leading the victorious throngs. Should the bronze wall rise a
third time, under Phoebus's authorization, a third time let it perish, de-
stroyed by my Argives, a third time may the captive wife mourn her hus-
band and sons. (3.3.61–68)

The recent history of the civil wars assumes a coherence and clarity when
viewed as tragic iteration: since the time of Laomedon's betrayal of the
gods, the *pax deorum* has been disturbed. Rome has been repeating and
expiating the crimes initiated at Troy, and it is up to the present generation
to avert another cycle.

The possibility of *prohairesis* or "action taking the form of a decision,"
which the Roman audience now faces, conforms to such a generic para-
digm: understood in Aristotelian terms, the *praxis* or "doing" set in motion
by *prohairesis* constitutes the tragic action (*Poet.* 1449b36–50b9).[69] *Prohai-
resis* is not the same concept as free will: as Jean-Pierre Vernant and Pierre
Vidal-Nacquet have argued (1988, 49–84), the relationship in tragedy be-
tween so-called individual agency and fate is, at best, one of complicity.[70]
Such tragic complicity, as we shall see, obscures the degree to which this
view of Roman history is in fact imposed on its audience. All the same, by
making the present a consequence of Laomedon's decision in the past and
suggesting that "choices" present themselves anew, Horace brings his au-
dience to the same conditional identification with characters of the heroic
age with which spectators responded to Greek tragedy.

The foreshortening of time, as Juno's speech brings the present into a
face-to-face relation with an otherwise distant mythological past, suggests
the same superimposition of the heroic age and contemporary time that
marked the audience's experience during a fifth-century performance at
the City Dionysia in democratic Athens (Vernant and Vidal-Nacquet 1988,
23–48). To be sure, the heroic age constituted a more legitimate history
for fifth-century Athenians than for first-century Romans. But the impor-
tant point is that Greek tragedy presented a unique fusion of time frames,
a fusion related to political process: on the one hand, the heroic age gave
expression to conflicts or issues of the polis in the familiar, but temporally
removed, language of mythic history; on the other, the performance of

69. See Gellrich 1988, 106–8, for the idea that tragedy depicts only an action once taken,
not the psychological activity of deliberation that precedes and makes possible the *prohairesis*.
Vernant and Vidal-Nacquet (1988, 56–57) further define *prohairesis* as a decision that "rests
upon . . . a rational desire, a wish (*boulesis*) informed by intelligence and directed, not toward
pleasure, but toward a practical objective that thought has already presented to the soul as a
good."

70. Liebeschuetz (1979, 93 n. 1) comments, in his discussion of Vergil's and Horace's
"tragic vision" of the civil wars: "That the gods influence the minds of wrongdoers to choose
conduct which will bring punishment was a Greek view."

these tragedies before an audience of 15,000 Athenians, together with the internal dynamic of the chorus's relation to the protagonists, evoked the democratic context of the fifth century. The illusion of political participation encouraged by such conditions of performance served to reinforce acquiescence in the various ideologies of the polis being explored and negotiated on stage. In Horace's Roman context, one such ideology is that the audience needs symbolic purification as a result of its guilt; and the belief in and fulfillment of such a need are among the effects at which Horace's construction of history as a tragedy aims.

Horatian lyric explicitly superimposes time frames and relates poetry to political process in the Regulus ode, where the dramatic monologue of the captive general before the Senate provides a historical exemplum. Horace's version of the episode presents Regulus advising the Senate to reject the Carthaginians' offer to ransom captive Roman soldiers.[71] The grisly monologue advocating sacrifice itself dramatizes the issue of Crassus's soldiers still held by the Parthians during Horace's own day. In this way, the specific audience of the Senate within the poem encodes the larger audience of Horatian lyric. Moreover, a Roman reader's identification with Regulus's audience is encouraged by the epithet *auctor* (3.5.46), which, though applied to Regulus, immediately brings Horace to mind. Thus, dominated by speeches that lend them an overtly dramatic quality, both 3.3 and 3.5 map the dynamic of speaker and audience within the fictive lyric context onto the reader's (or spectator's/listener's) relationship with the text. The rhetorical element of both Juno's and Regulus's speeches suggests a deliberative address to a council of decision makers even as the Trojan backdrop invokes the tragic situation of divinely determined choice.[72]

The movement from "heaven" to "earth" in the sequence of 3.3, 3.4, and 3.5, notwithstanding the allegorical assertion of Olympian (i.e., Caesarian) will in the Gigantomachia, implies that Regulus's circumstances at some level issue from the tragic view that Juno articulates. The speeches of both characters inadvertently address and implicate the present generation even as they figure in poems that chart a trajectory of tragic and generational decline. And 3.6, as an indictment of the present generation, completes the sequence so that Roman history becomes a tragic mythos with a beginning (the time of Romulus), middle (the wars with Carthage), and end (the corrupt present). We should note that money, in particular, lends

---

71. Horace alters the version of Regulus's heroism found in Cic. *Off.* 1.39, 3.99, by presenting Roman soldiers held by Carthaginians rather than Carthaginian generals held captive in Rome. Quinn (1980, 254) adds that Horace has adapted details from the speech by T. Manlius Torquatus (Livy 22.59–61) concerning the ransoming of prisoners at Cannae.

72. Witke (1983, 45) remarks that Juno speaks about a future that can be averted, given the proper response. For Regulus's speech as deliberative oratory, see G. Kennedy 1972, 399.

unity to these three time frames and relates to potentially "tragic" choices. The gold that Juno warns should be left in the ground constitutes a prominent source of Roman ignominy—the ransom money—in 3.5. We shall return to the implications of the literal "disembedding" of this gold, but here we must recognize that the "fallen state" of Rome's captive soldiers is linked to the very conditions whose violation, Juno asserts, will bring further destruction. That Rome did not in fact accept the Carthaginian terms does not dilute Horace's construction of this tragic mythos of history: on the contrary, the poet specifically alters history to emphasize the depraved condition of the Roman soldiers—that they are still alive and thus capable of being ransomed accounts for their fallen state; by tampering with facts in this way, by writing about what could have happened rather than what did, Horace achieves the "universal truths" of tragedy. The consequences of 3.5 can be inferred from the situation described in 3.6, where money figures anew: the degenerate present age is characterized by the adulterous woman who essentially sells her favors to the high-bidding businessman or ship's captain, the "lavish purchaser of shame" (*dedecorum pretiosus emptor,* 3.6.32). Thus, the vision of progressive decline with which 3.6 ends (45–48), though a deterioration encompassing only four generations, recapitulates the greater temporal frame of Roman history that spans the development of 3.3 through 3.6.

Horace also emphasizes the centrality to these poems of the rhetorical or performative component of tragedy by a pointed allusion to the ode to Pollio. There, as we recall, the poem builds the effects of a performance of tragic history into the lyric action: the speaker's dirge for the civil wars is both an imagined response to Pollio's dramatic recitation—as a choral lament that suggests a cathartic experience—and a kind of usurpation of its voice and vision. In the final stanza of this ode, the speaker draws his Muse up short and bids her to sing a lighter strain:

> sed ne relictis, Musa procax, iocis
> Ceae retractes munera neniae,
>   mecum Dionaeo sub antro
>   quaere modos leviore plectro.

But lest, wanton Muse, you set aside light themes and handle anew the office of the Cean dirge, seek with me measures of a lighter strain deep within the Dionaean grove. (2.1.37–40)

At the abrupt foreshortening of Juno's speech in 3.3, the speaker addresses his Muse in a similar vein and orders her to lighter themes:

> non hoc iocosae conveniet lyrae.
> quo, Musa, tendis? desine pervicax

> referre sermones deorum et
> magna modis tenuare parvis.

But this will not suit the playful lyre: where are you headed, Muse? Stop
stubbornly relating the speeches of the gods and diminishing great
things with small measures. (3.3.69–72)

Not only does the gesture of reproachful address to his Muse here es-
tablish a direct connection with the Pollio ode, but similar epithets describe
her in each case. Whether displaying the "wanton" impudence of *procax* or
the "headstrong" obstinacy of *pervicax*, the Muse has a mind of her own—
willful, perversely resistant, and not to be controlled by the symposiastic
poet of lyric. This abrupt and formulaic "break-off," the Pindaric *Abbruchs-
formel*, asserts anew the generic domain of lyric and informs the audience
that Juno's speech is different, taking up the concerns of the high style of
epic and tragedy.[73] But most significant for my argument is that Pindar's
address to the Muse occurs in *Pythian* 11, where the poet has digressed
from his epinician praise by recounting the life of Orestes (16–41). Re-
gardless of whether *Pythian* 11 was composed before or after the perfor-
mance of Aeschylus's *Oresteia* in 458, Horace surely would have associated
Pindar's lyric with the dramatic version of the story. Orestes embodies the
tragic double bind of divine determination and human responsibility, and
Horace's Pindaric allusion in these lines connects him (an absent referent)
both to the general tragic orientation of Juno's vision and to the specific
need for purification. The original *puer vindex* (avenging boy) invoking the
protection of Apollo, Orestes constitutes the mythic counterpart to Octa-
vian before his ideological transformation into Augustus. Significantly, as
3.3's reference to Augustus's future deification implies, such a transfor-
mation is already in process: the guilt of Octavian's own vindictiveness is
displaced onto a mythological past that, as 3.6 suggests, has been reenacted
by the Roman people (but not their ruler).

There are other signs of such conversion of recent history into tragic
myth. The cyclic repetition whose origin Juno places in Laomedon's be-
trayal is found in the very first stanza of the Pollio ode:

> Motum ex Metello consule civicum
> bellique causas et vitia et modos
> ludumque fortunae gravisque
> principum amicitias et arma . . .

The civil conflict that began with Metellus's consulship, the causes of
war, its evils, and its patterns, Fortune's game and the fateful alliances of
leaders, and arms . . . (2.1.1–4)

---

73. For the conflict between the *tenue* and the *grande* in Horace, see Lowrie 1997, 40–45.

The tricola that structure this stanza pair each of the elements in the two series of collective objects (Nadeau 1980, 179). The *gravisque / principum amicitias* (fateful alliances of leaders) concretely specifies the *bellique causas* (causes of war), clearly implying the first triumvirate and the betrayal by its members. In the time frame of Pollio's history, the origin of civil discord lies in this betrayal, but the dishonoring of pacts is echoed by the reference to Laomedon in 3.3 (*ex quo destituit deos / mercede pacta Laomedon*, 3.3.21– 22). The source of tragic cyclicity here seems to set time itself into motion— another characteristic of tragedy (Frye 1957, 213). The *ex quo* (from the time) of line 20 recalls the *Motum ex Metello . . . civicum* (civil conflict from the time of Metellus's consulship) of 2.1; the sense of temporal progression unleashed by a tragic fall coincides with the movement (*motum*) into verse. The weight of the *gravis . . . amicitias* (heavy, fatal alliances), like the fall of the tree in 2.13, crashes down and precipitates a movement into poetry. In 3.3, however, such historical origins have been displaced onto the crimes of the tragic past.

This idea of the fall, so central to any conception of tragedy, has as its corollary the notion of the tragic protagonist. In a rigorously Aristotelian vision of tragedy, the tragic protagonist suffers *peripeteia*, a reversal of fortune that is closely associated with *prohairesis* (Frye 1957, 210). Both 3.3 and 3.5 invoke this idea of a liminal decision, as if to suggest that Rome, as a tragic figure, has chosen her decline in the past and may continue her downward spiral in the future. As the speaker at the beginning of 3.5 implies by his lament for "the corrupt Senate and changed ways" (*pro curia inversique mores*, 7), the warning of Regulus has not prevented a fallen moral state. Already slipping and soon to fall (*labantis*), those with weak moral resolve find only temporary strength in the speech that Regulus gives. This implicit characterization of Rome as a tragic individual, rushing to her ruin, appears elsewhere in the Horatian corpus, often using the verbs *labere* (to fall, to slip) or *ruere* (to rush headlong). The sixteenth epode, for example, opens with the explicit image of Rome's headlong fall: "Already another age is worn down by civil war and Rome herself topples (*ruit*) from her own strength (*suis . . . viribus*)" (*Epod.* 16.1–2). The fourth Roman ode evokes this idea allegorically in its Gigantomachia. The giants' rebellion, an expression of pure force, fails for lack of temperate wisdom. The moral that is drawn suggests the decline of Rome: "Force deprived of counsel falls from its own weight" (*vis consili expers mole ruit sua*, 3.4.65).[74]

More broadly, the tragic protagonist's fall evokes the idea of ritual sacrifice and the slaying of a victim, bringing us back to Girard's sacrificial

---

74. See Newman 1967, 110 n. 3, for further citations of this trope in Augustan literature. See Commager 1962, 199–205, for Horace's appropriation of the motif from the first and eighth Pythian of Pindar.

crisis. As we recall, tragedy both imitates or reflects such a crisis even as it performs a mimetic sacrifice of its own, one intended to put an end to vindictive violence and to reestablish cultural differentiation. Similarly, the Horatian construction of Roman history as "tragic" both describes a fallen state and, through the trope of lyric sacrifice, converts that condition into a sacral offering.

The erosion of cultural distinctions, the sign of such a crisis, appears in many guises in these poems. The bristling confusion of the Titans' multiple arms in the Gigantomachia of 3.4, for example, like their attempt to pile Pelion on Olympus indiscriminately, allegorically reflects the same (if later) state of cultural disintegration as do the images of corrupt morals and sacrilegious ways in 3.6. That ode, in turn, displays the fallen state of Rome against which Regulus warns in 3.5. Complaining that his soldiers, if ransomed by the Roman Senate, would "confound peace with war," Regulus laments the collapse of perhaps the most important distinction underwriting Roman identity. The "destruction spreading into the future age" (*perniciem veniens in aevum*), which would be brought on by accepting the Carthaginian terms, metastasizes in 3.6 into a flood of contamination that spreads through family, home, and fatherland: "the age fertile with sin first despoiled marriage and offspring and home; disaster stemming from this source flowed into the people and the country" (*fecunda culpae saecula nuptias / primum inquinavere et genus et domos; / hoc fonte derivata clades / in patriam populumque fluxit*, 3.6.17–20).[75] As we saw in the discussion of the ode to Pollio, the sacrificial crisis lends itself to images of infection, as well as of natural cataclysms. The next few stanzas, showing the effects of such contamination, develop the idea of the collapse of values as a crisis of distinctions: the young matron, contriving illicit loves from an early age, is so far corrupted that she does not discriminate in her already transgressive adulterous liaisons. And the opening stanza of 3.6 famously presents the deteriorated temples of the gods as a symbol of decline:

> Delicta maiorum immeritus lues,
> Romane, donec templa refeceris
> aedisque labentis deorum et
> foeda nigro simulacra fumo[.]

Though you are not to blame, you will expiate the crimes of your ancestors, Roman, until you rebuild the temples and the crumbling shrines of the gods, and restore their images, filthy now from dark smoke. (3.6.1–4)

The moral irresolution of the "wavering senators" (*labantis patres*) in 3.5.45 clearly echoes in both the crimes of previous generations, *delicta maiorum*, and the "crumbling shrines" (*aedisque labentis*).

---

75. With the OCT I read *clades* in line 19 rather than Shackleton Bailey's *labes.*

The image of religious monuments in decay suggests the collapse of cultural distinctions in other ways. As visual symbols of national power, monuments express by their very skyward projection a sense of vertical hierarchy. In the second stanza of 3.6 the speaker asserts the importance of this hierarchy—of a vertical distribution of cultural roles. The speaker reminds his addressee, the blamelessly corrupt Roman, that "by subordinating yourself to the gods, you rule" (*dis te minorem quod geris, imperas,* 5). This stanza looks back to the very opening of the cycle of odes, where Hellenistic theory of kingship combines with allusion to the end of civil conflict: "Fear-inspiring kings rule over their own flocks; over kings themselves Jove wields authority, illustrious for his triumph over the Giants, and controlling all with a nod" (*Regum timendorum in proprios greges, / reges in ipsos imperium est Iovis, / clari Giganteo triumpho, / cuncta supercilio moventis,* 3.1.5–8). The well-ordered state—with the king as shepherd of his people, holding himself second to Jove—turns into the allegorical Gigantomachia, resolved by the assertion of Olympian authority. The orderly hierarchy of the first two lines rests on the successful *triumpho* that follows.[76] *Triumpho,* with all its political charge for the Roman military imagination, immediately brings to mind the referent—the real story—of the allegorical narrative told later, in 3.4. It recalls the triumph avoided by Cleopatra in 1.37, even as it intimates that cultural order, the hierarchical distribution of roles, partially depends on the military superiority of a single man. It is this vision of order, I believe, that the Roman Odes seek to justify. The audience must be persuaded to acquiesce in—even to desire—this hierarchy. The rhetorical strategy of such persuasion is twofold: first, these poems articulate a social vision, one of distinctions or boundaries—the *discrimina ordinum*— whose violation has led to the endless cycles of the civil wars. Second, the Roman Odes involve their audience as undeserving yet entirely implicated participants in the national tragedy: once implicated, the audience needs symbolic purification, which will, in turn, reestablish the *discrimina ordinum.*

The audience's participation becomes explicit in the sixth Roman ode. Here the ultimate cause of Rome's fall is religious impiety: the gods, angered by human indifference, have bestowed (*dederunt*) a multitude of evils on sorrowing Hesperia (3.6.7–8). And yet, as we have seen, the theme of impiety specifically connects the *nefas* of civil war, as a crisis of distinctions,

---

76. I disagree with Syndikus (1973, 16–17), who dismisses any hierarchy of power in this stanza, claiming that the kings possess no real power—all is ruled by Jupiter. For Witke (1983, 21), Jupiter becomes *Necessitas* and all are equal before Fate. On the Hellenistic theory of kingship, see G. Williams 1968, 160–70; Santirocco 1986, 118, with n. 27, for further bibliography. See Zanker 1988, 150–52, for Augustus's preoccupation with the discrimination and stratification of social orders.

with sexual crimes. Adulterous liaisons despoil the marriage bed, which becomes the source of the flood of civil destruction (*hoc fonte derivata clades / in patriam populumque fluxit*). The young maiden contriving illicit passion looks back to the violations of Paris and Helen, and takes her place on the stage of the tragic cycle. As Andrew Wallace-Hadrill remarks, this is an ideological vision that plays explicitly on the potential for guilt created by the transgression of sexual taboos (1982, 35–36). But the conventional scholarly focus on the historical referents of this ode—whether it reflects failed moral legislation of 28 B.C.E. and whether Augustus's restoration of the temples was already in process—has perhaps obscured the full significance of the discourse of guilt and expiation, and thus sacrifice, of the first stanza (see Fraenkel 1957, 261; Witke 1983, 66); for we can take Wallace-Hadrill's observation further. The sacral character of these lines, with their emphasis on expiation, recalls the opening of the entire cycle—the ritual silence demanded by the "priest of the Muses"—even as it conforms to the ritual implications of the tragic construction of history as a mimesis of sacrifice. For living Romans not only embody the "crisis" in their transgressions, they also, as the last generation of the "Republic" in its fallen state, constitute the metaphorical victims of sacrifice: the present generation of Romans, though guiltless, commits "crimes" that pay for or expiate (*lues*), as a sacrifice might, those of the past generation (*delicta maiorum*).[77] The syntax asserts that such payment will continue until the temples are restored, but within the cycle of odes as a whole, the Horatian persona as *sacerdos* provides the context for ritual. If the youth of Horace's audience— the "boys" (*pueri*) and "unmarried maidens" (*virgines*)—attend to his poems, the tragic frame will make possible their conditional identification with "the fall of Rome," their own sacrilege superimposed on that of their forefathers: and they themselves, as audience to their "tragic fall," will experience the tragic cleansing that will put an end to the cycle. Though the poetic representation initially constructs them as victims of the past, it also constructs the past as a way of releasing them from that victimhood. In addition to the pointedly expiatory diction of *luere*, we should note that both the "virginal" status of the *virgines* at the cycle's opening and the "innocence" implied by *immeritus* as an epithet for the contemporary Roman are rhetorically consonant with the initial ritual purity, and abiding innocence, of a sacrificial victim (see Wissowa 1902, 351). In keeping with the fluid dynamics of sacrifice, the audience, as though witnessing an actual

---

77. Liebeschuetz (1979, 94) comments regarding Paris and Helen's sexual crimes in *Odes* 3.3: "adultery was the instrument through which they were punished." See also Thome 1992, 88, for discussion of Cic. *Sull.* 76, where the vicious excesses of the Catalinarians are described as expiation for their previous crimes.

rite, experiences purification through temporary identification with the victim—the representation of their own fallen selves.[78]

Returning to the ritual context of the cycle's opening, we recall that *sacerdotes* refers to priests as public dignitaries of the state whose civic role was to advise the Senate on religious matters and to officiate at sacrifices. By employing the term *sacerdos* (used in its nominative form only once more in the *Odes* to refer, in 3.3, to Rhea as the mother of Romulus), Horace draws attention to the role of priests in public expiation, a duty explicitly prescribed by Cicero in *De legibus:* "Sacrilege which cannot be expiated shall be held to be impiously committed; that which can be expiated shall be atoned for by the public priests" (*sacrum commissum, quod neque expiari poterit, impie commissum esto; quod expiari poterit, publici sacerdotes expianto,* 2.9.22).[79] In Horace's poem, the duty of public expiation combines with that of civic counsel. The rhetorical speech acts of Juno and Regulus in 3.3 and 3.5 constitute advice and warning—ultimately spoken by the Horatian *sacerdos*—that simultaneously counters impiety and frames history in terms of a tragic cyclicity. Juno speaks to the gods "in council" (*consiliantibus,* 3.3.17); and the language describing Regulus's "counsel given at no other time" (*consilio numquam alias dato*) echoes that of the opening stanza of 3.1, "songs not previously heard" (*carmina non prius audita,* 2–3), thus furthering this identification: these poems, as *carmina* "troped" into sacrifices by the figure of Horace as priest, convert a national condition—a crisis of distinctions—into a form of public expiation. Indeed, we may even understand the *consilium* given by the Muses in 3.4 in such terms:

> Vos Caesarem altum, militia simul
> fessas cohortis abdidit oppidis,
>   finire quaerentem labores
>   Pierio recreatis antro,
>
> vos lene consilium et datis et dato
> gaudetis almae.

In your Pierian grove, you refresh and remake lofty Caesar, as he seeks to end his toils, as soon as he has hidden away his weary troops in towns; you both give gentle counsel and rejoice in giving it. (3.4.37–42)

---

78. On such identification, by which the witnesses to a sacrifice must visualize the victim's death as their own, see Feldherr 1998, 138.

79. Trans. Keyes 1928, Loeb edition. Although Cicero's text provides laws for an "ideal state," many of them were based on actual Roman law and practice. Moreover, though no acts of official expiation were recorded after 37 B.C.E., Augustus's reinstitution of the *lustratio,* a form of purificatory ritual performed in connection with the *census* in 28 B.C.E., demonstrates a concern with public acts of purification after the civil wars. See Aug. *Res Gestae* 8.2; Liebeschuetz 1979, 96; Feldherr 1998, 117. On the actual purificatory acts implied by the phrase *lustrum condere,* see Ogilivie 1961. For further bibliography on priests and expiation, see nn. 3 and 4 above.

Caesar himself is "re-created," suggesting his transformation from the *puer vindex* of the years preceding Actium into Augustus the merciful, a metamorphosis that recalls by its diction—*recreare*—the snakes in the hair of the Eumenides in *Odes* 2.13, even as it implies Orestes (born anew at Delphi) and the purifying effects of religious ritual.[80] Yet such a re-creation of Octavian already exists in these poems; more precisely, it consists in the very displacement of his guilt and responsibility (shared by those who engaged in the rivalrous competition for power) onto the Roman people. Finally, there may be an echo of Cassandra in the phrase "songs not previously heard," an echo picked up by the phrase *Troica sacerdos* (3.3.32): "the Trojan priestess," though referring to Rhea Silvia (as conflated with Ilia), cannot fail to bring to mind the most famous and ill-fated Trojan prophetess of them all.[81] Cassandra, who embodies the very paradox of tragedy—the inescapable doom it represents and the redemption effected by mimesis—is not far from the overall spirit of the Roman Odes.

Thus, for a Roman audience familiar with the conventions of tragedy and sensitive to religious practices of their own culture, these poems constitute an expiation for the past, a purification that issues from the rhetoric of sacrifice performed as a speech act. And just as sacrifice reestablishes cultural differences, so these Horatian poems reinforce the distinctions between mortal, ruler, and god, thereby redefining social roles for the future. From an Aristotelian perspective, of course, the capacity to make such distinctions similarly derives from the experience of tragic catharsis as a response to dramatic mimesis.[82] Yet, as I have argued, by substituting for a sacrificial action these poems effect more than the Aristotelian notion of catharsis. Elsner's analysis of certain ancient responses to artistic images, as described by Pausanias (10.18.5), helps clarify this relationship of mimesis to ritual. Taking the case of the offering of the Orneatai at Delphi, where bronze figures representing a sacrifice and a procession were substituted for the actual rites promised to the gods—daily victims having become too costly—Elsner points out that such a "performative or ritual imitation complicates the dynamics of mimesis" because it presupposes an "*identity* . . . between . . . the act and its representation" (1996, 529; more generally, 526–29). Elsner concludes by claiming that such "supernatural

---

80. Apollo, protector of Orestes and patron of Octavian, figures prominently in 3.4.60–64, lines deriving from Pind. *Pyth.* 1.39–40: see Fraenkel 1957, 276–85, and Lowrie 1997, 249–52, for Horace's adaptation of Pindar. See Commager 1962, 224, on the Muses' recreation of Caesar in terms of Octavian's "new image" as Augustus.

81. Witke (1983, 19) points out that one reading of *carmina non prius audita* is texts whose advice, though spoken earlier, went "previously unheeded."

82. Catharsis, which follows a cognitive experience of a work of art, makes possible a refinement of the ethical sensibility that "conduces to an alignment of the emotions with the perception of moral qualities in the world" (Halliwell 1986, 196; more generally, 196–200).

identity of image and prototype" constitutes a "ritual-centred' discourse of sacred art" that "parts company with the 'aestheticist' discourse" of mimesis characterized by the "themes of deception, absence and illusion" (529). Though Elsner's main concern is mimesis as an imitation of a static work of art, his concept of a ritual-centered discourse that depends on the notion of *identity* applies precisely to the rhetoric of sacrifice in the Roman Odes. For as Horace invokes the motifs of tragedy as a *mimesis* of sacrifice, his role as *sacerdos* functions as a performative *metaphor,* the rhetorical trope that, above all, operates through identity and substitution.

THE GIFT OF IDEOLOGY

Now that we have examined how these poems invoke the rhetoric of sacrificial ritual, we can situate this religious transaction in the context of public *munera* and patronage, both literary and political. Despite the unending debate over the precise function of Greek tragedy, there is qualified agreement that the civic drama served as a form of ritual initiation into the prevailing ideologies of the city (Zeitlin 1990, 68–69; Goldhill 1990). The opening stanza of the Roman Odes clearly presents one such image of initiation, but we still must be careful in considering the function of *Odes* 3.1–6 in this light. These poems present material that is often interpreted as "Augustan" ideology—the apparent advocacy of martial virtue in 3.2 or the denunciation of promiscuity in 3.6 certainly conforms to, and has recently been taken to be complicitous in creating, the attitudes that fall under this rubric.[83] Nevertheless, insofar as ideology can be understood not as a static set of beliefs but rather as a "combative arena of persuasion and struggle" (Rose 1995, 62), we might better view the Roman Odes as poems whose main ideological function is again performative—to enact the tragedy of Rome's fall as a means of convincing a literate audience of the necessity of the Principate. That such persuasion occurs through poems whose dramatic monologues suggest the political oratory of Republicanism and civic participation only underscores the degree of complicity required by consent to this vision.

As critics remark, by presenting civil unrest as a consequence of religious impiety, the Roman Odes recast the actual political and socioeconomic causes of the wars in terms of divine fate and an inherited debt to the gods (see Gordon 1990a, 194–95). My own interpretation has claimed that for

---

83. For discussion of whether or not the Roman Odes effectively "reflect" Augustan ideology, see Pasquali 1964 [1920], 649–710; Büchner 1962; Klingner 1964a; and n. 67 above. For Horace as a participant in the creation of ideology, see Santirocco 1995. Lowrie (1997, 227 n. 4) comments that Syme's frequent quotes of Augustan poetry points up the ease with which poetry becomes assimilated to "history."

those willing to listen, the speaker's symbolic sacrifice will pay off this debt and reestablish the *pax deorum*. But the momentum of exchanges does not stop here, for Augustus himself is embedded in this rhetoric of human-divine gift relations. When Juno returns Romulus to Mars and permits the Roman hero to join the ranks of the gods, relinquishing her anger in the very same gesture (*iras et invisum nepotem . . . Marti redonabo*, 3.3.31–33), she makes the gift of deification a consequence of the implied expiation. The poem's earlier mention of Augustus's future godhead is parallel to that of Romulus here: the one will "drink nectar lying back" among deified "culture heroes" of the past (*quos inter Augustus recumbens / purpureo bibet ore nectar*, 11–12), while the other is allowed to drain "the juices of nectar . . . among the ranks of the gods" (*ducere nectaris / sucos . . . ordinibus patiar deorum*, 34–36).[84] The superimposition of the two figures suggests that Augustus's future divinity, as well as the conditional benediction for the Roman Empire, similarly issues from the appeasement of the angry goddess. We perceive here a dynamic of gift eliciting countergift—*do ut des*—that structurally parallels but inverts the idea of vindictive reciprocity: now that the *pax deorum* has been restored by the "gifts" of the Muses' counsel (*consilium et datis*) and the speaker's implied sacrifice, Juno will no longer punish the impious; although she, along with others, previously bestowed (*dederunt*) a multitude of ills on sorrowing Hesperia (3.6.7–8) and offered up Italians as sacrifices to the shades of Jugurtha (2.1.27–28), Juno will now reward the deserving—the man "just and resolute of purpose" (*iustum et tenacem propositi virum*, 3.3.1).[85] To be sure, such a reading requires us to consider Juno's speech from two perspectives: both as the effect of her expiation and, as argued in the previous section, as part of the tragic frame of Roman history, wherein the successive violations committed by the Roman people account for the fall of the Republic. Nonetheless, insofar as Juno's speech contributes to the construction of the past as mythic tragedy and thus allows for purification in the present, such expiation is implicit in what she says: for just as her language of Roman religious contract—"I will return" (*redonabo*)—is discursively linked to the Horatian speaker's own rhetoric of expiation and his posture as *sacerdos,* so too the superimposition

84. Most scholars see Romulus as a model for Augustus in this poem: see Commager 1962, 212–16; André 1969, 44; Witke 1983, 42–43; Lowrie 1997, 238. Syndikus (1973, 42–42), however, cautions against too easily identifying Augustus with Romulus, as the latter's name was conventionally applied to those giving new foundations to the state.

85. In the first half of 3.3, the deification of "culture heroes" such as Hercules, Romulus, Pollux, and finally Augustus, is presented as a consequence of *hac arte,* a phrase that refers to the "virtue" of the poem's first stanza—the tenacity of purpose. However, from a perspective of self-referential discourse, *hac arte* also implies the speaker's own capacity to immortalize—a connotation supported by *Odes* 4.8, a poem that explicitly addresses the fame of Hercules and Romulus as dependent exclusively on the poet for their continued glory.

of time frames in 3.3 causes predictions made in the mythic past of Romulus to apply allegorically to the Augustan present.[86] From the perspective of ideology, such contractual rhetoric seeks to persuade its audience of the legitimacy of Augustus's power—an *imperium* that, despite all the conditions attending its prophecy, is both divinely sanctioned and the consequence of debt made good.

To take another example, the persuasion and consent by which ideology functions surely inform the two uses of *merces* (payment, reward) in *Odes* 3.2 and 3.3. Variously interpreted in terms of political allegory, encomiastic convention, and the *kleos* of immortality, the rewards for silence held out by the speaker in 3.2.25–28 will forever resist hermeneutic certainty.[87] Their meaning is shrouded by the very inscrutability of the Eleusinian mysteries that metaphorically develop the image:

> est et fideli tuta silentio   25
> merces: vetabo, qui Cereris sacrum
>   vulgarit arcanae, sub isdem
>   sit trabibus fragilemque mecum
>
> solvat phaselon; saepe Diespiter
> neglectus incesto addidit integrum.   30
>   raro antecedentem scelestum
>   deseruit pede Poena claudo.

For faithful silence there is a sure reward: I will forbid anyone who has revealed the sacred rite of mysterious Ceres to reside in the same abode or to unloose the delicate ship with me; often Jupiter, disdained, has added the innocent to the guilty, but rarely does Vengeance, despite her crippled gait, not catch up to the impious, though he has a head start. (3.2.25–32)

As is often remarked, the silence both looks back to the "held tongues" of the audience that witnesses the symbolic sacrifice of the *sacerdos Musarum* in the first poem and presumably allows the voices of Juno and Regulus to be "heard" in the following poems. Given that purification rites of some form were an integral component of the Eleusinian mysteries, we can justifiably see one meaning of the *merces* as the reward of expiation, the payment that rights the imbalance initiated by Laomedon's having refused the

---

86. Witke (1983, 42) notes that "the word *redonabo* [3.3.33], in its religious sense of pardon, remit, condone, with implications of expiation and atonement, is of course to be construed with Augustus as much as with Quirinus."

87. See Davis 1983 for both a summary of the history of criticism on this stanza and his own argument that, in keeping with Pindaric conventions, it refers to the decorous silence the *laudator* should keep—knowing when to stop the *encomium*. On the ambiguity of Horace's statements concerning *virtus* in general in this poem, see Connor 1972.

merces promised to the gods who built Troy (3.3.22). Those who are silent and keep the contract (*fideli silentio*) will "hear" the persuasive voices of Juno and Regulus and will experience the tragic cleansing of guilt inherited from the past. Those who are "innocent" (*integrum*), like the *immeritus* Roman citizen of 3.6, will not be added by Jupiter to the guilty, the forefathers whose sins (*delicta maiorum*, 3.6.1) are expiated by the present generation. This reward of silence, understood as purification, counters the image of punishment with which *Odes* 3.2 ends—the Aeschylean vision of retributive and generational justice that, though delayed, inevitably catches up with the wicked. The purifying connotation of *merces* thus conforms to the Roman understanding of expiation in the directly economic terms of a symbolic expenditure that pays off a debt to the gods.

This reading parallels the more explicit vision of exchange in *Odes* 3.2— the soldier's sacrifice of life for glory: here, the *kleos* of immortality is won by the military courage, or *virtus,* that sacrifices itself for the state. In the first half of the poem, a form of social sacrifice brings the reward of "divinity," or access to the divine, whereas in lines 25–32, pious religious conduct converts divine vengeance into the divine beneficence that Juno displays in 3.3. Because Juno's relinquishing of Romulus so that he may become deified suggests the divine forgiveness born of expiation, it connects with and develops these two hermeneutic strands from the second poem.

In this context we may further understand the term *merces* much as Leslie Kurke has in analyzing Pindar's use of analogous terms appropriate to a monetary or "market" economy (see 1991, 240–56, on *Isthmian* 2): by applying a lexicon from a disembedded economy to an embedded transaction, Horace advocates a form of profit, but one achieved through sacrificial expenditure and "loss." The implied *devotio* offered by Regulus in 3.5 suggests a similar expiatory profit: only by sacrificing himself and his soldiers to the enemy will Rome be purged and cleansed of the *pernicies* (destruction, plague) that threatens the whole community.[88] In keeping with Juno's advice to leave gold quite literally "embedded" in the ground, Regulus depicts the dangers of ransoming his army, of redeeming a soldier with gold (*repensus auro,* 3.5.25): commodifying the soldier will undercut his "use value." In contrast, the metaphoric gleam of courage or true worth (*Virtus*) in 3.2.17–22 shines with untainted honor (*intaminatis fulget honoribus*) and opens heaven for those who do not deserve to die (*recludens immeritis mori caelum*). It is this *virtus* that brings immortality and then evolves into the attribute of *fides,* displayed in the trustworthy silence (*fideli*

---

88. See Thome 1992, 88, for this explicit connotation of *devotio.* Cicero (*Off.* 3.99) discusses Regulus's behavior initially in terms of *magnitudo animi,* or "greatness of spirit," the Latin equivalent of *megalopsuchia.* Fowler (1995, 252 n. 11) points out that *megalopsuchia* and *megaloprepeia,* "magnificent spending," are kindred concepts in Aristotle.

silentio) of the penultimate stanza. Regulus in 3.5 best displays the Roman *virtus* of 3.2 and the opening of 3.3, but the silent audience to his sacrifice have the *merces* or symbolic capital of its consequences—purification of the community.

And yet this silence, which the Roman Odes present in terms of religious metaphor, constitutes a kind of euphemism for the way in which the poems make their audience complicit with an ideological vision. Silence is a form of consent to how this cycle of odes naturalizes a "monarchic" ideology by recasting it in terms of a divine-mortal gift exchange: the deification of Romulus, and by implication Augustus, is both the reward and the precondition for expiation. By constructing the past in terms of tragic history and sacrifice, these poems present the increasing political domination of one man as a divine gift rendered necessary by the collapse of values, the erasure of cultural distinctions—the *discrimina ordinum*—that constitutes Girard's sacrificial crisis. Thus the allegorical Gigantomachia of 3.4, in which Olympian (Augustan) hierarchy asserts itself anew, restoring (or rather creating) the stratified social vision of gods, kings, and people presented in 3.1, evolves into the prediction in 3.5 of Augustus as a god incarnate who, having reestablished order in a country beset by civil conflict, is now ready to add Parthia and Britain to his empire.

Finally, this "re-creation" of the past, as an ideological strategy for legitimizing the present, disguises a certain economic calculation on the political level. It is really loyalty to Augustus that is at stake here, but the speaker, as priest, elicits adherence to the *princeps* by the symbolic expenditure on behalf of his people. As mentioned in chapter 1, Richard Gordon has drawn attention to the "voluntary" expenditures of priests in the early Empire as a means of creating *fides*, or loyalty—the symbolic capital garnered through giving.[89] Pierre Bourdieu suggests that such symbolic gifts possess value by virtue of the "wastage of money, energy, time, and ingenuity," or the labor devoted to the *form* and *presentation* of giving (1977, 194). We see this idea of the symbolic gift not only in the implied trope of the cycle of poems as sacrifice, with the speaker's emphasis on religious form, but also, as I have suggested, in the sacrificial ideology behind the martial courage advocated in 3.2 and 3.5.

Though the "patriotism" of the famous gnome "it is sweet and fitting to die for your country" (*dulce et decorum est pro patria mori*, 3.2.13) may be undercut by the lines that follow it, the idea of personal expenditure—the "expense of spirit"—nonetheless develops tellingly from a sequence of images ultimately connected to the speaker's own symbolic sacrifice. For the

89. Thus Gordon (1990a, 194) interprets the hyperbolic attention paid to the forms of religious sacrifice as a means of creating symbolic capital—or loyalty and a sense of obligation. Gordon here concurs with what he calls the "political" argument of Veyne (1990, 298–327).

idea of Homeric *kleos,* or glory earned in battle, evolves in 3.2 from the poem's opening image of character—or spirit—created through endurance and poverty; this image, in turn, follows on the closing stanza of 3.1, which figures the Sabine farm.[90] The careful placement of this image implies two related ideas: first, that the speaker's own "character" or "spirit," nourished on his humble estate, is expended in the symbolic offering of his poetry, a gift to his country that will earn him *kleos;* and second, that the ultimate source of that expenditure is the patronage of the Augustan regime. As I discuss in chapter 4, the echo in *Epistles* 1.7 of the phrase *dulce et decorum est* raises this issue of poetry as "expense" or "loss" in a context that challenges the emphasis on voluntarism in Roman descriptions of patronage. In 3.1 the speaker as *sacerdos* similarly hints that economic calculation may lie beneath a generous gesture.

For though he disdains material wealth and the anxieties it brings, the speaker ironically draws attention to the exchange value of the farm: "why should I raise high, in the style of the nouveau riche, a hall with columns intended to be envied? Why should I exchange my Sabine valley for burdensome wealth?" (*cur invidendis postibus et novo / sublime ritu moliar atrium? / cur valle permutem Sabina / divitias operosiores?* 3.1.45–48). As a symbol of the virtue of the restrained desire advocated earlier in the poem (3.1.25), the farm possesses an abstract value akin to the symbolic capital that the loss or expenditure of "riches" (*divitias*) would create: the speaker's stance may elevate the farm over material wealth, even as he implies that, judged by externals, it is in fact worth less than a hall in the style of nouveau ostentation; however, his rhetorical question effectively equates, in an image of exchange, the symbolic value of his property with the material value of wealth. Balancing with perfect symmetry the opening stanza featuring the priest, this final image of 3.1, the poet's property, may be said to participate in an implied circulation of symbolic capital, eventuating in the gift of expiation: for if the gift of the farm creates the symbolic capital of the poet's loyalty or obligation to the regime, then that capital is circulated further in the form of symbolic sacrifices on behalf of the people. These *munera,* in turn, indebt the people to the poet, and ultimately to the *princeps,* for the very act of canceling a debt to the gods. In light of this "movement" of the original capital of the farm, the formulaic "break-off" at the end of 3.3 (recalling Pindar's address to his Muse in *Pythian* 11, discussed above), takes on greater significance: for after the digression on Orestes, the Pindaric speaker claims, "Muse, if you have agreed to hire your voice for a fee, you must dart hither and thither, other ways than for Pythonicus and Thrasydaeus" (Μοῖσα, τὸ δὲ τεόν, εἰ μισθοῖο συνέθευ παρέχειν / φωνὰν

90. For criticism on the cyclic connections between the end of 3.1 and the beginning of 3.2, see Santirocco 1986, 116: Witke 1983, 31.

ὑπάργυρον, ἄλλοτ' ἄλλα ταρασσέμεν / ἢ πατρὶ Πυθονίκῳ / τό γέ νυν ἢ Θρασυδαίῳ, 41–44).[91] The passage implies that digression on other topics is necessary to offset a quid pro quo exchange of patronage. Horace's allusion to these lines both in 3.3, the ode that refers to Augustus's deification, and at the end of *Odes* 2.1, a poem that evolves from the praises of Pollio into the speaker's own sacrificial *munera,* underscores that public expiation and the tragic frame in which it is offered simultaneously obscure and serve the interests of patronal exchange.

This chapter has analyzed the discourse of sacrifice and tragedy in Horace's political poems from two related angles: on the one hand, tracing an evolution from *Odes* 2.1 and 2.13 into the Roman Odes, we have examined the performative aspect of Horace's religious rhetoric and found a "ritual-centered" discourse that fulfills the need for public expiation; on the other, we have situated this rhetoric in terms of its ideological function as serving to justify the Principate and its prophesied *imperium* as divinely sanctioned, as the "return gift" of the gods—the *pax Augusta* issuing from the reestablishment of the *pax deorum.* Subtly recalling but differing from the expiation of Orestes, the original *puer vindex,* the ideological makeover that re-creates Octavian as the divine Augustus displaces his guilt onto the people, making it a matter for their, not his, purification. Finally, we have seen that the posture of the Horatian priest has a further ideological function in that it serves to veil the economic interests of the regime in the creation of this vision of divine *imperium.* Such a poetic vision does not appear automatically to respond to the gift of land—or literary, imperial patronage—in a quid pro quo exchange; instead, it is structured in terms of voluntary expenditure, a discourse of priestly euergetism in which gifts to the people involve both *philanthropia* (benevolence) and *liberalitas* (generosity).[92] Though Gordon here refers to real goods, such as the provision of "games, feasts, monetary distributions and dispensations of oil or wine" (1990a, 194), as well as the construction of civic buildings—all forms of the so-called voluntary payments, or *summa honoraria,* that were incumbent upon priests on election—we might nonetheless understand Horace's sacrificial expenditure in the same terms.[93] For Horatian lyric, invoking the public spirit of Greek

---

91. I follow the translation and interpretation of Richard Stoneman in his notes to Conway and Stoneman 1991 [1972].

92. See Gordon 1990c, 219–31, for the Principate's increasing dependence on such a discourse of sacrificial euergetism, one particularly centered around the *princeps* himself.

93. Benveniste (1971, 278) connects *damnum* to the Greek verb *dapanān,* "to spend or consume," and to the Latin *daps,* "a sacrificial meal." He thus establishes the relationship between the "loss" suffered in compensation for a crime and the "loss" of conspicuous consumption in a voluntary sacrifice.

tragedy, fulfills a function in the Roman world similar to that of other public *munera*—buildings, games, and gladiatorial shows: targeting a literate audience versed in aesthetic conventions,[94] these poems promote a cohesive national identity and justify Augustus's power in a discourse that parallels the voluntary public gifts of Rome's leader.

94. As Jameson (1981, 106) remarks, "genres are essentially literary *institutions,* or social contracts between a writer and a specific public, whose function is to specify the proper use of a particular artifact."

CHAPTER THREE

The Gifts of the Golden Age

Land, Debt, and Aesthetic Surplus

"Golden Latin," a critical term for the prose and poetry of the late Republican and Augustan period, appears infrequently in contemporary criticism and the more recent handbooks of classical literature.[1] The reason, perhaps, lies in the current idea that labels reflecting qualitative distinctions serve ideological interests. Critical nomenclature and aesthetic discriminations tell us more, so one view would have it, about the assumptions, ambitions, prejudices, and politics of those who make such judgments than about the literary text or category in question. The term "Golden Latin" came into use at a time when English imperialism identified with the Roman Empire and when the *Aeneid* served as a paradigmatic text that justified visions of nationalism and colonial ambitions.[2] Though the term originally referred to a stylistic zenith of purity and homogeneity to which the Latin language had evolved, it also suggests the golden age imagery that played such an important part in Augustan ideology, or the image that those in power projected of themselves.[3] The golden age is both implicitly and ex-

1. For example, Conte (1994) employs the divisions of "Late Republic," "Augustan," and "Early Empire"; Kenney and Clausen (1982) use similar divisions. In contrast, Hadas (1952, 14) refers to the period 70 B.C.E.–14 C.E. as "the Golden Age," and 14–180 C.E. as "the Silver Age"; Wilkinson (1963) accords with this periodization.

2. Hallet (1993, 47) cites Teuffel (1870), followed by Cruttwell (1877), as the German and English scholars who first coined the terms "Golden Age" and "Silver Age" and who "furnish historical explanations . . . which indeed base aesthetic judgments on political factors."

3. On "ideology," see Eagleton 1991, 1–2, who gives sixteen definitions currently in circulation. Four are relevant here: (1) the process of production of meanings, signs, and values in social life; (2) ideas that help legitimate a dominant political power; (3) the conjuncture

plicitly identified with the benefactions of empire in Augustan literature, an identity that no doubt facilitated the retrospective veneration of Golden Latin by nineteenth-century Europeans. But such aesthetic discriminations reflect more than just the politics and ideology of nineteenth-century classicists: both Vergil and Horace, arguably the most "Augustan" poets, represent their own creativity in terms of gifts enabled and stimulated by those who ushered in a return of the *aurea saecla*. Hence, when images of the golden age serve to suggest the independence, creative fertility, or divine inspiration of Horace, the political implications of the iconography often complicate whatever the topos connotes about aesthetics.

We now turn to poems of the Horatian corpus that display the poet's rhetorical figuring of his identity as variously negotiating the cultural contradictions and ambivalences implicit in the status of the Sabine farm as a gift—a benefaction often depicted with details of the golden age or as a pastoral locale. This chapter and chapter 5 address poems in which the estate features explicitly; chapter 4 explores how Horace's Sabine property, as a suppressed term or "absent center," mediates the representation of his relationship with Maecenas in *Epistles* 1.

The literary criticism concerning Horace's estate has generally been of two kinds. One group of scholars has emphasized the poet's representation of his farm as a symbol of aesthetics, a source of creative inspiration and poetic integrity.[4] This approach not only presumes that the aesthetic components of a poem can be analyzed independently of its socioeconomic context but also takes for granted Horace's own independence: as a critical ideology for the Augustan period, aestheticism suggests a commitment to viewing the artist as unconstrained by contemporary political demands or social discourses. Patronage, in this view, is taken up in the poems only as a theme or motif, a rhetorical set of images determined by the internal demands of genre rather than by any pressures or discourses outside of the text.[5] Other critics, concerned with social issues embedded in Horace's poems, have focused almost exclusively on the role of the farm as a biographical source, a locus of admittedly tenuous information about the

---

of discourse and power; and (4) the process whereby social life is converted to a natural reality. For a discussion of poets as active participants in the creation of Augustan ideology, see Santirocco 1995, who argues against the tendency to see Augustan poets as either reflecting or opposing a preexisting set of ideological beliefs.

4. An exemplary but not exhaustive list includes Fraenkel 1957, 205–7; Commager 1962, 348–52; Schmidt 1977; Johnson 1982, 140–42; Thomas 1982; Davis 1991, 201–2; Putnam 1994, 357–75.

5. Note, for example, the claim of Zetzel (1982, 87): "a good case can be made for denying utterly the importance of patronage to Latin poetry. Not necessarily to the poets, I hasten to add, but to their literary productions."

poet's relationship with his patron.[6] Some, to be sure, are not so easily categorized. Eleanor Leach, for example, explores the depictions of the farm as literary topography—the verbal representations of spatial reality that invoke both the poetic context of genre and the cultural context of extraurban, villa society (1993b).

My own reading of these passages similarly mediates between the two approaches by examining the degree to which representations of the farm in Horace's text suggest an ideology about the artist and aesthetic production that simultaneously depends on, competes with, and often appropriates the terms of the socioeconomic discourse of patronage. My study seeks to elucidate the cultural assumptions that underlie, together with the rhetorical and poetic strategies that negotiate, the following paradox: on the one hand, the farm invokes the discourse of patron-client reciprocity—the very real gratitude that the Horatian speaker represents himself as feeling toward his benefactor, as well as the need to requite his gifts; on the other hand, the farm, the very gift that obliges, simultaneously allows Horace the liberty to renegotiate his debts. That is, while the gift of the estate serves to expropriate the labor of the poet in the form of the Roman Odes, it is precisely the aesthetic construction of the farm, either in the pastoral terms of a *locus amoenus* (lovely place) or in figures of the golden age, that provides the speaker a rhetorical means of resisting the demands of reciprocity and reclaiming his "spent" self.

To understand the poetic and historical contexts of these depictions of Horace's farm, we must first examine images of benefaction in Vergil's *Eclogues,* poems in which the golden age topos, and pastoral ease more generally, takes on explicit associations with patronal generosity.[7] Vergil's work provides a critical backdrop for understanding the passages in Horace in which the lineaments of a *locus amoenus* appear.[8] The allusions to the

---

6. Leach (1993b, 273) comments on Horace's allusions to his farm as "frequently scrutinized as successive watermarks in the history of his patron-client relationship." For this approach, see Bailey 1982, 36–37. Bradshaw (1989) opines that Augustus, not Maecenas, gave Horace his Sabine estate; after reviewing the evidence, Lyne (1995, 9–11) concludes that Horace had at least three properties and maybe five, arguing that Augustus was the source of more benefactions than Maecenas.

7. I look to Vergil's *Eclogues* as a model for exploring the kinds of issues considered by Patterson (1987, 7): "how writers, artists, and intellectuals of all persuasions have *used* pastoral for a range of functions and intentions that the *Eclogues* first articulated." For a discussion of the literary origins of the topos of the golden age in Augustan literature, see Reckford 1958; see Wallace-Hadrill 1982 and Zanker 1988, 167–93, on the ideology of the topos. Galinsky (1996, 90–100) stresses the importance of *labor* to the Augustan evocations of the *aurea saecula* after the fourth eclogue. See Castriota 1995, 124–44, on the topos in relation to the Ara Pacis. For further bibliography, see n. 30 below.

8. The escapist fantasy in *Epode* 16, recommending withdrawal to a remote isle of the blessed as a solution to civil war, displays many elements in common with *Eclogue* 4, the most

Vergilian context, I believe, have not been sufficiently remarked and are not fully understood. Yet as a "gift" from Maecenas, or from the Augustan regime at large, the Sabine farm has political and economic associations that evoke the *Eclogues'* most salient topical issue—the land expropriations of Octavian and Antony by which they settled the veteran soldiers after Philippi.[9]

Any reading of Horace's depictions of his estate must therefore take into account both the historical context of the land confiscations of the civil wars and the intertextual resonance of the *Eclogues* that responds to the same political background. As we shall see, the relationship between art, *otium* (leisure, unencumbered time), and the gift of property in Vergil's bucolic poems reflects a discourse of patronage similar in its assumptions and uses to the Horatian images of benefaction. For both poets, land is perceived as a gift whose value lies in its capacity to ensure *otium* and the consequent production of poetry. Because poetry is a means of displaying gratitude, its potential to serve the political interests of the benefactor is inscribed in the codes of social exchange: ideology, as a function of art, may be produced in the very same gesture as the aesthetic expression of *gratia*. My concern, however, is not with the content of political ideology per se but rather with how far such ideology intersects with the poetic treatment of this relationship—with the representation of patronal relations, not always inaccurately, in terms other than those of self-interested reciprocity. For such treatment displays what Pierre Bourdieu calls the "misrecognition" of the economics of exchange in a gift economy, revealing the degree to which these aesthetic texts at one level do function ideologically, insofar as they naturalize social and political distributions of resources.

Before turning to a close reading of the poems, we should consider the general question of how aesthetics and ideology are related. Contemporary reading practices that view works of literature as necessarily, even if

---

acclaimed vision of the *aurea aetas* in European literature. However, critics generally agree that the poem is a deliberate response to Vergil; and because it lacks any explicit relationship to benefaction or aesthetics, it is not relevant to my discussion. See Clausen 1994, 145–50, for the argument that Vergil's poem postdates Horace's.

9. For specific facts about the confiscations and resettlement of veterans, see Brunt 1971, 329–30; Keppie 1983. Though some of the land used for resettlement came from estates of those proscribed, according to Dio and Appian there were first eighteen and then sixteen more cities specifically set aside for land distribution to the soldiers who supported the triumvirs at Philippi. As Brunt and Moore (1967, 42) and Keppie (1983, 38–39) claim, soldiers of the Republic had no specific legal right to lands or monies on discharge; nonetheless, land distribution had historical precedent in the policies of Scipio Aemelianus and the Gracchi as well as in the settlement of Sulla's veterans. Cf. the discussion in Leach 1974, 117 n. 5, 131, and sources cited therein.

sometimes contradictorily, ideological, rooted in the social formations and material practices of a particular time, in many ways trace their own genealogy back to the Marxist aesthetics of the Frankfurt School and its uneasy alliance of German idealist aesthetics with a socially conscious criticism seeking to reveal the socioeconomic interests served by the text. Though committed to unveiling or unmasking the ideological distortions at play in any given work of art, some Marxist critics also attribute a modified autonomy to the aesthetic realm, arguing that the seeds of social subversion, or at least signs of the potential for different political and social arrangements, often coexist—as hermeneutic gaps, figural inconsistencies, or formal irresolutions—with the very aesthetic elements that serve the interests of the status quo.[10] This subversively utopic impulse of art essentially retains the romanticism of an idealist aesthetics such as Schiller's (here displaced from the harmony of form to the lack thereof), even as it is deployed within a critical practice that ultimately aims to view literary texts as fully embedded within the material and discursive practices of a particular historical period.

This critical genealogy is relevant to my analysis of the *Eclogues* and the Horatian uses of pastoral, particularly in the depictions of the Sabine estate in the *Satires* and the *Odes,* because these poems seem consistently to pose the question of the relations between aesthetic production and political power. Benefaction as a material practice that promotes art is, in the *Eclogues,* also a social system of land redistribution, a practice that serves to establish or legitimize the status and authority of military leaders as political figures. I argue that by assimilating a patronal ideology to the conventions of pastoral, Vergil's eclogues not only display a "misrecognition" of the economics of literary benefaction, they also render natural—or at least comprehensible and meaningful—the confiscations by which the military were settled after Philippi. Such a reading by no means discounts the numerous ways in which Vergil draws attention to those who suffer from the expropriations and the other effects of civil war. Indeed, part of the aesthetic miracle of these poems is the fragile dialectical resolutions they achieve, speaking on both sides of the issues: in the first eclogue and later, the perspectives of both the haves and the have-nots are represented even as the poems culminate in an imaginary and, for many readers, imperfect synthesis of the two.

In this regard, Fredric Jameson, whose work draws on the insights of the

10. For an overview of Marxism in literary studies, see Kavanagh and Jameson 1984. For Marxist approaches to antiquity, see Arthur and Konstan 1984 and Rose's introduction, "Marxism and the Classics" (1992, 1–42), to which I am indebted. Marcuse (1978) strongly adhered to the notion of the autonomy of art but also appropriated Schiller's view of the unity of form—a notion problematized by poststructuralist theory, as Brenkman (1985, 184) points out.

Frankfurt School, provides a useful interpretive paradigm: simply put, his double hermeneutic posits a simultaneous operation of contrary impulses toward freedom and repression in an aesthetic text (1971, 306–416). Given a text's material conditions of production, the modalities of such a double impulse are specific both to the work's historical moment and to the particular conventions of its genre. But broadly speaking, "repression" is the way in which a text participates in justifying and naturalizing the power relations of the status quo, thereby reinforcing the ideology of dominant social groups. Hence, the hermeneutic that Jameson calls "negative" uncovers the textual strategies or formal components of this complicity. On the other hand, as Peter Rose points out, "even if one concedes that the ideological function of art is in some sense to manage potentially disruptive discontents within society, then by definition art cannot manage what it does not in some way reveal and evoke" (1992, 36). The positive hermeneutic thus aims at bringing clearly into consciousness the ways in which a text acknowledges a version of reality that does not square with the ideology of those in power. Since art—to the degree that it functions as ideology— seeks to make relations of power appear essential and universal rather than historically, socially, and economically contingent, the positive hermeneutic uncovers precisely those textual details that point to the contingent.

The shifting and mercurial factions of power immediately following the assassination of Julius Caesar make it difficult to locate a stable or specific set of political relations whose right to dominance the *Eclogues* might be said to both interrogate and render "natural." However, as the Republic declined in the first century B.C.E. and increasingly became less a "reality" than a rhetorical concept or nostalgic ideal to be manipulated by the ambitious, political power came to rest with single individuals or the oligarchic few, whose public influence and status depended on their military backing. It is this type of political structure—power in the hands of a few who have force to defend their interests—and the social system of patronage and benefaction that supported it (particularly through land allotments to the military) that we intuit as ultimately naturalized by the *Eclogues*. From Jameson's perspective, this interpretation would constitute a negative hermeneutic, inasmuch as it reads the poems (if not their author) as endorsing, in however qualified a manner, the political system that essentially became a military dictatorship.

However, it is not my purpose here to provide an in-depth Marxist critique of the *Eclogues:* the voices of the dispossessed, marginalized, and unconvinced, and the contingencies that mark their fate, are quite visible in all of Vergil's work and have received much scholarly attention.[11] Rather,

11. In the *Aeneid*, for example, the positive hermeneutic is visible in the lyric pauses and in the interruptions of the epic's narrative telos to inaugurate the Roman Empire.

I read the golden age topos and pastoral motifs more generally as rhetorical figures that, in the context of the late Republic and early Principate, exemplify the aesthetic realm in its capacity both to naturalize and to interrogate social relations of power. Though I explore how these figures express a "dominant" ideology in Vergil—that is, an ideology in which the discourse of benefaction and political power intersect—I nonetheless argue that Horace alludes to Vergilian pastoral in a way that acknowledges its dark side. By invoking Vergil, Horace alludes to pastoral's imaginary resolutions even as he ambiguates and comments ironically on benefaction as a social system:[12] the gift of land carries both the cultural memory of expropriation and the obligation to reciprocate. Yet insofar as earlier images of Horace's estate, in the *Satires* and *Odes,* do conform to the ideology of benefaction as naturalized by the *Eclogues,* such images ironically lay the foundation for the rhetorical strategies by which the poet later resists or subverts what he reveals as a tacit, if distorted, code of reciprocity. Ultimately, as chapter 5's analysis of *Epistles* 1 demonstrates, Horace's pastoral allusions construct his estate in a way that both resists the vulnerability posed by the material world and simultaneously justifies his right to ownership, serving to inscribe the poet in the ranks of the landed elite. Horatian gestures of "freedom" are, in many ways, thus incorporated within and by the discursive structures of power they are meant to resist.

LAND, *OTIUM*, ART: *ECLOGUE* 1

Though Vergil by no means explicitly presents the securing of Tityrus's estate in the first eclogue in golden age terms, the pastoral theme of *otium* certainly connects the shepherd's relieved gratitude to the *deus* (god) at Rome with the prophetic visions of the fourth eclogue. The "pastoral vision" here secured for the individual, Tityrus, is later expanded into the universal topos of the peace and plenty of a golden age, as his private *otium* (as envisioned by Meliboeus) becomes a social utopia enjoyed by all in *Eclogue* 4.[13] In some ways, such translation of the contingent good fortune of one (or a few) into a social vision prophesied for all characterizes the

12. On this type of ironic allusion, see Hubbard 1995, 12

13. I am indebted to Perkell (1990a, 171–81) for her discussion of the "pastoral vision" in *Eclogue* 1 as a product of Meliboeus's own transfiguring imagination. For an elucidation of her terms "pastoral vision" and "pastoral design," the latter of which derives from Marx 1981 [1964], see Perkell 1996. For problems of dating and conflicts between the chronology of composition and the sequence of the *Eclogues* as a collection, see Van Sickle 1978, 2–37. Other discussions of the first eclogue from which I have profited are G. Williams 1968, 307–12; Putnam 1970, 20–81; Leach 1974, 113–42; Alpers 1979, 65–95; Segal 1981, 271–300.

distortions of ideology.[14] But these poems do more than suggest the process by which the ideological potential of Vergil's pastoral song derives, in part, from a system of patronage; they also naturalize that social discourse of benefaction by assimilating it to conventions of the bucolic landscape. This results in an idealized vision of benefaction—as a system that promotes social cohesion and community—and downplays the idea that ideology is produced as a return gift.

In *Eclogue* 1, the particular fictive situation of Tityrus and Meliboeus underscores the final consequence of the generosity of those in Rome: the gift of land secures *otium*, and leisure in turn makes possible art and aesthetic freedom. Indeed, though Meliboeus emphasizes his own loss of land and thus his experience of expropriation, the opening images in which he figures Tityrus describe the latter's musical activity rather than his possession of land:

> Tityre, tu patulae recubans sub tegmine fagi
> silvestrem tenui Musam meditaris avena;
> nos patriae finis et dulcia linquimus arva.
> nos patriam fugimus; tu, Tityre, lentus in umbra
> formosam resonare doces Amaryllida silvas.

Tityrus, reclining beneath the shady protection of the spreading beech tree, you practice your songs on a slender reed; but we leave the borders and sweet fields of our country, we are exiled from our land; you, Tityrus, comfortable in the shade, teach the woods to echo back "lovely Amaryllis." (1.1–5)

Scholars have long recognized the contrast between the two shepherds here as a dissonance between the civic turmoil of recent history and an ideal "pastoral vision," a conflict that characterizes the *Eclogues* as a whole. However, in addition to such structural or "binary" oppositions is a series of equivalences or exchanges—a particular economy of values that should be stressed. In setting his loss of property against Tityrus's song of Amaryllis, Meliboeus effectively equates property and song as values: for Meliboeus, the presence of land or property is automatically translated into its aesthetic equivalent—pastoral song.[15] This close relationship between land and song

---

14. Van Sickle (1978, 44–75) describes a linear, dynamic development of a "positive ideology" in the *Eclogues*.

15. See Goux 1990, 9: "Metaphors, symptoms, signs, representations: it is always through replacement that values are created. . . . Value is presupposed by formal identity and by indemnity, even if no real permutation, no give-and-take trade actually makes the substitution of equivalents visible[.]" In the first eclogue, *otium* is one value in a chain of signification; in this respect, the substitution is metonymic rather than metaphoric.

is reflected in the woods that Tityrus "teaches to echo back 'lovely Amaryllis.'" Here, the land's absorption and reproduction of song—a common motif of pastoral—equates the two in a form of metonymic substitution. In fact, in keeping with the chain of substitutions discernible in the eclogue's opening, song itself is represented by the woman, Amaryllis, who is the subject of the shepherd's tune. As though to point up the completeness of the land's conversion into song, the sound of *silvas* (woodland) quite literally echoes the vowels, sibilants, and liquids in Amaryllis's Greek name so that Theocritean art temporarily elides the presence of recent Roman history.[16] Thus, though land is the material substance that actually enables the shepherds' lives, it is also what Meliboeus transforms into an ideal and aestheticized pastoral vision. Meliboeus represents Tityrus as enjoying what I propose to call an "economy of *otium*": a system of symbolic exchanges that is materially based but in which the value of that material—land—is determined by its aesthetic returns. In such an economy, the land is itself appreciated for its aesthetic qualities, and possession of it ensures the owner the peace and tranquillity necessary for the pursuit of "letters" or the production of culture.[17]

Meliboeus's particular vision is poignantly stirred by the imminence of his loss (Segal 1981, 276–77). However, by idealizing the actually mundane and unlovely landscape that Tityrus is allowed to keep, the dispossessed shepherd's song also compensates to a degree, serving to transform the pain of expropriation into an aesthetic fullness. Indeed, a recent "positive" reading of the eclogue's final lines claims that the aesthetic power itself of Meliboeus's pastoral sensibility, as expressed in song, moves Tityrus at the end of the poem to make his offer of generous, if tentative, hospitality (Perkell 1990a, 176). Another way of putting this is to say that what is *dulce* (melodious, delightful) about Meliboeus's poetry becomes, ultimately, *utile* (useful). What appears at first as merely a swan song, a haunting but helpless response to the brutal realities of civil discord, turns out to have a social function.

For the purposes of my analysis, the interdependence of this social effectiveness of Meliboeus's song and Tityrus's hospitality is crucial. The final lines of the eclogue, as many recognize (though their explanations vary), achieve a temporary synthesis of the dialectical oppositions represented by

16. Amaryllis appears in Theocr. *Id.* 3.1, 4.36.

17. Cf. Cic. *De Or.* 1.224: *philosophorum autem libros reservet sibi ad huiusce modi Tusculani requiem atque otium.* D'Arms (1981, 79) points up the vocabulary used to describe luxury villas in the ancient sources: "*voluptas* (rather than *fructus*), *luxuria, voluptariae possessiones, amoenitas, otium* are recurring words and phrases." On the varied connotations of *otium* in the late Republic and Augustan era, see André 1966, 205–541.

the two shepherds. I see this harmony as arising from the conclusion's tentative proposal that the aesthetic values of Meliboeus's economy of *otium* work together with the actual, material benefactions of patronage to create community. Although the moment of community envisioned is only temporary, it nonetheless involves the extension of the sensibility of each character to include the other: on the one hand, the simple lyricism of Tityrus's offer displays not only his final receptivity to Meliboeus's predicament but also an openness to his aesthetic vision (Perkell 1990a, 179); on the other, Tityrus's offer is a gesture, albeit limited, that would allow Meliboeus to partake of the more concrete benefits of his friend's good fortune. Tityrus may need Meliboeus to awaken him to his social responsibilities, but Meliboeus needs from Tityrus the very material protection that he now offers.[18] The bucolic community in which Tityrus includes Meliboeus, glimpsed in the smoke rising from the rooftops at a distance, reflects more than pastoral empathy, for it suggests the social cohesion to which the ideology of benefaction aspires.

More than one stratified social structure is implied in this cohesion. Indeed, the *deus* or "god" at Rome who secures Tityrus his estate combines features of the patron with a discourse of Hellenistic king worship.[19] The benefaction of this particular god, accessible and ready to aid (*praesentis . . . divos*, 41), invokes the practice of exchange—the reciprocal giving of goods and services, between two parties of unequal status—that marks the Roman institution of patronage. In return for the grant of land (or the assurance that he may continue to inhabit it), Tityrus vows always to render a sacrificial victim once a month to the *deus* whose features will never fade from his memory. Given the Roman context and Tityrus's own dramatic perspective, the shepherd's divine nomenclature constitutes a hyperbolic expression of his overwhelming sense of gratitude. To call one's human benefactor "a god" is rhetorically consonant with the genre of the *eucharistikon,* a speech of gratitude usually addressed directly to the donor in question (Du Quesnay 1981, 98–103). However, such attitudes ultimately derive from the Greek-speaking world; when the Romans took over the land ruled by Hellenistic monarchs, the deification of benefactors became part "of their own stock of cultural responses" (102–4). In addition, then, to suggesting the practices of Roman patronage, the monthly sacrifice that

18. On the importance of "human needs and relations" in the pastoral world, see Alpers 1979, 225.

19. This observation is not meant to reduce the eclogue to an old-style set of allegorical correspondences, with Octavian the probable figure hovering behind the *deus*. The historical situation is important, but only as it is filtered through the fictive encounter of the two shepherds and their individual sensibilities.

Tityrus promises may derive specifically from the celebratory cult of Hellenistic rulers.[20] Within the dramatic fiction of the pastoral dialogue, Vergil has grafted a discourse of Hellenistic king worship—of which Tityrus himself would probably have been ignorant—onto a Roman context of gratitude and obligation to a patron. We shall return to the ideology of monarchy, similarly naturalized by assimilation to the pastoral landscape, in the discussion of *Eclogue* 4.

As Seneca points out in *De beneficiis*, a person can never really pay back his benefactor, and the debt incurs a lifelong sense of gratitude that binds the two together (2.18.5).[21] Hence, in place of a full reciprocation to the man of higher status, the beneficiary himself becomes a benefactor to others below him, and disseminates favors in turn. Such a patronal hierarchy is indeed suggested when Tityrus offers food and shelter to Meliboeus before he must leave. Although Meliboeus is the "free citizen," and Tityrus is or was the slave, the modalities of patronage invoked by land grants ultimately condition not only Tityrus's relationship to his *deus* but also the formal structure of relations between the two shepherds at the end of the poem.

Critics have censured the belatedness of Tityrus's offer and the merely pragmatic or contractual element of his sacrificial offerings to the *deus*.[22] And yet the eclogue tentatively (perhaps reflecting the hesitation of Tityrus's final words) endorses benefaction as the economic system that produces results. Tityrus originally goes to Rome in hopes of obtaining his liberty (*spes libertatis*, 32), either through manumission by *censu* or by securing his right to farm, because expropriation from the land would mean the loss of *ususfructus* (the right to the "fruits" rather than ownership of property) and the possibility of accumulating his *peculium*.[23] But as Tityrus's

20. See Clausen 1994, 48, and P. White 1993, 171–73, for the Hellenistic significance of Tityrus's vow to make monthly sacrifices to the *deus* in Rome. Drawing a distinction between benefactors and rulers, Du Quesnay (1981, 107) in fact rejects this view, deriving from Wissowa, and considers worship of the *Lar familiaris* to be the model for Tityrus's monthly sacrifices. Saller (1982, 23) emphasizes that the diction of patronage characterizes man-god relations in both the Republic and early Empire.

21. Seneca does not discuss the ongoing relationship between a benefactor and his beneficiary in terms of a *cliens-patronus* bond. However, as the introduction makes clear, my views incline to those argued by Saller (1982, 6): "We should not jump to the conclusion that patronage existed only where the terms *patronus* and *cliens* were used."

22. See Putnam 1970, 67; Coleman 1977, 90; Patterson 1987, 3. Leach (1974, 137–38) sees Tityrus as powerless, not callous. Arguing for a more positive reading of Tityrus's hospitality, Perkell (1990a, 175) nonetheless sees him as "ready to worship a new, private, urban god, for reasons of expediency."

23. *Peculium* is often used to refer to a "slave's savings" by which he might buy his freedom; more technically, Varro (*Rust.* 1.2.17) defines a slave's *peculium* as the right of pasturage that could be granted by a master to slaves. Finley (1973, 64) writes that "*peculium* was property

own description of his engagement in a "market economy" suggests, he has not in the past been successful at saving his money to purchase his freedom: not only was his former love a spendthrift, but he himself was lazy (*inertem*) and, most important, the town was ungrateful (*ingratae*) and decidedly not responsive to his sale either of sheep or cheese:

> Libertas, quae sera tamen respexit inertem,
> candidior postquam tondenti barba cadebat,
> respexit tamen et longo post tempore venit,
> postquam nos Amaryllis habet, Galatea reliquit.
> namque (fatebor enim) dum me Galatea tenebat,
> nec spes libertatis erat nec cura peculi.
> quamvis multa meis exiret victima saeptis,
> pinguis et ingratae premeretur caseus urbi,
> non umquam gravis aere domum mihi dextra redibat.

Freedom, which, though late, yet took notice of lazy me, after my whitening beard began to fall to the scissors, had regard for me nonetheless and came after a long time—after Amaryllis took me, and Galatea left. Indeed—I'll confess—while Galatea held me, there was neither hope of freedom nor the inclination to save. Although many victims left my enclosures and cheese was pressed for the ungrateful town, never did I return home with money in hand. (1.27-35)

There are several striking features in this brief glimpse of Tityrus's foray into the neighboring town to sell his goods. First, Tityrus applies to a commercial situation a word appropriate to a gift economy or to the exchange of benefits and favors: although he is presumably *selling* his goods for *aera* or bartering them for other items, he seems to be relying on the gratitude of the townspeople for the excess profit that would go to his *peculium*.[24] But

---

(in whatever form) assigned for use, management, and within limits, disposal to someone who in law lacked the right of property, either a slave or someone in *patria potestas;* . . . a slave . . . could expect to buy his freedom with the profits [of the *peculium*.] [.]" On *ususfructus* in Roman law, see Watson 1968, 203–21. Manumission by *censu* refers to the grant of freedom that could be given by the censor, every four years in Rome, to those slaves who presented themselves at the behest of their master. Freedom, if granted, would be accompanied by citizenship. See Treggiari 1969, 25–27. For discussion of the historical and legal realities behind Tityrus's journey to Rome to acquire his *libertas*, see Leach 1974, 120–21; Coleman 1977, 79, 82; Du Quesnay 1981, 115–36, and the sources cited therein.

24. Tityrus brings expectations of the "pastoral pleasance" to a market situation. For discussion of the pastoral economy as what I am calling a "gift economy," where monetary calculation and precise values are unknown, see Rosenmeyer 1969, 161–67, who notes that "In spite of the absence of labor from the pleasance, a gift in which the donor has invested some of his time and energy is especially welcome. Hence the cups lovingly chiseled, the pipes meticulously honed and waxed, and the garment newly oiled." He adds that "the emphasis is on their [the gifts'] aesthetic qualities[;] . . . they are rewards or signs of accreditation"

the excess associated with *gratia* and the concept of a return gift has no place in a system where commodities—in this case, cheese and sheep— have an exchange value and are sold at a market.[25] Second, Tityrus's use of the word *victima* to describe the sheep taken to the town market suggests the ritual of sacrifice and not a commercial transaction. *Pinguis* (fat) is likewise an epithet often used to describe an animal used in such a ritual. To be sure, the phrasing may simply reflect Tityrus's expectation that his sheep will be bought by priests or those who must make sacrifices but have no animals of their own.[26] Nonetheless, his use of the word *victima* here appears somewhat overdetermined. Tityrus is in the full flush of having just received a benefaction and is full of *gratia* to his benefactor. Such *gratia* expresses itself in images of sacrifice; thus whenever he mentions his benefactor, Tityrus includes images of the ritual offering of lambs that he will make in return (1.7–8, 42–43). The association of *victima* with these other images of sacrifice appears, for example, in the repetition of the verb *exiret:* Tityrus thinks in terms of sacrificial offerings ("though many fat victims left [*exiret*] my enclosures"), when he considers escaping the condition of slavery—"it was not possible for me to escape the status of a slave nor elsewhere discover gods so accessible and helpful" (*neque servitio me exire licebat / nec tam praesentis alibi cognoscere divos,* 41–42). Hence, despite the discrepancy between the commercial and gift economies, he impulsively views the former system, and its failure to gain him his *libertas,* through the lens of the economic system—benefaction—that has just blessed him. Finally, both of the goods that "fail" to produce *gratia* in the commercial context are the very ones that, as return gifts or generous gestures, are prompted by *gratia* within a gift economy: in addition to the "tender lamb," the sacrificial *victima* to be rendered to the *deus,* the *caseus* or cheese—thanklessly pressed for the townspeople—is one of the items Tityrus offers to Meliboeus at the end of the poem. In contrast to commerce, as dramatically presented by the poem, benefaction inspires *gratia,* the gratitude that, in an ideal world, lays the groundwork for community.

It is often remarked that ideology functions by canvassing alternative

---

(163–64). In this regard, pastoral gifts, though often "humble," nonetheless suggest the "prestige objects" of primitive gift economies.

25. Commentators often ascribe Tityrus's inability to save money for his *peculium* to the spendthrift ways of Galatea, his sweetheart before Amaryllis: e.g., Coleman 1977, ad loc. However, as Du Quesnay (1981, 122) rightly points out, "Tityrus presents the connection between his manumission and his relationship with Amaryllis as temporal, not causal (*postquam*)."

26. Servius refers *pinguis* to *victima,* but otherwise does not comment. For the idea that the process of sacrifice was necessarily mediated through the market, cf. Plin. *Tra.* 10.96.10: *Certe satis constat prope iam desolata templa coepisse celebrari et sacra sollemnia diu intermissa repeti passimque venire ⟨carnem⟩ victimarum, cuius adhuc rarissimus emptor inveniebatur.* I am grateful to C. Bennett Pascal for this reference.

systems of social and economic distributions of power and then rendering them, in a particular scenario, ineffective. This holds true within the first eclogue: for by presenting Tityrus's good fortune as the result of benefaction rather than a market economy, and by displaying the ineffectiveness of the latter when the shepherd wishes to buy his freedom, the poem essentially demonstrates the "inevitable" necessity of patronage as a socioeconomic system. One might object that the god's pronouncement in Rome, "*pascite ut ante boves, pueri, submittite tauros*" ("Pasture your cattle, rear your bulls as before, slaves," 45), merely ensures that the estate remain in the same hands as before and leaves uncertain whether or not Tityrus actually secured his liberty.[27] However, regardless of what Tityrus does in fact receive, several textual details combine to present benefaction in a positive light: the market system as a negative foil, the mention of the same "goods" that failed to gain Tityrus's liberty in a commercial context as positive expressions of *gratia* in a gift economy, the offer of pastoral gifts in a moment of tenuous community at the end of the poem. This endorsement is hardly absolute: it is presented dramatically, through Tityrus's perceptions and experience. Moreover, as Christine Perkell notes, it is only through the power of Meliboeus's sensibility that Tityrus awakens from the solipsism of his good fortune. The social cohesion enabled by an ideal view of benefaction—and only glimpsed in the final lines as an ironic alternative to, or commentary on, the divided fortunes of the two shepherds—is a specific response to song. But what begins as a response is also appropriated. For pastoral song succeeds in translating or assimilating the social and historical discourse of benefaction to the conventions of bucolic generosity and community. The effects of this assimilation are twofold: first, such an ending dramatizes the ideological potential of pastoral song (and its idealizing motifs) to overcome historical division and provide a shared set of values[28] —thereby showing art and benefaction to have similar goals; and second, the ending serves to naturalize the contingent power relations behind such benefactions, gifts that, if the eclogue is read allegorically, were quite possibly made with a self-interested view to such endorsement.

GRATIA AND THE POETICS OF EXCESS: *ECLOGUE* 4

The fourth eclogue provides another example of the way in which Vergil's pastoral absorbs the discourse of benefaction. Because self-reflexivity is a

27. Perkell (1990b, 45) argues that this uncertainty in the poem constitutes one of its "hermeneutic gaps" or "*loci* of indeterminacy"—terms derived from Wolfgang Iser's reader-response theory.

28. See Perkell 1990a, 179, on the "community of longing" for shared values effected by Meliboeus's pastoral song.

prominent attribute of bucolic poetry—activities and objects in the shep-
herds' landscape tend to refer to the production of song—it follows that
the spontaneous production that is typical of nature in a golden age topos
takes on an aesthetic character in the context of pastoral. Vergil, as we shall
see, assimilates the libidinal or emotional value of the concept of *gratia* to
these highly stylized excesses of the golden age. The connotation of *gratia*
as "goodwill," akin to the meaning of *voluntas,* as well as the original sense
of "acknowledgment"—the *réconaissance* or *éloge* that Joseph Hellegouarc'h
remarks in the concept of *gratia*—thus also come into play here.[29]

Vergil's most famous "pastoral" is a poem not originally conceived in
the bucolic mode. Written to celebrate Asinius Pollio's consulship in 40
B.C.E., the fourth eclogue's messianic predictions of the return of a golden
age, the rule of Saturn, anticipate and arguably provide a source for the
political use of the topos in the art and poetry of the 20s B.C.E. and later.[30]
Possibly influenced by the Sibylline prophecy of a new temporal order,
Vergil adapts the idea of a golden race in Hesiod and Aratus to the Roman
concept of a new *saeculum,* or "age." The identity of the child whose birth
and successive stages of life will coincide with generations of mythic histor-
ical time remains obscure; he is possibly a son of Asinius Pollio, but more
likely the offspring of the recent alliance between Antony and Octavia (a
marriage that was to be short-lived). This political union was intended to
cement through kinship the treaty of Brundisium, negotiated with the as-
sistance of Pollio in September of 40 B.C.E., between the political rivals
Antony and Octavian. Thus, Vergil's poem draws both from the genre of
the epithalamium, in celebration of the recent wedding, and from the bas-
ilikon, adapted to the Roman occasion of Pollio's consulate: the praise of
Pollio includes and is partially displaced onto the praise of the child who
will rule as a king (Du Quesnay 1977, 56–57). Despite the eventual disso-
lution of the treaty, the marriage, and the accord between the factions of
the Caesarian party, the attributes of the golden age here—the lion lying
down with the lamb, the voluntary fecundity of nature—resemble the em-
blems of peace that later decorate so much of the sculpture of the Princi-
pate and early Empire. Recent scholarship has stressed the mutability of

29. See Hellegouarc'h 1963, 202, on the association of *gratia* with *éloge* and thus *laudes.* I
discuss the association between *gratia* and libidinal excess in chapter 1. See Saller 1982, 21,
on *gratia* as "an attitude rather than an action."

30. *Eclogue* 4 has generated vast critical commentary. I have particularly profited from
Putnam 1970, 136–65; Leach 1974, 216–44; Du Quesnay 1977, 25–99; Van Sickle 1978, 55–
75; Segal 1981, 265–70; Arnold 1994; Hubbard 1995. For broader discussions of the concept
of the golden age in Augustan ideology and literature, see n. 7 above. Both Galinsky (1996,
90–100) and Barker (1996) argue against taking the fourth eclogue as a blueprint for later
appearances or evocations of the golden age topos.

this mythological topos;[31] the fourth eclogue differs from later literary narratives of the golden age in its emphasis on nature's spontaneous fertility without the need for human labor. This feature not only characterizes Hesiod's description, one of Vergil's major sources; it is also dramatically consistent with the social relations of patronage in which the poem is embedded.

To begin with, in contrast to the dramatic fiction of shepherds engaged in song, the occasion of the fourth eclogue draws attention to the poem as a means of honoring Pollio, possibly Vergil's patron at this time.[32] The speaker introduces a grander, more amplified tone, using a pastoral metaphor:

> Sicelides Musae, paulo maiora canamus!
> non omnis arbusta iuvant humilesque myricae;
> si canimus silvas, silvae sint consule dignae.

Sicilian Muses, let us sing in a slightly higher mode, more lofty matters!
Orchards and humble tamarisks do not please all; if we sing about
woods, let them be a forest worthy of a consul. (4.1–3)

The consulate as a political occasion clearly demands a grander strain, but the honor accorded to Pollio in this poem also flatters him as a patron of poets. In particular, the theme of the golden age looks back to Pollio's appearance in the third eclogue (Segal 1981, 251–52, 261; Arnold 1994, 146–47). There, Damoetas's appreciation of Vergil's patron as a reader expresses itself in the invocation to the Muses to "fatten a calf" for him (*vitulam lectori pascite vestro*, 85). When Menalcas tops this display of gratitude by flattering Pollio's talent as a poet himself, and invokes the preparation of a bull as sacrificial offering, Damoetas responds with lavish praise that pulls out all the stops: he wishes that the one who appreciates Pollio's verse arrive in a place that the poet already inhabits, a land where honey flows and the thornbush bears spice—*adunata,* or impossibilities, that

31. As Barker (1996, 436) suggests, "in the myth of the golden age one is confronted less by a fixed symbol than by a mobile discourse—that is, by a composite of different positions taken by different Romans at different times around the idea of a returning golden race."

32. Pollio's role as a patron of the *Eclogues* is by no means indisputable, given the ambiguity of lines 6–13 in *Eclogue* 8, where the speaker claims that his songs began at the command of the addressee's bidding (*iussis / carmina coepta tuis*). The patron here has often been understood as referring to Pollio, because Vergil describes his addressee as a poet of tragedy, and Pollio was the most famous tragedian of his day. However, Clausen (1994, 234–37), following recent scholarship, attributes the reference to Octavian, who was known to have begun an *Ajax* and whose travels at the time of this eclogue's composition better square with the lines describing the patron's journey.

evoke a golden age topos.[33] Thus Damoetas flatters Pollio, through a metaphor that suggests he has already achieved perfection of pastoral technique. Though both the initial lines of *Eclogue* 4 and this exchange in *Eclogue* 3 are thought to be additions to the poems as originally composed, intended to help integrate them into a unified book (Clausen 1982, 310–11; 1995, 126), the alteration only enhances an effect already present. The amplification of tone, the more grandiose strain of *Eclogue* 4 is, at some level, already inscribed in a discourse of benefaction: without conflating Damoetas with the *Eclogue* poet or the author himself, figures who operate on different contextual levels,[34] we may still read the elevation of tone in part as an impulse or function of *gratia*—the appreciation felt in response to Pollio's patronage of Vergil as a poet. Damoetas's desire for the discriminating reader qua poet to join Pollio, already set in the metaphorical land of honey and *adunata*, structurally parallels the *Eclogue* poet's invocation of the Muses' assistance, in the next poem, to sing *paulo maiora* worthy of a consul.

Moreover, though the comparative *maiora* refers in its immediate context to the difference between the lowly tamarisk and more stately woods, and thus metaphorically to the contrast between humble and grand themes, it also strongly connotes the idea of excess or surplus value associated with *gratia*. As I discussed in chapter 1, when Cicero distinguishes between monetary exchange and a gift economy, he alludes to the paradox that *gratia*, though returned, leaves behind an excess or residue, a trace of itself—something that, in fact, causes the favor to increase in value.[35] Specifically, Cicero's distinction suggests the consequences of the idea that one who receives a benefit or kindness can never fully pay back his benefactor and be free of the debt: *gratia* as expressed in a concrete form of return, as "return favors," may very well exceed the original gift; and, because a feeling of gratitude is left over despite the return favors, causing the social relationship to outlast the exchange, *gratia* suggests a value of libidinal excess.[36] Indeed, we perceive one aspect of such excess assimilated to the conventions of pastoral in the amoebean competition between Damoetas

---

33. Verg. *Ecl.* 3.84–89: Damoetas: *Pollio amat, quamvis est rustica, Musam: / Pierides, vitulam lectori pascite vestro.* Menalcas: *Pollio et ipse facit nova carmina: pascite taurum, / iam cornu petat et pedibus qui spargat harenam.* Damoetas: *Qui te, Pollio, amat, veniat, quo te quoque gaudet; / mella fluant illi, ferat et rubus asper amomum.*

34. See Leach 1974, 245–76, on the various roles played by the "Eclogue poet."

35. "A man has not repaid money if he still has it; if he has repaid it, he has ceased to have it. But a man still has the sense of favour, if he still has the sense of favour; and if he has the sense of the favour, he has repaid it" (Cic. *Off.* 2.69; trans. W. Miller 1913, Loeb edition).

36. Seneca (*Ben.* 2.18.5) makes the same distinction as Cicero; he concludes that to the benefactor (as opposed to the creditor), *at illi e plus solvendum est, et nihilo minus etiam relata gratia cohaeremus; debeo enim, cum reddidi, rursus incipere, manetque amicitia.*

and Menalcas: in a rivalrous display that resembles the agonistic prestation, or the competitive giving, of a potlatch, each shepherd invokes a progressively more lavish image—calf, bull, land of milk and honey—to mark his favor with, and appreciation of, Pollio. Here the motives of amoebean display—to exceed and thereby best one's competitor—combine with the wish to requite Pollio and produce a final extravagant, and thus "excessive," image of gratitude. The phrase *paulo maiora* of the next eclogue thus resonates ironically as understatement not only within its own context but also in relation to this earlier sequence of images that serve as competitive and increasingly lavish expressions of *gratia,* and that first associate Pollio with the golden age.

In addition, *paulo maiora* might suggest the actual excess involved in a return gift or acknowledgment of a benefaction pure and simple. Again, as we saw in chapter 1, Cicero quite explicitly relates *gratia* and the idea of increase when he discusses the appropriate response to an unlooked-for benefaction: "for no duty (*officium*) is more imperative than that of proving one's gratitude (*referenda gratia*). But if, as Hesiod bids, one is to repay with interest (*maiore mensura*), if possible (*si modo possis*), what one has borrowed in time of need, what, pray, ought we to do when challenged by an unsought kindness? Shall we not imitate the fruitful fields, which return more than they receive?" (*Off.* 1.47–48).[37] The use of the comparative *maior* in both contexts is slim evidence of a connection, but Cicero's analogy to Hesiod and agriculture is relevant in many ways to Vergil's description of the golden age in *Eclogues* 4.[38] Given that Pollio is not only a consul in this poem but also possibly the person who as a patron first encouraged Vergil to write bucolics, the phrase *paulo maiora* suggests Hesiod's advice to give back more than one has received. *Paulo,* unattested elsewhere in Vergil, could allude to Cicero's qualification of *si modo possis,* his acknowledgment that repayment in "greater measure" is difficult and not always possible. More important, for all that Hesiod's advice occurs in the context of the human toil of the iron age, Cicero's analogy to crops growing in natural and spontaneous increase suggests the voluntary surplus of the golden age. To be sure, Cicero presents the increase of *gratia* in terms of nature's response to the labor of planting or the "gift" of seed—that which is analogous to the unprompted or unsought benefaction. However, the emphasis on both the apparent spontaneity of the original gift—it is not expected or induced—and the similarly spontaneous "excess" of the return suggests

37. Trans. W. Miller 1913, Loeb edition.

38. The idea of measurement in relation to Rome comes up in the first eclogue, when Tityrus admits that the city confounded his pastoral sense of dimension: *sic canibus catulos similis, sic matribus haedos / noram, sic parvis componere magna solebam. / verum haec tantum alias inter caput extulit urbes / quantum lenta solent inter viburna cupressi* (22–25).

two prominent features of golden age motifs: nature's bounty and the absence of coercion.[39] Hesiod's advice to give back more than one has received is, in many ways, a translation of nature's generosity in the golden age into the ethical realm of human relations (see esp. *Op.* 352–60).

I propose, then, that the discourse of patronage conditions more than just the loftier tone of the eclogue. *Gratia,* which expresses appreciative responsiveness either as an attitude or in the concrete terms of a return gift, metaphorically characterizes the very activity of nature's spontaneous profusions in this depiction of the golden age. In sympathetic response to the child's birth, at first the earth spontaneously produces little gifts (*nullo munuscula cultu*) of flowers, ivy, and acanthus (18–20). The word *munuscula,* appearing nowhere else in the Vergilian corpus, initially suggests the offerings of the shepherd-lover in a pastoral context displaced to the symbiotic relationship between earth and child (Putnam 1970, 146). Significantly, however, it also connotes the symbolic gifts of Roman social relations.[40] Cicero uses the word to describe a speech as a "little gift" he has written in defense of Deiotarus, his old host and friend, which he later sends to Dolabella.[41] Caelius employs it ironically to refer to a charge brought by a defendant against his accuser,[42] a usage that underscores its usual positive connotation as a symbol of relationship. Suetonius describes Augustus's distribution of *munuscula* to the residents of Capreae, again suggesting the bond symbolized by the gift (*Aug.* 98.3). Horace uses the word, though somewhat negatively, to describe an unsolicited gift in *Epistles* 1.7.17. Indeed, though I am choosing to read *munuscula* in the fourth eclogue as an expression of *gratia,* it is also possible to read these gifts as spontaneous benefactions. Spontaneity and the absence of coercion are visible in other motifs: the goats returning home unbidden, a common feature of golden age descriptions; or the sheep famously changing the color of their wool by their own will (*sua sponte*), a fanciful invention of Vergil's own that he adapted from Etruscan prophecy (Du Quesnay 1977, 42). Suggestive of either benefaction or *gratia,* the emphasis on voluntarism and the lack of calculated interest behind these gifts of nature accord with

39. For a list of passages in the Greco-Roman tradition that contain these specific features as part of the golden age, see the *conspectus rerum* in Gatz 1967, 229, and the specific headings 1. *terra sua sponte victum ferens* and 1.b) *variae res se ultro offerentes.*

40. See Veyne 1990, 216: "petty gifts maintained the relation of clientage, which often consisted in an exchange of services very widely separated in time. In order that the obligation to return the service received might be kept up, there had to be a bond of affection between protector and protégé, and this affection was symbolized by petty gifts which seemed to create the bond but in fact merely served to maintain friendship and the memory of a service which still awaited its reward."

41. Cic. *Fam.* 9.12.2: *Sed ego hospiti veteri et amico munusculum mittere volui.*

42. Cic. *Fam.* 8.8.1: *Nemini hoc deferre munusculum maluit quam suo accusatori.*

the prescriptive and ideal view of giving and receiving presented by Cicero and Seneca (see Sen. *Ben.* 1.2.2, 2.17.7).

The ease with which a golden age discourse could assimilate such Roman attitudes to the bucolic landscape helps account for the later adoption of such motifs as symbolic of the Augustan regime. For it is precisely the patronal aspect of the imperial rule ushered in by Augustus's regime, as it became established in the 20s B.C.E. and later, that is "naturalized" by the topos of the golden age or pastoral motifs more generally.[43] In *Eclogue* 4, nature's enthusiastic response to the advent of the young child and the stages of his maturation serves literally to provide the initial lineaments of a naturalizing discourse for the authoritarian rule of a single man who will "rule the world" (*reget . . . orbem,* 17); such a discourse gains power from originating in and evoking the recognizable terms of Roman social relations. Rather than appear as imposed by force, authoritarian rule evolves as a form of gift or distinction, a glorious age (*decus hoc aevi,* 11) that is freely bestowed or "sent down from heaven" (*caelo demittitur alto,* 7) and voluntarily received. The amplified tone and vatic register of the speaker, as a reflex of honor and index of *gratia* for Pollio, parallels nature's expressions of gratitude and symbiotic responsiveness to the child as a metaphoric "gift" of Pollio's consulship: the external frame of the poem's occasion is repeated in the structural relationship between the child and nature.

Yet ironically, Vergil's deployment of the topos here presents nature's superfluity as an excess that becomes aesthetic. What begins as the libidinal excess of gratitude expresses itself in images that self-reflexively connote poetic production. As we have seen, in sympathetic response to the child's birth the earth spontaneously produces little gifts of flowers, ivy, and acanthus. Their aesthetic associations are heightened by analogy to the Greek word for flower, *anthos,* which can allude to poetry (Arnold 1994, 147). But aesthetic production is also seen as cumulative: the golden age is a place of extremes, and so we find an organic world pumped full of hormones to the point of monstrous, or at least "unnatural," output. Not only does honey—a symbol of pastoral poetry—drip from trees (cf. Theoc. *Id.* 1.146), but nature expands beyond her bounds: iridescent sheep, effort-

---

43. For example, the issue of coins with Octavian in 41 B.C.E., and later Augustus in 17 B.C.E., in conjunction with the image of *cornucopiae,* suggests precisely the role of the emperor as ultimate benefactor. See, too, my discussion of Horace's epistle to Iccius (1.12.28–29) later in this chapter. Galinsky (1996, 111) cautions that the images on coins cannot be "interpreted indiscriminately as betokening a Golden Age suggestive of the fourth *Eclogue*" and cites the tradition of such iconography dating back to 207 B.C.E. and the Second Punic War. Such caveats and observations notwithstanding, Vergil's poem associates nature's fertility with a discourse of benefaction, a connection elsewhere visible in Augustan iconography and literature.

lessly changing hue to produce a splendid array of colors, spontaneously do the work of culture and thereby make obsolete the expensive labor of dyes. Since nature's bounty is all-providing, the entire economic substructure that may be said to underlie the production of culture becomes otiose in this vision: "Even the trader will yield from the sea, and the seafaring pine will no more exchange goods; all the earth will bear all things" (*cedet et ipse mari vector, nec nautica pinus / mutabit merces; omnis feret omnia tellus,* 38–39). The economic exchanges that provide the Roman world with the luxurious foreign dyes so highly prized by the aristocracy yield here to the spontaneous and voluntary changes of nature: "No longer will wool learn to dissemble various colors, but the ram himself, in the meadows, will change his own fleece, now to a charming reddish-purple, now to golden yellow" (*nec varios discet mentiri lana colores, / ipse sed in pratis aries iam suave rubenti / murice, iam croceo mutabit vellera luto,* 42–44). The repetition of *mutabit* in these two sentences points up not only nature's appropriation of human economic work but also the exchanges of value that, in the economy of *otium,* evolve into art: the idealized landscape here provides the economic surplus that constitutes the conditions of *otium,* and such leisure, in turn, is immediately translated to an aesthetic level—here symbolized by the sheep in their technicolor dreamcoats.[44]

The landscape as a place of aesthetic production thus recalls the effects of Meliboeus's transfiguring imagination in the first eclogue. Here, however, the capacity to transform, to metamorphose, literally to change (*mutare*) appearances or *colores* originally emanates not from loss but from an impulse of *gratia.* The *Eclogue* poet again invokes this assimilation of the libidinal excess of grateful joy to the aesthetic fertility of the pastoral landscape when he claims: "Behold how all things rejoice at the coming age! O, may the end of a long life remain for me then, and enough breath to glorify your deeds!" (*aspice, venturo laetentur ut omnia saeclo! / o mihi tum longae maneat pars ultima vitae, / spiritus et quantum sat erit tua dicere facta!* 52–54). The rejoicing of all things (*laetentur ut omnia*), including the speaker's own wish to celebrate, looks back to the phrase *omnis feret omnia tellus,* which leads into the sheep as emblems of aesthetic production. The desire to praise the future deeds of the child thus derives from the same responsive sympathy as do the metamorphosing sheep. Epideixis, or the rhetoric of praise, is here symbolized by the ovine *colores* (a symbolism distinct from the meaning of *colores* in Roman rhetoric, discussed below). Thus, even as the eclogue provides a naturalizing discourse for political

---

44. Rosenmeyer (1969, 214–17) notes that the golden age topos, replete with the *adunata* of "animal skins that come in technicolor hues," honey from oaks, and the lion bedding down with the lamb, becomes a feature of the pastoral tradition only with the fourth eclogue. Vergil's sheep have often been considered a breach of aesthetic decorum.

relations, it playfully dramatizes the status of this golden age vision and its ideological claims as an aesthetic product.

We might push this reading further and suggest that the potential for the aesthetic to manufacture consent, to elicit the voluntary acceptance of contingent social formations as natural, is perhaps self-reflexively represented by this figure of Vergil's famously "indecorous" sheep. For the *aries* spontaneously changing the color of his coat presents in a kind of hybrid form the image of a citizen, needing no intervention from the law above, conflated with art as a means of persuasion. This veiled reference to the operations of ideology becomes clear when we consider two other distinct connotations of the ram's *colores*. On the one hand, the activity of dyeing to produce colorful hues is associated, in the literature of late Republican Rome, with an extensive poetic discourse of sin, deceit, and corruption (see Putnam 1970, 153–55; Barker 1996, 445–46). Here, in the golden age, the wool will not have to be taught "to deceive," or falsely represent, various colors (*nec varios discet mentiri lana colores*). Sheep changing their own color, as a replacement for the maritime trade that once brought in the expensive dyes, thus implies a liberation from the trafficking and economic exploitation that led to moral decline. In this respect, sheep qua citizens are choosing, autonomously (*sua sponte*), to live in a way that is virtuous and free of sin. On the other hand, the *colores* also connote the figurative embellishments and excesses of Roman rhetoric (Arnold 1994, 149). Even more specifically, as one commentator remarks about the use of *color* in Quintilian, it is the technical term for "the particular aspect given to a case by skilful manipulation of the facts"—the gloss or varnish that may even alter the truth (Peterson 1891, on Quint. *Inst.* 10.1.116.). Hence, in the fourth eclogue the *colores* ironically suggest the aesthetic means by which spontaneous good conduct and the acceptance of the child as king are encouraged. That is, the various *colores* imply Vergil's own pastoral art, with all its rhetorical figuration, as it provides the naturalizing discourse that brings the freely choosing citizen into alignment with the governance of the single man. However, such authoritarian rule is only a vision, intimated rather than spelled out by the celebration of the child in conjunction with the return to a golden age.

Given the probable date of the fourth eclogue's initial composition, this poem should not be read as a conscious endorsement of Octavian and what later became the Augustan regime: in 40 B.C.E., Antony was the man of the moment (Clausen 1994, 125).[45] But the *Eclogues* were no doubt continuously modified with both additions and deletions until the moment of their

---

45. Du Quesnay (1977, 38) remarks that many of Vergil's Epicurean friends from Philodemus's community at Naples fought on the Republican side at Philippi and, after their defeat, turned to Antony rather than to Octavian.

publication in 35 B.C.E. As Wendell Clausen suggests, this process—particularly changes made after relations between Antony and Octavian deteriorated—may well have produced some of the mysterious allusiveness of the fourth eclogue (see Clausen 1994, 125–26; 1982, 315–17). The fanciful sheep may have been added later and may be commenting ironically on the extremity of the poem's hopeful vision as Vergil initially composed it.[46] One way in which the eclogues function to legitimize or naturalize political structures is through the very *absence* of overtly specific and identifiably consistent contemporary references: thus, though Antony may hover behind the original epithalamium of *Eclogue 4*, with his offspring the recipient of the implied basilikon, it is Octavian whom many perceive as the *deus* of *Eclogue* 1. And because neither figure is named outright, the poems can represent a political structure—in this case the phenomenon of "Caesarism" or the charismatic single leader—headed now by one, now by another individual. That the topos of the new *saeculum* or "age" inaugurated by a single "ruler" was originally associated with Julius Caesar (see Du Quesnay 1977, 61) underscores the vanity of seeking allegorical precision. Rather, we should note that the basilikon of *Eclogue* 4 and the sacrificial practice of Hellenistic ruler cult in *Eclogue* 1 are both embedded, in different ways, in a Roman discourse of benefaction and assimilated to a pastoral context.

The backdrop to this assimilation is, of course, the redistribution of land to the various veterans supporting these powerful military figures; and whereas the first eclogue unflinchingly confronts, if only to resolve temporarily, the painful and inequitable practice of expropriation from the land, the fourth treats the issue indirectly but no less ideologically. As we noted earlier, pastoral abundance has resonances both generally with responsive gratitude and specifically with the "initial" gift in a patronal exchange. And so, if land grants were one means of securing loyalty to the Caesarians' program, particularly the loyalty of veteran soldiers (as well as of poets), then a topos of a natural economy of spontaneous surplus would serve to gloss over and mystify the material reality of confiscations that made many of those grants possible.[47] Moreover, we know that Vergil's

---

46. See Hubbard 1995, 6, for this reading. If these lines were added later, I would tentatively suggest yet one more connotation of the changing *colores:* in 35 B.C.E., Octavian had superseded Antony as the man of the day, and Vergil may well be referring to a shift—and possibly his own—of political sympathy, a necessary (perhaps voluntary) reorientation of his own allegiances.

47. See n. 9 above for specific facts on land confiscation. To be sure, the collection as a whole starkly acknowledges the effects of expropriation. Nonetheless, in the fourth eclogue, human authority is entirely sanctioned by nature in a dialogic interaction: the spontaneous flowers that spill into the cradle at the poem's beginning suggest the same interactive endorsement as the image at the end (so ambiguously reflective of this dialogue) of the child recognizing—either with his own or by her smile—his mother's face. As a powerful semiotic

eclogues were performed and are likely to have circulated individually be-
fore being collected and "published" as a single volume in 35 B.C.E. If so,
the circulation of the fourth eclogue may well have produced an effect
similar to the numismatic iconography of the late 40s: after the resettle-
ment of veteran soldiers who fought in the siege of Perusia, Octavian issued
a coin that figured his image as *divi filius* (son of a god) on the obverse
and Fortuna with rudder and *cornucopiae* on the reverse (Galinsky 1996,
114). Though employed on coins long before Vergil's and subsequent de-
pictions of the golden age, the *cornucopia*, in the context of the expropri-
ations, constitutes an ideological distortion of contemporary issues, com-
municating the pleasures of the newly endowed rather than the grievances
of the freshly dispossessed.

The manipulation of property law that such confiscations entailed may
have prompted two of the most striking features in Vergil's later versions
of the golden age: the lack of laws and the absence of private property.[48]
To be sure, such defining absences were always implicit in the Greek tra-
dition of the topos, whether the perverted and antisocial "paradise" of the
Cyclops in Homer (see E. Cook 1995, 98–99) or the prototypical account
of Hesiod. The anxiety connected with justice, inheritance, and the be-
queathing of property that motivates the speaker of the *Works and Days*,
toiling to make ends meet in the fallen age of iron, implicitly assumes a
golden age free of such concerns. And the Cynic and Pythagorean cry "back
to the golden age," with its rejection of the structures and institutions of
the polis, certainly voices a critique of private property (Detienne 1979,
60–66). Nonetheless, that Vergil brought these implicit features to the fore,
proclaiming the imminent return of an age in which laws and property
divisions are unnecessary, fits his particular, late Republican or triumviral
context. On one level, the prophecy constitutes a utopian fantasy born of
a sincere desire to be free of the effects of civic turmoil; but such a vision
also weakens, or at least casts in a different light, any criminality in the
confiscation of land. Expropriation may be necessary to bring about a social
order in which prosperity will be had by all.

This necessity is intimated, albeit in a distorted fashion (there is no
outright reference to land confiscation), in the fourth eclogue: traces of
sin (*sceleris vestigia*, 13) will become inactive under Pollio's consulship yet

---

emblem of "nature," the image of maternity here contributes to the overall effect of pastoral
as mystifying the real facts of dispossession that surface in the first and ninth eclogues.

48. For discussion of these attributes of the golden age in particular, see Wallace-Hadrill
1982, 22–28. Gatz (1967, 229) notes that the absence of private property is a Roman inno-
vation. Keppie (1983, 59–66) cites the agreement at Bononia backed by the *lex Titia* as the
authority by which Octavian and Antony carried out the confiscations that enabled resettle-
ment of the veterans who fought at Philippi.

remain to initiate a second cycle of civilization preceding the final return of the golden age; in this postlapsarian state, the girding of towns with walls and the cutting of furrows in the land suggest the divisions of private property.[49] Thus it is property itself, rather than its seizure and expropriation, that constitutes a crime. Precisely that point is made in the description of Saturn's kingdom in the *Georgics:* "Before Jove there were no farmers turning over the soil; it was not lawful even to mark or divide the field with a boundary."[50] The motif that the land belongs to all thus underplays the deprivations suffered by those who are individually dispossessed.

Alternatively, from the perspective of the recipient, the topos of communal ownership is paradoxically reassuring. A gift of property may never adequately ensure ownership, for the benefactor may never loosen his hold over the recipient.[51] But to anticipate a return to an era of plenty, in which the earth's spontaneous profusions are enjoyed by all, shifts the focus from any uncertainty about ownership and sense of constraint felt by the recipient to an ideology of disinterested voluntarism on the part of the benefactor. Once again, we see such attitudes, reminiscent of the language of Roman social relations, in the first book of the *Georgics:* "people would acquire things for common use, and the earth gave all things more freely then when no one was asking" (1.127–28).[52]

Karl Galinsky has recently stressed the uniqueness of the golden age vision in the fourth eclogue, claiming that its view of an age of indolence, in which nature provides spontaneously and no human effort is required, is replaced in subsequent versions by the conditional dependence on human labor. He points out that the description of the age of Saturn in the *Georgics,* quoted above, is a world to which Jove introduces *labor* as a means of inciting civilization. The hard-earned profits and pleasures of the farmer, the fruits of toil, constitute the real golden age. A similar conditionality is present, he argues, in the plastic arts, where images of agricultural fertil-

---

49. Verg. *Ecl.* 4.31–33: *pauca tamen suberunt priscae vestigia fraudis, / quae temptare Thetim ratibus, quae cingere muris / oppida, quae iubeant telluri infindere sulcos.*

50. Verg. *Geo.* 1.125–28: *ante Iovem nulli subigebant arva coloni: / ne signare quidem aut partiri limite campum / fas erat; in medium quaerebant, ipsaque tellus / omnia liberius nullo poscente ferebat.* Comparing these lines to other passages in Vergil in which Saturn (the ruler of the Golden Age *ante Iovem*) is the original legislator (*Aen.* 8.321–32), and toil and hard work characterize the true Italian "golden age" (*Geo.* 2.532–40), Wallace-Hadrill (1982, 23–24) relates these "internal incoherences" in the accounts to "embarrassment" over "the security of property, the unequal hierarchy of rank and the strict legislative structure which the Augustan regime in fact ensured" at a later date.

51. For Augustus's wish to maintain a close "patronal" relationship with his veterans, see Keppie 1983, 114–22.

52. As Sen. *Ben.* 2.2.1 repeatedly stresses, the best benefaction is the one that is not explicitly sought: *Molestum verbum est, onerosum, demisso vultu dicendum, rogo,* and *properet licet, sero beneficium dedit, qui roganti dedit.*

ity—often *cornucopiae*—are closely juxtaposed with those of Roman arms. Peace and prosperity depend on Roman military might. The evidence suggests, he concludes, that "there was no attempt to obscure, through a plethora of blissful images, the realities of the age" (Galinsky 1996, 118).

I would qualify these claims: images of pastoral abundance may not have obscured the realities of the age, but they certainly constituted an element of an ideological discourse that rendered the presence of militarism necessary and even natural. The coexistence of these seemingly antithetical images—military arms and fruitful fields—encourages a belief in their codependence, an idea that goes back to the early Roman concept of the citizen as both farmer and soldier. And just as these images were ideologically linked in the plastic arts of the Principate, so we have seen that Vergil's novel use of literary pastoral provides, if not an easy justification for, at least a way of understanding land confiscations and the resettlement of veterans in the late forties. David Halperin's comments on the attributes particular to pastoral as a genre also suggest that it is especially suited to the work of ideology: "A kind of contrast . . . intimate to pastoral's manner of representation is that between a confused or conflict-ridden reality and the artistic depiction of it as comprehensible, meaningful, or harmonious" (1983, 68). Rather than elide dark realities, Vergil's daring reshaping of Theocritean pastoral builds the dissonance between the confusions of history and the harmonies of art into the very structure of many of the eclogues. Vergilian pastoral "manages" contradictions through imaginary resolutions even as it calls attention to, and comments on, their imaginary status.[53] In this respect, the social and economic conflicts that ideology resolves or negotiates lend themselves to pastoral.

So far we have examined pastoral images only in terms of their capacity to endorse or at minimum render "meaningful" the contingent power relations of the triumviral period and the uneven distribution of resources that maintained that power. Viewed through Jameson's negative hermeneutic, the system of benefaction by which those resources (specifically land) were transmitted is naturalized by its assimilation to the pastoral landscape. Yet poetry cannot be reduced to a seamless articulation of ideology, for aesthetic texts are necessarily overdetermined by rhetorical excess; that is, they manifest certain elements of diction, formal structure, registers of imagery, and gaps or lacunae that contradict, reveal, or even resist the ideological distortions supporting the social formations of a particular period.

To some degree, this idea of subversion shares its origins and intellectual ground with the language and effects of deconstruction. For it is precisely

---

53. See Rose 1992, 36, for such management as a feature of all ideology, a process that Jameson's negative hermeneutic makes explicit.

the "excess" and play of the aesthetic realm (as symbolized by Vergil's excessive sheep) that make it possible to deconstruct, and hence subvert, the terms that constitute a particular ideological discourse. In other words, in poststructural theory, aesthetic play refers to the effect of language as an overdetermined (and hence unstable) system of signification. Aesthetic excess is embedded in the consistently rhetorical nature of language, where linguistic signs ultimately receive value only from the deferred presence of other signs whose "supplementary" function both "defers" and potentially undermines (differs from) the initial meaning.[54] As Geoffrey Hartman comments, "Literature destabilizes, by overdetermination or indeterminacy— by what seems to be an excess (figurality) or a defect (equivocation)—the 'real character' of communication" (1978, viii).[55] Those who practice deconstruction tend to find in the free play of signification a text so "undecidable" and "decentered" that political implications become moot, but a positive hermeneutic could use a deconstructive tactic to illuminate ways in which aesthetic play provides resistance to hegemonic discourses.

When Horace invokes either a pastoral or a golden age motif as ways of figuring his relationship to his estate, these generic allusions introduce a certain rhetorical instability to his poems: this figural excess, I believe, is connected both to the aesthetic connotations of pastoral as a genre in general and to the historical moment of Vergil's *Eclogues* in particular. As in Vergil, the estate gives rise to an economy of *otium,* in which land is valued for its aesthetic returns and the socioeconomic context of patronage may be comfortably assimilated to pastoral conventions. On the one hand, these Horatian poems conform to an ideal vision of benefaction and demonstrate Bourdieu's notion of the misrecognition of the economics behind gift exchange; on the other, they simultaneously reveal how the farm, as a site of pastoral aestheticism and hermeneutic multivalency, provides the rhetorical strategies by which the speaker resists ideas of debt, constraint, and potential deprivation paradoxically associated with the estate as a gift.

THE MAN PROTESTETH TOO MUCH: *SATIRES* 2.6

The multivalency implicit in the golden age representations of the farm appears most prominently in *Odes* 1.17, but the libidinal excess associated with the estate as a gift informs the opening of *Satires* 2.6.[56] In this pious

54. Derrida's (1978) concepts of "play" and "supplementation" contribute to "undecidability" when, in de Man's (1979a) analysis of the rhetoric of literature, its "performative" aspect works against its "constative" aspect, or what it states.

55. See also Preminger and Brogan 1993, s.v. "deconstruction."

56. Such excess value is apparent not only in the concept of *gratia,* but also in the "goodwill" or *voluntas* of the benefactor. Cf. Sen. *Ben.* 1.5.2–3: "There is a great difference

thanksgiving for the bounty of the gods, the speaker claims that fortune has blessed him with more than the modest plot of land and little bit of wood that had been his wish:

> Hoc erat in votis: modus agri non ita magnus,
> hortus ubi et tecti vicinus iugis aquae fons
> et paulum silvae super his foret. auctius atque
> di melius fecere. bene est. nil amplius oro,
> Maia nate, nisi ut propria haec mihi munera faxis.   5
> si neque maiorem feci ratione mala rem
> nec sum facturus vitio culpave minorem,
> si veneror stultus nihil horum, 'o si angulus ille
> proximus accedat qui nunc denormat agellum!
> o si urnam argenti fors quae mihi monstret, ut illi,   10
> thesauro invento qui mercennarius agrum
> illum ipsum mercatus aravit, dives amico
> Hercule!', si quod adest gratum iuvat, hac prece te oro:
> pingue pecus domino facias et cetera praeter
> ingenium utque soles, custos mihi maximus adsis.   15

This was in my prayers: a measure of land not so large, with a garden and near the house a spring of pure water and above this [in addition] a little patch of woods. The gods have given me more and better. It is good. I ask for nothing more, son of Maia, except that you make these gifts lasting [truly mine]. If I neither make my property greater by crooked calculation, nor have diminished it through the vice of waste, if foolishly I pray for none of these things: "Oh, if that nearby corner could be added, which now skews my farm's shape! Oh, if lucky chance would reveal to me a pot of money, as it did for him, who once the trea- sure was found plowed the same field as an owner which he had as a hired laborer, made wealthy by his friend Hercules!" If what is here now pleases me, grateful for it, with this prayer I ask: fatten the master's flock and all else but his talent, and, as you are accustomed, always be my greatest guardian! (2.6.1–15)

For all that this satire continues to furnish commentators with a rich source of biographical knowledge about the poet, savvy readers have been careful to acknowledge Horace's conscious manipulation of a humble persona.[57] Horatian satire, particularly in the second book, performs a defensive func-

---

between the matter of a benefit and the benefit itself: and so it is neither gold nor silver nor any of the gifts which are held to be most valuable that constitutes a benefit, but merely the goodwill of him who bestows it. . . . But a benefit endures even after that through which it was manifested has been lost."

57. Lyne (1995, 17–20) emphasizes Horace's "image-management" because of his self-consciousness over earlier Republican sympathies.

tion: it protects the author from charges of crass ambition and, as one critic has recently suggested, "at once manages and exposes the anxieties attending . . . [the poet's] social ascent" (Oliensis 1997, 90). Having acquired an estate in the country, seven years after his initial acquaintance with Maecenas, the poet takes pains to deflect and deflate any perception that the farm constitutes payment in a quid pro quo exchange of goods for poetic services. Such deflection employs many strategies and can be discerned in both the diction and the events that Horace either includes in or omits from his description.[58]

Traditionally this poem has been understood as a kind of "thank-you letter" to Maecenas for the grant of the Sabine farm. Those who object to this view claim that nowhere is Maecenas actually addressed; nor does the speaker explicitly claim that he has been given something (Bradshaw 1989, 161). However, the use of the euphemism "gods" to refer to those in power, particularly in their capacity to dispense favors and the benefactions of land, appears later in the satire itself, in reference to the settlement of soldiers in Sicily after the battle of Actium. We have also seen this euphemism employed as the "exaggeration" of the grateful rustic, Tityrus, in the first eclogue. As noted there, such deifying language is common in acknowledging one's benefactor, following the rhetorical convention of the *eucharistikon* or "speech of gratitude," and it is in keeping with Seneca's claim that "those who make benefactions resemble the gods" (*qui dat beneficia deos imitatur, Ben.* 3.15.4).[59] And yet, though this poem does express *gratia* to Maecenas as well as the regime in general, the opening displays a tension between the dramatic enactment of the conventions of an ideal discourse of benefaction and a rhetorical resistance to benefaction's more negative realities. Thus, despite the attempt to represent his relationship with Maecenas as conforming to an ideology of voluntarism, the rhetoric reveals the speaker's anxiety that his newly acquired gift translates too easily into the connotative values of both debt and compensation.

On the one hand, the speaker repeatedly and in various guises emphasizes a discrepancy between his own wishes and the more fulsome resources of his implied benefactors. Whether in the restrained diminution of *non ita magnus* (not so large) and *paulum* (a little), or the humorous wish for the simple fare of beans, the kinsmen of Pythagoras (*faba cognata Pythagorae,* 63), or, finally, the fable of the country mouse and city mouse, the author's autobiographical persona consistently identifies with images of modest needs. Indeed, the primary meaning of *modus* in this passage, "quantity" or

58. See now Oliensis 1998, 46–51. Though I have profited much from Oliensis's discussion of this poem and the *Satires* in general, I had essentially completed my manuscript before the publication of her book.

59. See Du Quesnay 1981, 102 and passim for Tityrus's *eucharistikon.*

"measure," yields easily to a secondary sense of "limit" or "boundary," a sense that underscores the word's etymological relationship to "modest."[60] What Horace stresses in his opening words of solemn gratitude is that the gods' beneficence has gone beyond the limit of his prayers (*auctius atque / di melius fecere*).

Such a claim—that the gift exceeds the expectation or wish of the recipient—suggests a certain voluntarism on the part of the giver: the excess implies that the speaker may not be able to requite the benefaction and thus that it was made without a calculated interest in recompense. It brings to mind Cicero's advice that benefactions are more honorably made to men of good conduct than to those of fortune, for "the needy person, if he is also a good man, may indeed be unable to requite his gratitude, but he can certainly have it." And Cicero goes on to describe the poor man who has received a gift: "If, however, you do anything for a poor man, he thinks that you are observing not his fortune, but himself" (*Off.* 2.69–70).[61] Indeed, the speaker's willing identification with humble needs, his open display of appreciation, and his desire to maintain a virtuous restraint concerning his property all present an ideal vision of benefaction in which neither giver nor receiver looks to profit in a self-interested way. This matches Vergil's description of the golden age in the *Georgics:* "the earth gave more freely then, when no one was demanding it." The deifying language displays the same libidinal excess as a function of gratitude, as do the comparative adverbs (*auctius, melius*) in regard to the gods' "more liberal" beneficence. Such a portrait of benefaction flatters the giver and thus expresses *gratia* as a dedicatory inscription might; but because Maecenas is not explicitly mentioned, the expression of gratitude is not immediately implicated in a quid pro quo reciprocity.

However, if we look more closely at the dense rhetoric of wish and gratitude here, we see fissures in this posture of humble desires rewarded. The opening seems to invite a deconstructionist reading: whereas some commentators understand *paulum silvae super his* as referring to the spatial location of the woods over the poet's land, others take it to mean "in addition to," "over and above," "in excess of" the land with its garden, spring, and house (Brind'Amour 1972). The semantic ambivalence of the preposition

---

60. Given the reference to resettlement of veterans later in the satire, it is significant that *modus* is the term used for the plots of land distributed to soldiers as well as for the yield of a plot of land.

61. Although the literature on benefaction condemns giving in order to profit from a return, there is nonetheless an explicit form of calculation in the benefactor's assessment of the merits of the beneficiary. The gift should be appropriate to the standing and need of the recipient: see Cic. *Off.* 1.45, 2.61–3, 2.69–71. Hence, from the perspective of "ideal benefaction," to surpass such decorous matching of gift to receiver would further display the good will—voluntarism—of the giver.

super suggests the subversion of the poet's modest wish—his "measure of land not so large." And the poem immediately provides more evidence that can support an interpretation relying on linguistic ambiguity. To begin with, Horace claims that he asks for nothing more, except that Mercury should make the poet's gifts enduring or *propria*. Again, scholars have interpreted this to mean that Horace does not ask for a quantitative increase in what he now has, but only that he may continue to enjoy his fortune (*nisi ut propria haec mihi munera faxis,* 5). The following two lines (6–7) would seem to confirm the poet's desire that the quantity of gifts remain the same. But Horace then goes on to give two examples of what he should not ask—foolish requests whose avoidance becomes the condition for the poet's license to make a reasonable prayer to Mercury. One of these requests is for money that, when found, allowed a mercenary farmer to buy and own the land that he previously tilled for hire. Horace has rather conspicuously failed to explain why this would be a foolish wish, but Porphyry fills us in: Mercury had wryly commented that such a man could never be happy because he performed precisely the same labor on his land after he bought it as he had before. Horace does not include this "moral" to the story, however, and from the perspective of symbolic capital or the markers of status in the Roman world, ownership would be far more desirable than merely working for hire.[62] Without the moral, the wish appears not so unreasonable.

Indeed, since the substance of this "foolish request" involves the question of ownership, it causes the previous wish that Mercury make enduring (*propria*) the poet's gifts to take on an ironic resonance: *propria*, of course, could refer to the poet's full ownership and possession of his gifts as easily as it could mean "constant" or enduring. To be sure, *propria* occurs here in a formal prayer, a context that encourages the sense of *perpetuus* or "enduring."[63] Yet it is also partly through the negative exemplum of the foolish request that *propria* has been interpreted as meaning "enduring" and not "one's own" in line 5: the desire for full ownership provides one term of the binary opposition that defines *propria* as the other term—enduring use. However, the actual semantic ambiguity of the word suggests that the speaker's overt wish is, at some level, haunted by the foolish wish that he should not make and whose avoidance becomes the condition for

62. Thus Cicero (*Off.* 1.150) writes, "Again, all those workers who are paid for their labour (*mercennariorum*) and not for their skill have servile and demeaning employment; for in their case the very wage is a contract to servitude" (trans. M. Atkins from the edition by M. T. Griffin and E. M. Atkins [1991]). K. White (1970, 348) provides grim details concerning the unprotected position of the hired laborer in times of sickness or when weather interferes with his work. He is, in many respects, inferior to a slave.

63. See Kiessling and Heinze 1961b, ad loc., who quote from Val. Max. 4.1.10: '*satis bonae et magnae sunt: itaque precor ut eas perpetuo incolumes servent.*' On *propria*, see *OLD*, s.v., 1, 2.

his prayer of line 13. One might say that as a "forbidden wish" the desire to own can only be expressed negatively and distortedly.[64] Both requests— the permissible wish that the gifts be enduring and the taboo wish based on the example of the *mercennarius* (hired laborer)—are bound together as a series of convoluted rhetorical contingencies. Like the man who buys the property he tills, Horace covertly desires his property to be his very own.

Given the historical background of land expropriations at this time, the poem's own mention of the resettlement of veterans (2.6.55–56), and Horace's own probable background (losing his family estate in the earlier dispossessions after Philippi and gaining an estate that may have been seized from another owner), the wish to own securely would hardly be unexpected (see *Ep.* 2.2.49–52). But the ease with which the victors at Actium both seized and gave away property would only prove the futility of the idea of secure ownership: continuous use would be all that one could really hope for. Ofellus, the peasant-philosopher of *Satires* 2.2, provides an ironic example: he had previously been a landowner, but he now works as a tenant farmer on the same plot, now measured off for another (*metato in agello . . . mercede colonum*, 114). Having most likely lost his land in the expropriations after Philippi, Ofellus is a man who "continues to use" his land even as, in an inversion of the forbidden wish in 2.6, he has moved down the ladder from one who owns (or "has bought")—*mercatus*—to one who tills for hire, *mercennarius*.[65] As Ofellus muses, the turmoil of the civil wars only underscores the degree to which ownership and private property are "cultural" constructions: "now the land is deeded to Umbrenus, recently it belonged to Ofellus; it will belong to no one absolutely, but passes, now to me now to another, for use" (*nunc ager Umbreni sub nomine, nuper Ofelli / dictus, erit nulli proprius, sed cedit in usum / nunc mihi, nunc alii*, 133–35). As an emblem of diminished status, Ofellus serves as a mirror image showing the reverse of Horace's upward mobility. Yet even though not owning reflects a lowered

---

64. Such contradictory wishes resemble Freudian compromise formations, the distorted and compromised ways in which covert and forbidden desires make themselves known. The use of the term *mercennarius*, as the person with whom Horace negatively identifies, strikes me as similarly overdetermined: in addition to a hired farm laborer—the overt meaning in the context of Horace's negative exemplum—*mercennarius* of course can refer to the "hired" mercenary soldier, a figure whom the satire's later reference to land allotments for the veterans of Actium might very well bring to mind, even if Octavian's soldiers did not strictly fall into such a category.

65. While *colonus*, or "tenant," is generally distinguished from *mercennarius*, or "wage laborer," for purposes of translation, Foxhall (1990, 97) reminds us that tenants cannot be clearly "separated from other labourers: debt bondsmen, slaves, 'serfs,' wage labourers and even 'independent' peasants may also have been entangled in some kind of tenancy relationship."

status, the idea of ownership has become, in many ways, an empty concept indistinguishable from use.[66] Horace's new status as the beneficiary of an estate is fragile, and the contortions of his prayers reflect his uncertainty.

The darker implications of Horace's good fortune may similarly be revealed in the allusion of the phrase *di melius fecere* to the first eclogue and Tityrus's statement *deus nobis haec otia fecit* (the gods are responsible for this leisure, 6). Just as Tityrus's own blessings are inextricably bound up with Meliboeus's losses, both within the poetic counterpoint of the text and within its historical context, so Horace's allusion here evokes the dispossessed farmer as an implied presence. Moreover, Tityrus's status as a slave who regains the continued use of his land rather than the explicit purchase of his freedom may be hinted at in the figure of the hired laborer. The wish to buy land may be no more practical than Tityrus's desire to buy his liberty. In both poems benefaction, rather than acquisition through purchase, is the economic system that secures results, and the giver appears to maintain his hold on, thereby exercising control through, his gifts.

From another perspective, when we consider that it is the *wish* of the hired laborer, his desire to own, and not his identity that the speaker of the satire claims to disavow, then the opposition between gift and contract begins to break down. We might read this, again, as the poet's anxiety surfacing in an analogy that he invokes simply to repudiate—his fear that his acceptance of the estate draws him symbolically near to the role of the *mercennarius*, the hired laborer. Mercury is in fact the god of commerce, of exchange; and as Eduard Fraenkel observed, the language of the first line of *Satires* 2.6, *hoc erat in votis* (this was in my prayers) recalls the formula of prayer, "as if the poet were saying *hoc modo nunc voti compos factus* (or *damnatus*) *sum* [having acquired my wish, now I am bound by my vow]" (1957, 138). Such language suggests that the speaker, *voti damnatus* by the grant of the estate, is in the very condition of obligation that provided, according to Marcel Mauss's early speculations, the origin of a contract, of *nexum* and *actio*: "The mere fact of *having the thing* puts the *accipiens* in an uncertain state of quasi-culpability (*damnatus, nexus, aere obaeratus*), of spiritual inferiority and moral inequality . . . in relation to the one delivering (*tradens*) the contract" (1990 [1950], 52). Though the development of a market economy eventually disembedded such transactions, the system of benefaction retained the traces of moral obligation and commitment that characterize gift exchange and the origins of contract. As Mauss speculates regarding *mancipatio*, the "thing handed over continues, in part and for a time, to belong to the 'family' of the original owner. It remains bound to

---

66. Augustus later passed much legislation to make property ownership more secure. See Nicolet 1984.

him, and binds its present possessor until the latter is freed by the execution of the contract, namely by the compensatory handing over of the thing, price, or service that, in turn, will bind the initial contracting party" (50). When Horace announces in *Epistles* 1.1.19 that he "is attempting to subordinate things to himself rather than himself to things" (*mihi res non me rebus subiungere conor*), he suggests that very sense of "being bound" or *nexus* by the possession of property—*res*—that lies at the origin of Roman notions of contract.[67] Indeed, just as we may recognize the diction of gifts in such "contract" words as *tradere, reddere,* and *vendere,* all of which retain the root verb *do, dare,* so the term *munera,* or *munus* in its singular form, by which the speaker refers to the "gifts" of Mercury, derives from the root **mei,* or "exchange." In keeping with such etymological roots, *munus,* understood as "political office," requires expenditure on *munera* as spectacles and games (Benveniste 1973, 79–80). *Munus,* as "a gift carrying the obligation of an exchange," therefore draws together a series of discursive strands in the Horatian *corpus* and the exchanges they imply: the gift of the estate, the public office of *sacerdos,* and the sacrificial expenditures which that office required.

Perhaps because of these implications of the estate as "gift," the rhetoric and diction of both the poet's gratitude and his denial of any desire for more appear to undo the overt meaning of his statement. On one level, the poet *does* wish to have a form of ownership over the farm, to make it "his own," and thus he does wish for *more*—more than simply to have use of the estate for the rest of his life.[68] *Res,* or property, in the form of *munera,* or gifts, and the future implications and obligations that these transactions signify for the poet create an ambiguity or contradiction in the poet's stance of humble gratitude. The implicit contract that accompanies *munera* belies the ideology of voluntarism even as it reveals *gratia* as a form of obligatory debt to be paid in time. This "debt of gratitude" partially accounts for the covert wish to own the farm outright, and anxiety over such debt may be found in yet one more connotation of *munera propria*—as gifts "suitable" or appropriate to Horace's modest nature, and thus not obliging him unduly.[69] In contrast, the advantage of outright ownership lies in the complete absence of any obligation—the independence guaranteed by the

67. Commentators or translators generally read *res* here as referring to external circumstances, but Treggiari (1979, 53) reminds us that the word also suggests property. For the language of binding in relation to benefaction in Cicero's correspondence, see chapter 1, n. 45, and the corresponding text.

68. Jonathan Swift's rendition of the opening of *Satires* 2.6 (possibly modified by Alexander Pope) would imply a similar covert wish, one that his version in fact brings to the fore.

69. I am grateful to one of the anonymous readers for the University of California Press for this point.

commodity. And related to such independence is the freedom—a relative one, to be sure—from fear about the capricious whims of authority, the fear that the one who gives may just as easily take away.

The *Epistles* and *Odes* provide further evidence for this complex of ideas. *Epistles* 1.16, the letter to Quinctius, begins with an extended description of the topography of the Sabine farm and ends with a scene adapted from the *Bacchae,* in which Pentheus threatens to strip the "good man" of all his belongings. However, since virtue is an internal *bonum* (good), the removal of external *bona* has no effect on the integrity of Dionysus—the "man" enslaved by Pentheus. And when Pentheus threatens to throw Dionysus in chains, the prisoner calmly and ironically replies that the god will free him when he wishes. Horace's interpretation of this line to mean "I will die" presents death as the only absolute liberty available in the face of absolute power.[70] Read in conjunction with the references to Jove at the end of *Epistles* 1.18 and 1.19, this image of Dionysus stripped of his goods suggests more than the poet's characteristic concern with independence of will and thought, for it must be set against the autobiographical image of the author, literally self-present with his farm, at the beginning of *Epistles* 1.16. As a material good the farm is an external *bonum* and thus subject to the same caprices of power as are Dionysus's belongings. A similar, though by no means so sinister, image of arbitrary power appears at the end of *Epistles* 1.18. That poem, an explicit meditation on the institution of *amicitia,* ends with a cameo of the poet, accepting his vulnerability to the whims of Jove but maintaining equanimity for himself.[71] While this reference to Jove may simply denote the gods, the allusion to the "ears of Jove" by an angry would-be poet in *Epistles* 1.19.43 suggests that the Olympian god in *Epistles* 1.18 may also connote Augustus. Moreover, the identification of the politically powerful with the gods is a trope of the literature of this period, registering in colloquial slang the awareness of the concentration of power in the hands of a few (Reckford 1959, 196). In *Satires* 2.6, as discussed in the introduction, Horace presents himself as constantly hassled in the streets by those who perceive him as "closer to the gods" and hence more privy to the state's handling of the pressing affairs of the moment:[72] here, the passerby asks whether Horace knows of a possible invasion by Dacians, or the use of Sicilian land for the resettlement of veterans—pointing again to the

70. For discussion of the end of this epistle, see Johnson 1993, 45–46; Bowditch 1996, 474–75.

71. Hor. *Ep.* 1.18.111–12: *sed satis est orare Iovem qui ponit et aufert, / det vitam, det opes: aequum mi animum ipse parabo.*

72. Hor. *Sat.* 2.6.51–56: *'o bone, nam te / scire, deos quoniam propius contingis, oportet, / numquid de Dacis audisti? . . . quid? militibus promissa Triquetra / praedia Caesar an est Itala tellure daturus?'*

practice of expropriation. By the time of the *Epistles,* of course, it is unlikely either that Horace will give back or that Augustus, as the supreme authority, will take away, but the consciousness that the latter *could* exercise his power over Horace, should he wish to, appears in the sequence of the final lines of *Epistles* 1.16, 1.18, and 1.19.

A similar awareness of the caprices of material fortune, if not explicitly the whims of authority, appears in *Odes* 3.29. Here, the speaker's invitation to Maecenas to join him at his Sabine estate evolves into a meditation on the vicissitudes of time, whose unpredictability the poet likens to the Tiber—at one moment flowing calmly, at another gathering up and "whirling together smoothed stones and uprooted trunks and livestock and houses" (*nunc lapides adesos / stirpesque raptas et pecus et domos / volventis una,* 36–38). As at the end of *Epistles* 1.16, where Pentheus threatens to remove the disguised Dionysus's property—his livestock, money, couches, and silver (*pecus, rem, lectos, argentum,* 1.16.75)—so the metaphor of a river's raging dispossessions in *Odes* 3.29 ironically responds to the poem's earlier evocation of the Sabine estate in specifically pastoral terms. Though the farm is not mentioned explicitly, the speaker has invited Maecenas into the country for respite at the hottest time of the year, when "the weary shepherd with his sluggish flock seeks the shade and stream and thickets of rough Silvanus, and the silent bank is untouched by the wandering breeze" (*iam pastor umbras cum grege languido / rivumque fessus quaerit et horridi / dumeta Silvani, caretque / ripa vagis taciturna ventis,* 3.29.21–24). Surely the marker of the estate here, as a pastoral retreat, should be read against the references to the river of time and the unpredictability of Fortune, who, "delighting in her cruel commerce . . . redistributes insecure rewards, generous now to [the poet], now to another" (*Fortuna saevo laeta negotio/ . . . transmutat incertos honores, / nunc mihi, nunc alii benigna,* 49–52): pastoral allusion in this context conjures up the fragile fortunes of Vergil's shepherds as it ambiguates the practice of benefaction; the gift of pastoral *otium* remains haunted by the cultural memory of the confiscations. And though we should resist glibly identifying Maecenas here with *Fortuna*—indeed, the statesman should beware her capricious ways as much as the speaker—we may nonetheless remark that the adjective *benigna,* or "generous," also appears in its nominal form in the first epode, where the poet directly acknowledges Maecenas as the source of his material well-being: "sufficiently and more has your generosity enriched me" (*satis superque me benignitas tua ditavit,* 1.31). Moreover, as I discuss in the next chapter, the gesture of renunciation that the speaker makes at the end of *Odes* 3.29—"I give up what she has given me, should Fortune shake her wings and fly away" (*si celeris quatit / pennas resigno quae dedit,* 53–54)—employs the very same diction as the poet's controversial claim in *Epistles* 1.7 that he would return everything (*cuncta resigno*) if constrained by benefactions.

Thus, as physical property, or *res,* the estate ironically signifies potential loss in two ways: as a material gift of the regime, the farm is a reminder of the arbitrary seizure of property by which many such dispensations were made and by which they could just as easily be revoked; in addition, as the opening to *Satires* 2.6 reveals, the farm symbolically expropriates the poet's person, laying claim to his labor by fulfilling his wish. Nonetheless, as I argue fully in chapter 5, Horace counters such potential loss by representing his estate as a *locus a-moenus,* a place that makes possible both the poetic fantasy of a plenitude of self and a resistance to the exchanges implied by gifts.

The aestheticizing of the farm involved in such a representation appears earlier in the Horatian *corpus,* in both *Satires* 2.6 and *Odes* 1.17. The satire presents the farm both as a place undergoing the transformation from real locale to textual space and as a pastoral refuge from the hazards of the city. When we consider again the phrase "this was what I sought in prayers" (*Hoc erat in votis,* 2.6.1), we may note that *hoc,* or "this," is what linguists call a shifter: it acquires meaning from its unique moment of utterance. Its meaning therefore shifts, depending on the context of utterance and on the speaking subject or "I" activating the particular speech. In Horace's satire, *hoc* does indeed refer to its own linguistic context insofar as it gestures forward to the description of what *had* been in the poet's wishes—the small plot of land, garden, spring of pure water, and patch of woods—a vision now exceeded by the present reality of the estate. But as a deictic (or "pointer") that is inherently unstable or empty, filled with meaning only through context, "this," as the commentator Edward Morris suggests, also points to the scene that Horace observes before him in the moment of writing (1939, ad loc.):[73] the poet has retreated to his "refuge in the hills" and now, as he gazes out over his land, asks "what sooner should I celebrate with my satiric and pedestrian Muse?" Poised on the very edge between the phenomenal reality before him and the conventions of description, Horace underscores his initial act of topographical representation with his use of the deliberately ambiguous *hoc* as well as with his rhetorical question. On the one hand, from the extratextual perspective of the physical property— "this" estate upon which the speaker gazes—the poet is bound: as noted above, *hoc erat in votis* implies *voti damnatus,* the state of obligation to the *deus* or, in the language of contract, to the "giver" (*tradens*). And yet, on the other hand, the poet's brief sketch of his dream farm initiates the topos of the Sabine property as an idealized landscape, a topos that will develop, in the *Odes* and the *Epistles,* into a *locus amoenus* that draws on a literary

73. See Benveniste 1971, 218–22, on shifters and deixis. Kiessling and Heinze (1961b, ad loc.) comment that the *hoc* refers to a unity composed of the discrete elements in the following description amassed into a whole.

typology. Just as the poet's desires shape the representation of the farm in
the first few lines, so his imagination of the country—as an escape from
urban *negotia* and the client's duties—associates it with the sleep (*somno*)
and leisure time (*inertibus horis*) of pastoral *otium* (60–62).

When we then consider the second prayer that Horace makes to *Maia
nate* in relation to the first, a relationship between the farm, language, and
independence (if not plenitude) begins to emerge. Horace's first wish is
that the farm be *proprius*—enduring—or, as I have suggested, in fact his
very own. The condition of his prayer, again, is the restraint and modesty
of his wishes, a limit that has already been exceeded by reality (and perhaps
undermined by the language of the wish itself). But if he is content with
what he has (13), Horace is then entitled to a second wish, and with this
he directly invokes Callimachean aesthetics and the *Aetia*: "fatten the mas-
ter's flock and all else but his talent, and, as you are accustomed, always be
my greatest guardian!" (*pingue pecus domino facias et cetera praeter / ingenium,
utque soles custos mihi maximus adsis,* 14–15). Only slightly altering the con-
ventional trope that distinguishes the fat flock from lean language, this
particular gesture of Alexandrian affiliation calls up Vergilian pastoral and
specifically the intervention of Apollo at the beginning of *Eclogue* 6: "Tity-
rus, a shepherd should feed and fatten his sheep, but sing a finespun song"
(*pastorem, Tityre, pinguis / pascere oportet ovis, deductum dicere carmen,* 6.4–5).
Apollo's advice, coming after the speaker claims he was about to sing of
reges et proelia (kings and battles), equates, if provisionally, the *Eclogue* poet
with the figure of Tityrus. We are thus led back, through a web of allusions,
to the first eclogue and its identification of land with *otium* and the con-
version of such leisure, in turn, into song. Such intertextuality suggests that
one way in which the speaker makes the farm his own—*proprius*—is to
convert it into a pastoral locale that has affinities with a particular literary
tradition. Horace aesthetically appropriates the farm for himself—exercis-
ing over it the rights of representation—at the same time as he acknowl-
edges the actual source of his gift in the figure of *Maia nate* (Mercury born
of Maia), god of commerce and exchange, the vowels and consonants of
whose name suggest "Maecenas."[74] By inserting the farm into the motif of
the *recusatio*, the speaker also declares his wish that the estate not compro-
mise his aesthetic independence regarding genre. Insofar as the estate does
participate in a circuit of exchange and eventuates in poetry, let those
poems remain lean, the poet says, let them be Alexandrian in style to suit
a Callimachean *ingenium*. Once again, Horace lays a certain claim to the
farm, asserting his rights of aesthetic property—of propriety or decorum.
Given that the references to land settlements for the veteran soldiers date

---

74. Referring to *Odes* 1.2, where Mercury and Octavian are conflated, Bradshaw (1989,
163–64) argues that the allegorical figure here suggests Augustus, not Maecenas.

the satire to 31 or 30 B.C.E., following the battle of Actium, the poet's invocation of Callimachean style may very well be more than a conventional gesture: written during the 20s B.C.E., the specifically political poems of the *Odes,* and the so-called Roman Odes in particular, provide lyric endorsement (however conditional) of the Augustan regime. Horace here acknowledges his patron in the wish that *Maia nate,* Maecenas, remain a *custos,* but the poet specifies that his work will be lyric and not epic.

Satire 2.6 is thus the first poem in the corpus that takes up the theme of the farm as a gift, transformed by the poet into a topos with generic allusions to pastoral. Such imaginative transfiguration recalls both the economy of *otium* that underlies Meliboeus's assessment of Tityrus's land and the aesthetic fertility to which the libidinal excess of gratitude is assimilated in the fourth eclogue. For Horace's idealizing of his farm is initially an expression of gratitude, an instance of praise poetry that indirectly compliments Maecenas on his magnanimity: Horace acknowledges his patron by displacing the praise due him onto his gift—"what sooner should I make illustrious (*illustrem,* 17)," the poet asks in reference to his land—and by showing the pleasure that the estate brings him. The libidinal excess that accompanies the gift (*auctius atque / di melius fecere*), and that is returned in *gratia,* may be said to contribute to the idealizing vision of the country and thus parallel, if not in fact become, the excess associated with aesthetics. In *Ode* 1.17, to which we now turn, the aesthetic excess associated with the topos of the golden age is even more explicitly embedded in the gift-exchange modalities of patronage.

THE *CORNUCOPIA* AND HERMENEUTIC ABUNDANCE: *ODES* 1.17

> Velox amoenum saepe Lucretilem
> mutat Lycaeo Faunus et igneam
>   defendit aestatem capellis
>   usque meis pluviosque ventos.
>
> impune tutum per nemus arbutos   5
> quaerunt latentis et thyma deviae
>   olentis uxores mariti,
>   nec viridis metuunt colubras
>
> nec Martialis haediliae lupos,
> utcumque dulci, Tyndari, fistula   10
>   valles et Usticae cubantis
>   levia personuere saxa.
>
> di me tuentur, dis pietas mea
> et Musa cordi est. hic tibi copia
>   manabit ad plenum benigno   15
>   ruris honorum opulenta cornu.

hic in reducta valle Caniculae
vitabis aestus et fide Teia
   dices laborantis in uno
      Penelopen vitreamque Circen.   20

hic innocentis pocula Lesbii
duces sub umbra, nec Semeleius
   cum Marte confundet Thyoneus
      proelia, nec metues protervum

suspecta Cyrum, ne male dispari   25
incontinentis iniciat manus
   et scindat haerentem coronam
      crinibus immeritamque vestem.

Often Faunus swiftly changes Lycaeus for lovely Lucretilis and all the
while keeps the fiery heat and rainy winds away from my goats. Through-
out the protected grove, safe from harm, the wives of the smelly he-goat
stray seeking the hidden arbute and thyme, and the kid-goats fear nei-
ther green snakes nor warlike wolves, when, Tyndaris, the sloping valleys
and smooth rocks have sounded deeply with the sweet panpipe. The
gods protect me, my reverence and my Muse are dear to them. Here
lush abundance of the riches of the country will flow to the full for you
from the generous horn. Here, in a hidden valley, you will avoid the
heat of the Dog Star, and on Teian lyre will sing of Penelope and glassy
Circe contesting over one man. Here, in the shade, you will drink glasses
of innocuous Lesbian wine, and Bacchus, son of Semele, will not mix in
wars with Mars, and you will have no fear of impudent Cyrus, that he
might attack you, unfairly matched, with unrestrained hands and tear the
garland, clinging to your hair, and your innocent clothes. (1.17.1–28)

An invitation to Tyndaris to come and enjoy the sympotic delights of Hor-
ace's estate, this ode combines pastoral and golden age motifs to present
an idealized landscape. As in the fourth eclogue, the topos here emphasizes
the safety of the environment—sheep wander unthreatened by wolves or
snakes—even as Tyndaris is assured that rough Cyrus will be kept away.
Though critics have cited the accoutrements of the golden age, and dis-
cussed Horace's representation of his farm here as a privileged domain of
aesthetics,[75] the implications of the central image of the *cornucopia* in such
a context have not been fully explored. An image of pastoral plenty that
came to symbolize the riches of the *pax Augusta,* the *cornucopia* appears
prominently in two works of the early Empire, the cuirassed statue of Au-
gustus found at Prima Porta and the cameo known as the Gemma Augustea.

---

75. Cf. the discussions of Fraenkel 1957, 205–7; Commager 1962, 348–52; Schmidt 1977;
Davis 1991, 199–205; Putnam 1994. On the history of the *locus amoenus* in classical literature,
with reference to this poem, see Schönbeck 1962, 186–93.

As noted earlier, *cornucopiae* were also prominently displayed on coinage of the triumviral period. Because of the larger political context of this image of fertility, as a rhetorical figure in Horace's poem it embeds aesthetic production in the gifts of imperial patronage.

Appearing in the central stanza of the poem—the point of transition from a magic landscape of animal life protected by Faunus in the first half to the world of lyric, epic, and excluded elegy of the second half—the *cornucopia* emphasizes what Lewis Hyde calls the passage of the gift (1979, 45–49): in this case, the image of plenty marks the process by which the benefaction of land, the reward of genius, is transformed into song and passed on. On the one hand, the gods of this central stanza refer back to Faunus, the rustic divinity responsible for transforming Horace's estate into a charmed landscape, exchanging (*mutat*) Mt. Lycaeus for pleasant Lucretilis. On the other hand, the phrase *di me tuentur* (the gods protect me), as it leads into the ideologically charged image of the *cornucopia,* also suggests the gifts of the regime. Just as Horace's *ingenium* (talent, genius) is in the care of the god Mercury—a stand-in for Maecenas and those he represents in *Satires* 2.6—so here the gods protect (*tuentur*) the poet, because his piety and muse are dear to them. To be sure, Horatian claims about the sacrosanctity of the poet are commonplaces and need not imply a political or socioeconomic context. But the specific diction of patronage is telling and, taken with the pastoral imagery, connotes a political source similar to the palpably historical gods of Tityrus in the first eclogue. Then, too, the poet's *pietas* here recalls the speaker's claim in *Satires* 1.6 that his upright life and blameless character (*vita et pectore puro,* 64) gained him entrance to Maecenas's group. Finally, the *cornucopia* appears elsewhere in the Horatian corpus in a context that explicitly ties the abundance of the gods to patronal relations and the plenty of the *pax Augusta.*

For example, *Epistles* 1.12, the letter to Iccius as procurator of Agrippa's estates in Sicily, urges its addressee to enjoy his *ususfructus,* the rights to the use of produce of the land he oversees, as "no greater abundance could be bestowed by Jove" (*non est ut copia maior / ab Iove donari possit,* 2–3). As we saw in the introduction, when the letter later recommends Pompeius Grosphus as a friend whom Iccius should "make use of," the social relations of patronage are expressed in openly economic terms: the "going rate of friends is cheap, when good men are in need."[76] Both social and economic abundance are then given a political inflection: in the coda of Roman news at the end, references to recent military victories, by Agrippa and Tiberius over the Cantabrians and Armenia respectively, are followed by the statement that golden plenty pours out grain from her full horn (*aurea fruges /*

---

76. Hor. *Ep.* 1.12.22–24: *utere Pompeio Grospho et, si quid petet, ultro / defer: nil Grosphus nisi verum orabit et aequum. / vilis amicorum est annona, bonis ubi quid deest.*

Italiae pleno defudit Copia cornu, 28–29). Here, a possible allusion to a good year for the grain crop, welcome news after the famine of 22 B.C.E., expands into a symbol for the prosperity that comes with peace—albeit a peace wrought and ensured by armed conquest. Notwithstanding the potential irony that Italy's fortune depends on the subjugation, and implicitly the economic exploitation, of other countries, this ending renders Jove's *copia* at the beginning in distinctly political terms. Augustus is the ultimate if unmentioned patron (on 1.12, see Putnam 1995). Similarly, in *Odes* 1.17 the gods' protection suggests the material prosperity that Horace enjoyed as a beneficiary of the Augustan regime.

In addition, the *cornucopia* symbolizes aesthetic abundance. To some degree, the image alludes to a commonplace of ancient rhetoric: both Cicero and Quintilian refer to the dazzling variety of literary tropes—that is, the dense "rhetoricity" of literature—in terms of "abundance" or *copia*.[77] In Horace's poem, the *cornucopia* connotes such profusion of figural language as well as its consequent potential for contradiction. A concrete emblem of *plērōsis,* or the fullness associated with a god's presence, the *cornucopia* complements both the divine epiphany of Faunus and the music of his pipe echoing from the smooth rocks. The abundance of continuous sound implied by *personuere* develops into the "song within song" image of Tyndaris's lyric domestication of epic in the fifth stanza: as Gregson Davis points out, lyric here includes epic, reduced to an elegiac rivalry between Penelope and Circe (1991, 203). Tyndaris herself, a patronymic suggestive of Helen, is emblematic of both the source of epic conflict and its transmutation into poetry—in this case, lyric (Putnam 1994, 371). Further, the landscape echoing with music, a frequent image of pastoral, is enacted by the succession of performers—Faunus yielding implicitly to the speaker, who yields in turn to Tyndaris. Aesthetic abundance here resides in the profusion of genres, as elements of pastoral conform to a lyric *convivium* in which both elegiac rivalry and epic violence are contained.

Odes 1.17 locates the origin of this aesthetic excess in the gifts of the patronal system. The "generous horn" (*benigno cornu*) from which *copia* flows recalls Maecenas's *benignitas* in *Epode* 1 even as it anticipates the poet's reference to his "abundant vein of talent" (*ingeni / benigna vena*) in *Odes* 2.18. But just as the *cornucopia* functions on a purely symbolic level in *Odes* 1.17, referring to no actual thing in the poem's narrative or sequence of events, so the complex hyperbaton of this stanza points up the elusive transition from material gift to aesthetic production. Suggestive of Faunus's initial transformation of the farm into a charmed landscape echoing with song, the gods here both symbolize aesthetic talent and reward that talent;

---

77. Cf. Cic. *De Or.* 3.30.121; Quint. *Inst.* 10.1.5–6: *opes sint quaedam parandae. . . . Eae constant copia rerum ac verborum.* I am grateful to Robert Grudin for these references.

pastoral riches issue both in return for the talent and again, symbolically, as the creative source itself. And in keeping with Faunus's swift movement, which sets the momentum at the poem's opening, what we might call the flow of signifiers gathers the specific separate entities into one: gods, muse, speaker, and pastoral fruit constitute so many different signs for the same elusive referent, linked to creativity. The superabundance of signs is yet another reflection of the nature of the referent: for what is creativity but the mysterious production of something out of nothing? That is, creation differs from simple substitution, direct exchange, or transformation insofar as it produces something extra. Without venturing too deeply into the language of deconstruction, one might say that the *cornucopia* thus provides the aesthetic supplement to the center of the poem, a center whose signifying "abundance" actually conceals an absence under its surface.

Though the precise origin of such signifying excess remains elusive, the excess is a property of aesthetics that the poem also figures as libidinal. And this libidinal element, in turn, connects with Cicero's comments on *gratia:* because *gratia* can refer to both a favor repaid *and* the sense of favor that remains after repayment, it parallels the libidinal excess that attaches to the object, increasing in value as the spirit of the gift is passed on. In ideal terms, because the gift is prompted by feeling—Seneca claims that a person should "love his benefactions"[78]—it carries a libidinal value in addition to its material worth; it is in response to this nonquantifiable libidinal value that the receiver is prompted to give in excess of the original gift. Surely this concept of the essential movement of the gift, or the spirit of the original gift, appears in the swift succession of figures who inhabit Horace's magical landscape in *Odes* 1.17: what Faunus gives to the speaker, the speaker gives to Tyndaris. The rich abundance of the farm flows (*manabit*) for the addressee, and she, in turn, at first receiving will then produce song of her own. The aesthetic excess that we see as a profusion of generic echoes in Tyndaris's song thus arises from, or at least parallels, the accumulation of libidinal value—or energy—as the gift changes hands. And just as Lewis Hyde argues that the libidinal element of the gift expands to include the parties involved in a form of collective ego (1979, 16–17), so the hyberbaton of the central stanza entwines gods, speaker, and addressee in a cameo image of the tripartite relationship of patron, poet, and audience. We have here an ideal view of benefaction, one in which economic transaction provides for social cohesion.

Yet despite this positive image, the *cornucopia* of this poem also suggests the potential for its own subversion as an ideologically charged symbol for

---

78. Sen. *Ben.* 2.11.5: *Si gratos vis habere, quos obligas, non tantum des oportet beneficia, sed ames* (If you wish to have gratitude from those whom you lay under an obligation, you must not merely give, but love, your benefits).

imperial patronage. Here we might turn to a more negative understanding of libidinal excess, one more akin to Georges Bataille's sense of the violence of eroticism. For in addition to its conventional sense, the "horn of plenty" is a fairly obvious symbol of ejaculation, an expenditure of sexual libido. The poem suggests that libidinal surplus not transmuted into art—that is, aesthetic excess—may very well lead to sexual violence. As an invitation to Tyndaris to come and enjoy the symposiastic delights—drink, song, and erotic feeling—of the Sabine farm, the poem, as many have remarked, presents eros in an ambiguous light. On the one hand, the poet offers Tyndaris cups of innocent Lesbian wine (*innocentis pocula Lesbii*), symbols of the light and playful passion of Sappho and Anacreon. These gifts will, in turn, encourage voluntary giving from Tyndaris: sexual favors will not be wrested from her, but rather offered up willingly in response to the speaker's gifts. Indeed, it is precisely the effects of too much wine that the speaker promises to keep away from Tyndaris at his retreat. Bacchus will not, along with Mars, mix elegiac violence into the cups of innocent lyric.[79]

On the other hand, this safe haven of the golden age is defined through the excluded presence of the elegiac lover at the end of the poem. Such definition through difference is paralleled in the poet's careful choice of adjectives: for though innocent (*innocentis*) wine, not Cyrus's incontinent (*incontinentis*) hands, characterizes the poet's estate, the words' distinct meanings depend on minor differences in lettering. Such traces or echoes of one word in another reflect the aesthetic play symbolized by golden age fertility and the *cornucopia*. Similarly, the poem's inclusion of the image of violence ensures its presence despite Cyrus's exclusion from the farm. This presence-in-absence dynamic, on the levels of both form and diction, underscores the ambiguity that some critics remark in the speaker's intentions.[80] Despite his claims, too much wine may yet bring on the more violent eroticism of a Cyrus. This uncertainty—are the speaker's intentions less honorable than he claims?—reflects still another form of abundance, the ambiguity that results from contradictory implications.

This analysis may seem to depart from the subject of patronage, but it is precisely the connotative multiplicity symbolized by the *cornucopia* that, as I argue in the next chapter, allows Horace to refashion his relationship with Maecenas. Indeed, the negative effects of donation that Pietro Pucci has remarked in Horace's gifts to Tyndaris in this poem, subjecting her to

---

79. Putnam (1994, 363) observes that the phrase *proelia confundere* is a witty turn on the "standard idiom *proelium committere* or *facere*," and underscores the "wrong mixing" that the speaker promises to avoid.

80. Dunn (1990) claims that the *invitatio* is governed by the rhetoric of seduction causing Cyrus's violence to function as the speaker's threats. See, too, the comments of Connor (1987, 28–31) on the figure of Cyrus.

the "seduction of his world" (1975, 280), are the effects of indebtedness that he himself chafes beneath and attempts to escape in the *Epistles*. The violence of Cyrus may be read not just in terms of Horace's will to subjugate Tyndaris but also as the symbolic incorporation of all that resists and would violently rend the ideological veil of voluntarism, the circle of generous giving so seductively and beguilingly imaged in the central strophe.

In this chapter I have argued that the discourse of libidinal excess and voluntarism that defines the gift—or an ideal, prescriptive view of benefaction—can be seen as assimilated to the pastoral economy and aestheticized landscape of the *Eclogues;* moreover, this process serves to naturalize benefaction as both an economic and ultimately a political system. When Horace invokes Vergilian pastoral in *Satires* 2.6, he introduces into his representation of his estate both the naturalizing discourse of the *Eclogues* and their darker underside—the pressures of civil turmoil, in particular the confiscations of land, that threaten to tear the imaginary resolutions of those poems just as they haunt the speaker's own rhetoric of benefaction. This ambiguating subtext to Horace's pastoral allusions is compounded by the contractual connotations of the gift and by gratitude as a burden of debt. Nonetheless, in regard to *Odes* 1.17 I have suggested that pastoral's assimilation of a patronal economy also provides Horace the rhetorical figures with which he transmutes the raw materiality of the estate as imperial benefaction into an image of aesthetic abundance; by so transforming his material *munus* into a *locus a-moenus,* a place that is "not for profit," Horace appropriates the libidinal excess of patronal voluntarism and creates an imaginative site of copious connotation. For even as Faunus suggests the gods of patronage, he also implies the poet himself: at the end of 1.16, the speaker claims that he seeks to "exchange angry lines for sweet" (*nunc ego mitibus / mutare quaero tristia,* 25–26), a change that Faunus's substitution (*mutat*) of pleasant Lucretilis for Lycaeus surely makes good. A discursive site of hermeneutic plenty, the farm, as we shall see in chapter 4, enables the poet to resist—even as he reveals—the discourse of quid pro quo exchange to which his relationship with Maecenas threatens to regress.

CHAPTER FOUR

From Patron to Friend
Epistolary Refashioning and
the Economics of Refusal

Toward the end of the twenty-ninth ode of his third book the Horatian speaker claims to praise Fortune as long as she stays, but should she shake her wings and fly away, he will renounce her gifts, wrap himself in his virtue, and take poverty as his dowry. This philosophical indifference to fortune's vicissitudes draws the first three books of the *Odes* to a close; and, as the final poem (excepting the proud *sphragis* where Horace compares his achievement to a monument of marble), it anticipates many of the issues that the *Epistles* will take up. The trope of Epicurean self-sufficiency—here figured as the warm (and Stoic) shawl of virtue and the marriage gift of poverty—appears in the epistolary poems as the ultimate benefaction bestowed by the poet on himself. Such independence, in turn, depends on a dialogue with the audience, whether that be the specific lyric or epistolary addressee or a more generalized public "readership"—those whom the poem implicitly establishes as consumers of poetry. The Horatian subject, particularly in the *Epistles*, takes shape in a performance of rhetorical counterpoint in which the speaker often invokes his audience as a foil for his self-definition.

The "Grand Maecenas Ode" anticipates this process of definition. Following the convention of an *invitatio*, *Odes* 3.29 bids Maecenas to leave the heat and ostentation of the city, and take refuge in the cool simplicity of the Sabine farm. Halfway through a formulaic list of why, when, where, and what to bring, the poem betrays convention; rather than ending with a gesture to R.S.V.P., it embarks on a detached philosophical meditation. This shift from personal address to ethical stance describes the movement of many of the *Epistles*, whose addressees frequently offer the occasion for Horace's homespun Hellenistic treatment of Roman social issues. The structural resemblances, however, extend further, for oscillating from

stanza to stanza in the first half of the poem are binary oppositions: Mae-
cenas, Rome, and corruption are set against Horace, his estate, and virtue.
Though individual epistles engage an eclectic range of philosophical top-
ics, they often make the Sabine farm into a geographical metaphor, or
figurative locus, for the pursuit of the good life. This equation, in turn,
justifies the epistolary genre, as the Horatian speaker frequently converts
the distance between writer and addressee into an occasion for meditating
ethical differences. Moreover, the request entailed by this lyrical *invitatio*
anticipates the inverse structure of the first and seventh epistles, where
Horace refuses Maecenas's demand to write more odes and justifies to his
patron his absence from Rome. *Odes* 3.29 thus does more than prefigure
many of the structural alignments that inform the *Epistles,* the synchronic
relations that buttress their ethical exploration: it also points to a dia-
chronic development, stretching from the first three books of the odes into
the *Epistles,* of Horace's relationship with Maecenas.[1]

The historical backdrop implied by this development deserves mention.
The *terminus ante quem* conventionally given for the publication of the *Epis-
tles* is 20 or 19 B.C.E. By that time, Horace had been a member of Maece-
nas's "circle" or *cohors* for some fifteen years and, judging from the gratitude
the poet expresses in *Satires* 2.6, in possession of an estate in the country—
generally called "the Sabine farm"—for more than ten years.[2] The evidence
of Suetonius, coupled with interpretations based on the poems themselves,
suggests that the patronal relationship originally secured by an act of ben-
efaction had become an external structure, or form, within which the feel-
ings or emotive content of real friendship had developed. It is the ambi-
guity of such a relationship, one in which the formal structure could still
impose itself, that Horace's epistolary poems to Maecenas explore. As forms
of *recusationes,* these "refusal poems" are unusual in that they ground their
demurral not by claiming inadequacy to the task but rather by referring to
a past debt made good.

Indeed, as chapter 2 demonstrated, the religious rhetoric of sacrificial
expiation serves not only to justify the necessity of the Principate but also
to lend an ideological veil to the "economic" exchanges involved in the
production and consumption of such poetry: rather than being a response
to the debt imposed by benefaction, the poet's sacrificial expenditure is
voluntary, in keeping with a discourse of priestly euergetism. In turn,
through such circulation of symbolic capital, the *pax Augusta* appears as
the consequence of expiation, the reestablishment of the *pax deorum* (peace

---

1. Santirocco (1986, 153–68) traces a similar development of Horace's relationship with
Maecenas in the *Odes.*

2. See chapter 3, n. 6, and the introduction, n. 9, for evidence concerning the Sabine
estate.

or blessing of the gods), rather than the bloody ascent and militaristic domination of one man. The previous chapter explored the ideological veil of voluntarism from the perspective of the gift of land itself, arguing that Horatian depictions of his estate, drawing on Vergilian pastoral, reveal "gaps" or "fissures" in the veil even as they ultimately conform to the prescriptive view of benefaction as a disinterested form of giving. In this chapter, I suggest that Horace both threatens to rend the veil completely, revealing—even exaggerating—patronage in all its naked economic interestedness, and at the same time "repairs" the fissure, the gap between ideology and objective structure, by aligning it with different levels of audience.

Specifically, I analyze the epistles to Maecenas—1.1, 1.7, and 1.19—as poems that aesthetically refashion the patronal relationship into one of a more egalitarian friendship. The chapter is divided into four main sections. In the first, I review the conventional scholarly approaches to the problem of autobiography in the *Epistles* and then give my own account of the Horatian subject in these poems. In the second, I give a reading of the first epistle in terms of this "autobiographical subject" and its engagement with economic issues of debt, credit, and symbolic capital. My third section examines how this view of the Horatian subject bears on the other poems to Maecenas, and in particular how it explicates the problematic assertion in *Epistles* 1.7 that Horace, if pressed by the demands of patronage, is willing to return all benefactions to his patron. In the fourth section, I examine more closely the abundant economic imagery of the seventh epistle and the ways in which it interacts with the ambivalence of Horace's status identifications.

Because critics have, for the most part, viewed the letters to Maecenas either as straight autobiographical documents asserting independence or as essentially fictive explorations of the relationship of patronage, they have ignored the unique way in which the hermeneutic process of reading the *Epistles* is involved in the new configurations of identity that the poet claims for himself.[3] Scholarship has not, in short, sufficiently taken into account the role of audience in the production of meaning.[4] As we shall see, in the

3. The autobiographical view was popular early in the twentieth century when "biographical criticism" was still in vogue and "sincerity" was considered a major critical issue rather than a rhetorical effect. Thus Courbaud (1914) and Fraenkel (1957, 310) saw the letters as autobiographical and "real," whereas critics of the last few decades—Becker (1963), G. Williams (1968), McGann (1969), Macleod (1983), and Kilpatrick (1986)—have inclined toward seeing the *Epistles* as fictions that draw in varying degrees from experience. Johnson (1993), however, reads the poems as a form of "psychobiography," albeit filtered through Horatian art and irony.

4. Though disagreeing as to their biographical accuracy, most scholars of the *Epistles* have explored them for their philosophical statements and orientation: e.g., for Courbaud (1914),

seventh epistle in particular, audience determines the different systems of images that the poet employs as he refashions his relationship with his patron. Signifying the ambivalence of Horace's social identifications, these different registers of imagery simultaneously make possible a revelation of patronage as a system of calculated interest, even exploitation, and a complicity with its ideology of social cohesion.

EPISTOLARY SUBJECTIVITY

Whenever the question of the status of the *Epistles* as autobiography comes up, critical attention has until recently focused on whether the letters were "real" or not. For Gordon Williams this is "too crude" a question to ask, and he concludes that they "had no practical function as letters" and that the "overt literary intention of the *Epistles* is the real one" (1968, 24).[5] M. J. McGann discusses this question in terms of the letters' effectiveness in the real world: "To say that the epistles are not real letters is to hold that they were not intended to have consequences in the 'real world,' that their statements, their questions, and their advice have no entailments for the persons addressed" (1969, 89). His position seems to hamstring the power of fiction by insisting that only if the letters were actual correspondence could they impress their readers or addressees. On the contrary, as I suggest in my conclusion, the cameo glimpses of Horace on his farm were intended to have an effect on readers other than those specifically addressed. And because little is known about the addressees of many of the letters, it is difficult to imagine their individual responses.[6] Maecenas, however, figuring as the addressee of no fewer than three of the *Epistles* and as the care-worn politician of *Odes* 3.29, a poem that ushers in the themes and structures of the philosophical letters, is a personage whose historical status invites us to infer more about him as a reader. With subtle echoes of diction and imagery extending over the range of these poems, Horace uses the *Epistles* to attempt a redefinition of his relationship with Maecenas. Although this transformation takes place in the temporal space of the suc-

---

the *Epistles* stage the poet's development from Epicureanism through Stoicism; Maurach (1968) and McGann (1969) see the *Epistles* as exemplifying essentially Stoic ideas, with the latter emphasizing Panaetius as a model. Macleod (1983) and Kilpatrick (1986) see the ethics of *amicitia* as the major concern.

5. See n. 3 above, for a summary of the critical positions. See Kilpatrick 1986, xvi, on the *Epistles* "as dramatic poetry [akin to] Browning's monologues." For Johnson (1993, 10–11), the epistolary speaker's implicit claim—that "the masks are suddenly put away for good and all"—constitutes a "theatrical gesture."

6. Notwithstanding such uncertainties, Allen et al. (1970) discuss the addressees of *Epistles* 1 and conclude that they were "'safe' and 'Augustan' politically" (265).

cession of letters, and thus in narrative time, it involves Maecenas's partic-
ipation as an actual reader interpreting Horace's poetry.

To trace how Horace's relationship with his patron changes over the
course of the *Epistles*, we must address the autobiographical nature of the
poet's persona. The issue of "sincerity" has been effectively laid to rest by
critics of classical texts over the past few decades,[7] but the question of con-
nections between the postures assumed by poets in their verse and the
cultural codes or conventions of their historical context obviously remains
central. For the purposes of this chapter, I consider the autobiographical
persona to be an aesthetic effect, in keeping with linguists' definition of
subjectivity as constituted in language. And if, as Michel Foucault's work
has argued, subjectivity is the product of cultural discourses that are his-
torically specific,[8] then Horace's autobiographical persona would find ex-
pression in those discourses particular to his period. Moreover, subjectivity
as the effect of articulations employing the pronominal shifters "I" and
"you" points to the fundamentally dialogic, and therefore dyadic, structure
of such discourses (Benveniste 1971, 233–30). To use a slightly different
terminology, the subject positions available in language always exist relative
to a second term of a dyadic relationship. The dyadic discourses particular
to Horace's Rome, which he manipulates to effect a modified independ-
ence from Maecenas over the course of the *Epistles,* are the relation be-
tween patron and protégé, the relation between participants in a more
philosophical and therefore egalitarian "friendship" (*amicitia*),[9] and the
relation between a *praeceptor* (instructor)—often Epicurean—and his pupil.
Each of these relationships, in turn, has a coherent system of associated
images, diction, and rhetorical conventions that the poet exploits.[10]

My recourse to linguistics—and to the dyadic model of subjectivity

---

7. Veyne (1988) is one of the more recent defenders of the high degree of artifice and
convention in Latin poetry. Davis (1991, 78–184) analyzes autobiographical events in the *Odes*
as a rhetorical trope that confers poetic authority on the speaker, conforming more to the
rhetorical demands of such aims than to any regard for biographical truth.

8. Foucault (1970, 380) writes, "for the signifying chain by which the unique experience
of the individual is constituted is perpendicular to the formal system on the basis of which the
significations of a culture are constituted: at any given instant, the structure proper to individ-
ual experience finds a certain number of possible choices (and of excluded possibilities) in
the systems of the society."

9. For clarity, in this chapter I generally use *amicitia* to refer to a philosophical ideal of
friendship unmediated by political considerations. However, as already discussed in the intro-
duction, the concept of *amicitia* can embrace a full spectrum of personal relations from those
of patronage proper to a kind of Ciceronian ideal of identity of interests, values, and opinions.

10. Thus Horace manipulates his culture as a semiotic system shared by his readers. Cf.
Geertz 1973, 14: "as interworked systems of construable signs . . . culture is not a power . . .
[but] a context, something within which they can be intelligibly—that is, thickly—described."

offered by Emile Benveniste in particular—rather than to the more usual psychoanalytic paradigms of the subject associated with Jacques Lacan or Julia Kristeva is motivated by two considerations. First, though a Lacanian model in fact shares with Benveniste the notion of subjectivity as coterminous with language, as well as a concept of the "split subject" whose discourse reveals in its gaps and fissures a latent level of connotation, the "postmodern" subject of Lacan depends on a totalizing view of the subject's relations in the "Symbolic order" as ultimately conditioned by the castration complex. Such psychoanalytic constructions of the subject threaten to distort the discursive particularity of the cultural codes of antiquity by reducing their significance, in the final analysis, to the confines of the bourgeois "family plot." Second, by combining a dialogic understanding of the subject—the linguistic expression of personhood—with a Foucauldian view of discursive practices, I hope to provide the most suitable hermeneutic paradigm for understanding Horace's epistolary negotiations of "patronal pressure," a paradigm that emerges from the aesthetic form through which those poetic maneuverings are carried out.

The epistle is the genre in which the dyadic construction of the subject appears most visibly. Its essence involves the mechanics of communication, rendering it the generic articulation of Benveniste's "dialectic reality" of the subject: "Consciousness of self is only possible if it is experienced by contrast. I use 'I' only when I am speaking to someone who will be a *you* in my address. It is this condition of dialogue that is constitutive of person" (1971, 224–25). Benveniste is making a universal claim here about the linguistic effect of subjectivity; by being true wherever the pronominal "I" is employed, such a claim risks becoming trivial when applied in particular contexts. But the epistle as an aesthetic genre heightens, or raises in a kind of bas-relief, the contours of the dyadic relationships informing the writing subject. Even the everyday epistle, intended as a practical means of conveying information, illustrates with remarkable clarity this language of the self, for correspondence as such mediates, and thus simultaneously fixes in relation to each other, two subject positions. As Stanley Stowers points out, the letters of Greco-Roman antiquity reflect specific social codes of behavior, and thus locate the writer and addressee in their proper place (1986, 27). The distinction between "ordinary" and "aesthetic" letter is by no means easily drawn, especially in antiquity, when not only was the writing of ordinary letters something of an art form and subject to a theoretical taxonomy, but personal correspondence was also polished and refined for publication at large (18–19, 32–35). However, we can ascertain degrees of fictionality, if not of artistry; when the fiction is greater, and the constraints of "real" communication fewer, then the artistic license is broader.

Such license would permit greater manipulation of the dyads informing epistolary relations; and it would also give a poet the freedom to occupy subject positions that, although part of a discursive historical background, are not necessarily available to him outside of the fictional setting of the letter. Horace avails himself of this license in his epistles, employing the genre as a means of inverting or converting the dyadic relations that constitute him as a poetic subject. But such deliberate tampering does not in itself make his letters to Maecenas less autobiographical. Rather, these texts might be considered as linguistic resolutions—ways of negotiating the tensions in the cultural discourses by which Horace as subject finds himself defined: as Fredric Jameson writes, "the aesthetic act is itself ideological, and the production of aesthetic or narrative form is to be seen as an ideological act in its own right, with the function of inventing imaginary or 'formal' solutions to unresolvable social contradictions" (1981, 79).[11] As we shall see, the impulse toward an aesthetic resolution derives from the ideological terms themselves of the patronal discourse whose more negative realities Horace experiences as confining: Horace's resistance to the actual economics of patronage is enabled by a rhetorical excess or "aesthetic play" that, as we saw in the previous chapter, is associated with the gift of *otium* and the ideology of the golden age. Horace's poems thus both reinforce and challenge the social relations from which they arise.

This paradox reflects the degree to which the epistolary subject may occupy contradictory positions. As Kaja Silverman points out, Benveniste's linguistic theory allows for flexibility in the discursive construction of the subject, since with every articulation it is figured anew: "Benveniste's discontinuous subject may depend for its emergence upon already defined discursive positions, but it has the capacity to occupy multiple and even contradictory sites" (1983, 199). Horace uses this capacity in his epistles to Maecenas. Exploiting the twofold nature of the published epistle, a genre that assumes the expression of private intimacies even as it exposes them to a public readership, Horace writes a poem whose overt—or "public"— stance unravels for the audience of the elite: by occupying the role of a philosophical *praeceptor*, Horace encourages Maecenas to read a discourse of ideal *amicitia* or friendship beneath the surface gestures of a protégé, or a subordinate *amicus*. Horace occupies several discursive sites simultaneously to convert a hierarchical *patronus*-protégé relationship into the "horizontal" dyad of personal friendship.

The role of philosophical master that he employs brings up the question of doctrine in the *Epistles*. Much scholarly ink has been spilled in the attempt to pin Horace down to one or another creed; more recent scholars tend to agree only that the *Epistles* display an eclectic blend of predominantly Hellenistic philosophy presented by a persona as ironic and elusive

---

11. This production of narrative form essentially constitutes what Jameson considers a "first hermeneutic horizon."

as Plato's Socrates.[12] Indeed, for all its characteristic self-deprecation, the speaker's statement in the first epistle that he harbors in whatever philosophical port the storm might have blown him has a ring of truth.[13] And though such texts as Cicero's *De officiis* and *De amicitia* clearly influence the philosophical vision of the *Epistles,* their anecdotal style, their loose structure, and the persistently contradictory stance of the speaker make any single source improbable. Individual elements of a poem do suggest specific schools, however, and some have argued that an Epicurean ethos permeates the entire collection. The genre itself recalls Epicurus's use of the prose epistle as a vehicle for philosophical teaching.[14] The Greek philosopher notoriously disregarded poetry as insignificant to his vision of the "good life," but Lucretius certainly vindicated the Muses, who provided the persuasive finish necessary to his transmission of Epicurus's ideas. As this and the following chapter demonstrate, Epicureanism is, at the least, a strong influence on the *Epistles.* I single out certain Epicurean practices and principles for their relevance to the discursive site that the Horatian speaker takes up, both as a student and a teacher of philosophy. The frequent nexus of imagery in the *Epistles* comparing philosophical sayings to a liquid, and the student to a vessel that must begin clean, suggests the Epicurean practices of confession and memorization.[15] In addition, the Epicurean principle of withdrawal from public life, to the "Garden" (in Epicurus's day, at the outskirts of Athens), finds ample analogue in the Sabine farm. Finally, the democratic aspect of Epicureanism—its promise to aid the sufferings of all alike, regardless of gender or status—appears in the frequent tension in the *Epistles* between social hierarchies and philosophical egalitarianism.[16]

12. On Horace's synthesis of different philosophical schools as Academic—reflecting the Skeptics as well as Plato and Socrates—rather than merely eclectic in orientation, see Kilpatrick 1986, xvii, 116 n. 44. Mayer (1986) reads the epistolary Horace as essentially Socratic and considers the critical tendency to discover specific philosophical orientations in the poems to be flawed.

13. Mayer (1986, 58) draws attention to how similar in language, but not in context, this statement of Horace is to Cicero's complaint that young men cling to philosophical systems like shipwrecked sailors to rocks: *una alicuius quem primum audierunt oratione capti de rebus incognitis iudicant, et ad quamcumque sunt disciplinam quasi tempestate delati ad eam tamquam ad saxum adhaerescunt* (*Acad.* 2 [Lucullus] 3.8).

14. Heinze (1919; reprinted in Kiessling and Heinze 1961a, 367–80), made a case for Epicurus's letters as the primary model for Horace, a view that Becker (1963, 15–16) and others have since rejected.

15. See Nussbaum 1994, 126, 129, and sources cited therein. I am indebted to Nussbaum's entire discussion of Epicurean practice in her chapter "Epicurean Surgery" (102–39).

16. The literature on Horace and Epicureanism is vast, though most scholars dispute any concrete affiliation with a school or rigidly systematic exposition of particular tenets, and later

Before we trace the development of this conversion of the dyadic rela-
tionship between Horace and Maecenas, we should briefly consider the
Sabine farm as the material condition mediating, anchoring, and focusing
the intersecting cultural discourses composing that dyad. In the discourse
of patronage, the Sabine farm serves as a major *beneficium* that encourages
and expects, although its ideology does not demand, the compensating
gestures of *officia*. Moreover, the farm confers not only important economic
self-sufficiency and the "leisure" time of *otium*, but also the symbolic capital
of status attached to independent landholding:[17] the farm made Horace
eminently free in the Aristotelian sense—a freedom based on wealth and,
ultimately, on social status. And yet in the logic of gift exchange and con-
cealed economic interest, it is such benefactions that his epistles, particu-
larly the seventh, represent as potentially still obliging.[18] Hence, the re-
peated gesture of a philosophical independence that we see in these letters
often collides with the actual—as opposed to the ideological—code of pa-
tronage. In keeping with much of the advice in the *Epistles* endorsing a
course between two extremes, the independence voiced by these poems is
modified and conditional: for even if the Sabine farm represents the locus
of an Epicurean withdrawal from the political world and demands of Au-
gustan Rome, that world's beneficence is what makes such a renunciation
possible. And though this conditional independence marks the intersec-
tion of two cultural codes—the interdependence of patronage and philo-
sophical self-sufficiency—it is within the space of a third discourse, an ideal
and philosophical *amicitia*, that Horace communicates his complex posi-
tion to Maecenas. Finally, as the inequality characteristic of the *patronus-*
protégé relationship yields to the horizontal dyad of friendship, another
differential dyad emerges that supports this new formation: the *vulgus* that
aligns itself with Rome, Maecenas, and publicity in the first epistle becomes,

critics have tended to undermine earlier assertions of Horace's Epicurean orientation. DeWitt
(1939) made piecemeal identifications of discrete Epicurean sentiments, scattered throughout
the poetry; Merlan (1949, 451) claimed that Horace's Epicureanism is "whining" rather than
"virile"; Perret (1964, 95–98), Büchner (1969), and Gantar (1972) all reject any sustained
Epicurean affiliation or exposition on Horace's part. For a defense of Horace's commitment
to Epicurean ideas of friendship, see Diano 1968. See nn. 4 and 12 above for discussions of
the *Epistles* in relation to other philosophical schools.

17. Cf. Cicero's comments (*Off.* 1.151): "there is no kind of gainful employment that is
better, more fruitful, more pleasant and more worthy of a free man than agriculture" (trans.
M. Atkins from the edition by M. T. Griffin and E. M. Atkins [1991]). The estate is both a
discursive site of social inscription in the extratextual world of cultural discourses ("possession
of land signifies aristocratic identifications") and a variable locus of constructed meaning
within the poems.

18. Significantly, the word with which Horace claims that he has been enriched by Mae-
cenas's benefactions is *locupletem* (*Ep.* 1.7.15), whose root meaning is "rich in land."

by the nineteenth, the second-rate poets of little discernment. Through their envy, they bring into relief the contours of the elite aesthetic circle centered around Augustus.

This overall trajectory of my analysis clarifies the ways in which the uniquely Horatian invention of the verse epistle constitutes a "formal" solution to social contradiction. As a genre at once private and public, it enables Horace to resolve the conflict embodied by the material condition of his estate, employing semiotic registers that speak to different audiences. Unlike lyric, which may also be understood as a private rhetorical performance before the public gaze, the verse epistle permits its creator to draw on the letter's generic affiliations with philosophical practice: in keeping with the parainetic focus of the prose epistle, Horace's novel genre brings under its philosophical scrutiny the overlapping discourses of friendship and patronage whose dyads constitute its very form.[19]

DYADIC DISEQUILIBRIUM AND THE ALTERNATION OF DEBT: *EPISTLES* 1.1

The tensions of numerous cultural discourses are in play in the first few lines of the opening epistle. Whether historically "genuine" or not, a request from Maecenas for lyric poetry, possibly panegyric, serves as the occasion for Horace to justify his new interest—philosophy—in the genre that will provide the medium for its exploration:[20]

> Prima dicte mihi, summa dicende Camena,
> spectatum satis et donatum iam rude quaeris,
> Maecenas, iterum antiquo me includere ludo.
> non eadem est aetas, non mens. Veianius armis
> Herculis ad postem fixis latet abditus agro,   5
> ne populum extrema totiens exoret harena.[21]
> est mihi purgatam crebro qui personet aurem:
> 'solve senescentem mature sanus equum, ne
> peccet ad extremum ridendus et ilia ducat.'
> nunc itaque et versus et cetera ludicra pono: 10
> quid verum atque decens, curo et rogo et omnis in hoc sum.
> condo et compono quae mox depromere possim.

19. In the invocation of the epistle as a medium for philosophical instruction, the Horatian *epistolary* subject differs from the Horatian *lyric* subject. But the frequent presence of specific addressees in classical lyric, as well as the rhetorically persuasive nature of the speaker, make the I-you dyad often as pronounced in a lyric as in an epistle.

20. For discussion of whether a fictive or actual occasion prompted this epistle, see n. 3 above and the critical consensus that these epistles are "fictive" but may draw from experience. See my introduction and its nn. 1 and 3 for other interpretations of this opening.

21. With the OCT I read *totiens* in line 6 rather than Shackleton Bailey's *rediens.*

By my first Muse glorified, to be glorified by my last, you, Maecenas, seek to confine me again in the old school, though I have been gazed upon enough and already awarded the foil. My age, my temperament are not the same. Veianius, having hung up his arms at Hercules' temple door, hides, concealed in a field, to avoid beseeching the crowd, repeatedly, from the edge of the arena. There is voice constantly sounding in my cleansed ear: "Wisely free the aging racehorse in time, lest he stumble at the very end, short of breath, a sight to be mocked." And so, I now set aside poems and other frivolous pursuits. The true and the proper, this is my care and query, and I am completely involved in this; I am storing up and setting in order those things which soon I may bring out to use.
(1.1.1–12)

The tightly woven symmetry of the near golden first line displays the conflict between the demands of patronage and the prerogative of the Muse. On the one hand, Horace claims that Maecenas was honored (*dicte*) by his first Muse, and will be honored (*dicende*) by his last, and he thus complies with the convention of dedicating a book of poems to his patron. But by drawing attention to such honor as a poetic convention, Horace privileges his own artistry at the—quite literal—*expense* of his patron. Honor is owed to the patron, to be sure, but aesthetic artistry converts the poet's debt into that of his benefactor: for the separation of the adjectives *Prima* and *summa* ("first" and "last"), as modifiers of *Camena* (Muse), and their placement at the beginning and the middle of the line create two appositional phrases in which the words modifying Maecenas, *dicte* and *dicende,* are embraced and subsumed by those describing Horace's Muse. Such brilliant hyperbaton, the famous Horatian mosaic in an image of patron-poet interdependence, pointedly underscores that Maecenas owes his poetic life to the speech of his protégé. Although *dicende* might suggest a continuing debt on the part of the poet, such a future obligation, looking ahead to the nineteenth epistle similarly addressed to the patron, has already been met—once the collection of poems is published as a whole—in the temporal unfolding of the poetry book and the reading process: that is, Maecenas has received the first dedication and, rest assured, the line implies, he is to receive the last. But Horace's poetic inclination comes first, both in the line and in his generic choice (*Prima . . . Camena*); it centers the line, implying that obligations diminish from this summit. By thus manipulating the dedicatory convention, Horace grounds the overt justification for refusing his patron—"My age, my temperament are not the same"—in the credit or symbolic capital that he has accrued through his celebration of Maecenas: drawing attention to the debt that Maecenas has incurred in depending on the poet for immortality, Horace inverts the hierarchy of patronage and asserts that aesthetic values have priority over the social or political *officia* of a dependent.

Renouncing his patron is not an act of willful caprice; rather, the Horatian speaker claims to have taken up the pursuit of philosophy. And because the epistle is often the medium of such pursuit,[22] the generic transition from the *Odes* to the *Epistles* helps mediate between the two dyadic relationships of patronage and philosophical instruction. Horace refuses to align his identity as poet any longer with the role of a dependent, choosing rather to adopt first the position of student but ultimately that of teacher—the "doctor" of philosophy. The role of knowing *praeceptor,* dispensing the prescriptions of philosophy, is at this point only implicit, a consequence of genre; but the shift from an inferior to a superior position appears in the transition from the objectified Horace of line 2 to the series of emphatic first-person singular verbs, the pronominal "I"s, of lines 10–12. At first Horace compares the writing of verse to a gladiatorial school (*ludus*) and spectacle, whose elements of open visibility and personal compromise (or subordination to the patron) metaphorically suggest the more public genre of lyric encomia or "political" poetry that shapes many of the *Odes*. But the "proven" (*spectatum*) and "rewarded" (*donatum*) gladiator, weary of seeking the public's favors, now engages in gathering the fruits and distilling the wine of truth: four verbs of first-person agency—"I attend to" (*curo*), "I seek after" (*rogo*), "I store up" (*condo*), and "I compose" (*compono*)— accumulate quickly, asserting the poet's urgency in the philosophical enterprise on which, as though producing a wine from a cellar, he will soon draw (*depromere*). Though new to these pursuits, the speaker claims that he is bound to swear by the words of no master (*nullius addictus iurare in verba magistri*). And as the letter of a dependent to his patron proceeds to metamorphose into a more generalized parainesis to the good life—now lyrical, now satiric—it is clear that he himself identifies with the philosophical praeceptor.

In this transition from one role to another, the metaphor of the *gladiator,* as I suggest in my introduction, deserves closer scrutiny. Scholars have not sufficiently explored the discursive web of associations raised by this image of laborious showmanship sponsored by another.[23] They have tended to emphasize the irony of Horace's casting his situation in terms of such ex-

---

22. For an overview of the philosophical epistle in antiquity, see Stowers 1986, 36–40.

23. For example, P. White (1993, 137) downplays any possible political implications of the terms *ludus* and *ludicra* by referring the connotation of "game" to the more symposiastic verse of the erotic odes. But much evidence connects *ludus* to political poetry. First, Horace's own inverted *recusationes* or *revocationes,* at the end of the ode to Pollio and *Odes* 3.4, point up the frequent inextricability of political and erotic motifs as part of his lyric persona. Recent criticism has brought out the importance of the poetry scroll and the arrangement of a book as a whole; hence, in referring to light erotic poems, *ludus* may stand synecdochally for *Odes* 1–3 as a whole. Lyne (1995, 78, 187) comes close to suggesting such a metonymic function of the erotic poems.

treme servitude, rather than the economic implications of the image.[24] Irony no doubt exists in the discrepancy between the crude and bloody sport of the gladiator and the refined metrical rhythms of the poet, but the nexus of images connected to the idea of expenditure and debt suggested by a gladiatorial *munus* raises the issue of freedom in complex ways. To begin with, when Horace claims that in his new pursuit of philosophy he is sworn to no master, the word *addictus* has more than one implication. As commentators point out, the term can refer to one who has sworn by a gladiator's oath as well as to a person in a relationship of monetary debt to another. Thus, Horace's newfound—or keenly desired—freedom in the genre of the philosophical epistle is implicitly contrasted with a sense of past economic obligation in the figure of the gladiator. To be sure, most gladiators owed their labor to another because of slavery, not debt; nonetheless, the economic meaning of *addictus* reinforces Horace's use of the gladiatorial metaphor to express a past sense of obligation.[25] The poet's present status as not *addictus* tellingly echoes the words *dicte* and *dicende* in the first line, where honoring of the patron constitutes one means by which such debt is made good.

The echoes reach beyond this poem. In *Epistles* 1.18, Horace gives advice to his young friend Lollius, who is about to enter into a relationship of personal patronage with a *potens amicus*, "a powerful friend" or patron of higher status. At the poem's outset, the speaker intuits that Lollius fears becoming like the figure of the *scurra* who "repeats the speeches and sayings of the rich man" (*divitis iterat voces et verba,* 12), just as a "boy gives back dictated lessons to his master" (*ut puerum . . . dictata magistro / reddere,* 13). These two depictions of the role of a protégé or dependent—servile parasite and compliant schoolboy—contain marked verbal echoes (*verba, dictata, magistro*) of the phrase *addictus iurare in verba magistri,* "bound over to swear by the words of a master." Such patterns of diction become significant when we consider that the gladiator's oath (see Ville 1981, 248–49), the schoolboy's lessons, and the parasite's parroting all depend on repeated words and phrases. As I have argued elsewhere (1994), Horace's advice to Lollius contains a subtext concerning the poet's own experience of patronage; such a reading strengthens the echoes between these two epistles, which suggest that embedded in the rhetorical figure of a gladiatorial oath,

24. Kilpatrick (1986, 2) suggests that the "ironic" comparison to a "superannuated gladiator" alludes to the similar image in Cic. *Sen.* 5.14. For Kilpatrick the irony refers more to the element of age (i.e., Horace is still writing very good poetry) than to the constraint of the gladiator. See my discussion of this passage in the introduction.

25. See Ville 1981, 228–64, for the evidence concerning origins and status of gladiators: they were originally prisoners of war, and then variously slaves, men condemned by the law, and finally "free" men who took the gladiator's oath voluntarily.

where the reproduction of phrases is at issue, may be a certain referential literalism regarding the production of poetry.

Moreover, the image of the *ludus*, or "gladiatorial school," to which Horace resists returning, naturally implies the *munera*, or "gladiatorial shows," for which the poet, gazed at sufficiently, has been presented with the foil signifying his discharge. Although *munus* specifically denotes a gladiatorial spectacle, such shows were often presented in association with athletic games (*ludi*), public banquets (*epulae*), or sacrificial feasts (*viscerationes*), at which the flesh of the victim was shared among the guests (Ville 1981, 386–87). And the *ludicra* that the speaker claims he sets aside along with verse in line 10 may also refer to theatrical shows and public entertainment. Significantly, the image of *ludi* performed for a patron's approval—he makes a "thumbs up" gesture—also appears in *Epistles* 1.18. Here, too, the diction suggests the writing of poetry, and specifically political verse, since the *ludus* put on by Lollius is a *naumachia* (mock sea battle) of Octavian and Antony's showdown at Actium.[26] In turn, these images of gladiatorial and other forms of spectacle in *Epistles* 1 invoke instances in the *Odes* where the language of public games and display is used. As we have seen, the word *munus* is employed by Horace to refer to funereal offerings in the ode to Pollio, the poem that anticipates the role of tragic sacrifice and expiation in the Roman Odes. These "political" poems may therefore be specifically alluded to by the gladiatorial imagery in the *Epistles:* gladiatorial shows, or *munera,* have their origin in the ritual sacrifices for the dead that the Pollio ode invokes as symbolic expiation for the civil wars.[27] These associations all underscore the idea of public expenditure as a primary metaphor through which Horace conceives the political poetry of the *Odes,* a trope that involves both patron and poet. On the one hand, the patron's munificence to the poet indebts him and causes him to become *addictus,* even as such patronage leads to an expenditure or *munus* for the sake of the public. The gladiatorial metaphor may thus be interpreted as Horace's humorous demystification of the ideal of voluntarism and disinterestedness in literary patronage as practiced by Augustus and Maecenas. On the other hand, the poet's aesthetic labor puts his benefactor(s) in his debt. As we shall see,

26. Hor. *Ep.* 1.18.58–66: *Ac ne te retrahas et inexcusabilis absis, / quamvis nil extra numerum fecisse modumque / curas, interdum nugaris rure paterno; / partitur lintres exercitus, Actia pugna / te duce per pueros hostili more refertur; / adversarius est frater, lacus Hadria, donec / alterutrum velox Victoria fronde coronet. / consentire suis studiis qui crediderit te, / fautor utroque tuum laudabit pollice ludum.* Here, the gesture of the raised thumb to indicate the patron's approval aligns him, as in *Ep.* 1.1, with the public. As commentaries point out, this is the first known reference to such a gesture, one whose origin and precise form are still contested.

27. On the origin of gladiatorial *munera,* see Auguet 1994 [1972], 19–25; Hopkins 1983a, 3–7; Barton 1993, 13.

the seventh epistle probes and challenges this dynamic of exchange most explicitly.[28]

But here, in the first epistle, the disequilibrium that marks this alternation of debt is countered (and modified) by the overriding rhetoric of the speaker's lesson of equality—both before the law of human nature and of eligibility for the treatment of philosophy. Philosophical study "helps the poor and rich alike, even as neglected, it will harm the young and old with no discrimination" (*aeque pauperibus prodest, locupletibus aeque, / aeque neglectum pueris senibusque nocebit*, 25–26). This disregard for difference recalls that of Epicureans, whose egalitarianism reflects their ideal of friendship.[29] The Epicurean indifference to distinction—whether of gender or political status—in its celebration of the horizontal relation of friendship provides a structural model, if not a concrete source, for Horace's exploration of this paramount Roman discourse. When at the end of the poem, with characteristic slipperiness, the Horatian speaker slides once more from impersonal proselytizing to personal address, resuming his dialogue with Maecenas, we witness again the collision of several dyadic relationships:

> si curatus inaequali tonsore capillos
> occurri, rides; si forte subucula pexae   95
> trita subest tunicae vel si toga dissidet impar,
> rides: quid mea cum pugnat sententia secum,
> quod petiit spernit, repetit quod nuper omisit,
> aestuat et vitae disconvenit ordine toto,
> diruit aedificat, mutat quadrata rotundis?   100
> insanire putas sollemnia me neque rides,
> nec medici credis nec curatoris egere
> a praetore dati, rerum tutela mearum
> cum sis et prave sectum stomacheris ob unguem
> de te pendentis, te respicientis amici.   105
> Ad summam, sapiens uno minor est Iove, dives,

---

28. The more economic (and contractual) the exchange becomes, the less ambiguous the disequilibrium of debt. Kurke (1991, 225–39) analyzes how Pindar applies rhetorical tropes from a disembedded economy of wage and profit to an embedded economy of aristocratic expenditure on the Olympian games. In some instances, Horace may be said to do the opposite: he takes images from the embedded economy of public expenditure on the gladiatorial *munera* and uses them to suggest the economic calculation behind patronage: he has already (*donatus iam rude*) earned his withdrawal from public themes and performance, and thus he has paid off his debt. Significantly, the speaker of *Epistles* 1.1 also compares himself to a retired racehorse: *hippotrophia*, or conspicuous expenditure on horse racing, had strong associations with tyranny in the Greek world. See Kurke, 215–16, for further references.

29. This egalitarianism holds among members, prospective or otherwise, of the school. The manifest hierarchy in the relationship of master to students in Epicureanism is discussed by Nussbaum (1994, 119).

> liber, honoratus, pulcher, rex denique regum,
> praecipue sanus—nisi cum pituita molesta est.

If I run into you when my hair is cut unevenly, you laugh; if it happens that the shirt under my brand-new tunic is worn-out, or if my toga, ill-fitting, sits askew, you laugh: what about when my thought is at war with itself, rejects what it sought, seeks again what it just now abandoned, seethes and is out of sync with the entire system of life, when it destroys, builds, changes squares to circles? You think that I rage my usual fits and you neither laugh at me nor think that I'm in need of a doctor or guardian appointed by the praetor, though you are the caretaker of my affairs and get angry over a crookedly cut nail on the friend who depends on you, who looks to you for all. In sum, the wise man is second to Jove alone—he is rich, free, honored, handsome, finally a king of kings, and, particularly, healthy, except when he has a runny nose. (1.1.94–108)

After a long satiric section that ends with an image of seasickness that spares the rich man no more than the poor (*aeque nauseat*), the Horatian speaker turns personal once again, pointing out the superficiality of Maecenas's treatment of his protégé. With diction recalling the claim that the differences of class and age are external and irrelevant to a person's qualification for philosophy, Horace objects that Maecenas notices only imperfections of appearance—his "uneven haircut" (*inaequali tonsore capillos*), "an ill-fitting toga" (*toga . . . impar*), "a crookedly cut nail" (*prave sectum . . . unguem*)—and is insensitive to the busy workings of his mind. Indeed, the adjectives describing the poet's disheveled look, *inaequali* and *impar*, suggest more than simply a poet at odds with himself: they tellingly imply the stratified and unequal nature of the patronal relationship. A patron's dependents are a visible indication of his own status (Wallace-Hadrill 1989, 83), and Horace thus implies that Maecenas cares only how such bad grooming might reflect on himself—that is, when he exercises his spleen over a badly cut nail, he cares about Horace only as a "client." But many dyadic discourses cross here, with Horace occupying first one position and then another, creating an instability of tone matched by an oscillating syntax. With the same erratic impermanence that marks Horace's mental wanderings—a mind that "scorns what it sought, seeks what it abandoned" (98)—the poet's persona vacillates from satiric philosopher to disgruntled protégé to respectful friend and back to a philosopher who mocks his own claims. Nor are these positions mutually exclusive: as the satiric philosopher shifts to the misunderstood protégé, the criticisms of the latter rely on the didactic prerogative of the former. The necessarily superior tone of reproof subsides only with the pendulum swing from the end of line 104 to line 105, where the accessory syntax of the prepositional phrase, *de te pendentis*, *te respicientis amici* (the friend who depends on you, who looks to you for all), mirrors the admission of dependence and respect. Assuming the independent voice of the philosopher, Horace teaches his patron to care for his protégé less as a public beneficiary or client, whose appearance reflects on his benefactor, and more as a private friend. In a sense, Horace teaches Maecenas to be *his* private doctor.

The vacillating subject—as client or protégé, friend (*amicus*) or praeceptor—is another means of manifesting the disequilibrium of debt or expenditure between Horace and Maecenas. By the end of the first epistle, the philosophical advice that Horace has given his patron, albeit in a general satirical form, constitutes further expense on the part of the poet that entitles him to his patron's private solicitudes. The poet's exhausting mental workings cause him to be as "spent" mentally as the gladiator is physically from his labor at the poem's opening. We shall see this sense of earned entitlement again in the seventh epistle, where the poet's right to refuse requests is figured as both the freedom based on the fulfillment of past obligation and as a further indulgence granted by the patron turned friend. For the independence that Horace displays in writing the *Epistles* rather than more odes paradoxically depends on Maecenas's generosity. In the first epistle, as we have seen, this symbiosis stirs the most refined and decorous Latin artistry: the elegant hyperbaton of the first line—with the temporal modifiers of Horace's Muse weaving in and out of the vocatives of his patron—asserts not only the priority of the poet but the dependence of such willfulness on his benefactor as well. Grammatical inflection again mirrors this syntax of relationship in line 105—*de te pendentis, te respicientis amici*. But in the seventh epistle, Horace communicates this complex position to Maecenas as the reader of a latent discourse, a subtext speaking to him as a friend beneath a surface discourse that addresses him as a patron.

One effect of the opening poem is to prepare Maecenas for such latency in the seventh. The very first image of the retired gladiator suggests the opposition between public and private genres: the retired gladiator, Veianius, tired of beseeching an audience, hides concealed in a field (*latet abditus agro*), having hung up his arms to Hercules (1.1.4–6). This imagery may seem to refer only to the generic distinction between the *Odes* and the *Epistles*, but the emphasis on secrecy and concealment points to more than just the privacy of the epistolary genre and the "life in retreat" of Epicureanism.[30] The opposition reappears at the end of the epistle, where

---

30. Of course, letters became "public" as soon as they were "published"—that is, when authors allowed people other than their friends to make copies (see Starr 1987); and, as Allen et al. (1973, 130) stress, letters were often "public enough property that Cicero could caution

Maecenas's concern with Horace's clothing displays public fastidiousness at the expense of private emotion. Here, the idea of concealment in the diction of the poem's opening lines structures the dialogue between speaker and addressee: Maecenas is being asked to read beneath the surface, to pay attention to Horace's hidden interiority.

To this point, however, the oppositions between public and private, appearance and reality, suggest only metaphorically a parallel with the cultural discourses of a politically nuanced patronage and the more philosophic *amicitia*, and with the generic choices associated with them. But before Maecenas as an actual reader arrives at the seventh epistle, where these discourses inform a contradictory tension between the semantics of the text and its subtext, he is prepared by the preceding poems in yet another way: they cause him to associate specifically with the epistolary genre the very interiority that Horace asks him to recognize. Such an association would be immediate, given that ancient epistolography often described the function of the letter as the "sharing of two selves." As Stowers notes, this idea is conveyed clearly in a letter of Seneca to Lucilius: "I thank you for writing to me so often; for you are revealing your real self to me in the only way you can. I never receive a letter from you without being in your company forthwith" (Sen. *Ep.* 40.1; Stowers 1986, 29). In Quintus Cicero's comment to his brother Marcus, "I behold all of you in your letters" (*te totum in litteris vidi*, Cic. *Fam.* 16.16.2), we also see the capacity of the epistle to bring the "whole self" into the mind of the addressee.[31] Horace builds on this a priori generic convention, using imagery developed from the related epistolary type—the philosophical exhortation.

When Horace claims that he seeks the true and proper and stores up (*condo*) things from which he soon may draw (*depromere*), he asserts more than his independence as a poet; he also introduces what will be a dominant metaphor for the teachings of philosophy in many of his verse letters. He compares the philosophical content of the following epistles to a liquid—in this case, to wine. The comparison of poems to wine is, in many ways, a Horatian topos: the verb *condere*, for example, appears in *Odes* 1.20, where Horace invites Maecenas to come drink "Sabine stored in a Grecian jar" (*Sabinum . . . Graeca . . . testa conditum*, 1–3)—a symbol of the poet's verse, which depends on Greek forms.[32] In *Odes* 1.9, with a slight variation,

---

Atticus that a letter was meant just for him (*Att.* 8.9.1)." But I am emphasizing that the genre of the epistle, in contrast to the fiction—and sometimes reality—of the public performance of the odes, is predicated on the absence, and thus invisibility or concealment, of the author.

31. For the conventions of "real letters" invoked in Horace's *Epistles*, see Allen et al. 1973.

32. Much has been written on Horatian poems figured as wine. On *Odes* 1.20, see Pavlock 1982, 81; Cairns 1992, 88.

the speaker bids Thaliarchus to "fetch" or "decant" (*deprome*) a four-year-old wine from a Sabine *diota,* the Greek word for a two-handled jar.[33] *Odes* 3.29, another lyric invitation, pointedly announces that a "smooth wine in a jar still unopened or unturned" (*non ante verso lene merum cado,* 3.29.2) awaits Maecenas in the country. The poetic context of this image—that is, the poem that draws the *Odes* to a close and anticipates the themes of the *Epistles*—suggests that the "wine" here connotes the philosophical content contained in the verse epistle—a genre or "jar" not previously "turned" (*non ante verso*) before Horace. Aesthetic form as a container for the substance of a "philosophical liquid" further recalls a familiar image of Lucretius, in which the brew of Epicureanism is likened to a medicine whose bitterness doctors disguise by "smearing the edges of a cup with honey" (*oras pocula circum / contingunt mellis . . . liquore,* 1.937–38). Thus Lucretius relies on the "sweet honey of poetry" (*musaeo dulci . . . melle, DRN* 1.947) to attract his reader's mind to the language of his argument and then to see through and grasp the nature of the universe.

The relationship of poetic language to philosophical content is a notorious crux for Lucretian studies, particularly as Epicurus himself regarded clarity as the most important characteristic of speech and thus thought prose, rather than poetry, should be employed for philosophical instruction.[34] Though the honeyed figures of rhetoric have the potential to mislead, Lucretius claims that his poetic language is intended to clarify rather than obscure Epicurean philosophy.[35] Nevertheless, Epicurus's suspicions haunt Lucretius's medicinal simile; and as an image, it lends focus to the conflicting conceptions of language in the *Epistles.* In the first, the sayings of philosophers are viewed as "charms" (*piacula,* 1.1.36), "songs" (*decantata,* 64), and mysterious chants (*verba et voces,* 34), which are able to "renew" (*recreare,* 37) the sick individual. Philosophical language can thus be internalized, taken like a liquid, so that it will work inside the soul like a medicine in the stomach. Such a view is in keeping with both the medical imagery of Epicureanism and the memorization of Epicurus's sayings

---

33. On the "Sabine jar" as applying to both the wine and the jar, see Edmunds 1992, 31.

34. Cf. Diog. Laert. 10.13, 10.120. As Asmis (1995, 21) claims in reference to this view, "It is the function of clear speech to communicate clear opinions that are verifiable by each student on the basis of sensory experience." Such a view implies that language ideally is a transparent medium expressing its signified content.

35. As Asmis (1995, 33–34) points out, Lucretius "aims to dispel the darkness of his listeners' ignorance by illuminating the discoveries of Epicurus with the language of poetry." Nonetheless, the image of honey *does* address the figural and rhetorical nature of poetic surface, and thus the capacity for deception, multivalency, and the need for interpretation. The problematic role of poetry in the practice of Epicureanism in the late Republic is addressed by the essays collected in Obbink (1995).

practiced by his students.[36] But against this understanding of language as transparent, unproblematically united with its referent, is another, suggested by the honey of the Muses: words as rhetorical surface, capable of deception.

The conception of language as a liquid explains why Horace develops the metaphor of philosophy as a wine or potion in conjunction with images of a person's receptivity to wisdom. Indeed, the voice that whispers in Horace's purged ear to retire the aging horse before its fall precedes the speaker's own reference to his philosophical wine cellar. Here the equation is indirect, but elsewhere, as in *Epistles* 1.2 to Lollius, the analogy is clear. After warning that the "vessel" (*vas*) must be "clean" (*sincerum,* 54), the philosopher-poet bids Lollius to drink in the teacher's words with a pure heart: *nunc adbibe puro / pectore verba puer* (67–68). Epictetus is said to have similarly observed that "the writings and teachings of philosophy, when poured (*influxissent*) into a false and low-lived person, as though into a dirty and defiled vessel, turn, change, are spoiled."[37] Horace combines this idea with the convention of the philosophical epistle "as the literary genre through which the living example of the guide and the shared lives of teacher and student could best be communicated" (Stowers 1986, 38). So when he writes that he is seeking the true and the fitting and that he "is all in this" (*omnis in hoc sum*), and then follows with the metaphor of distilling truth or storing wine, the phrase may also refer to Horace's self as being fully within, "self-present" in, the language of philosophy—*in hoc.* Horace can thus be said to liken his interior self to a liquid that a reader, such as Lollius in the second epistle, will take within as he "imbibes words in his pure heart." As I argue in the conclusion, Horace figures the image of his epistolary self as a gift to be received by his readers. Again, the tenets of Epicureanism suggest this idea of internalizing the teacher so that the student may always have reference to his or her character and principles.[38] Not only does the phrase *omnis in hoc sum* recall Quintus's comment to Marcus, "I see all of you in your letters" (*Te totum in litteris vidi*), but as Benveniste points out in his essay on shifters, *hoc* is a word that refers to the temporality of its own linguistic context (1971, 219). We shall see that Horace's identification of his pursuit of philosophy with the linguistic space and time of these poems themselves becomes explicit in *Epistles* 1.7 Here

36. See Nussbaum 1994, 125–28, for discussion of the Epicurean sources, Phld. *Peri Orges* XLIV, *Peri Parrhesias* 6, 20, 54, 63–64, and the analogy of philosophy to a form of therapeutic medicine.

37. Epictetus, frag. 10; trans. Oldfather 1952, Loeb edition.

38. See Nussbaum 1994, 132, on the importance of memory and repetition in Epicureanism: students were to learn the *Kuriai Doxai* by heart. By relying on memory, a student could take "the teaching inside himself or herself so that it [would] 'become powerful' and help her in the confrontation with error."

in *Epistles* 1.1, however, the poet's present self is both held in abeyance from the patron's demands—it is *omnis in hoc*—and implicitly contrasted with Horace's past lyric being, an entity that Maecenas metaphorically possessed. In many ways, the project of the *Epistles* is a philosophical reclaiming of this past self. The seventh letter explores precisely this relationship between the self—as bodily presence, lyric persona, and epistolary subject—and the benefactions that lay a claim to it.

THE DUPLICITOUS SPEAKER OF *EPISTLES* 1.7

This enigmatic epistle is often regarded as the "most personal and occasional of the entire collection" (Kilpatrick 1986, 8). Most critics have considered the poem as a concrete record of Horace's declaration of independence from Maecenas, whether as a letter actually sent or as a poetic treatment of his repudiation of further obligations as a dependent.[39] Taking as its occasion Maecenas's longing for his friend who has stayed too long in the country, the poem proceeds to explore the issue of patronage in a series of exempla. No other epistle contains so many fables and illustrative exempla (Fraenkel 1957, 336), and as a poem also noted for its highly personal content it presents an interesting tension between seeming unmediated "autobiography" and the interpretive uncertainties of *ainoi* (illustrative tales, stories, fables). The use of such exempla for didactic purposes recalls the second epistle to Lollius: there, Horace claims that Homer offers a better source of philosophical instruction than do Chrysippus and Crantor.[40] Although the concerns of the equanimous soul in that epistle are general and the seventh focuses specifically on the social issue of patronage, the two poems share a reliance on didactic exempla and thus raise similar questions of interpretation.

But the second epistle also anticipates the autobiographical element in the seventh poem. The Epicurean imagery of a medicinal liquid in this poem to Lollius, together with the epistolary function of bringing the writing self before the addressee, suggests that Horace's claim in the first poem—*omnis in hoc sum*—is also meant to apply to Maecenas's experience as a reader of the sequence of *Epistles* 1.1 through 1.7. In other words, for Maecenas as a reader, Horace is just as much present in the language of

---

39. I have profited from the following extended discussions of *Epistles* 1.7: Büchner 1972 [1940]; Gunning 1942, 303–20; Fraenkel 1957, 327–39; Hiltbrunner 1960; Wimmel 1969; Kilpatrick 1986, 7–14; Berres 1992, and see 216–18 for a review of the scholarly positions.

40. Mayer (1986, 67) emphasizes that Horace turns to Homer for philosophical instruction because he prefers "the vivid moral tales of a writer known to all" and repudiates "sectarian squabbles and opaque jargon." Homer may have been "known" to all, but familiarity with his work, in contrast to the populist "fable" of the fox in the cornbin of *Epistles* 1.7, would be a mark of aristocratic allegiance.

the second epistle as he is in the first. When the poet, or his consciously manipulated persona, admits at the beginning of the seventh epistle that he has deceived Maecenas by staying away longer than he had promised, his reference to "real" time seems to apply metaphorically to the linguistic time of the preceding epistles: *Quinque dies tibi pollicitus me rure futurum,* / *Sextilem totum mendax desideror* (1.7.1–2). Having promised to be away in the country for five days, Horace, a liar, is wanted for all of the sixth month; and, as the seventh epistle makes clear, he will be away for a long time yet. As in the first poem, Horace equates his self with his epistolary exploration of philosophy, and his physical absence from Rome metaphorically expresses his perseverance in a new genre that denies the claims of his patron: Horace has been away for six epistles—his clever accounting (five days, sixth month, seventh epistle) converting a sabbatical into both a source for and an effect of his generic departure.[41] However, unlike the first epistle, where language appears to be an unproblematic vehicle for the liquid of the self, a merely transparent container that safeguards philosophical queries and advice for the consumption of the reader, Horace here calls himself a *mendax,* or "liar," as if to underscore the potential for deceit possessed by any representation of the self in language. Indeed, the fiction or occasion of physical absence on which his epistolary persona depends resonates with the Lacanian notion that such linguistic representations are always haunted by absence and the slippage of meaning. Because the letters are only linguistic representations of a Horatian self, they involve the aphanisis of the "real," intending Horace: a persona is always necessarily something of a *mendax*. A letter does not unproblematically bring the self to the perceiving self of the addressee. In this regard, the epistolary persona poses many of the same problems as a poet's lyric "voice," understood not as a "transparent expression of self, but as a figure of self" that leads to "all the problems of figuration." As William Batstone's analysis of the rhetorical self suggests, the "figure" of voice may, like metaphor, "mean by not meaning what it says; its path to truth may be through an explicit error" (1993, 149).[42]

On one level, the figure of the Horatian *mendax* poses hermeneutic problems akin to the paradox of the Cretan liar: such a riddle resists any conclusive interpretation because it "disempowers poetic assertion in the pro-

41. Curiously, though scholars note the playful game between the promise of "five days" and the extension into the whole of the "sixth month," they have not seen the *seventh* epistle as partaking in this temporal accounting and thereby conflating literary or epistolary time with "actual" time.

42. See Batstone 1993 generally for an analysis of the problematic lyric "voice" as a rhetorical "figure of self."

cess of making a poetic assertion" (Batstone 1993, 132).[43] If Maecenas was
the attentive reader to which his literary discernment in his entourage of
poets attests, he would have picked up on Horace's complexly allusive self-
accusation as a *mendax*. Long familiar with Horatian irony and evasion,
Maecenas might well have been suspicious of a poem whose speaker begins
by calling himself a liar, and then proceeds to claim his independence even
at the price of giving up all he has received as a dependent.[44] Such wariness,
however, would not have been a reader's initial attitude toward the *Epistles*.
When the didactic speaker at the end of the first epistle encourages Mae-
cenas to read beneath a superficial appearance to the interior confusion
of Horace's soul, the poet's confessional nakedness seems analogous to
what the genre of the *Epistles* offers. Because Horace frequently mentions
his nails when discussing his art,[45] the crookedly cut nail that offends Mae-
cenas's decorous sense of dress might suggest the erratic composition of
the *Epistles*, with their radical shifts in tone, seemingly loose structure, and
haphazard sequence of material. There, Horace would be saying: "Disre-
gard any roughness of construction—it is only a reflection of the tumult
in my soul—and *this* is what you should be reading beneath the surface."
But such a reading presumes, again, the transparency of linguistic form as
supplying unproblematic access to meaning. As I have argued above, such
a reading accords with the Epicurean imagery of a fluid passage of thought
from the poet to his addressee,[46] and it could have been Maecenas's un-
derstanding of the passage—until he came to the seventh epistle. Here,
Horace's use of *mendax* warns Maecenas to suspect the overt statements of
the poem, not to find meaning beneath the *transparent* surface of form but
to interpret beneath a sometimes illogical opacity of signification. And as
if to encourage this kind of reading, not only does Horace employ a con-
spicuous signifying system—the exempla of fable, anecdote, and epic nar-
rative—he also exploits the connotative range of his diction and the rever-
sal of logical expectations set up by his syntax to undermine his overt
claims. Thus Horace prevents unmediated accessibility not just by physically

43. Reference to the "Cretan paradox," attributed to Epimenides, appears prominently in
the first hymn of Callimachus, where the speaker is in a quandary as to how to celebrate Zeus,
whose birthplace the Cretans, ever liars, claim to be Mt. Ida.

44. Berres (1992, 219) sees the difficulty in distinguishing between Horatian levels of
ironic versus nonironic speech as a major interpretive problem posed by this letter.

45. Cf. Hor. *Sat.* 1.10.70–71, where the poet addresses what Lucilius would experience if
he were writing in Horace's time: *et in versu faciendo / saepe caput scaberet, vivos et roderet unguis;*
and *Ars P.* 292–94: *carmen reprehendite quod non / multa dies et multa litura coercuit atque / perfectum
decies non castigavit ad unguem.*

46. See Diog. Laert. 10.13 for the high value that Epicurus placed on clarity of expression.
See Stowers 1986, 38.

withdrawing from the city but also by putting up poetic resistance to easy interpretation. The number and variety of readings that this epistle has attracted indicate that hermeneutic resistance is innate to the poem, one of whose functions is precisely to complicate the issue of intentionality and the ontological, performative status of poetic assertion. With that caveat, rather than succumb to the circular logic of the Cretan conundrum, I propose the following reading, which depends on a duplicity of discourse and intended audience.

After calling himself a liar, Horace proceeds to ask for Maecenas's indulgence for staying away in the country, an indulgence that his patron would give Horace both when he is actually sick and when he is fearing sickness:

> atqui
> si me vivere vis sanum recteque valentem,
> quam mihi das aegro, dabis aegrotare timenti,
> Maecenas, veniam, dum ficus prima calorque   5
> dissignatorem decorat lictoribus atris
> dum pueris omnis pater et matercula pallet
> officiosaque sedulitas et opella forensis
> adducit febris et testamenta resignat.

> But if you want me living sound and well, the indulgence that you grant me when I'm ill you will give me fearing to become so, Maecenas, while the season's first figs and fierce heat adorn the undertaker with his black retinue, now when every father and dear mother grows pale for their children, and conscientious duty and legal hairsplitting draws on fevers and unseals wills. (1.7.2–9)

Painting a comic cameo of Rome in the summer (G. Williams 1968, 20), Horace claims that the insufferable heat, combined with the demands of *negotia* (business duties), make him afraid to come to the city. Horace's persona is clearly speaking as a dependent, requesting from Maecenas the same solicitous care for his physical health as he sought, at the end of the first epistle, for the confusion of his soul. Blaming the summer, then introducing the next sentence with the conditional conjunction *quodsi*, Horace sets up an expectation that he will return in the winter:

> quodsi bruma nives Albanis illinet agris,   10
> ad mare descendet vates tuus et sibi parcet
> contractusque leget. te, dulcis amice, reviset
> cum Zephyris, si concedes, et hirundine prima.

> But when wintry snow blankets the Alban fields, your bard will go down to the sea and go easy on himself, and huddled up will read. You, sweet

friend, he will see again with the spring winds, if you will allow it, and
the first swallow. (1.7.10–13)

But just as Horace has betrayed his promise to stay away for only five days—
or five epistles—so too does he set up both syntactically and with his ima-
gistic opposition of summer/winter an expectation for his return that he
then betrays. He will return only with the spring winds and the first swallow.
The appellations used by the poet chart the movement from one role to
another that such delays effect: Horace stays away as Maecenas's *vates,* a
word that suggests the role of public poet rejected in the first epistle, but
in his withdrawal he will read (presumably philosophy) and will return, in
the spring, to see Maecenas as his *dulcis amice.* If Maecenas cares about his
vates as a friend, as the didactic philosopher has asked him to do in *Epistles*
1.1, he will condone the absence of his dependent from Rome.

The most significant betrayal of language occurs later in the poem—a
betrayal that also depends on Maecenas's understanding as a friend and
that centers on the interpretation of the verb *resigno.* The adjective *contrac-
tus*—understood here as withdrawn into oneself or "huddled up"—indi-
rectly alludes to the later deception. For its meaning recalls the end of *Odes*
3.29, where the speaker claims that if Fortune flies away, he will renounce
her gifts (*resigno quae dedit,* 54) and wrap himself in his cloak of virtue (*mea
virtute me involvo,* 55). The verb *resigno* is used twice in the seventh epistle.
As we have seen, the word first comes up in the parodic picture of Rome's
death-dealing heat, where the city's pressing demands lead to fevers and
then unseal wills (*testamenta resignat*). Later, it appears in an ambiguous
phrase, *cuncta resigno,* that follows the fable of the fox and the cornbin and
that has generally been understood as a hypothetical, if problematic, ap-
plication of the moral of the exemplum to Horace's situation: just as the
fox who wishes to exit the cornbin should leave as thin as when he entered,
so Horace should "give back all" (*cuncta resigno*) of Maecenas's gifts if he
wants to be free of obligations (29–36). Some critics claim that Horace
could not possibly have meant what he writes, arguing that the epistle is
merely a fictional exploration of patronage that uses Maecenas's relation-
ship with Horace as the particular occasion (G. Williams 1968, 21–22;
McGann 1969, 95–96). Ross Kilpatrick, who has written one of the more
recent studies of the *Epistles,* offers a suggestive, though narrowly exclusive,
alternative reading of this controversial line, one that depends on the prin-
ciple of decorum and suitability that informs the entire epistle (1986, 11–
13). My own reading, though not intentionally conceived to mediate be-
tween these two lines of argument, is informed by both interpretations
insofar as it rests on a duplicity of discourse.

The betrayal of expectation that marks the opening of the epistle prepares for this duplicity, and we see it again in the second use of the conditional conjunction *quodsi* in Horace's humorous *adunata:*

> quodsi me noles usquam discedere, reddes   25
> forte latus, nigros angusta fronte capillos,
> reddes dulce loqui, reddes ridere decorum et
> inter vina fugam Cinarae maerere protervae.

But if you wish me never to leave, you will return my strong body, my black hair on a once narrow forehead, you will return my knack for sweet speech and elegant laughter and for mourning, in drink, bold Cinara's flight. (1.7.25–28)

Setting up a condition that Maecenas must meet should he wish Horace never to leave him, the poet betrays his reader's expectation by making an impossible demand—the return of lost youth. And despite what may be the humor of this trope—an *adunaton* or "impossibility"—mockingly applied to the poet's appearance, it brings up an issue of irrevocability that seriously affects our understanding of the fable then told:

> forte per angustam tenuis vulpecula rimam
> repserat in cumeram frumenti pastaque rursus   30
> ire foras pleno tendebat corpore frustra.
> cui mustela procul 'si vis' ait 'effugere istinc,
> macra cavum repetes artum, quem macra subisti.'
> hac ego si compellor imagine, cuncta resigno.

Once it happened that a little fox had crept through a narrow crack into a cornbin, and having eaten his fill, with glutted body was trying to return outside in vain. A weasel some way off said to him, "if you wish to escape from there, you need to seek again the small opening as thin as when you entered." If I am arraigned by this picture, I give back everything. (1.7.29–34)

This fable is most striking in that its overt meaning seems to invert the irrevocability of the situation that introduces it: Maecenas cannot give back Horace's youth, but Horace, if he should be accused with this *imago,* would give back all that he received from Maecenas. Proponents of this interpretation understand *resigno* in a commercial sense, as in to sign money from one account to another—to enter money "in favor of someone else" (*OLD,* s.v., 2b)—and hence to hand over or resign.[47] They adduce as support for

---

47. For those who essentially subscribe to this commercial reading of *resigno* and its derived implications of "handing over" or "giving back," see Courbaud 1914, 282; Fraenkel 1957, 334; G. Williams 1968, 21–22; McGann 1969, 95–96; Johnson 1993, 44.

this reading the similar usage in *Odes* 3.29, where Horace claims to sign off Fortune's gifts—*resigno quae dedit.* The consistency with which this idea of return comes up in the seventh epistle makes such a reading to some extent inevitable: it recalls the similar use of *reddere* (to return) in the lines introducing the fable, and it anticipates similar diction in the exempla that follow.

Thus we would understand the poet's challenge a few lines later, *inspice si possum donata reponere laetus* (39), as a variation on the same claim—"Try me: I'm quite capable of cheerfully returning everything that has been given me." This interpretation would be in keeping with Maecenas's view of Horace's modesty, often praised (*saepe verecundum laudasti*), if put to the test (McGann 1969, 51). The Homeric example of Telemachus, refusing the initial gifts of Menelaus (*tua dona relinquam*, 43), also appears to support this reading; and the long tale of the lawyer Philippus and the auctioneer Vulteius Mena, which takes up the latter half of the epistle, concludes with a moral that one return to circumstances appropriate to a person's stature: "The one who recognizes, at last, how much affairs that were abandoned are better than those sought, let him return in time (*mature redeat*) and seek again (*repetat*) what was left behind. Each person should measure themselves by their own standard" (1.7.96–98). This last story alludes in many ways to what we know of Horace's life, particularly to his relationship with Maecenas, making an allegorical correspondence as "compelling" as the fable of the fox in the cornbin. In the first place, Horace's father was a *coactor,* a person who mediated between the auctioneer—Vulteius Mena's profession—and the buyer.[48] A freedman of independent means, he may well have influenced Horace's imaginative creation of the poor but self-sufficient Mena. Moreover, when Philippus comes upon Vulteius Mena, he is cleaning his own nails with a knife; as remarked above, Horace links his fingernails symbolically to his poetry, and the image here could then suggest an aesthetic independence existing before the compromising benefactions of the state. Most persuasive for this seductive symmetry of tale and biography is the farm in the Sabine country that Philippus, loaning money, encourages Mena to buy, and that proves his undoing. Even when a closer scrutiny of the callous and cavalier treatment of Mena by Philippus shows the exemplum to be, like that of the Calabrian host (14–19), *ex contrario,* some would still interpret the summarizing moral to mean that Horace, if pressed, would return the Sabine farm.[49]

48. For Horace's father, see *Sat.* 1.6. For discussion of Suetonius's biography of Horace and various elements of the received Horatian *vita*, see Fraenkel 1957, 1–23; Anderson 1982, 50–73, 1995; Mayer 1995; G. Williams 1995.

49. Critics (e.g., Kilpatrick 1986, 122) often point out that of all the exempla, only the

This episode, in turn, echoes the fable of the fox; and the theme of a loss of independence recalls the gladiatorial image of the first epistle, where Horace feels that Maecenas threatens to shut him in (*includere*) an old profession that puts him on display. The public/private dynamic of that initial metaphor opens the way to another understanding of the seventh epistle, as it brings up yet another image of compromised freedom in Horace's verse letters—the fable of the horse and the stag in the tenth epistle. The horse, in order to beat the stag, takes on a rider; but the price of winning the contest is the loss of his independence.[50] Frederick Ahl makes this image central to his study of the duplicity of discourse in poets during the Empire (1984). His essay stresses how the overt meaning appeals to the vanity of the emperor, while a clever manipulation of allusive diction and meter produces a latent discourse undermining the professions of the surface. This paradigm is equally applicable to Horace, but the alignment of audience with discourse is reversed: in Horace, the elite literary circle around Maecenas enjoys the private understanding, accessible perhaps to only the more astute of the reading public.

As I have discussed above, Horace prepares Maecenas for reading beneath the surface with his didactic reproof at the end of the first epistle. The betrayals of expectation that mark the first half of the seventh epistle would further warn the reader, Maecenas, to treat with skepticism the two most emphatic, and therefore suspicious, statements: *hac ego si compellor imagine, cuncta resigno,* and *inspice si possum donata reponere laetus.* Having earlier promised (*pollicitus*) and deceived (*mendax*), why shouldn't Horace be lying now?[51] Indeed, the first use of *resigno* in the vignette of Rome in the summer suggests a reason for Horace's deceit: should Horace give back the Sabine farm, the most prized and prominent of the *donata* or "gifts," the act would be a death for him; to sign all his property over to Maecenas would be tantamount to unsealing a will, *testamenta resignat.* The echo of this verb in the noun *dissignatorem* (undertaker) further underscores this subtext.[52] Giving back all, *resignare cuncta,* would necessitate returning to the city, a place that causes death. Thus, for Horace to apply the

---

one involving Telemachus is not *ex contrario.* Contrast Berres (1992, 236), who claims that the Philippus-Mena story comes the closest to Horace's and Maecenas's relationship, with the poet as jokingly reflected in Mena but Philippus an inaccurate stand-in for Maecenas.

50. For the nexus of these images of compromised freedom, see McGann 1969, 34, 56.

51. The self-accusation at the beginning of the epistle is clearly intended jocosely, as a way of excusing the speaker's change of mind and decision to stay away from Rome. But the use of such a strong epithet surely has a bearing on the later statements that seem so impossible to accept at face value.

52. This subtext may also suggest the poet's genuine intention to give back all his property to Maecenas on his death. In fact, Maecenas died first, and Horace left his estate to Augustus: see Suet. *Vita Hor.*

"lesson" of Vulteius Mena—returning to an abandoned but more suitable situation—would be as impossible as for Maecenas to return Horace's youth. The irrevocability of time that betrays and undermines the conditional possibility of Horace's never leaving Maecenas qualifies in turn both the fable of the fox in the cornbin and its narrative variation in the story of Vulteius Mena: while these illustrative *exempla* appear to allow for turning back—the weasel uses the future *repetet,* and the speaker's summarizing moral employs the jussives *redeat* and *repetat*—the possibility of return depends specifically on timeliness (*mature);* and the time to have given back benefactions received, in particular the Sabine farm, is past.

The lack of any explicit mention in the text of Horace's Sabine farm—the poet refers only to *cuncta* (everything) and *donata* (things given)—makes it the absent referent that enables this duplicity of discourse. Just as the absence of any concrete material referent for the *cornucopia* in *Odes* 1.17 makes it a center of signifying abundance, so the ellipsis in this epistle permits the farm to take on contradictory connotations. On the one hand, the estate is the gift that mediates between Horace and Maecenas in the cultural discourse of patronage, the central term whose relinquishment would presumably free Horace from any obligation as a dependent to return to Rome. On the other hand, since the binary opposition implicit in the cultural dyad of patronage is superimposed on the opposition Rome/country (the *patronus* is in Rome while his dependent stays in the country), the Sabine farm slips from being a medial to a polar term. Within the fiction of the letter, Horace implies that the *rus,* or country, that has detained him for all of the sixth month is one of two small resort towns: "small things suit a small man: regal Rome does not please me now, but leisurely Tibur or peaceful Tarentum" (*parvum parva decent: mihi iam non regia Roma, / sed vacuum Tibur placet aut imbelle Tarentum,* 44–45). But this use of *parva* is telling, for Horace has used the same term elsewhere to describe the Sabine farm (*parva rura, Odes* 2.16.37); moreover, since the self-restoring Sabine estate figures in so many of the *Epistles* as the *rus,* the place removed from Rome that creates epistolary distance, the association here is hardly far-fetched. Also, as Catullus 44 suggests, the more fashionable way of referring to the Sabine territory was by the name of Tibur, the town closest to that region. Because the Sabine estate is not explicitly mentioned, the surface reading of a dependent renouncing all obligation to his patron by offering to return all his gifts is possible. But the gift itself enables that gesture,[53] as

53. Macleod (1983, 284) claims that the Sabine estate allows the gesture of independence, but asserts that *cuncta* refers only to "the luxury and grandeur of city-life." Büchner (1972 [1940], 104) makes the similar claim that *donata,* in the phrase *donata reponere laetus,* refers only to "reichen römischen Einkünfte oder die materiellen Vorteile seines Aufenthaltes in Rom." For objections to reading *cuncta* in a restrictive manner, see Berres 1992, 223–25.

the Sabine farm now provides the pole from which Horace claims freedom from the demands of patronage, whether that entails generic independence or physical absence.

It is this position of compromised liberty that Horace communicates in his subtext, a position that depends on Maecenas's understanding as a friend. Kilpatrick's reading of the line *hac ego si compellor imagine, cuncta resigno* could participate in this latent discourse: in his view, Horace uses *resigno* in a legalistic sense, responding to the fable as an accusation of greed not by returning everything but by saying "I refute the entire charge" (*omnem criminis fidem resigno*).[54] Such a meaning is perhaps present in Horace's use of the word, and it does provide a key to an understanding of the poem that focuses on Horace's modesty and refusal to accept any further gifts that might oblige him.

But to read the poem exclusively this way overlooks how the simultaneously public and private audience inherent in the epistolary genre informs Horace's diction. Although the source of the accusation is obscure, the word *procul* (at a distance) implies an envious onlooker (Büchner 1972 [1940], 104),[55] to whom Horace addresses only one of his two messages. To an envious public Horace says, "If pressed, I'll give it all back," while a latent subtext reads, "that's a ridiculous charge—I refute its credibility; and, besides, it's impossible." Such duplicity is supported within and outside the poem; not only does Horace call himself a *mendax* at the very outset of this letter, but the nineteenth and twentieth epistles refer explicitly to the private audience that Horace's work enjoyed before it ventured into the hands of the reading public. In the nineteenth epistle the poet again stands accused: not of living off the boons of the regime but, when he declines to give public recitations, of saving his poems for Jove's ears alone (*Iovis auribus ista / servas*, 1.19.43–5). And the *sphragis* poem, addressed to the book of epistles themselves as if they were a young slave (*liber*, 1.20.1), pities his impatience to walk the public streets, to see a world beyond the few people to whom he has already been exposed (*paucis ostendi gemis et communia laudas / non ita nutritus*, 1.20.4–5).[56] Moreover, the gladiatorial image of the first epistle echoes in the brawl from which Horace escapes at the end

54. Kilpatrick (1986, 12) bases his reading on the use of *resignare* by Cic. *Arch.* 9 to mean "destroy or invalidate" in the phrase *omnem tabularum fidem resignasset*, "destroyed completely the reliability of the records."

55. Kilpatrick (1986, 11) reminds us that a similar expression of envy is made in *Satires* 1.9 and 2.6. Also noteworthy is *Epistles* 1.14, where Horace avoids in the country the envy of the city dweller. This avoidance of envy by dwelling in the country makes more problematic the gesture of returning all gifts, the country estate included, as a way of avoiding the accusation of greed from an envious onlooker.

56. For a discussion of *Epistles* 1.20 in terms of the tension between public and private that informs the "published" epistle, see Oliensis 1995.

of the nineteenth, when he cannot refute the charge of hoarding his work for a private audience: "To avoid being cut by the fighter's sharp nail, I shout 'I dislike that place' and demand a time-out" (*luctantis acuto ne secer ungui, / 'displicet iste locus' clamo et diludia posco,* 1.19.46–47). Thus, the "double" audience that the epistles as a genre enjoy—the private circle of friends and the greater "public" at large—itself partially determines the duplicitous statements of the speaker.

Finally, we should note that because the poet rejects the visibility that attends lyric performance and poetry of the polis, the "publicity" and exposure that the first epistle associates with the lyric genre becomes, as the *sphragis* poem suggests, a matter of publication—the book severed from the author's control and made available to a general readership through the written text alone.[57] Publication shifts the tension between public performance and personal—or "private"—epistle to a contrast of public textual commodity versus private *recitatio.* Such reorientation underscores the effect of these epistles—the point with which we began—in their aesthetic refashioning of Horace's relationship with his patron.

In the first epistle, Horace associates his *dicte* Maecenas with the public audience to whom the political poems are directed, and thus with literary patronage as a form of sponsorship on behalf of the state: in this scenario, though a gladiator and hence a slave, Horace is the medium through which his patron speaks to a general audience, creating an image of the stratified system or hierarchical network of patronal relations. The nineteenth epistle, by contrast, finds Maecenas not *dicte* but *docte;* he is a discriminating connoisseur of the poetry scene, but with a discernment that, the epithet implies, Horace's artistry has sharpened, tested, and *taught* over the course of the epistolary collection. Having taken the upper hand as philosophical *praeceptor,* the poet establishes an egalitarianism of aesthetic discernment: *Epistles* 1.19, by calling Maecenas *docte,* flatters him as having the capacity to distinguish between the speaker and the *servum pecus* (servile crowd) of his *imitatores* (19).

At the end of 1.19, literary discrimination—shared by poet and Maecenas alike—is juxtaposed with *grammatici* and poets who, in an electoral metaphor, seek acclaim in the manner of patrons hunting for votes (*plebis suffragia*), by their public munificence on meals and the gift of worn-out clothing (*impensis cenarum et tritae munere vestis,* 37–38). Introducing the brawl from which the poet seeks a *diludia* in line 47 when he refuses to participate in a public recitation, this image again recalls the gladiatorial *ludus* of 1.1 in its rejection of poetry as a form of expenditure, as euergetism

57. For the argument that the aristocratic elite of the late Republic and early Empire manipulated this tension between performance and publication in the effort to maintain social hegemony, see Habinek 1998, 103–21. I am indebted to this discussion.

implicitly directed toward political ends. As the image of *Epistle* 1.19 mocks poets who, in terms of the analogy, themselves act as patrons, using gifts to canvass support, so the allusion to the first epistle lends a certain literalism to the comparison: the echo of Horace's own "worn-out shirt" (*subucula . . . trita,* 1.1.95–96) at the end of 1.1 in the phrase "gift of worn-out clothing" (*tritae munere vestis*) suggests that it is the patronal use of poets, in forms of public display, that the speaker rejects. Public consumption of verse, at least Horatian verse, is now instead a matter—ironically—of "private" consumption at home (*domi*), where the speaker is pleased that his commodified text is "read by the eyes" (*oculisque legi*) and "held in the hands" (*manibusque teneri*) of those with freeborn discrimination (*ingenuis*) (1.19.33–34). Though these lines follow on the proud statement that Horace has "made public" (*vulgavi*) the Greek meters of Alcaeus in Latin verse, and thus refer to the reading of the *Odes* rather than to the *Epistles* as a published text, they are in keeping with the distinctions of the *sphragis* poem: the poet rejects the public audience of literature as spectacle and writes either for the readers of the published text or for the private audience of the powerful, the *recitationes* enjoyed by the ears of Jove. By withdrawing from face-to-face contact with the public at large, and simultaneously emphasizing the aesthetic discrimination required of readers of the written text, the poet redresses the imbalance of a patron-client relationship and establishes in its place, in his close circle of *amici,* an elitist sympathy of privileged readership and aesthetic taste.

So far my argument has established, in a preliminary fashion, the following points. First and foremost, Horace's poems actively contribute to transforming his relationship with Maecenas from one jeopardized by the duties and disequilibrium of patronage to one more egalitarian and permissive. Second, these two conceptions of their relationship, though situated on a continuous spectrum, are aligned with particular—albeit notional—levels of public and private audience. Third, it is the very absence in this context of any mention of the Sabine estate, otherwise conspicuous in the *Epistles,* that permits the connotative ambiguity (similarly aligned with audience) regarding the speaker's seeming intention to return all benefactions. Thus, as a subordinate protégé, the poet discloses and affirms the reality of the reciprocity ethic of patronage by making the price of his independence the return of his patron's gifts. At the same time, Horace undercuts his claims to be able to make good on such a gesture by making his country estate, the place away from Rome, the implied ground from which he speaks.

Finally, as we have seen, the speaker further undermines his claims by his own demand for the return of his past self. When the poet introduces time as an element of exchange, he reveals that a purely economic understanding may inform a more public and formal conception of patronage but no longer applies to his relationship with Maecenas. Horace's refusal to return to Rome denies Maecenas the physical companionship often expected of a protégé or dependent, and stirs or creates in his patron the feelings of desire predicated on absence that are characteristic of friendship.[58] The imagery of the descent to the sea that describes the poet's first betrayal of his addressee's expectation supports this idea of the conversion process and its relation to time. Not only does Horace stay away as Maecenas's *vates* and then return invoking the language of *amicitia*, but this absence takes place over the winter season, a time that metaphorically suggests the death of one identity and the creation of another.[59]

THE ECONOMICS OF SOCIAL INSCRIPTION

Now that I have laid out the framework of my own analysis of this enigmatic epistle, it remains to examine more closely how the connection between Horatian identity and notional audience is inscribed in the economic imagery of the poem. As we shall see, the philosophical uses of Homer in the second epistle reappear as ideological inscription in the seventh: here the anecdote about Telemachus is intended to assert the poet's parity with his aristocratic readership. Homeric gift exchange is invoked as the proper analogue for the ideology of voluntarism to which the aristocratic elite aspires in its practice of benefaction. The economic calculation that may lie beneath the language of affective and affected *amicitia* is a view of patronage that Horace simultaneously reveals to Maecenas and challenges him to repudiate.

Contractus *and the* Nexum

Diction referring to a patronal relationship stripped of the affective ambiguities of friendship runs throughout *Epistles* 1.7.[60] The potentially

58. Cicero's *De amicitia* suggests the degree to which absence of the friend is an integral and defining constituent of ideal *amicitia;* see the discussion in Leach 1993b. Absence, of course, is the sine qua non of the epistolary genre; as a defining constituent of *amicitia* it also plays a strong role in *Epistles* 1.10.

59. The image of the sea and water may well invoke rituals of cleansing, a process also involved in religious or philosophical ideas of conversion and renewal: on the ritual bath in the sea prescribed by the Eleusinian mysteries, see Bowie 1993, 241.

60. Scholars note that the actual patron-client relationship, while not legally binding, was nonetheless more openly—and *visibly*—expressed as an "exchange relationship." Wallace-Hadrill (1989, 66, 82–83) discusses the importance of the *visibility* of clients in the *atrium* of their patrons, and Dixon (1993, 453) comments: "The implicit exchange was therefore not only an exchange of concrete gifts and favours but the return of gratitude, widely expressed as praise of the donor. . . . The erection of public statues and inscriptions recording benefactions is more typical of such clearly unequal and public relationships." Thus actual *patrocinium* closely approximated, if it did not actually constitute, a "contractual" relationship.

problematic *contractus* that describes Horace as he reads by the sea reso-
nates with a very specific legal connotation, if we understand patronage as
an economic system of exchange.[61] As mentioned in the introduction, Mar-
cel Mauss claims (and Roman legal historians concur) that the practice of
debt-bondage, or *nexum,* constitutes an early form of contract law: the per-
son receiving a loan temporarily relinquishes his person and its labor to
the creditor until the debt is paid off (1990 [1950], 49).[62] Though on one
reading *tuus vates* suggests a personal and intimate tone, the proximity of
the phrase to *contractus* implies, if subtextually, the contrary: an impersonal
contract created by the original benefaction of the farm. In his capacity as
public poet—as a *vates*—Horace (or at least his labor) would, in the logic
of the *nexum,* quite literally belong to Maecenas and justify the use of the
possessive pronoun.[63] Such an interpretation recalls the claim of *Epistles*
1.1, where Horace is no longer (he implies) *addictus,* or bound over, to a
master, even as it finds further support in the jocular *adunaton* demanding
the return of Horace's hair, strong body, and decorous laughter.

But these lines do more than identify the poet's past physical self as a
possession that the patron would, ironically, have to return should he wish
never to be without Horace's bodily presence. For the autobiographical
image here acquires properties associated with genre: sweet speech, grace-

61. Critics and commentators generally understand *contractus* to mean "huddled up"
(*OLD,* s.v., 1a), or "sparing," "living in a constricted fashion" (*OLD,* s.v., 2): cf. Mayer 1994,
ad loc. Preaux 1968, ad loc., adds: "C'est l'idéal de l'εὐθυμίη démocritéenne sous l'éclairage
de la *parsimonia.*" Kiessling and Heinze 1961a, ad loc., understand it similarly as "ganz auf
mich selbst zurückgezogen." Surprisingly, given the legal and commercial language of other
images in the epistle, none of these commentaries remark any connotation of a literal "con-
tract," though such a meaning is present in the noun *contractus,* which itself derives from the
past participle of *contraho,* a verb that can mean to enter into a formal legal or commercial
agreement (*OLD,* s.v., 6).

62. Watson (1975, 111) defines the *nexum* as "an act *per aes et libram* by which a free man
was bound to a creditor and was subject to his control until an amount of bronze which had
been weighed out was repaid." As Watson goes on to specify, Varro, *Linq.* 7.105 discusses a
difference of opinion between Manilius and Mucius, siding with the latter to the effect that
"the person bound by *nexum* did not become the property, the slave, of the creditor" (112).
The distinction thus appears to be one between having a right to the *labor* of the debtor and
actually *owning* his person. Varro traces the etymology of the term *nexum* to *neque suum* in
order to point up the difference between *nexum* and *mancipatio,* the latter referring to an
actual transfer of ownership of property—in this case the *res* of a person—and thus slavery.
But given the difference of opinion in our available sources, as well as the subtextual and
metaphorical use of the language of contract in Horace, this distinction does not negate the
basic implications of *contractus.*

63. In a chapter on *ususfructus,* Watson (1968, 203) discusses a legal joke in Plaut. *Cas.*
836–37: "There seems to be a deliberate contrast, for humorous purposes, between *mea est*
and *meus fructus est* [;] . . . a claim to the right to the fruits is put in opposition to a claim of
'ownership.'" G. Williams (1990, 264) emphasizes that the coercive phrases like *noster esto* in
comedy derive directly from the language of patronage.

ful laughter, and the lament of Cinara's elusive ways all figure as metony-mies for the erotic odes—the echo of *dulce ridentem Lalagen* (sweetly laugh-ing Lalage, *Odes* 1.22.23) is unmistakable—and the sympotic Horace, as I have argued, necessarily implicates the more public *vates*. Indeed, the po-litical odes of the Horatian *vates* are implied directly: the sequence of the two adjectives *dulce* and *decorum* in the line *reddes dulce loqui, reddes ridere decorum et* (*Ep.* 1.7.27–28), surely also alludes to the most memorable (and disturbing) line of the Roman Odes, *dulce et decorum est pro patria mori* (It is sweet and fitting to die for one's country, 3.2.13), even as it suggests the dedication of *Odes* 1.1 to Maecenas as *dulce decus meum* (2). In light of Horace's demand, all of these associations present the *Odes* as a kind of commodity that can be equated with the physical self of the poet. We may also see an allusion to both the *Odes* and the *Satires,* the first book of which was dedicated to Maecenas as well, in the contrast between speaking sweetly (*dulce loqui*) and laughing appropriately (*ridere decorum*). Thus Horace, by way of humorous response to his patron's demands, presents an image of his aesthetic labor as reified or objectified in these allusions to generic selves as commodities that are now in Maecenas's—or, more broadly speak-ing, the Augustan regime's—possession. And the specific allusion to the Roman Odes would further the identification of poetry as *munus*-turned-commodity in this revelation of the concealed contract of gift exchange. In keeping with the gladiatorial image that introduces the volume of *Epis-tles,* Horace's lyric labor is a "gift" of sacrifice for the sake of the country—*pro patria mori*—that the poet, with irony, now demands back. By making such a demand, Horace demystifies sacrifice as an act of voluntarism, in-verting the process of "symbolic alchemy which transmutes the price of labor into an unsolicited gift" (Bourdieu 1977, 173).

In terms of a "contract," then, Horace humorously (and wistfully) pres-ents his account as paid: Maecenas has no right to demand further *officia* from the poet, for the latter already paid off his debt on the farm by writing the *Odes*. We might say that Horace takes the public understanding of "for-mal" patronage as one of economic exchanges and subtly represents the contract as both honored and no longer relevant. For it is a hypothetical public to which the weasel from afar (*procul*) gives voice, and it is precisely their potential charge of continued indebtedness that Horace refutes in addressing Maecenas: as the "third party" necessary to witness the original transaction, the weasel perceives Horace as guilty, or *reus*—in a state of culpability for having accepted the *res* of the farm.[64] To this public, the poet

---

64. Mauss (1990 [1950], 51–52) discusses culpability in regard to early Roman law cited by Festus: "First, the contracting party is *reus,* he is above all the person who has received the *res* of another, and thereby becomes his *reus,* ie. the individual who is linked to him by the thing itself[.]" Moreover, as Watson (1968, 134) confirms, the handing over of property,

says, "I will sign it all back to his account"; but to Maecenas himself, Horace says, "You give me back my time and labor as reified in the *Odes* and *Satires*."[65] That is, Horace subtly suggests that it is Maecenas, and more broadly the regime, who is now in debt to the poet. The verb used by Horace three times here, *reddes* (you will return), appears once more in just this form in *Epistles* 1.13, where the poet gives instructions, with exaggerated and mock anxiety, to the figure Asinius who is to "deliver sealed papyrus rolls" (*reddes signata volumina*, 1), presumably *Odes* 1–3, to Augustus.[66] The repetition of this verb in these two letters only furthers the identification of poet and verse in a context in which the poems as reified object participate in the transactions of patronage, with their implicit contract—the concealed economics—of gift exchange: though the *Odes* enjoyed an audience beyond the *primi urbis* alone, the representation of them as a physical bundle to be conveyed to the emperor underscores their concrete function as return gift. And the gift ideology of patronage as one that, in fact, conceals the calculating expectations of return here colors the semantic scope of *reddere:* beneath the immediate contextual meaning of *reddes* in *Epistles* 1.13, as "you will deliver" or "you will hand over," is the monetary sense of repaying a loan or discharging a debt. This economic implication draws the uses of *reddere* in the seventh epistle together with the diction of bookkeeping and accounts that we see in the assertions *cuncta resigno* (I sign everything back to your account) and *inspice si possum donata reponere laetus* (See ["look at my account"] whether I can repay your gifts).[67]

Aera *versus* Lupini

Other images in the seventh epistle expose the economic calculation behind patronage as both a public reality and a fact to be repudiated in the name of friendship and the ideology of voluntarism. One such image stands out in apparent contrast to the many *ainoi* concerned with the art of giving.

---

the ceremony of *mancipatio*, takes place in front of five witnesses— suggesting that both the symbolic public of the "weasel" within the poem and the reading public of the *Epistles* are witnesses to Horace's statement.

65. For discussion of *Satires* 1 in terms of "propagandistic" value, see Du Quesnay 1984.

66. See Oliensis 1998, 189, for this phrase as an echo of Augustus's claims to have forced the Parthians to "return the spoils and standards" (*spolia et signa reddere*) of the Romans. Pointing to Augustan coinage of the time that celebrate the occasion, Oliensis suggests that Horace's "privately minted coin shows his 'standard-bearer' in a Parthian posture, deferentially bowing before the emperor."

67. See Sen. *Ep.* 81.9–10 (discussed in chapter 1) for the distinction between the language of a monetary loan, where *reddere* would be used, and that pertaining to benefaction and the returns it elicits, where the verb *referre* would be used, signifying the "voluntary" nature of expressions of gratitude. Cf. also Sen. *Ben.* 6.5.2. For *inspice* as a bookkeeping term, see Mayer 1994, ad. loc. For *reponere*, see *OLD*, s.v., 5.

After asserting that Maecenas did not make him *locupletem* (wealthy) after the fashion of a Calabrian host who gives away what he does not value, Horace draws the following terse and elegant conclusion from the exemplum:

> prodigus et stultus donat quae spernit et odit:
> haec seges ingratos tulit et feret omnibus annis.
> vir bonus et sapiens dignis ait esse paratus,
> nec tamen ignorat quid distent aera lupinis;
> dignum praestabo me etiam pro laude merentis.

The prodigal fool makes presents of what he scorns and despises; a field so planted has yielded and will always bring forth ingratitude. The good and wise man says he is ready to give to the worthy, and yet he is able to discern the difference between real money and counterfeit. I will also show myself worthy on a par with the honor earned by the giver. (1.7.20–24)

The first two lines clearly comment on the lasting ingratitude that an un-valued gift yields, but the following lines have occasioned much debate among the commentators. If the "good and wise man" refers to the patron, and thus, by implication, Maecenas, the *aera* (money) as distinguished from *lupinis* (counterfeit coins) could represent one of three elements in a patronal transaction: the benefactions given to a deserving man, the worthy recipients themselves, or the "gifts"—*officia* or otherwise—rendered as acknowledgment by the recipient in return.[68] What immediately strikes the reader familiar with the ideology of benefaction is the use of a monetary image in evaluating one of the constituents of the process. For all that Seneca in *De beneficiis* fastidiously and repeatedly separates the loaning of money and the practice of benefaction, successful giving requires assigning values and thus invokes the metaphor of currency. To some degree, this language of evaluation reflects a more pervasive phenomenon that began in the second century, a redefinition of the semantic scope of words describing monetary processes to include notions of aristocratic "goodness, reputability, and largesse" (Habinek 1998, 49).[69] That being said, the

68. Critics generally understand the distinction between *aera* and *lupini* to refer to the benefactions bestowed by the giver: see Büchner 1972 [1940], 92–93; Fraenkel 1957, 330–32; G. Williams 1968, 20; Macleod 1983, 284. However, Kiessling and Heinze 1961a, ad loc., read the distinction as referring to the worth of the receiver himself, a view derived from one scholiastic tradition.

69. As Kurke (1995, 36–64) notes, archaic and classical Greek texts use similar imagery to express ideas of aristocratic worth. However, the novelty of coinage created a certain suspicion, with the result that the dichotomy of essentialism (money consists of precious metal) and functionalism (money is exchanged and symbolic) breaks down according to class lines; references to coinage are conspicuously absent from archaic Greek lyric.

confusion in our passage over which element the *aera* represent only underscores how deeply calculation and a law of equivalences permeate the system of benefaction: *aera* may refer to gift, recipient, or return acknowledgment because, in terms of exchange value, each of these possesses a worth that responds to and elicits the corresponding worth of the other. The gift is appropriate to the internal worth of the recipient, whose character produces an acknowledgment appropriate to the value of the gift and the original benefactor.[70] The line *dignum praestabo me etiam pro laude merentis* further accentuates the equivalence of all these constituents of the patronal relationship: the return "gift" of acknowledgment, implied as the effect of the *dignum praestabo me* (I will show myself worthy), corresponds or answers to (*pro*) the glory—the symbolic capital of generosity—of the one who merits such reciprocation. Although the art of benefaction ideally eschews the sharp, if arbitrary, distinctions in value ensured by money, currency as the symbol of the concept of worth is readily used to illuminate the speaker's anecdote. The use of money as the metaphor's vehicle suggests the underlying monetary economics of its tenor, the relationship between a patron and his dependent.

The distinction between *aera* and *lupini* as a metaphor specifically for the return gift or acknowledgment of the original recipient also brings to mind the particular offerings that this epistle renders to Maecenas. When Horace claims *cuncta resigno,* we are reminded that the verb *resigno* can mean *rescribere* ("to write back" or "to transfer by writing from one account to another") in the economic sense. *Rescribere* itself suggests the very act of writing in which the poet presently engages. As Mark Shell suggests, the tropic nature of language is analogous to the symbolic value of money: "Literary works are composed of small tropic exchanges or metaphors, some of which can be analyzed in terms of signified economic content and all of which can be analyzed in terms of economic form" (1978, 7).[71] The monetary metaphor in Horace's epistle displays both economic form and content. Moreover, as a metaphor of economic content, the *aera* and *lupini* suggestively allude to a larger scale of exchanges of meaning in the epistle. For when Horace employs a series of fables, anecdotes, and metaphors for the art of benefaction, he offers Maecenas comparisons that may or may not be valid to the poet's own autobiographical experience. In short, he

70. This formulation is essentially in keeping with the theory of proper benefaction or liberality as articulated in Arist. *Eth. Nic.* 4.1119b18–1123a33 and Cic. *Off.* 1.45–49. See the discussion in Fraenkel 1957, 330–32; Kilpatrick 1986, 10.

71. The distinction between content and form applies to tropes containing money (if there is money or some kind of economic content in the vehicle) and to tropes generally, because each refers to an exchange of value and hence is economic in form. See the remarks of Goux (1990) discussed in chapter 3, n. 15.

presents his patron with allegories whose potentially counterfeit status must be determined by the one who interprets them. And it is precisely this status that conditions other statements of the poem: just as the Vulteius Mena episode and the fable of the fox in the cornbin do not, as negative illustrations, receive full value from the referent or "signified" of Horace's life, so his claims must be suspect as well. Even the betrayal of syntax to which the conditional conjunction *quod si* leads in lines 10 and 25 constitutes a form of counterfeit logic. When, presumably, Maecenas has recognized Horace as a *mendax,* and is thus able to distinguish between the *aera* and *lupini*— the real and fake coin—of anecdote, metaphor, and fable, he perceives the potentially counterfeit gesture of Horace's offer to "give it all back." Thus, Horace does more than reveal and confound the contractual economics underlying patronage as an ideology of disinterested voluntarism. He also breaks the contract of language, separating the sign from its referent as one might the inscription from the actual value of a coin.[72] His words, at least for those without the power of discrimination, are *lupini* that he presumes to pass off as *aera.*

This analogy between the words offered by a poet to his patron and the *aera* of legitimate currency returns us to a specific ritual that accompanied the dissolution of the *nexum,* or state of debt-bondage. Quoting Festus, Mauss claims that the original transaction is sealed by the gift of a bronze ingot, or *aes nexum,* given by the *tradens* (the lender, the seller) to the *accipiens.* Later, when the *accipiens* "discharges himself from the bond, not only does he carry out the service promised or hand over the thing or its price, but, in particular, on the same pair of scales and before the same witnesses, he returns the same *aes* to the lender, to the seller" (Mauss 1990 [1950], 139 n. 10). The offer to return his patron's benefactions, to discharge himself of his debt, metaphorically becomes in this epistle the very *aes* (in this case *lupini*) that would have accompanied the actual transfer.[73] Because of this analogy between *aera* and language, we can say that the gesture or offer to give back the goods received replaces the property itself. Or, in keeping with the relationship between inscription and the substance of coinage (a relationship that enables the development of paper currency), the promise made in language (writing) becomes dissociated from the actual referent—the act of return. This distinction between the writing that signifies and may confer value and the actual worth of a coin's metal— its substance—is implied here only when we apply the metaphor of real

72. Shell (1982, 15) comments on this separation: "when the ingot itself disappears, and all that remains is the inscription—the literature—is the numismatic inscription still substantially valid, as is symbolic paper money?"

73. The network of images in the text suggests this reading regardless of whether Horace intended such an equation.

versus counterfeit (or play) money to the various exempla and their relevance to Horace's life.

The power of the inscription to turn valuable metal into money as a medium of exchange, and thus the importance of credit attributed to an inscription, suggests the semiotic nature of coinage: it represents or substitutes for something else.[74] This idea of substitution, which underlies both currency (real or counterfeit) and language, and which is invoked by the distinction between *aera* and *lupini,* appears in various ways when the poet refers to his separation from his patron. Just as the letter itself serves to substitute for the physical presence of the poet, a missive that only represents him, so the epithets by which Horace refers to Maecenas and which are "tokens" of his gratitude hold true (so the poet implies) even when the two are absent from each other:

> saepe verecundum laudasti, rexque paterque
> audisti coram, nec verbo parcius absens:
> inspice si possum donata reponere laetus.

Often you have praised me as modest, and you have been called both king and father by me in your presence, nor, away from you, am I more sparing of my epithets: see, now, if I am able, cheerfully, to return your gifts. (1.7.37–39)

These lines most overtly engage the issue of Horace's credibility and make Maecenas the guarantor of the poet's statement that he could *reponere donata*. Horace's modesty and gratitude for past gifts, qualities witnessed by Maecenas himself, are such that he is quite capable of making good his earlier offer, *cuncta resigno*. And yet the workings of credit and credibility here are more complicated than they first appear. Invoking the initial issue of Horace's attendance on Maecenas in Rome, these lines also suggest that the language of gratitude, though separated from the immediate context of speaking and hearing, still carries value; in other words, credit must be accorded to the epithets *rex* (king) and *pater* (father) as symbols of Horace's gratitude, as the *aera* of return acknowledgment, despite their separation from the context of Maecenas as witness—*coram* (face-to-face)—that originally guarantees their worth. Horace shows himself worthy (*dignum praestabo me etiam pro laude merentis,* 24) through speech and, by implication, through poetry, not by returning in person to Rome. And poetry as a substitute for Horace's presence seems implied by more than the epistle itself:

---

74. Shell (1978, 66–67) points out that the first known inscribed coin bears the inscription *Phaneos eimi sema* (I am the *sema* of Phanos), on one side, and the image of a stag, a "heraldic badge of the goddess Artemis," on the other. The *sema* can refer both to the linguistic inscription or the stag and to the coin itself, making it "twice semiotic."

the reading of *audisti* for the verb omitted from the phrase *nec verbo parcius absens* suggests not only the sense of "hearing well of oneself" or "being well-spoken of" but also the actual practice of hearing verse recited.[75]

Thus, the poet's demonstration of worthiness as equivalent to the glory of his patron is an issue of the credit accorded to language: the credit, belief, or investment with value that language demands is superimposed on the issue of Maecenas's own credit or symbolic capital as a benefactor; and Maecenas's reputation—his credibility—depends, to some degree, on the credibility or sincerity of Horace's own words of praise. And the workings of credit extend further than the authenticity of sentiment behind praise spoken or written *in absentia*. The credit that the poet himself has earned through the aesthetic celebration of his patron guarantees his ability to return his benefactor's gifts. The credibility of the latter statement— *inspice si possum donata reponere laetus*—is underwritten, so to speak, by the sincerity of his previous recognition of his patron.

It is here that *aera* and *lupini,* as marking the distinction between effective signifying value and falsehood or worthlessness, come into play. For the separation from an immediate context that would guarantee or secure the meaning of some form of "signifier" is what invokes the problems of interpretation and the potential for deceit or counterfeit. That the capacity to make distinctions of value applies to language as well as to benefactions is reinforced by verbal repetition in the epistle: the negated adverb *parcius* (more sparingly), referring to the prodigality of Horace's praise and acknowledgment of his patron even when absent, looks back to the epithet *prodigus* (extravagant, wasteful) for the man who does not value what he gives away (20), as well as ahead to the exemplum from Homer, where Telemachus, by claiming that Ithaca is not very grassy (*prodigus herbae*), justifies his refusal of Menelaus's inappropriately ostentatious gifts (40–43). These verbal echoes suggest not that Horace offers *lupini*—or worthless words—when he calls Maecenas *rex* and *pater,* but that absence or separation from the context that initially guarantees the value of these words (spoken face-to-face) demands greater credulity, or credit, and thus raises the possibility of counterfeit status.[76] That is, because the epistle itself has replaced face-to-face interaction (*coram*), the *ainoi* of the epistolary context, though seemingly adduced to "clarify" and "illustrate," may in fact

75. *OLD,* s.v. "audire," 5b, 6b. According to Mayer 1994, ad loc., *audisti* is a "lexical Grecism" and *que . . . que* is perhaps modeled after *te . . . te,* lending these lines an epic tone. This reading would further support my argument that the Telemachus anecdote, the one analogy from epic, is intended to appeal to Maecenas's aristocratic sympathies.

76. Another implication of the speaker's claim to be no less sparing of praise when he is away from Maecenas is to validate the words of praise spoken *coram*. In this regard, "writing" may confer value on speech.

destabilize the "autobiographical" assertions. Hence, the statement that follows, *inspice si possum donata reponere laetus*, also must be understood as potentially misleading.

Like Father, Like Son: Telemachus and the Power of Refusal

On the one hand, *inspice* (examine, see) looks back to *coram* and suggests the *presence* of witnesses in an economic transaction. In this sense, the imperative would be directed at Maecenas and would issue the challenge "Try me, I'm as good as my word."[77] On the other hand, *inspice* also looks forward to the exemplum from the *Odyssey* that follows. This anecdote, too, signifies outside of its original context: removed from the surrounding epic story of Telemachus's visit to Menelaus to acquire news of Odysseus, it is here applied to a discussion of patronage. Exchanging one context for another, the exemplum demands from the reader—Maecenas, the larger reading public of ancient Rome, or ourselves—that we determine whether, like *aera,* this epic anecdote "gives an honest value" and is backed up by its referent (the assertion that Horace will give it all back) or, like *lupini,* the story does not translate into the real value of meaning. In other words, the imperative *inspice,* followed by the exemplum from Homer, points not to witnesses to an actual act of return but to a demand that the reader interpret whether any intention to return is present.

As I argued earlier, for those who believe the Homeric exemplum, like the fable of the fox in the cornbin, to imply that Horace would return all benefactions, the poet is being a *mendax* and passing off *lupini* as *aera.* But for those who perceive the lie and see the Horatian persona as up to something more complex, the anecdote in a sense does give back real value beneath its seeming falsehood.[78] Part of the complexity of the exemplum lies in the contrast between the original context of aristocratic gift exchange and the immediate one of patronage presented in the language of monetary accounts. Not only is *inspice* used of witnesses to an economic transaction, but *reponere* can also apply to the absolution of monetary debt (Preaux 1968, ad loc.). Yet the exemplum itself refers to gifts refused because of their extravagant inappropriateness to the situation of the receiver. Moreover, as one critic has recently suggested, such a refusal amounts not to a manifestation of decorum but rather to a breach in the etiquette of gift exchange (Lyne 1995, 154). For although the wise man should give appropriately to the merits of the recipient, the code of Homeric gift

---

77. Berres (1992, 228) emphasizes that Horace invokes Maecenas as a witness to the poet's capacity to make good his claim, but also stresses that Horace responds to those who might suspect his economic motives.

78. The truth or value of the Horatian lie here suggests the nature of poetry in general—communicating some form of truth or meaning through the deceptive surface of rhetoric.

exchange and particularly of guest-host relations lays an obligation on the recipient to accept what is offered.[79] Hence, by displaying his own lack of decorum, Telemachus in fact matches the indecorousness in the extravagant giving on the part of Menelaus. In matching gaff for gaff, Telemachus may very well illustrate Horace's ability to requite Maecenas on the level of indecorous behavior. Such a reading may seem to take to an extreme the simple observation that Telemachus is rude, but it nonetheless accords with one meaning of *reponere*—to repay or pay back injuries or benefits (*OLD*, s.v., 5)—a sense very close to the straightforwardly economic meaning of repaying a debt. The poet thus behaves in a way ironically consonant with his earlier statement: "I will also show myself worthy on a par with the honor earned by the giver."

The above reading may exaggerate the ambiguities of the statement *inspice si possum reponere donata* when read against the backdrop of the Homeric exemplum and the larger context of the epistle, but it accurately points up the problematic deferral and deflection of the value of Horace's statement—what it actually means—onto the anecdote from Homer. Hence, the distinction between *aera* and *lupini* may reflect the binary opposition of true and false in a way that does not always neatly divide the *ainoi* one from the other. Rather, the *value* of these fables and anecdotes lies in the complexity of their implications when applied to Horace's experience.

A final reading of the Telemachus anecdote is suggested by the *rex* and *pater* by which Horace refers to Maecenas and which stand as the testimony, and linguistic embodiment, of gratitude—a form of *aera* or return. These conventional epithets for a patron find an almost asymmetric correspondence in the Homeric exemplum that follows: although Telemachus turns down Menelaus's gifts, making the son of Atreus into a Maecenas figure, the associations of "king" and "father" would better apply to Odysseus. Moreover, the manuscript reading of *sapientis* (wise) rather than *patientis Ulixi* (enduring Ulysses) recalls the phrase *vir bonus et sapiens* (the good and wise man) in line 22, where the good benefactor is defined and associated with Maecenas.[80] One explanation of this asymmetrical correspondence may lie in the particular nature of the "goods" that Telemachus receives from Odysseus: the son acquires the father's name, the

79. For example, when Glaucon and Diomedes exchange armor in *Il.* 6.234–36, considerations of economic disparity between the gifts, though noted by Homer, are completely subordinated to the obligation to give and receive in keeping with the code of *xenia* that obtained between their fathers. For the psychology of the pressure to accept in gift-exchange societies, see the comments of Mauss (1990 [1950], 41) on the potlatch of the Kwakiutl tribe. On the appropriateness of the gift, see n. 70 above.

80. This manuscript reading also likely alludes to Philodemus's treatise *On the Good King According to Homer.*

genealogical bloodlines of family, and something of the father's *kleos,* or reputation. Moreover, Telemachus's justification for turning down Menelaus's gifts—Ithaca's unsuitability for horses—leads into the pithy conclusion, *parvum parva decent* (small things suit a small man), a phrase that sets up a parallel between Ithaca and the Sabine farm.[81] Though only implicit, it reinforces an overall representation of Maecenas's good patronage in terms of aristocratic and familial inheritance. Even as the poet represents his patron's present offer in the negative terms of Menelaus's excessive wealth, Horace allegorically grounds his capacity for refusal in terms of the symbolic capital that Maecenas's past patronage has accorded him: in Homer, Telemachus's refusal prompts the smiling recognition from Menelaus that the son has behaved with the practical forethought of his father. Thus, we see that an inherited disposition, the landed "patrimony" of Ithaca, and finally a freedom to breach social etiquette—a liberty based on Odysseus's *kleos* rather than on Telemachus's own stature—all combine to represent the aristocratic standing, the symbolic capital with which Maecenas has endowed Horace and which then allows him, paradoxically, the power of refusal. The understanding of *reponere donata* to mean "store up gifts"— Kilpatrick's interpretation (1986, 12)—would, in my reading, refer to this accumulation of symbolic capital that Horace then uses to assert his independence.

Discriminating readers perceive the aesthetic complexity of this Homeric *exemplum:* they separate the real value (*aera*) from the false (*lupini*), which the less astute reading public would understand as the apparent assertion of the poet's ability and willingness to return all Maecenas's benefactions. Such a public would automatically identify the Telemachus anecdote with the fable of the fox in the cornbin, as well as the Vulteius Mena story, failing to note how far the real value of the one exemplum differs (*distat*) from the false value of the others. Horace's counterfeit gesture, like Odysseus's disguises, ironically tests the worth of his readership: those who believe him foolishly count him discharged, while those who perceive the deceit have their capacity for aesthetic discrimination confirmed. It is no coincidence that the verb for perception in Greek—*aisthanomai*—is the etymological root of "aesthetic." By perceiving the problematic nature of the exempla that might illustrate or validate the speaker's assertion, discriminating readers do in fact receive a certain compensation for their engagement with the epistle. As speaker and reader alike align themselves with the "true" value that the Homeric exemplum reveals, aesthetic perception and aristocratic ideology reinforce each other.

81. Hor. *Odes* 2.16.37–38, *mihi parva rura et / spiritum Graiae tenuem Camenae,* is traditionally understood as referring to the Sabine farm and the conflation of humble needs with Callimachean aesthetics.

Moreover, the distinction between *aera* and *lupini* is inscribed in the first three *ainoi* even in terms of the material that they represent as ingested or exchanged: *lupini* were used as play money on the stage, but they were also the fodder of livestock and a staple of the poor man's diet.[82] Hence, as both a symbol of the worthless gift and the simple food of the common man, the *lupini* derive from the same semiotic register as the pears left for the pigs in the story of the Calabrian host or the corn that the fox consumes. In contrast, those who know the Homeric story remember that Telemachus receives a bowl of precious metal—*aes*—in place of the rejected horses and chariot (*Od.* 4.590–619). In Homer, this bowl is a *keimelion*, a precious object retrieved from Menelaus's innermost chamber. The aristocratic world of gift exchange is thus the model in which the poet chooses to inscribe his own experience, likening the institution of *amicitia* to the guest-host relations of Homeric *xenia*. As Leslie Kurke claims in her discussion of Pindar's epinician allusions to the epic relations of *xenia*, the "invocation of the Homeric model is not merely a literary allusion but an ideological gesture common to the poet and his aristocratic group" (1991, 139).[83] Similarly, the echo of *aera* in the *keimelion* of the background to the Telemachus anecdote both identifies good patronal relations with the aristocratic equals of Homeric *xenia* and gestures toward a shared elite culture.

Philippus and the Power of Return

The Vulteius Mena story provides a sharp contrast to an aristocratic ideology of gift exchange—one whose pretense to voluntarism in its own right permits the refusals of a Telemachus.[84] Whereas the figures in the Homeric exemplum are more or less equal, the difference in social station between Philippus and Mena is clear. Indeed, despite the emphasis on Mena's independence as a *coactor*, it is the difference in status that causes Philippus

82. For *lupini* as food of the common man, see Préaux 1968, ad loc., with sources cited there.

83. Kurke (1991, 145) discusses the symbol of the Homeric *keimelion* as a trope by which Pindar represents the power of poetry as an enduring utterance.

84. Although reciprocity was very much the rule of *xenia*, the delay between gift and countergift enables the ideology of voluntarism and friendship to conceal the economic aspect of the exchange. Finley (1953, 237) makes this distinction but inverts the emphasis: "In essence, Homeric gift-giving was normally a bilateral action, not a unilateral one. Although it retained the outward appearance of a free, voluntary act, it came very near to being obligatory." See also the comments of Donlan (1993, 150) on Menelaus's wish to make gifts to Telemachus. Donlan defines guest-host friendship in terms of "generalized reciprocity," a category of exchange employed by Sahlins (1965), where the "giving is (ideally) altruistic. There is no overt pressure for a return. Those who can, give; those who need, take. The emphasis is on social solidarity, and the "material" aspect is minimal" (Donlan 1993, 140). See chapter 1, n. 7.

not to brook a refusal of his invitation, thus initiating the relationship. The terms of *patronus* and *cliens* are openly used, and the Sabine property is fully acquired through the combination of a loan and a gift of money, not simply as a benefaction. Moreover, unlike Horace's own farm, associated with the freedom of *otium,* Vulteius Mena's estate is figured only in terms of labor and profits—the business or *negotium* of agriculture: Mena's exhausting efforts display Hesiod's vision of the farmer's work once the world has passed from a golden age of spontaneous surplus. And the relationship of patronage between Mena and Philippus swiftly becomes openly economic: the loan of money for the farm has turned Mena from an independent working man into a debtor, again suggesting the relationship between the *nexum* and the far end of the spectrum of patronage.[85]

Livy's description of a man suffering from such debt-bondage (2.23.3–9) bears an uncanny resemblance to the run-down condition of Mena when he bursts in on Philippus and demands "patron, return me to my previous life" (*patrone . . . vitae me redde priori,* 1.7.92–95). Mena is described as *scabrum intonsumque* (scabrous and unshorn, 90); he is anxious about his losses (*offensus damnis*), for his farm has been destroyed: "His sheep were stolen, his goats perished from disease, his crop deceived his expectations, his ox was near dead from ploughing" (*oves furto, morbo periere capellae, / spem mentita seges, bos est enectus arando,* 86–87). In Livy, the conflicts *inter patres plebemque* just preceding the war with the Volsci in 495 B.C.E. are brought to a head when one of those *nexos ob aes alienum* (bound in labor for their debts) rushed into the Forum:

> His dress was covered with filth, and the condition of his body was even worse, for he was pale and half dead with emaciation (*foedior corporis habitus pallore ac macie perempti*). Besides this, his straggling beard and hair had given a savage look to his countenance (*promissa barba et capilli efferaverant speciem oris*). . . . When they asked the reason of his condition and his squalor, he replied . . . that during his service in the Sabine war not only had the enemy's depredations deprived him of his crops, but his cottage had been burnt, all his belongings plundered, and his flocks driven off. Then the taxes had been levied, in an untoward moment for him, and he had contracted debts.[86]

Though *nexum* was obsolete by the time Horace writes, the similar details in these two descriptions and the emphasis on Philippus's power to "return" (*redde*) Mena—as though he were a physical possession—by relieving him of his debt suggests traces of this archaic economic practice.

---

85. See Cornell 1995, 291, on early patronage: "The goods and services exchanged can be materialist in the crudest sense, when the patron provides the barest means of subsistence, and the client is obliged to provide labour services. At this point the relationship shades into servitude, and it is probably not incorrect to see *nexum* as an extreme form of patronage."

86. Trans. Foster 1919, Loeb edition.

The imperative *redde* here also returns us to Horace's earlier use of the verb in his jocular *adunata* demanding that Maecenas give back the poet's youth. There, too, we found subtextual traces of primitive contract law in the diction articulating the poet's present relations with his patron. The echo of these earlier autobiographical statements in the later anecdote demands, once again, that the reader distinguish between the *aera* and *lupini* of the epistle's *exempla*. As many critics recognize, the Vulteius Mena episode is clearly not an unmediated reflection of Horatian experience, and thus it can be aligned with the fable of the fox in the cornbin. Yet the many correspondences with Horace's life offered by specific details in the story suggest that it is an extreme, if inexact, *exemplum* intended for those who believe Horace's statement that he could return his gifts. In this final anecdote, Horace fully exposes the implicitly contractual element to benefaction by using the actual language of patronage in what becomes a situation of monetary debt.[87] This revelation is directed—notionally, at least—at a public readership that might consider the poet a paid hack of the regime. For Maecenas, however, the Vulteius Mena episode stands as a model of bad patronage, an *exemplum ex contrario* to be repudiated in the name of *amicitia*, or friendly, voluntary relations among the elite. Whereas Philippus has the power to "return" Mena, through the monetary relation of actual debt, to his previous life, the element of time has so radically altered Maecenas's relationship to Horace that the poet can no more give back his patron's *donata* than the latter can give back the poet's youth and labor reified in the *Satires* and the *Odes*.

Otium *and Hermeneutic Exchange*

As noted above, the lack of direct reference to the Sabine farm makes possible the poet's duplicitous representations. It is, in fact, the poet's resistance to turning what the estate represents for him—*otium*—into mere exchange value that enables it to signify in contradictory ways. Claiming that he would not traffic in *otium*, Horace refuses to convert his symbolic capital—the leisure of landed wealth—back into material capital: "I would not trade (*muto*) my leisure (*otia*) for all the wealth (*divitiis*) of Arabia" (1.7.36).[88] *Otium*, as we saw in chapter 3, is the source of aesthetic produc-

---

87. Mena is called a *cliens* (75) and Philippus is *patrone* (92). The latter usage is unusual; during this period *patronus* generally refers only to a lawyer, a master of a freedman, or the benefactor of a town.

88. On the surface, this line appears to refer only to the leisure time of the man unconstrained by the duties and burdens of excessive riches and thus can be taken as evidence that the speaker *would* return the farm, or *cuncta donata*, should they constrain his *otium*. However, *otia* also refers to the farm, as the tellingly similar line from the first Roman Ode implies—*cur valle permutem Sabina / divitias operosiores* (3.1.47–48). Here it is the Sabine property quite explicitly that the speaker discusses in terms of potential exchange for *divitias* or riches.

tion, the leisure and respite from the demands of *negotia* that may eventuate in art. Significantly, the verb used by Horace in his apparent refusal, quite literally, to *negotiate* his freedom—*mutare*—is the word that Vergil employs to juxtapose the overseas trade of the merchant with the natural and aesthetic surplus of the golden age in the fourth eclogue. In that poem, the precise equivalences of commerce yield to the spontaneous profusions of a golden age economy.[89]

The libidinal, nonquantifiable quality of *gratia*, as I discussed in chapters 1 and 3, ideally eludes such precise calculations of a monetary economy and displays the same tendency to excess as the *Eclogues'* representation of the golden age.[90] As a rhetorical figure the trope of the golden age, and more specifically the *cornucopia*, articulates the same ideology of disinterested giving to which the emotion of *gratia* responds. Horace's estate as place of polysemous connotation—gift, ground of independence, object of status, symbol of debt—recalls the *cornucopia* of *Odes* 1.17 as emblem of signifying abundance and excess of libidinal feeling. By appropriating the semiotic register of benefaction as one of natural abundance,[91] Horace thus converts his farm, an image of *otium*, into a site of rhetorical or aesthetic play that secures his freedom.

On the other hand, we have also seen that the terms of a monetary economy may be said to structure the aesthetic form of *Epistles* 1.7. Hence, monetary equivalence and aesthetic excess are, so to speak, two sides of the same coin. For though the farm may be implicitly valued as *aera* (real coin) rather than *lupini* (counterfeit) by the giver, Maecenas, its value for Horace lies not just in monetary exchange but also in aesthetics and its "endlessly tropic and infinitely hermeneutic" transactions (Shell 1978, 85).[92] Yet only as an absent center does the material farm allow these infinite substitutions of meaning, this perpetual aesthetic supplementation. As property conspicuous for its absence, the farm justifies the metaphor of coinage: although real estate constitutes "visible property," the farm's very invisibility

89. In *Eclogue* 4, *nec nautica pinus / mutabit merces* (38–39) yields to *aries iam suave rubenti / murice, iam croceo mutabit vellera luto* (43–44).

90. See Cic. *Off.* 2.69–70 and Sen. *Ben.* 2.25.1: "For what so much proves a grateful heart as the impossibility of ever satisfying oneself, or of even attaining the hope of ever being able to make adequate return for a benefit." Cf. Sen. *Ben.* 5.4.1: "No one can be outdone in benefits if he knows how to owe a debt, if he desires to make return[;] . . . so long as he holds the desire to give proof of a grateful heart, what difference does it make on which side the greater number of gifts is reckoned?" (trans. Basore 1935, Loeb edition).

91. See *Off.* 1.22, where Cicero recommends that human beings imitate the natural abundance of the earth in their distribution of benefits and services.

92. See Shell 1978, 63–88, for discussion of the simultaneously aesthetic and economic nature of coinage and the inherently economic nature of the exchanges performed by metaphorization and symbolization in thought.

in this text lends it the power of money as "invisible property." Hence, despite Horace's efforts in resisting an economy of monetary equivalence, one that would allow Maecenas to trade on the exchange value of his ben-efactions, the endless substitutions made possible by the farm's absence demonstrate the inescapability of money as a form determining Horace's thought. In this case, Horace's freedom from the economic realities of patronage depends, in a sense, on a system of linguistic tropes—metaphor, simile, and analogy—that themselves operate as money does. We might say that in the dialectical fashion of a Marxist hermeneutic, any freedom from the economic realities of patronage contains the ideological terms of that system within the very impulse toward liberation. The farm as absent center or invisible property implies both the natural excess of the *cornucopia* and the hermeneutic transactions akin to monetary exchange.

The idea that Horace's gestures toward a modified freedom should draw both from the ideology of voluntarism *and* from symbolism of pure eco-nomic reciprocity accords with the twofold nature of his audience and the fundamental ambivalence of his self-identifications. On the one hand, in keeping with the populist impulse of the fable as a genre, Horace's offer as "client" to return his patron's gifts reveals and rejects any underlying contractual character they may represent. We hear about such use of the animal fable, the particular type of *ainos* that Aesop wrote, in the comments of Phaedrus. A slave and freedman of Augustus, Phaedrus claimed that the fable "was invented . . . to enable the slave to give expression in a disguised form to sentiments which he dared not speak out aloud for fear of punish-ment."[93] Moreover, as G. E. M. de Ste.-Croix points out, Aesopic fables were a literary genre whose simplicity particularly found favor with "those who lacked the elaborate literary education needed for a proper understanding of a large part of Greek and Latin literature" (1981, 444). Horace uses the fable both as a form of protest and as an *ainos* that appeals to a particular level of audience. On the other hand, it is precisely by appealing to an "elaborate literary education" that Horace places himself on equal footing with Maecenas. By inscribing himself in the aristocratic gift-exchange cul-ture of Homer's *Odyssey*, Horace recasts their relationship as one of egali-tarian *amicitia* distinguished by an aesthetic of giving.

Gregory Nagy's analysis of the function of *ainoi* in Greek society may shed further light on Horace's use of such tales, *exempla,* or fables to make

93. De Ste.-Croix 1981, 444; he goes on to comment that "it was not only slaves whom Phaedrus had in mind as the disguised heroes of fables. One of his pieces, about a frog dreading a fight between two bulls, is introduced with the words, 'The lowly are in trouble when the powerful quarrel' (*humiles laborant ubi potentes dissident,* I.30.1)." Shell (1978, 113) notes that Aristotle (*Rhet.* 2.20.6) warns against Aesop's fables as subversive of the political order.

distinctions between two different communities or readers. Nagy interprets *ainos* in the occasional context of the praise poetry of Pindar, distinguishing the term from epic *kleos* or "glory." As a mode of discourse, *ainos* includes praise, its function in Pindar; but more broadly it constitutes a "marked speech-act, made by and for a marked social group" (Nagy 1990, 31). Hence, *ainos* may refer not only to praise poetry but also to the instructive speech of admonition (parainesis), as well as to animal fables such as that of the fox in the cornbin. In Pindar's hands, the *ainos* constitutes a "difficult code that bears a difficult but correct message for the qualified and a wrong message or messages for the unqualified," a form of communication that likens it to the *ainigma* (enigma) that, as Nagy points out, is an etymological derivative (148–49). Moreover, the use of *ainoi* in the Greek lyric poets, particularly in Pindar, is directed specifically at a community of the *sophoi*, those who are wise or skilled at decoding poetic messages; the *agathoi*, those "noble" in terms of their ethical standards; and the *philoi*, those physically and emotionally close to the poet (148). As I have argued, Horace employs two different levels of *ainoi*, one directed at the "aristocratic elite" and another that addresses those of less discernment, less education, and (because the fable is a genre associated with slaves) less social status. Surely Horace's use of the *ainos* accords with its function as a marked speech act as he carves out his two communities of readers, riddling and ambiguating his poem, at once claiming his elite status and yet conscious of his freedman father's origins.

In this chapter, my overarching argument has demonstrated that Horace both reveals his sense of the economic calculations behind benefaction and also reinscribes himself in an aristocratic ideology of voluntarism. Against the open acknowledgment of the exchanges that constitute patronage, the poet invokes temporality, a "commodity" that resists the logic of reciprocity and disrupts the law of return. It is time away from his patron that Horace initially seeks, just as he jokingly asks for the return of the past should Maecenas still consider him in debt. Time's irrevocability—time as the ultimate benefaction, or *officium* (duty), for which there is no return—serves, paradoxically, to enforce the ideology of voluntarism that the poet exposes as the false consciousness of patronage: despite the poet's offers, it is too late to give back benefactions received. Once exposed as ideology, such voluntarism then becomes a defining component of the more egalitarian *amicitia* ("friendship," in this case) that replaces the patronal relationship. The aristocratic sense of time *not* spent as an *officium* is, of course, *otium*. As we shall see in the next chapter, it is the farm as a place of *otium* that allows Horace to distinguish himself from his bailiff and further his identification with the landholding elite.

CHAPTER FIVE

The Epistolary Farm
and the Status Implications
of Epicurean *Ataraxia*

In the previous chapter we saw that the gifts of Maecenas implied a con-
sequent loss or dispossession of Horace's sense of self. The nexus of asso-
ciations invoked by the various uses of the word *reddere*, particularly in the
seventh and thirteenth epistles, suggests that the act of receiving a gift also
expropriates. Insofar as it encourages reciprocation, it symbolically places
the recipient in the debt of the giver, thereby giving his or her person over
to the benefactor. I have also claimed, in chapter 3, that the subliminal
fear of actual expropriation surfaces at the end of *Epistles* 1.16 and 1.18, in
the figures of Pentheus and Jove as capable of taking away something—
property, liberty, or life—from a person. That discussion explored how
Horace, even in the earlier representations of his estate, *Satires* 2.6 and *Odes*
1.17, begins to invoke the aesthetic connotations of pastoral that transform
the farm from a place associated with debt, loss, or potential expropriation,
either real or psychological, into a site of interpretive plenty. Such a site,
as we saw in chapter 4, lends the Horatian speaker a modified discursive
agency insofar as it allows him a certain copiousness of rhetorical selves: as
"client" or lesser *amicus,* as friend, as philosophic instructor, the speaker
invokes different levels of *ainoi*—parainetic stories that discursively resist
the symbolic condition of a "reified self," the person as *reus* or bound by
the *res* of benefactions received, to which the actual, material practice of
patronage may lead.

This chapter develops my interpretation in regard to the two poems of
the *Epistles* that feature extended descriptions of the estate: 1.14, Horace's
letter to his bailiff, and 1.16, the letter to Quinctius. In these poems, Horace
invokes either details from a golden age topos or the more inclusive generic
frame of pastoral to identify with a vision of plenitude. Both poems stress
the distinction between the farm as a place implicated in a market economy

of real goods or *fructus* and its role as an aesthetic source in an economy of *otium*. Though critics of the *Epistles* have remarked the emphasis on a real-world economy in these poems, and have even noted how the speaker distinguishes himself from such a vision, they have not explored the extent to which this distinction is framed in terms of Epicureanism and issues of social and political status.[1] Here I pursue two lines of argument: first, that the plenitude of the self, the capacity of the farm to render aesthetic or philosophic returns that give the poet back to himself (*mihi me reddere*), as the opening of *Epistles* 1.14 claims, derives from an economy of *otium* and the specifically Epicurean associations of Vergilian pastoral; and second, that despite the egalitarian emphasis of Epicurean philosophy, the speaker manipulates it as a means of negotiating his anxiety over status affiliation. Ultimately, as we shall see, the discourse of philosophic freedom from externals—whether understood as material goods or political liberties—paradoxically serves to justify Horace's entitlement to such indicators of privilege.

We first saw the economy of *otium* in relation to Meliboeus's response to Tityrus's good fortune in Vergil's *Eclogue* 1: the sense of protection and aesthetic fullness enjoyed by Tityrus derives, in fact, from Meliboeus's own transfiguring imagination, which is a response to his expropriation. This dynamic between privation, song, and plenitude, however, has deeper roots in bucolic poetry.

PASTORAL AND PRIVATION

One topic of both Theocritean and Vergilian pastoral is desire for the beloved; hence, the shepherd's song is itself often predicated on the absence or loss of the love object. *Eclogues* 2, 8, and 10 all arise as laments of, or for, unhappy or unrequited love. But song also becomes a way of relieving desire, either concretely through the hope that the words may exercise a charm over the beloved or more abstractly by situating eros in a larger cosmic order that diminishes its intensity.[2] Alphesiboeus's reply to Damon in *Eclogue* 8, for example, presents song as magically potent, capable of causing love's requital and drawing the beloved back into the lover's presence. But if we consider Corydon's passion for Alexis in *Eclogue* 2—a poem modeled on Theocritus's *Idyll* 11, the Cyclops's comic lament for Galatea— our view of how *carmina* relieve or work against the lover's sense of deprivation becomes more complex.

Unlike the Theocritean original, Vergil's poem makes no mention of

1. For discussion of these epistles, see esp. Hiltbrunner 1960; McGann 1960; Voit 1965; Thomas 1982; Kilpatrick 1986, 89–102; Leach 1993b.

2. See the comments of Segal (1981, 142) on Lycidas's desire in Theoc. *Id.* 7.

song as a *pharmakon,* instead displaying eros in an "elegiac" light (Putnam 1970, 90, 93–96; Kenney 1983), a more plaintive and less humorous mode than that of his Greek predecessor. In addition, the delusions of love in this poem conform to Lucretius's depiction of erotic desire at the end of book 4 of *De rerum natura.* Indeed, insofar as Corydon's passion resembles (and anticipates) the longing of elegiac love in Propertius and Tibullus, that similarity is largely the result of the common influence of Lucretius and an Epicurean view of eros. Although little survives of Epicurus's own writings about love, the evidence implies that he classified it as an "empty desire" based on false belief.[3] Corydon, as we shall see, becomes aware of his delusion, but many details of *Eclogue* 2 suggest that he initially demonstrates the Epicurean conception of eros as an empty striving that knows no limit.[4]

For example, in introducing Corydon's lament the speaker describes his artless words (*haec incondita,* 4) as hurled out with "empty passion" (*inani studio,* 5); and at the end of the poem, the shepherd himself queries, *quis enim modus adsit amori?* (what limit could be set to passion? 67). Moreover, that Corydon's eros focuses on Alexis, his master's "pet" and an emblem of urban refinement, suggests Epicurean notions of the city and "civilization" as the source of false belief. To be sure, the city often constitutes that against which the pastoral ideal is negatively defined. Nonetheless, the dialectic between the ease and plenitude of pastoral *otium* (or what Christine Perkell calls the "pastoral vision") and its threatening "counterforce," a tension characteristic of the "pastoral design," is here construed as a dramatic exposition of Epicurean ideas.[5] When Corydon becomes conscious of the folly of his longing, evincing the sense that such passion undermines pastoral's ideal harmony between humans and nature, he cries out, *heu heu, quid volui misero mihi? floribus Austrum / perditus et liquidis immisi fontibus apros* (Alas, alas, what was my wish? Crazed I've inflicted the south wind on my flowers and sent bulls into my pure springs, 58–59). Suggesting that passion disrupts both the literal milieu of the pastoral environment (*fontes et flores*) and the song making that such images traditionally symbolize,[6] the phrase

3. For a discussion of the evidence for the Epicurean classification of erotic love, as distinguished from sexual impulse, see Nussbaum 1994, 151–54.

4. See Nussbaum 1994, 153–54, for the transformation of a natural, "non-necessary" desire like sexual impulse into an empty desire: "This alteration brings about (1) strained or intense eagerness, and (2) an unsatisfiable, unlimited character."

5. Perkell (1996, 135) defines the "pastoral vision" as the "description of an individual speaker's longed-for ideal" and the "pastoral design" as the "meaningful structure" of the whole poem, which contains what "Marx [1981 (1964)] calls the 'counterforce,' the alien reality that obtrudes upon the imagined ideal and signals its imaginary status."

6. For the aesthetic associations of *flores* and *fontes,* as the "sources and products of poetic inspiration," see Leach 1974, 149, who also notes the echo of Lucr. 1.927–30: *iuvat integros*

would seem also to allude specifically to Lucretius's description of a lover's sense of remorse at the dissipation of his life: "from the very center of the fountain of delight, there rises something bitter that brings anguish in the midst of flowers, perhaps because the mind perceives and regrets its craven wasting of youth and years" (*medio de fonte leporum / surgit amari aliquid quod in ipsis floribus angat, / aut cum conscius ipse animus se forte remordet / desidiose agere aetatem lustrisque perire*, 4.1133–36). Drawing on the literary tradition that associates *fontes et flores* with aesthetics, Vergil has recast the Lucretian fountain and flowers of passion's delight, ruined by self-conscious remorse, as emblems of the "pastoral vision" before the onset of eros.

But even though Corydon continues to burn with love (*me tamen urit amor*, 68) at the end of his lament, the process of the song itself appears to bring about a resolution by awakening him to his predicament. And he experiences more than deepened awareness: when he consoles himself that he "will find another Alexis" (*invenies alium . . . Alexin*, 73), and turns his mind to the more practical activity of weaving a basket (*quin tu aliquid saltem potius, quorum indiget usus, / viminibus mollique paras detexere iunco*, 71–72),[7] Corydon displays the inclination to abandon his "empty desire" and turn to activities and loves that may give him some real satisfaction. Perhaps this slight reflex of human will, following on the deeper insight into his condition, explains the Lucretian allusion in the otherwise conventional priamel of erotic pursuit that precedes the final lines of the poem: "The wild lioness pursues the wolf, the wolf chases the goat, the wanton goat seeks the flowering clover, and, O Alexis, Corydon seeks you: each is drawn by his own desire" (*torva leaena lupum sequitur, lupus ipse capellam, / florentem cytisum sequitur lasciva capella, / te Corydon, o Alexi: trahit sua quemque voluptas*, 63–65). As commentators point out (without exploring the connection), the proverbial "each drawn by his own desire" echoes a similar phrase in which Lucretius explicates free will as the result of the "swerve" of atoms: "if atoms do not make a swerve, then, I ask, what is the source of free will, torn from fate, by which we proceed where desire leads each (*quo ducit quemque voluptas*)?"[8] Despite his incongruity—the rustic well-versed in Epicurean doctrine—Corydon exemplifies an understanding of human will in

---

accedere fontis / atque haurire, iuvatque novos decerpere flores / insignemque meo capiti petere inde coronam / unde prius nulli velarint tempora musae.

7. "Why don't you at least turn to weaving, with flexible rush and branches, something that need requires."

8. Lucr. 2.253–58: *si . . . nec declinando faciunt primordia motus/ . . . unde est haec, inquam, fatis avulsa voluntas / per quam progredimur quo ducit quemque voluptas?* On the erotic priamel and the Lucretian allusion, see Clausen 1994, ad loc.; the sensibility of *voluptas* here also recalls the effects of Venus as a "force of nature" in the proem of *DRN* 1.1, 15–16: *ita capta lepore / te sequitur cupide quo quamque inducere pergis.*

his attempt "to turn his mind to another," as Lucretius advises in his diatribe against erotic passion, when he encourages the lover "to flee the images and drive away the food of passion" (*sed fugitare decet simulacra et pabula amoris / absterrere sibi atque alio convertere mentem,* 4.1063–64).[9] The lover in Lucretius is then advised to sate his longing for a particular woman by replacing her with a *vulgivaga . . . Venere* (1071), a common prostitute who can relieve him of his physical craving.

In keeping with the tendency of Epicureanism to demystify what it deems to be illusions of the imagination, Lucretius's argument at the end of book 4 attempts to reveal the biological, animal actuality of sex that lies beneath the distorted fancy of desire. Like the appetite for food, sexual desire is classified as natural, though it differs insofar as it is not necessary; therefore, it can be sated and relieved, even as hunger or the need for sleep disappears as soon as it is satisfied.[10] This capacity for satiety, for a natural plenitude of being, characterizes both the animal and the vegetal life of Vergil's pastoral milieu: goats are described as *saturae* (well-fed, 10.77), or *distentas lacte* (swollen with milk, 7.3); the fields "have drunk enough" (*sat prata biberunt,* 3.111); and, as in Corydon's own evocation of the *locus amoenus,* flowers fill baskets to the brim (*plenis . . . calathis,* 45–46).[11] Sexual desire also appears in the context of appetite in Corydon's priamel of erotic pursuit. The final image of a goat, peacefully feeding on the clover, suggests the limit that characterizes natural appetite, but not eros. Hence, although the herdsman's desire never completely reduces to an animal sexuality, converting the bower into what Thomas Rosenmeyer calls "the conditions of a stable," the intensity of eros in this eclogue begins to yield to the basic Epicurean ethos of well-being, or *ataraxia,* that makes pastoral song possible.[12]

9. For the Epicurean ethos of the pastoral environment in general, see Rosenmeyer 1969, 98–129. Clausen (1994, 74) quotes John Dryden's remark in his preface to *Sylvae* (1685): "Virgil's Shepherds are too well read in the Philosophy of Epicurus." Corydon's visions of Alexis, despite his absence, may also reflect the lines just preceding Lucretius's advice to find a replacement: *nam si abest quod ames, praesto simulacra tamen sunt / illius et nomen dulce obversatur ad auris* (for if what you love is absent, images of that one are nonetheless continuously present and the sweet name turns in your ears, 4.1061–62). Du Quesnay (1979, 59) attributes this idea that "the lover sees his beloved even when he is absent" to the Alexis epigram of Meleager.

10. The idea that sexual impulses (unlike the frenzy of erotic desire) may be sated informs Lucretius's Epicureanism but does not figure in Epicurus's own writings. Nonetheless, Nussbaum (1994, 154) concludes that Lucretius essentially fleshes out Epicurus's idea that "erotic love is the product of a corruption of natural sexual impulses by false beliefs."

11. Though such satiety may sometimes be in jeopardy from the "counterforce" that threatens the pastoral environment, it nonetheless is situated in the "real" world of natural appetite in a way that erotic love is not.

12. Rosenmeyer (1969, 83) claims that *Eclogue* 2 employs the genre to show us "love as a

To be sure, the phrase *alium . . . Alexin* paradoxically implies Corydon's emotional resistance to his willful intention to seek "another," for the particularity of Alexis as the love object returns, at the end of the poem, with an insistence that recalls the beloved's name (given at the end of line 1) and undermines the concept of an *alium,* or "other." However, as Bernard Frischer has argued in his analysis of *Eclogue* 7, Corydon in that poem embodies attributes of the Epicurean wise man, a condition that implies a transformation and psychological development from the earlier Corydon of the second eclogue. These two figures display enough parallels and continuity to merit viewing them as the same person, but their different levels of psychological equanimity and artistic accomplishment point to some intervening transformative experience.[13] In *Eclogue* 7 Corydon, as one who possesses Epicurean wisdom, produces a series of pleasurable images of the *locus amoenus* (45–46, 53–55); these affect Thyrsis's senses in a way that awakens him to his *stultitia,* or foolishness, and thus initiate the process of his conversion to Epicurean *ataraxia* (Frischer 1975, 233–41). In keeping with this argument, I suggest that it is through his own evocation of the pastoral *locus amoenus* that Corydon at the end of *Eclogue* 2 begins to experience the transformation responsible for his "wiser" self of *Eclogue* 7. The passage that immediately precedes his realization that Alexis would have no interest in a rustic existence, caring nothing for pastoral gifts (*nec munera curat Alexis,* 56), shows that Corydon's singing in *Eclogue* 2, though not specifically introduced as a *pharmakon,* has been instrumental in awakening his self-awareness and points the way to the possibility for relief.

When Corydon summons Alexis with a conventional invocation (*huc ades, o formose puer,* 45), he evokes the lush world of the *locus amoenus* as a means of advertisement, a way of attracting the addressee to the pleasures of the here and now in the pastoral bower.[14] The shepherd lures his beloved with the promise of pastoral gifts (*munera*)—lilies, violets, and poppies woven with herbs and borne in baskets by the nymphs of the forest, and fruits, laurel, and myrtle gathered by Corydon himself:

> huc ades, o formose puer: tibi lilia plenis   45
> ecce ferunt Nymphae calathis; tibi candida Nais,

---

momentary aberration" and that in general "sex, in its cruder forms, is allowed to color the context marginally, without reducing the pastoral bower to the conditions of a stable" (85).

13. Frischer 1975, 77: "Die Unterschiede sind nur verständlich innerhalb des Rahmens einer einzigen, einheitlichen Persönlichkeit, aber sie implizieren—wie auch der Schluß der Ekl. II (Verse 69–73),—daß auch Corydon bedeutende Veränderungen durchgemacht hat seit seinem ersten Auftreten."

14. Du Quesnay (1981, 45) notes that such invocation is not only common in Theocritus but is essentially a variation of the *kletikon,* or speech of invitation.

pallentis violas et summa papavera carpens,
narcissum et florem iungit bene olentis anethi;
tum casia atque aliis intexens suavibus herbis
mollia luteola pingit vaccinia calta.   50
ipse ego cana legam tenera lanugine mala
castaneasque nuces, mea quas Amaryllis amabat;
addam cerea pruna (honos erit huic quoque pomo),
et vos, o lauri, carpam et te, proxima myrte,
sic positae quoniam suavis miscetis odores.   55

Come here, o beautiful boy: look, the Nymphs bear baskets full of lilies
for you; for you the lovely Naiad, gathering pale violets and poppy blos-
soms, joins them with narcissus and the flower of sweetly smelling fennel;
then, weaving in casia and other sweet herbs, she adorns the fine hya-
cinth with tawny marigold. I myself will gather the apples whitening with
tender down, and chestnuts, which my Amaryllis used to love; I'll bring,
too, wax-skinned plums: this fruit will be honored also. You too, laurels,
I'll gather, and you, neighboring myrtle, since you mix sweet scents
when placed thus. (2.45–55)

The passage is striking for the voluptuous and sensory presence of its im-
ages: color and smell abound with a concentrated potency suggested by
the very fullness (*plenis*) of the baskets (*calathis*). Such plenitude is a hall-
mark of pastoral—or, more accurately, the "pastoral vision"—but it differs
from Corydon's earlier boasts, also marked by abundance, concerning his
wealthy status: for the emphasis on unity and composition in the "garland"
of the nymphs, a rhetorical set piece recalling Meleager, is tied to aesthetic
polish, the attribute that Corydon's words initially lacked (*incondita haec*).
Intexans (49), *suavis* (49, 55), *pingit* (50), *positae* (55), *lauri* (54), and *myrte*
(54) all have aesthetic connotations, the latter two as plants conventionally
mentioned together by poets.[15] Moreover, though Corydon's vaunts of be-
ing rich in sheep and flowing with milk display pastoral plenitude, they
exaggerate and misrepresent his situation—he is no owner of flocks,
just as he is no Amphion in his musical prowess (20–24).[16] Regarding
his own attributes, Corydon displays a deluded sense of self, a boastful
conceit that, when he looks into the sea, invokes the Epicurean theory of

15. For the allusion to Meleager's garland, see Leach 1974,148; Du Quesnay 1979,59;
Clausen 1994, 79. For the emphasis on unity in this floral arrangement, see Putnam 1970,
105.

16. See Verg. *Ecl.* 2.19–22 for Corydon's boasts: *nec qui sim quaeris, Alexi, / quam dives pecoris,
nivei quam lactis abundans. / mille meae Siculis errant in montibus agnae; / lac mihi non aestate novum,
non frigore defit.* On the pompous and misleading conceit of Corydon as "an owner" of his
flocks, see Putnam 1970, 96; Clausen 1994, ad loc.

sense perception to back his claim to be handsome—"if the image never deceives" (*si numquam fallit imago*, 27).[17] On the one hand, this phrase is deeply ironic, for the entire *imago* that Corydon creates about himself is deceptive (Putnam 1970, 98); on the other, according to Epicurean theory, it is the shepherd's evaluative belief regarding his visual image, rather than the sensuous *imago* perceived, that is in error. In contrast, the *imago* of flowers, fruit, and foliage, though artfully arranged and thus still somewhat idealized, does not so greatly involve human estimation or inference; in fact, the aesthetic arrangement makes possible a more accurate perception of the natural riches of a pastoral existence. It is to this second *imago* that we should attribute Corydon's realization of his disaffection from the pastoral world. In the Epicurean theory of motivation, *imagines* prompt the mind to action; here, the vision of natural plenitude awakens Corydon to a more realistic appraisal of his situation and directs him to the proper bucolic activities of pruning his vines and weaving—or, in symbolic terms, to pastoral song rather than the *incondita* of erotic longing.[18]

Indeed, when Corydon leaves off his lament and turns to this typical, pastoral pastime of "weaving" (*viminibus mollique paras detexere iunco*), the infinitive *detexere* recalls the earlier participle *intexans,* which describes the naiad's plaiting together the lush cluster of casia, herbs, hyacinth and marigold that the shepherd offers to Alexis. The naiad's arrangement, as we noted, invokes Hellenistic poetry and the garland of Meleager in particular. But weaving had long symbolized art in Greco-Roman literature; and in Latin verse, where Horace's chewed nails evidence the attention paid to *callida iunctura* (skillful joining), weaving often connotes the supple arrangement of individual words. Thus Corydon's use of *detexere,* as it echoes the naiad's plaiting, conjures up the image of a basket of language that contains the riches of pastoral. The potency of the *imago* of flowers depends on the concentration of sensuous words in a few lines, as though the hexameter verse were stretched to its limits (or filled to the brim) with images of nature. And so when Corydon's song advertises such fullness through its linguistic representation, these verbal *imagines* of the pastoral world, initially intended to persuade the beloved to join his lover in the *locus amoenus,* instead bring Corydon back into a harmonious relationship with nature.

17. See Clausen 1994, ad loc.: "There is a moment of delicate irony here; . . . in Epicurean dogma, the senses are infallible and error arises from the viewer's opinion or inference."

18. Penwill (1994, 79) offers a "modern" analogy for the way these *imagines* affect and motivate the human *mens:* "Like a radio receiver tuned to a particular frequency, the mind will pick up those of the countless *imagines* flying around *ad quae se ipse paravit* ('towards which it has prepared itself,' 4.804). If I need to go shopping, my mind is by that perceived need 'prepared' to receive an *imago* of myself getting up and walking out of the door: the *imago* moves my mind which then moves my body." On Corydon's neglect of the "pastoral practice" of poetry as symbolized by the "half-trimmed" or *semiputa* vine, see Putnam 1970, 112.

As Lucretius stresses, Epicureanism held that the mind must conceive an *imago* of the desired activity in order for the will to action to follow suit (*inde voluntas fit; neque enim facere incipit ullam / rem quisquam, ⟨quam⟩ mens providit quid velit ante. / id quod providet, illius rei constat imago*, 4.883–85). Corydon's response to the *imago* of his own (or his maker's) making suggests both this concept of motivation and the philosophical uses of poetics that mark Lucretius's didactic poem.

The evocation of the sensory presence of nature also serves to annul the absence of the beloved. The natural plenitude that Corydon enjoys and offers to his beloved belongs to a pastoral register of theme and tone that discredits, or presents as foreign, the elegiac longing defined by privation. In this way, the fabric of the song intended to attract the beloved may in fact provide a vision with which the lover identifies, thereby transforming love's deprivation into art: the song becomes an aesthetic compensation for the beloved's absence or indifference.[19]

Love, as Anne Carson points out, is expropriative (1986, 32–33). In Freudian terms, it robs from the libidinal pool of the ego and redirects the libidinal cathexis of narcissism away from the self to another. Eros, in short, erodes the boundaries of the self. As I have suggested, the shepherd's involvement with his own song in the Vergilian version of Cyclopean lovesickness serves to overcome Corydon's unrequited, if comic, passion. By turning his attention to the bucolic *munera* (gifts) of his environment, Corydon fashions an *imago* of pastoral plenitude that makes desirable the natural satiety of Epicurean *ataraxia* rather than the state of limitless craving defined by *eros*. Hence, though desire may expropriate—causing the erosions of self-"possession"—the unique properties of pastoral give back.

Whereas Vergil's second eclogue captures some of the song-as-*pharmakon* quality of Theocritus's eleventh idyll, the brief excerpt of the Cyclops's monologue in the ninth eclogue points up the Roman poet's historicizing innovations to the genre. For Vergil reworks the pastoral trope of song as compensatory by testing it against the expropriation of land rather than the loss of the beloved. *Eclogue* 9 presents the figure of Menalcas, traditionally associated with Vergil, as failing to regain his land through his *carmina*—more specifically, through dedicating his poems to Varus. Here, the economy perceived in the first eclogue is reversed: rather than land as enabling and transformed into poetry, as Meliboeus imagines Tityrus's situation, song is a gift that is not successfully exchanged for land.[20] This information is conveyed by Moeris in conversation with Lycidas, as the two

19. For the more explicit function of song as *pharmakon* in Theocritus, see Rosenmeyer 1969, 84, 151.

20. As many have remarked, Meliboeus's imminent dispossession of land prompts his own song. See my discussion at the beginning of chapter 3.

struggle to remember bits and pieces of songs. Fragments of Theocritean song alternate with replies that refer to Roman events: the inclusion of the Cyclops's invitation to Galatea to join him in a lush *locus amoenus* is followed by four lines referring to the star associated with Julius Caesar, whose influence promises continuing fertility in the pastoral world (9.39–50). On the one hand, the Cyclops displays his vernal riches as already in the timeless here and now of the eternal present; the emphatic triple repetition of *hic*, introducing the props of the *locus amoenus* like the crowded decor of a stage set—flowers, water, tree, and shade—underscores the fullness of place as dependent on the moment of the speaker's utterance.[21] On the other hand, Lycidas answers Moeris's appropriation of Cyclopean (and pastoral) presence by offering not the present but the future: as critics have pointed out, his suggestion that Moeris sing of pastoral in a contemporary context proffers the possibility that the idyllic sphere may yet coexist with history, safeguarded—and indeed ultimately "led"—by the beneficent divinity of a Caesar. It is the star of Caesar, after all, that gladdens the fields with corn and causes the grape to deepen—or to "draw on" (*duceret*)—its hue.[22] Though the poem's overall frame tells against this reading, the vision of nature's symbiotic relationship with authority recalls the golden age of the fourth eclogue. In *Eclogue* 9, however, the dispossession from property caused by the political sphere thematically resonates in the loss of the capacity to make song itself: in response to Lycidas, Moeris laments that both his voice and his memory fail him. Song may overcome erotic deprivation in Theocritean pastoral, and it may stimulate Tityrus's generosity in the first eclogue, but in the ninth it is ineffective against the material loss that undermines the very conditions of its existence.[23]

This understanding of the ninth eclogue helps establish the relationship between song and expropriation in Vergilian pastoral as an intertextual backdrop to Horace's invocation of the genre in the *Epistles*. Contrary to the ninth eclogue, however, Horace's poems offer pastoral images as an effective means of attaining a sense of invulnerability to loss. In this regard, the epistolary speaker's use of bucolic *imagines* is more in keeping with, though not identical to, the parainetic—if serendipitous—function of the *locus amoenus* in *Eclogue* 2.

21. See Benveniste 1971, 219, on "indicators" such as *hic*: "The essential thing, then, is the relation between the indicator (of person, time, place, object shown, etc.) and the *present* instance of discourse."

22. Verg. *Ecl.* 9.47–49: *ecce Dionaei processit Caesaris astrum, / astrum, quo segetes gauderent frugibus et quo / duceret apricis in collibus uva colorem.* Clausen (1994, ad loc.) notes that the usual idiom is *colorem trahere*.

23. Putnam (1970, 323) notes that "the ruin of the land is reflected in the progressive degeneration of Moeris from creative singer, to mere repeater of his and others' songs, to one whose voice has fled."

THE ECONOMY OF *OTIUM* AND THE MATERIAL CONDITIONS
OF THE *AEQUUS ANIMUS: EPISTLES* 1.14

In Horace's fourteenth epistle, pastoral images have explicit associations with Epicureanism. Claiming that his Sabine estate restores him to himself (*mihi me reddentis agelli,* 1.14.1), the Horatian speaker suggests a form of self-renewal in which he discovers again an original wholeness. That wholeness implies, in turn, the state of the "witness" to which Epicurus's disciples aspired—the natural and sensuous character of the animal or newborn child before it has been corrupted by *paideia* (education). Such sensuous well-being evidences the basic *ataraxia,* or freedom from unnecessary desires, that constitutes the goal of Epicurean praxis.[24] Horace's choice of his *vilicus,* or the chief slave of his estate, as the addressee of the fourteenth epistle also suggests Epicureanism: the ideal community was egalitarian, and the assistance of philosophy was extended to all who could muster the means to spend time in the Garden, regardless of social status, sex, or political liberty.[25]

As a form of philosophical *praxis,* Horace's poem engages the problem of desire for another's circumstances and the resulting loss of equanimity. But what initially appears as a philosophical meditation on the *aequus animus* (balanced mind) in fact constitutes a set of rhetorical strategies by which Horace justifies his affiliation with the landowning and propertied elite. Images of pastoral plenitude restore Horace to himself and negotiate his own anxiety concerning the farm as a gift, but they depend on a highly stratified social structure and slave economy.

Like so many of the more "autobiographical" epistles, *Epistles* 1.14 has often been cited as a source of information about the Sabine farm. Historians, making use of literary evidence with characteristic ease, have even relied on it to testify to the particular mix of slave and tenant labor that is said to have predominated on agricultural estates of the period.[26] This glimpse into the actual economy of the farm comes at the very beginning of the poem and sets up one pole of the dialectic that runs throughout. The speaker proposes a contest, or agon, between his bailiff and himself

---

24. On the newborn child or animal as the "witness" for what constitutes healthy functioning in Epicureanism, see Cic. *Fin.* 1.30. Also see the discussion in Nussbaum 1994, 106–10. Significantly, the reliability ensured by such "witnesses" is often construed in language that implies "wholeness"—*integer, incorruptus,* etc.

25. On the "student body" of the Garden, see de Witt 1954, 95–97; Frischer 1982, 62–65; Nussbaum 1994, 117–18.

26. See Finley 1976, 106. Foxhall (1990, 103) remarks that the "profiles of the ideal bailiff in the agricultural treatises imply that real-life bailiffs were prone to develop. . . . low level-patronage networks"; that is, a bailiff, though a slave, might become a patron figure to tenants on the estate that he ran.

that will test their respective degrees of spiritual health—the degree to which each suffers *mempsimoiria*—"fault-finding" or, more generally, discontent with one's lot.[27] As the epistle develops, the speaker claims that such discontent derives from the *animus* that refuses to accept its own circumstances and envies the lot of another. The dramatic occasion for this meditation on desire as enslavement, however, sets the poem in the context of political rather than spiritual liberty: having once been a city slave who longed for the country, the *vilicus,* granted his wish and promoted to a position of higher status as Horace's bailiff, now wishes to return to the city; and although the speaker proffers a diagnosis of spiritual slavery with a sympathetic and even chummy egalitarianism,[28] he speaks as a free man to a slave who does not enjoy the same political liberties—in this case, the liberty of movement—as his master.

The rhetorical gambit of the agon temporarily conceals this political disparity in status, and the populist impulse behind Epicureanism initially sets Horace and his bailiff on equal footing as potential patients in need of philosophical therapy. Such equality in affliction is matched by an evenly balanced allotment of lines to the predicament of each, a taut and rhythmic dialectical movement that governs the poem's opening:

> Vilice silvarum et mihi me reddentis agelli,
> quem tu fastidis habitatum quinque focis et
> quinque bonos solitum Variam dimittere patres,
> certemus, spinas animone ego fortius an tu
> evellas agro et melior sit Horatius an res.   5
> Me quamvis Lamiae pietas et cura moratur
> fratrem maerentis, rapto de fratre dolentis
> insolabiliter, tamen istuc mens animusque
> fert et amat spatiis obstantia rumpere claustra.[29]
> rure ego viventem, tu dicis in urbe beatum[.]   10

Bailiff of my woods and of the farm that gives me back to myself, a place you scorn, though it houses five families and usually sends five worthy homesteaders to the market at Varia, let us have a contest, and see whether I pluck out thorns from my mind more efficiently than you from the field, and whether Horace or his property is in better shape. Although I am detained by my concern and reverence for Lamia, inconsolably mourning his brother, snatched away by fate, nevertheless my

27. For discussions of the epistle's treatment of this theme, see Hiltbrunner 1967; Kilpatrick 1986, 89–96.

28. Kilpatrick (1986, 93) claims that the "epistle's assumed egalitarian tone" obscures the fact that the addressee is a slave. Hiltbrunner (1967, 300) notes that the emphasis on the first-person plural in *certemus* (4) and *miramur* (18) provides a counterweight to the pronominal distinctions of *ego* and *tu* in lines 2, 4, and 10.

29. With the manuscripts I read *amat* in line 9 rather than Bentley's emendation, *avet.*

mind and soul carry me there and yearn to break the barriers obstruct-
ing the track. I say that the man in the country is happy, while you claim
it is the man of the city. (1.14.1–10)

Horace achieves an elegant symmetry of dissatisfied desire here. Attending
to a friend's mourning in Rome, the speaker writes longingly of the country
to his *vilicus* who, in turn, wishes for the pleasures of the city.[30] As the image
of the first line suggests, the speaker suffers separation from his farm, which
"returns him to himself," as a division of his own being. In psychological
terms, his cathexis of his estate as part of his ego is so intense that a visit
to Rome feels like a loss of himself. The speaker's desire is pictured as a
racehorse eager to burst the barriers and cover the spaces separating him
from his goal, an image that suggests the Platonic horses of the soul and
the fierce wish to reunite with the complementary other.[31] It suitably recalls
Vergil's recasting of erotic desire in terms of expropriation from the land
in the *Eclogues* even as the Platonic allusion makes the wish for union a
quest for knowledge. Desire for the land here connotes a wish for the philo-
sophical study that returns Horace to himself, giving him the same pleni-
tude that he recommends to Lollius at the end of *Epistles* 1.18.[32] Moreover,
Horace's sense of loss and consequent desire is doubled in the image of
Lamia's inconsolable mourning for his brother.[33] Grief over a brother's
death may, in turn, allude to Catullus 101 and the way in which poetry as
funereal gift there attempts to surmount distance and (vainly) to com-
pensate for absence.[34] Similarly, if perhaps more successfully, the letter to
the bailiff substitutes for the farm's absence, even as the pastoral song of
the shepherd provides images of a world of plenitude that dilute or dis-
place the desire of the singer.[35] Horace's letter, in fact, performs the very

---

30. Fraenkel (1957, 311) argued that the lines concerning Lamia's mourning, as the "oc-
casion" for Horace's absence from the farm, display "the stamp of reality." However, most
commentators, including Kiessling and Heinze (1961a, 114), have seen the *vilicus* as a fictive
addressee. See also Becker 1963, 21–22.

31. Hiltbrunner (1967, 302) also notes the allusion to the chariot out of control at the
end of Verg. *Geo.* 1.512.

32. Hor. *Ep.* 1.18.96–101: *Inter cuncta leges et percontabere doctos / qua ratione queas traducere
leniter aevum/ . . . quid minuat curas, quid te tibi reddat amicum*[.]

33. Kenney (1977) argues that Lamia is mourning his brother's loss to an obsessive rela-
tionship of elegiac love rather than his actual death. If so, the effect of desire as predicated
on loss or absence is *tripled* in the figure of the brother.

34. In Catullus's stately yet personal poem, verse serves both as ritual offering to the dead
and as vain consolation for the living. The many lands and seas through which the Catullan
speaker travels in order to present his words suggest geographic distance as a metaphor for
separation from the dead. Horace's poem alludes to Catullus through the image of Lamia's
grief by raising similar issues of language as a means of "reproducing" or substituting for the
absent "beloved" or desired object.

35. But, as Carson (1986, 92) notes, the letter also stimulates: "Letters are the mechanism

philosophizing that is figured as the function or product of the land. In other words, the speaker here works through to the state of the *aequus animus* (a "balanced mind"), a condition he attributes to the presence of the farm—*mihi me reddentis agelli*—by engaging in a philosophical agon with his bailiff.

The Locus Amoenus, *Epicurean* Voluptas, *and the Parainetic Image*

Separation from the estate means distance from its caretaker, which provides the premise for correspondence. Geographic distance is also at the heart of the problem, since the desire to be elsewhere afflicts both writer and addressee. The letter, as capable of crossing to that elsewhere, is thus particularly suited to the affliction at hand—the discontent with place. The speaker claims, in an assertion reinforced by the epistle's overt argument, that such discontent derives from a flaw in the "mind that never escapes itself" (*animus se qui non effugit umquam*, 1.14.13). For it is the mind that determines the appraisal of place, and in this case the precise vision of the farm: "Those places you consider desert and unfriendly, desolate wild, one who thinks alike with me calls lovely, just as he hates what you think beautiful" (*nam quae deserta et inhospita tesqua / credis, amoena vocat mecum qui sentit, et odit / quae tu pulchra putas*, 19–21). Here we see the apparent symmetry between Horace and his bailiff, underscored by the repetition of the pronouns *ego* and *tu* of the opening, beginning to break down. Unlike the bailiff, who wished for the country when he was a city slave and now, as the *vilicus* on Horace's estate, is eager to return to the city, Horace is consistent with his own desires and leaves reluctantly whenever unwanted business drags him to Rome (*me constare mihi scis et discedere tristem, / quandocumque trahunt invisa negotia Romam*, 16–17).[36] Moreover, in keeping with this consistency (ironically undercut by other epistles), the speaker has given up his former ways as a dandy for good, and is satisfied with a simple meal and a nap by the stream:

> nunc, age, quid nostrum concentum dividat audi.
> quem tenues decuere togae nitidique capilli,
> quem scis immunem Cinarae placuisse rapaci,
> quem bibulum liquidi media de luce Falerni,
> cena brevis iuvat et prope rivum somnus in herba.
> nec lusisse pudet, sed non incidere ludum.[37]

---

of erotic paradox, at once connective and separative, painful and sweet. Letters construct the space of desire and kindle in it those contradictory emotions that keep the lover alert to his own impasse."

36. Becker (1963, 21) notes: "Mit dem Gegensatz zwischen Stadt und Land, der damit eine neue Variante erhält, verbindet sich der Gegensatz zwischen Einst und Jetzt."

37. With the manuscripts I read *ludum* in line 36 rather than Shackleton Bailey's *lusum*.

Come now, hear what splinters our agreement. One whom a fine-woven
toga and sleek hair once suited, who, though giftless, you know used
to please greedy Cinara, and to drink clear Falernian at noon, a simple
meal and a nap next to the stream now pleases. There's no shame
in having played the rake, only in not putting an end to the play.
(1.14.31–36)

This description of the poet's present life—simple needs met, napping
by the river—must be interpreted through the linguistic lens of *amoenus,*
the adjective through which the poet's *animus* perceives his estate. There
is a circularity to his claim of having achieved a spiritual equanimity
whereby his mind is at peace with itself, for the image of pastoral content
that he adduces as an example is, in a sense, that from which his cerebral
calm derives. No doubt the actual farm provides the soothing balm of na-
ture just as its material benefits keep the poet from want. But Horace also
constructs the farm as a *locus amoenus,* a rhetorical ecphrasis or typology of
place to whose conceptualization he draws attention when he claims that
whoever thinks as he does calls it lovely (*amoena vocat mecum qui sentit,* 20).
Hence, in a manner that brings to mind Paul de Man's speculations about
autobiography, the details that Horace then adduces to describe his life on
the farm—details that purport to be autobiographical "referents"—appear
somewhat determined by the literary and cultural associations of the word
amoenus.[38] That is, on the one hand, Horace's philosophic claims are sug-
gestive of the Epicurean belief that the mind, not the senses, is liable to
error and "false belief," as exemplified by the *vilicus* (in contrast to himself);
on the other hand, language—and in this case the associations of
amoenus—seems to structure not only his perceptions but also the details
of his existence.

Before reviewing these associations, we should examine the previous
image of Horace—his past self, the decadent playboy of the *Odes*—to which
the speaker gives a full three lines. This vision of Horace the rake, flashily
dressed and drunk at noon, which precedes the image of his present life
of simple needs and indulgences, implies a construction of self shaped by
the emphases of lyric with Alexandrian affiliations: *tenues* and *nitidi,* de-
picting the fine weave of the poet's toga and the sleek shimmer of his oiled

---

38. The comments of de Man (1979b, 920) are particularly relevant to the "referential
productivity" of Horace's Sabine estate in relation to the biography that critics construct from
the poetry: "We assume that life *produces* the autobiography as an act produces its conse-
quences, but can we not suggest, with equal justice, that the autobiographical project may
itself produce and determine the life and that whatever the writer *does* is in fact governed by
the technical demands of self-portraiture and thus determined, in all its aspects, by the re-
sources of his medium? . . . is the illusion of reference . . . something more akin to a fiction
which then, however, in its own turn, acquires a degree of referential productivity?"

hair, lend this autobiographical object the high polish of Callimachean refinement. The triple repetition of the accusative relative pronoun *quem* and the ironic assessment of self through the eyes of another ("you know," *scis*) underscore this objectification that transforms the poet into a cameo picture with the same mosaic finish as his *Odes*. In this aesthetic equivalent of "clothes make the man," the verb *decuere* (suited, were appropriate to) contributes to the representation of life's phases as a series of activities determined by—decorously appropriate to—the conventions of genre, in this case the style and subject of sympotic lyric. And to point up the conflation of literary and biographical decorum, the poet claims *nec lusisse pudet, sed non incidere ludum* (It's no shame to have played around, only not to put an end to play), a statement whose repetition of the verb *ludere* in the noun *ludum* plays on the word's associations with poetry.[39] As he asserts in the first epistle, Horace is done with *ludi;* the generic reference there reinforces the connotation here.

But this gesture of renunciation, the poet's turn away from the levities of lyric, invokes the problematic of loss and privation that so haunts the more autobiographical epistles. As the genre whose premise is the mimesis of presence, the moment embodied in the illusion of the speaking presence of voice, lyric aims to stop time, at least to freeze and then to allow for the eternal reactivation of that moment during a reading or a performance. By inserting lyric into an autobiographical narrative in which the succession of genres marks temporal evolution, the speaker ironically undermines (and confirms the need for) the insistent message of the *Odes: carpe diem.* Seizing the day and lyric's promise of the eternal moment recede into a phase of personal history; and while this image of the *Odes* as embodiment of a past self does not explicitly evoke loss—the speaker here voices no regret—the figure of Cinara recalls the seventh epistle, where the deprivations and depredations of time *are* figured as irrevocable.[40] Moreover, as an ambiguous declaration of independence from Maecenas—an interpretation that I explored in the previous chapter—the seventh epistle imbricates the issue of presence, both as physical actuality and as lyric illusion, in the exchanges of patronage. To Maecenas's request for Horace's company, we recall that the poet replies: "But if you wish me never to leave, you will return my strong body, my black hair on a once narrow forehead,

---

39. Given the *vilicus*'s own desire for a brothel—*fornix* (21)—perhaps the phrase claiming the speaker's end of "play" echoes the similar comment made by Aristippus and quoted by Montaigne: "Aristippus parlant à des jeunes gens qui rougissaient de le voir entrer chez une courtisane: 'Le vice est de n'en pas sortir, non pas d'y entrer'" (quoted by Connolly 1981 [1944], 27).

40. De Man (1979b, 929–30) argues that lyric is ultimately privative (or defacing) insofar as it enacts the trope of *prosopopeia* in which the presence of language necessitates the aphanisis of the real.

you will return my knack for sweet speech and elegant laughter and for mourning, in drink, bold Cinara's flight" (1.7.25–28). We saw that here, as in the fourteenth epistle, an autobiographical image acquires properties associated with genre: in this case, time has both stripped the poet of a youthful physique and robbed him of his lyric speech. The poet's insistence on the impossible—that his patron return the past as lyric presence in exchange for the poet's return to Rome—equates the *Odes* as embodiment of a past self with the *officia* demanded by patronage. Moreover, Horace's lyric self in *Epistles* 1.7 includes the political odes. The diction in *Epistles* 1.14 suggests the same: the poet's claim that he "pleased Cinara" though giftless (*immunem Cinari placuisse rapaci*, 1.14.33) looks forward to the *sphragis* to the collection, *Epistles* 1.20, where the verb *placuisse* is repeated in the same metrical position in the statement *me primis urbis belli placuisse domique* (1.20.23).[41] Thus, on the one hand, the image of the poet who pleases with words as his only gift—he is otherwise *immunis*—is common in the elegists;[42] and this, in conjunction with the attribution of adjectives denoting Alexandrian style to Horace's person, suggests that he pleased Cinara through verse. On the other hand, *placuisse* (to have pleased), appearing in *Epistles* 1.20 in reference to the "first men of the city," immediately calls to mind the political odes. As an echo of the passage in *Epistles* 1.14, which in turn recalls the figure of Cinara in *Epistles* 1.7, the verb suggests the same metonymic relationship between the erotic and political poems of *Odes* 1–3 discussed in the previous chapter. Most important, the web of associations linking all three passages invokes the dynamic of loss and recovery, or loss and compensation, that I have analyzed in relation to the use of the verb *reddere* in *Epistles* 1.7 and 1.13.

The first line of the fourteenth epistle, where the farm is described as *mihi me reddentis agelli*, must therefore be read back against these implications of *reddere* in the letters to Maecenas and Asinius (or ultimately Augustus). In the context of *Epistles* 1.14, the farm gives Horace back to himself when the poet leaves the *negotia* and *officia* associated with Rome and returns to his estate. But, as was evident in chapter 4, identifying Rome with a loss of self is also an issue of generic choice: the world of Rome represents the public world of politics and the imperial vision or civic focus of some of the odes. Horace's refusal to return to Rome in *Epistles* 1.7, as he declines to perform the *officium* of physical companionship, recapitulates the refusal to engage any longer in the metaphorical performance of the *Odes*, recalling the image of the aged gladiator with which *Epistles* 1.1 opens. Against this trajectory of physical withdrawal from the city sketched

41. Cf. a similar phrase in *Ep.* 1.17.35: *principibus placuisse viris non ultima laus est.*

42. E.g., the speaker of Propertius 1.8A triumphs with elegiac song over the gifts of a rich rival.

by the narrative time of the epistles, *Epistles* 1.13 delivers the *Odes* to Augustus in Rome—*Augusto reddes signata volumina, Vini* (1.13.2). Given these various contexts of patronage as a series of transactions, where person, property, or poetry are all exchanged *as* property in 1.1, 1.7, and 1.13, we might say that the farm returns Horace to himself insofar as earlier it had given him away: the textual traces of early Roman contract law in Horace's diction suggest that receiving the farm from Maecenas, and the Augustan regime at large, has meant for the poet a return giving of himself in the form of the *Odes*. In gift exchange the distinction between things and people becomes blurred: the giver's person animates and anthropomorphizes the gift.[43] When Horace represents himself in *Epistles* 1.7 and 1.14 as literally embodying his poems, he also suggests that the verse embodies him— and so the repetition of *reddere* in the context of the delivery of Odes 1–3 to Augustus in *Epistles* 1.13 would imply. It is this division from his self that the farm now makes whole.

We can now return to the adjective *amoenus* as the linguistic lens through which the speaker perceives and constructs his farm as the place that restores his plenitude. *Amoenus* does not appear in the *Eclogues*, but Horace's use of the word in *Odes* 1.17 certainly associates it with pastoral and a golden age vision. There, it describes the mountain Lucretilis above Horace's farm and reflects the magical transformation effected by Faunus when he leaves his Arcadian habitat. In *Epistles* 1.16, the poem that I discuss next, *amoenus* is clearly associated with elements of the golden age. Here in *Epistles* 1.14, the letter to the bailiff, *amoenus* draws a certain connotative range of reference from these other appearances in the poems that give the fullest descriptive topography of the Sabine farm.[44] To add to this internal evidence, we have other telling uses of the word in works with which Horace

---

43. As suggested in chapter 4, Horace's figuring of his past self, his *time* and labor, in the reified terms of his poetry, causes the "gift" of poems to approach the status of a commodity. Sahlins (1972, 180–81) comments on this alienation of the human soul and labor in the object: "If Mauss, like Marx, concentrated singularly on the anthropomorphic qualities of the things exchanged, rather than the (thinglike?) qualities of the people, it was because each saw in the transactions respectively at issue a determinate form and epoch of alienation: mystic alienation of the donor in primitive reciprocity, alienation of human social labor in commodity production."

44. *Epistles* 1.1.83–85 plays with the etymological connection of *amoenus* with *amor: 'nullus in orbe sinus Bais praelucet amoenis,' / si dixit dives, lacus et mare sentit amorem / festinantis eri.* Here, the expensive building that extended over the waters at Baiae, the famous resort town frequented by the upper classes, indicates the owner's *amorem* for the *locus amoenus.* In this case, the adjective *amoenus* suggests the luxury villas outside of Rome that became such a prominent feature of the social life of the late Republic and early Empire: see D'Arms 1981, 79, and the descriptions he cites in Varro *Rust.* 1.13.6–7; Vell. Pat. 2.33.4; Cic. *Att.* 12.25.1. In contrast to this idea of human cultivation of natural beauty, *Ep.* 1.10.6–7 uses *amoenus* simply to describe the attributes of a rural scene: *ego laudo ruris amoeni / rivos et musco circumlita saxa nemusque.*

would have been familiar. As Ernst Robert Curtius points out in his discussion of the *locus amoenus* as rhetorical ecphrasis,[45] *amoenus* is the adjective Vergil employs in the *Aeneid* to depict nature at her most lovely. Significantly, two of the Vergilian uses refer to the Elysian fields—the idealized landscape par excellence—and two others to the Tiber, emblem of the pristine Italian countryside before it is torn by war. Horace's own inclusion of *amoenus* in lines exemplifying a "purple patch" in the *Ars poetica* (14–18) further suggests his sense of the word's capacity to conjure up an idealized natural world that was becoming a rhetorical convention. In addition, we have Varro's claim that "Those places are called *amoena loca* because they offer only love."[46] Verrius Flaccus informs us that such places are "without product, . . . that is, without profit, where no material profit is paid out."[47] Servius, taking his cue from Varro and Carminius, adds in his commentary on *Aeneid* 5.734 that "'amoena' . . . *loca* are places full of pleasure (*voluptatis*) alone, as it were 'without claims on one's services or duty' (*amunia*), where no profit is extracted."[48] Although Servius's concise distinction between pleasure and profit was clearly not available to Horace, we find this very opposition in the dialectical structure of the epistle: the contrasting points of view with which the poet and his bailiff assess the farm. Indeed, the agon proposed by Horace, revealed to be a discrepancy of perspective, may well allude to the opposing points of view, and material conditions, of Tityrus and Meliboeus. Certainly the verb *certere*, by which the speaker refers to his contest with the bailiff, is often employed in the *Eclogues* in the pastoral context of singing competitions.[49] However, Horace's contest is of a different order, and the emphatic repetition of pronouns at the beginning (*ego . . . an tu*, 4; *ego . . . tu*, 10) pointedly recalls the celebrated *tu . . . nos . . . nos . . . tu* of *Eclogue* 1.1–4. In Horace's poem, we might say that the speaker combines Meliboeus's *perspective*—his perception of land in terms of leisure and pleasure—with Tityrus's *status* as the person entitled to the privilege of such enjoyment.

We shall return to the social implications of this allusion, but I wish first

---

45. Although the ideal landscape evoked by the word *amoenus* goes back to Homer, Curtius (1973 [1953], 192) implies that the use of the Latin adjective to suggest a world of literary convention begins with Vergil. Noteworthy, however, is Lucretius's use of *amoenus* to characterize Mt. Helicon as source of poetic inspiration (1.117–18): *Ennius ut noster cecinit qui primus amoeno / detulit ex Helicone perenni fronde coronam.*

46. Isid. 14.8.33: *amoena loca dicta Varro ait, quod solum amorem praestant, et ad ⟨se⟩ amanda alliciant.*

47. Ibid.: *sine munere sint, . . . id est sine fructu, unde fructus nullus exsolvitur.*

48. Serv. *In Verg. Comm.* 5.734: *'amoena' sunt loca solius voluptatis plena, quasi 'amunia', unde nullus fructus exsolvitur.* Citations in nn. 46–48 are drawn from *Thesaurus Linguae Latinae* (hereafter *TLL*), s.v. "amoenus."

49. Cf. Verg. *Ecl.* 3.31; 4.58; 5.8, 9, 15; 7.16; 8.3, 55.

to stress that Servius's distinction—and his association of *voluptas,* or plea-sure, with the *locus amoenus*—makes an important (if possibly chance) con-nection to the prominence of pleasure in Epicureanism. In the second book of *De finibus,* as Cicero challenges key tenets of Epicurean ethics from a Stoic standpoint, he questions the doctrine that even mental pleasures derive, originally, from physical experience. Asking Torquatus whether "nothing ever delights [him] for its own sake" (*ipsum per se nihil delectat*), Cicero lists a series of *leviora*—things and activities of a more trivial nature than virtue, integrity, and other moral abstractions:

> I will suggest less serious matters, reading or writing a poem or a speech, the study of history or geography, statues (*signa*), pictures (*tabula*), scenery (*locus amoenus*), the games (*ludi*) and wild beast shows (*venatio*), Lucullus's country house (I won't mention your own, for that would give you a loophole of es-cape; you would say it is a source of bodily enjoyment); but take the things I have mentioned—do you connect them with bodily sensation? Is there noth-ing which of itself affords you delight? Persist in tracing back the pleasures I have instanced to the body—and you show yourself impervious to argument; recant—and you abandon Epicurus's conception of pleasure altogether. (2.33.107)[50]

The activities that Cicero lists here might be placed on a spectrum between those pertaining to language and those involving sight or vision. The reading or writing of a poem or speech and the study of history or geography are fol-lowed by the plastic and visual arts (*signum, tabula*), then the *locus amoenus,* then the cruder spectator sports (*ludi, venatio*), and finally the pleasures of villa society (*villa Luculli*). The placement of the *locus amoenus* after sculpture and painting underscores its aestheticized, ecphrastic character, and its in-clusion in the list points up the related distinction, relevant to many of these activities, between the observing or perceiving subject and the object or spec-tacle observed. Cicero here throws down the philosophical gauntlet to Tor-quatus, asking him to relate either intellectual or aesthetic pleasure, or the more crudely emotional excitement derived from spectacles, to the body.

In a sense, this is precisely what the Horatian speaker in *Epistles* 1.14 does. Though he may not provide a seamless vindication of doctrine—he is, after all, a pupil of no single master (1.1.14)—his writing of an epistolary poem, philosophical in its emphasis, is a cerebral experience of the Sabine farm, his own *locus amoenus,* that he relates to bodily satisfaction. For in keeping with the Lucretian formula of the poet's call to understanding, "Come, now, hear what divides our agreement" (*nunc age, quid nostrum concentum dividat audi,* 31), the associations of the word *amoenus*—through which Horace's rather than his bailiff's experience is structured—are Ep-icurean in their emphasis: the simple meal and the nap by the stream in

50. Trans. Rackham 1914, Loeb edition.

the grass of course suggest the time (noon) and place of pastoral song, but they also, as actions that fulfill "necessary" desires, signify an Epicurean freedom from disturbance either physical or mental, the *ataraxia* expressed by the dictum that the wise man suffers neither awake nor asleep.[51] The phrase *somnus in herba* (sleep in the grass, 35) may well allude to the phrase *somno mollior herba* (grass softer than sleep), employed by Corydon in *Eclogue* 7.45, in his singing contest with Thyrsis: as discussed above, in his study of the Epicurean dimension of this eclogue Frischer conceives of Corydon as an embodiment of qualities associated with the Epicurean "wise man." In turn, the opening of *Eclogue* 7, where Daphnis sits in repose beneath a rustling ilex, recalls the *locus amoenus* in Lucretius 2.29–31: *cum tamen inter se prostrati in gramine molli / propter aquae rivum sub ramis arboris altae / non magnis opibus iucunde corpora curant* (when nevertheless, strewn about on the soft grass near a stream of water, beneath the branches of a tall tree, they care for their bodies pleasurably with little effort).[52] Surely the speaker of *Epistles* 1.14 also alludes to this passage: the phrase *prope rivum* (near the stream) condenses Lucretius's *propter aquae rivum*, even as *in gramine* becomes *in herba* (on the grass). Thus Horace makes reference to other poetic evocations of Epicurean *ataraxia*, even as the enjoyment of his own *locus amoenus* suggests certain of Epicurus's precepts.

The emphasis on humble fare, though characteristically Horatian, recalls the discussion in *De finibus,* preceding the passage quoted, on the equal pleasure to be derived from inexpensive and costly things (2.28.91). This image of Horace's well-being also recalls the wholeness claimed at the beginning of the poem (*mihi me reddentis agelli*). But though Epicureanism aspires to discovering a kind of prelinguistic original child or animal self within, the philosophic process in many ways depends on language.[53] One of the ways in which the farm succeeds in restoring Horace to himself is by its participation in his epistolary exploration of philosophical and social issues. Through allusion to a pastoral retreat—or *locus amoenus*—the farm helps crystallize the benefits of the good life in a potent visual image of an *otium,* where even moving stones, provoking the mirth of neighbors, becomes a form of diverting play.[54] The neighbors' laughter here not only contrasts with the envy of city dwellers, but it also implicitly points up the distinction between Horace and his bailiff: for the poet, such work is almost

---

51. Both the emphasis on plain and simple eating and the idea of undisturbed functioning in sleep as well as in waking are components of the *ataraxia* discussed in Epicurus's *Letter to Menoeceus* 130, 135.

52. See Frischer 1975, 245, for discussion of *Eclogue* 7 in relation to this passage.

53. E.g., the practice of confession and the repetition of the master's sayings show language to be instrumental to the process of achieving *ataraxia.* See Nussbaum 1994, 128–35.

54. Hor. *Ep.* 1.14.37–39: *non istic obliquo oculo mea commoda quisquam / limat, non odio obscuro morsuque venenat: / rident vicini glaebas et saxa moventem.*

a form of recreation, insofar as the farm is *a-moenus,* or "without duty," whereas for the *vilicus* it is part of the *munera,* or duties, of his position. By imaging his estate in this way, a choice to which he explicitly draws the reader's attention, Horace accesses for himself the properties associated with Epicureanism's *ataraxia.*[55] The mental state of the *aequus animus,* Epicurean in its emphasis on the absence of disturbance, partially derives from the poet's intellectual appreciation of the image—as memory—of his physical contentment, a perception structured by the associations with pleasure (*voluptas*) attached to the word *amoenus.*[56] In a manner that recalls the ideal effects of the pleasant *imago* of pastoral riches on Corydon in *Eclogue* 2, it is the farm as an aesthetic and philosophic construct, not as a place of *fructus* (material profits) associated with the bailiff, that returns Horace to himself.

Similarly, at the end of *Epistles* 1.18, the speaker advises Lollius to study and learn "what returns you to yourself as a friend" (*quid te tibi reddat amicum,* 101). The use of the verb *reddere* here looks back to the opening of 1.18, where the *scurra* parroting his patron's words is compared to a schoolboy repeating lessons for his master (*puerum . . . dictata magistro / reddere*).[57] Given that this epistle is all about the dangers of losing one's individuality in a relationship of *amicitia,* the repetition of *reddere* again implies that patronage, or friendship with the powerful, involves the self in a system of exchanges. And the almost identical diction of the two phrases in 1.14 and 1.18—*mihi me reddentis* versus *te tibi reddat*—suggests that for Horace, it is the farm as image within the letters—the "study" of the estate and its incorporation into his philosophic excursions—that restores the poet and compensates for any symbolic losses associated with the debts of patronage. The duties and obligations originally associated with the estate as a *munus,* a "gift" for which Horace returned poems in his official capacity (*munus*) as priest of the Muses, no longer make demands on the poet. Rather, the farm as *a-moenus,* or outside the realm of political office, profit, and ne-

55. In Horace's perception of the estate, the quality of *amoenus* does not rule out physical activity: indeed, as I am arguing, there is a pointedly Epicurean inflection or cast to the farm's *amoenitas*—one conducive to *ataraxia* not as a "state of stagnant inactivity" but rather, as Nussbaum (1994, 109) clarifies in her discussion of this philosophic goal, as "the continued undisturbed and unimpeded functioning of the whole creature."

56. Significantly, Epicurus's own comments on his deathbed suggest that he viewed the potency of pleasant memories and thoughts as a means of overcoming physical pain: "My continual sufferings from strangury and dysentery are so great that nothing could augment them; but over against them all I set gladness of mind at the remembrance of our past conversations" (Diog. Laert. 10.22; trans. Hicks 1925, Loeb edition). See, too, the discussion in Nussbaum 1994, 111 n. 13.

57. Hor. *Ep.* 1.18.12–14: *sic iterat voces et verba cadentia tollit, / ut puerum saevo credas dictata magistro / reddere vel partis mimum tractare secundas.*

gotiation, ironically "returns" the poet to himself. At the end of *Epistles* 1.18, the speaker claims that "I will provide a balanced mind for myself" (*aequum mi animum ipse parabo*, 112).[58] There, the speaker himself is the one who gives, but the syntax again recalls the opening of the fourteenth epistle where the "giver" is the farm. Taken together, these phrases underscore the fundamental identification of the poet's sense of plenitude, his estate, and epistolary representations. By converting his estate into a *locus amoenus* in language, a place that does not obligate him in the civic duties (or *munera*) of the state, the poet discursively represents himself as "restored" to a condition of plenitude.

The Material Conditions of the Aequus Animus

Can we so easily leave the bailiff behind? The difference in perspective running throughout the epistle suggests that at the very least the *vilicus* is necessary as the didactic example of a troubled soul in need of the lessons of philosophy. And in terms of Horace's sense of self as discovered and accessed through language, his subjectivity—as master of both his estate and his desires—depends on the rhetorical counterpoint provided by his addressee.[59] The bailiff's social position becomes an easy metaphor for his enslaved spiritual condition (Kilpatrick 1986, 89). However, such figuration of political or social status in terms of philosophical—more specifically, Epicurean—definitions of freedom, and the use of this metaphor to provide a pointed contrast to the speaker's psychological health, suggests a form of rhetorical exploitation that parallels the way in which actual labor enables his pursuit of philosophy. The bailiff, both rhetorically and actually, contributes to the speaker's plenitude, a fullness associated with Epicurean ideas of satisfied desire but an image contemplated through the lens of the *locus amoenus*.

At the beginning of the epistle, the contest proposed by the speaker suggests a kind of equivalence of labor, at least in degree of effort if not in

---

58. Following on the line that refers to Jove's capacity either to give or to take away, the poet's statement here not only makes an assertion of equanimity in the face of potential loss but also appropriates the structure of patronal relations and transfers them to the psychological domain. By taking over the role of both giver and receiver, Horace in fact replaces the *ego à deux* of the patronal relation, the dyad that threatens to tip power in one direction or the other, with the vision of himself as a divided whole drawn together and properly balanced by the gift of the *aequus animus*.

59. For subjectivity as the effect of the pronominal dialectic of speech containing an "I" that necessarily assumes a "you," see Benveniste 1971, 223–30, and my earlier discussion in chapter 4. Perret (1964, 113–14) similarly suggests that "it is only in relation to another person that one manages to grasp oneself, to know oneself as a subject." Cf. Kilpatrick (1986, 89), who notes that the relationship "*allows* Horace the perspective to explore the liberated *animus* in contrast with the servile" (emphasis mine).

kind. But the equivalence resides only in a metaphoric borrowing from the bailiff's world of manual labor—an image applied via a convenient zeugma to Horace's mental effort. The contrast in their stations is in fact present from the first line. The bailiff, though scorning the farm, is associated with the market economy to which it belongs: rather than showing disdain, he should respect the robust size of the estate, substantial enough to send five households to the market at Varia. In addition to this detail, which securely places the bailiff in the world of commerce, his work is envisioned as pulling out thorns from the ground to prepare the fields for cultivation. Horace, in contrast, maintains a distance from his material affairs; his labor involves the cerebral effort of philosophy. Moreover, though the middle section of the epistle develops the idea of the *animus,* and hence the competition between Horace and his slave as persons with souls, the contest at the beginning of the poem replaces the *ego* versus *tu* opposition at the end of line 4 with the *Horatius an res* at the end of line 5. The bailiff's attitude toward Horace's property (*res*) can hardly merit censure when, as a slave, his very being constitutes part of that property.[60] The speaker has stacked the deck, and his language reveals an awareness of his advantage, for the spiritual ease that he enjoys depends on his freedom from the constraints of actual labor that define his bailiff. His reliance on his estate's productivity, and thus the labor of his bailiff, becomes more explicit as the poem proceeds.

In the course of listing the bailiff's complaints, the speaker cites the flooding of a stream after rain as further cause for resentment: the stream adds to the labor of the "lazy" (*pigro*) bailiff because it "must be taught with a great mass [of dirt] to spare the sunny meadow" (*rivus . . . / multa mole docendus aprico parcere prato,* 29–30). This exertion concludes the list of the bailiff's chores; lines 31–35 shift the focus to the speaker himself and how he differs from his *vilicus.* The literal text, quoted and discussed above, addresses the issue of time and its effect on desire: the symposiastic dandy of the *Odes* is now satisfied with a simple meal and a nap by the stream (*prope rivum somnus in herba*). Less obviously, the speaker's enjoyment of a comfortable spot on the grass by the brook is made possible by the bailiff, who has ensured the dryness of the sunny meadow by fortifying the stream's bank. The repetition of *rivus* in these two lines is no accident. It may be the speaker's role to teach philosophy, but it is the bailiff's job to teach the stream to spare the meadow so that Horace can appropriate it as the pas-

---

60. Aristotle (*Pol.* 1253b30) defined the slave as "property with a soul" (*ktêma empsuchon);* Varro (*Rust.* 1.17.1), as belonging to the "class of instruments that are articulate" (*instrumenti genus vocale*). I strongly disagree with Meyer's emendation of *res* to *rus,* a conjecture of Heinsius supported by Bentley. Not only is there no manuscript evidence to support it, but the change completely glosses over the ambiguity of the slave's status as "property with a soul" that this epistle explores.

toral image of his serenity. Taking the image of the speaker's contentment as a cameo of Epicurean quietude, we would have to conclude that such a philosophical posture depends in the poem on the bailiff's labor and the material output of the farm. The bailiff's physical labor in this instance recalls his earlier scorn and complaints about the estate's unsuitability for the production of wine and the difficult work of clearing land long fallow.[61] But in spite of the bailiff's deprecation, the farm appears to be a place of *fructus,* producing goods for the market at Varia, and Horace's poem would seem to belie Servius's claim: insofar as Horace's estate, as a *locus amoenus,* returns him to himself, such spiritual commerce depends on the very real economic returns ensured by his bailiff.

The speaker's own economy of *otium* is thus embedded in the conditions of material production—slave and tenant labor—that govern the actual farm. The speaker manages to achieve a certain freedom that compensates for the erosions of self associated with Rome as the locus of *officia* related to patronage, but that fullness of being is here seen to be determined a priori by the material benefaction of the estate and by the particular labor relations attendant on the farm.[62] The Marxist overtones of such an analysis are relevant to both this epistle and my overall argument.[63] The bailiff, as representative of the economic or organically productive aspect of the estate, points up the very real material conditions of Horace's independence. But this independence provided by the material gift is precisely what Horace owes to his patron and the regime; considered in the logic of patronage—that is, in terms of economic reciprocity and the debt of gratitude—it is in fact undermined by its own origin. The status implications of this continuing debt of gratitude—a beneficiary can never truly repay his benefactor and is thus subordinate to him—drives the speaker's contradictory desire first to identify with and then emphatically to distinguish himself from his bailiff.

There is one more important rhetorical ploy by which Horace, in *Epistles* 1.14, negotiates a certain freedom from these implications of patronage. Thus far I have argued that it is the sense of obligation, and all the various *officia* it entails, that "take" Horace away and diminish his sense of self; but the gift of land signifies potential loss in other ways. For land has brought

---

61. Geoffrey Schmalz suggests to me that the bailiff's frustration with the estate's resistance to the cultivation of vines may reflect the trend of increasing wine production in Italy during the late Republic and early Empire (conversation, May 1996).

62. In his chapter on Roman society and the multitude of functions that required attendance in Rome, Friedländer (1908–13, 1:211) comments: "In this social whirlpool, self-life became impossible: deeper natures fled into the country to have solitude and freedom."

63. For a discussion of the questionable relevance of a Marxist model of the economy to ancient society, see Konstan 1979; for a Marxist approach to Roman slavery in particular, see Konstan 1975.

status, not necessarily in the concrete form of providing Horace with eques-
trian standing,[64] but by attaching him to the circle of the politically powerful
and by establishing him as the owner of an estate whose agricultural pro-
duction qualifies him, in Cicero's view, as a "proper Roman gentleman."
Yet to require the gift of status serves as a constant reminder that one was
not born with it. The poet's self-consciousness about his freedman father
has been astutely analyzed by recent critics who suggest that Horace's ob-
sessive emphasis on his father's upright character, and his own resulting
virtue, masks his sense of inferiority concerning his birth (Johnson 1993,
18–32; Anderson 1995). Indeed, the autobiographical *sphragis* that ends
Epistles 1 describes this very attitude of psychological compensation:

> cum tibi sol tepidus pluris admoverit auris,
> me libertino natum patre et in tenui re
> maiores pennas nido extendisse loqueris,
> ut quantum generi demas virtutibus addas;
> me primis urbis belli placuisse domique[.]

> When a warm sun brings you more of an audience, let them know that,
> though born of a freedman father, of humble means, I stretched my
> wings further than the nest, and so may you compensate with my merits
> proportionately as you detract from my birth; tell them that I pleased
> the first men of the city both in wartime as in peace. (1.20.19–23)

Instructing his book itself to give the relevant facts about the poet's life,
Horace here presents a calculus of internal worth as making up for the
detractions of external birth.[65] Horace's overt concern with a philosophical
sense of freedom from desire in *Epistles* 1.14 betrays a similar psychological
calculus insofar as it reveals a paradoxical fear of enslavement to, or at the
very least anxiety about, the external status that the gift of land signifies
for him. We see this anxiety reflected, again, in an image of erosion or
detraction at the end of the epistle, where Horace claims that at the farm,
no one files away with an evil eye at his advantages (*non istic obliquo oculo
mea commoda quisquam / limat,* 38). The poet's sensitivity to such envy would
naturally be heightened by his own humble origins as the son of a freed-
man.

And so the vision of Epicurean freedom presented in the textual snap-

---

64. For the argument that Horace, like most of the poets of the late Republic, had eques-
trian status before any benefactions from the regime, see introduction, n. 25.

65. For recent discussions of the *sphragis* poem and the anxiety it displays about Horace
maintaining "authorship" and control of the epistolary collection, see Pearcy 1994, 457–64;
Oliensis 1995, 209–24. Misch (1950 [1907], 301) notes that the biographical information in
this poem is Horace's version, in "delicate miniature," of the Scholastic style of Alexandrine
biography.

shots of Horace's body—napping, working up a mild sweat in a capricious rearrangement of stones—in part responds to the political rather than the spiritual status of the slave. The politically, historically, and economically contingent fact of the bailiff's slave status is the mirror reverse of Horace's freeborn status: had Horace's father not had the economic wherewithal to buy himself out of slavery and to give Horace the education of a senator's son, and had Maecenas not chanced to pluck the poet from his position as a quaestor's clerk and given him a life of complete rather than occasional *otium*, the poet's legal status could have been his slave's; at the very least, his economic status would have been less prestigious. As it is, despite the philosophical inconsistency that erratic physical movement may signify for Horace, his is the political liberty to move to and from the country at will, whereas the slave, as much a *res* as the *saxa* or stones of the estate, can only be moved at the whims of his master. Horace's attempt to discover spiritual freedom over the course of the *Epistles,* literally to write himself into plenitude by envisioning his relationship to his farm in pastoral terms, thus responds—both actually, as a letter, and psychologically, as a compensatory defense—to this alter ego (the only addressee not named) who represents his sense of the fortuitous external contingencies that placed him where he was.

But Horace's recourse to Epicureanism (and Stoicism) and its definitions of internal liberties in fact naturalizes the political inequalities as essential ones. When the poet recommends in the final line of the epistle that "each should practice willingly the art or craft that he knows" (*quam scit uterque libens . . . exerceat artem,* 44) the adjective *libens* skillfully deflects attention from the socially contingent and external fact of political liberty to the internal, psychological attitude of cheerful acceptance. Art seems to be providing the ideological justification not just to willingly accept one's circumstances but even to embrace a given condition of labor for another. That is, Horace's poem endorses slavery by casting the issue of forced labor in terms of the innate aptitude and disposition of the laborer (we are not far here from Aristotle's theory of natural slavery in *Pol.* 1.1253b15–1255b40). Moreover, the line preceding this axiomatic injunction reduces the philosophical issue of desire experienced by the *animus* to an anthropomorphized envy felt by beasts of burden for the imagined lighter load of the other. The speaker's final advice is intended for both his addressee and a more general audience, but the immediate internal reference of the pronoun *uterque* (each of two) to the ox and the horse effectively lowers the slave's status from fellow human being who shares a philosophical ailment with Horace to property that performs work. The very absence of any actual "voice" on the part of the slave here is reinforced by his demotion from, in Varro's terms (*Rust.* 1.17.1), an *instrumentum vocale* (articulate tool) to an *instrumentum semivocale* (inarticulate tool). The focus of the poem has modulated from a "horizontal" issue, as Horace and his bailiff each long for the geographical locale of the other, to an assertion of hierarchical differentiation: responding to the bailiff's desire for another place, Horace reminds him to remember his place as slave.

This emphasis on political and social differences casts the two lines that refer to the divergent perspectives of Horace and his slave in another light. When Horace claims that one who agrees with him sees the land as *loca amoena*, whereas the slave believes it to be "desolate and unfriendly wilderness" (*deserta et inhospita tesqua*), a third party is introduced to the contrived debate. By aligning himself with Horace, he facilitates the transformation of the egalitarian tone of friendly dialogue (or imagined dialogue) into the didactic command of a superior to an inferior. For the third party, "who agrees with me [Horace]" (*mecum qui sentit*), constitutes a social presence, a person from that actual world of political realities whose external definitions of freedom Epicureanism disregards. Here the poem modulates from an initial evenly matched condition of spiritual malaise to a counterpoint of social affiliation and political status. The items on the list of the bailiff's pleasures and complaints that follows—the *fornix* (whorehouse, 21), *uncta popina* (greasy eating house, 21), and *meretrix tibicina* (flute-playing prostitute, 25), as well as the chores on the farm—appear to be socially determined or affiliated activities. *Amoenitas* (charm, pleasantness), the linguistic lens through which Horace and this third party perceive his estate and comparable places, in turn connotes more than the aestheticized *loca amoena* of pastoral and rhetorical ecphrasis. As John D'Arms's analysis has shown (1981, 78–86), *amoenitas* is a quality that men of landed wealth associate with their estates: the frequency with which this word comes up in such contexts in the correspondence of Cicero, for example, testifies to its social connotations. The Lucretian line *nunc age, quid nostrum concentum dividat audi* (31) thus conceals social and political disparities beneath its overt reference to differences of temperament. Although the speaker ostensibly sets the following description of his bygone days as a dandy in contrast with the pastoral picture of his present contentment, the references to the citizen's toga and the expensive Falernian wine imply political and social distinctions.[66] Yet by couching his criticism of the bailiff's own preoccupation with the entertainments of the city in terms of a philosophical refusal to be content with *quod adest* (what is at hand), the speaker makes essential rather than contingent the political and social disparity between him and his slave. This naturalizing rhetorical ploy helps shore up the boundaries of status definition—Horace is one of those *mecum qui sentit*,

---

66. See Zanker 1988, 162–66, for the importance of the toga as a sign of citizenship; see Cairns 1992, 100–105, on the expensiveness of Falernian and its associations for a contemporary audience.

who perceive and enjoy *amoenitas*—enabling him to experience the pleni-
tude provided by the pastoral construction of his estate as based on his own
"essential" worthiness.

THE *TENUIS IMAGO,* OR THE VULNERABILITY OF AN IMAGE: *EPISTLES* 1.16

Horace's anxiety concerning the Sabine farm as a gift, the implicit fragility
of his status as recipient of such a gift, and the desire to perceive the estate
in terms other than its material aspect appear as well in the sixteenth epis-
tle. In contrast to the letter to the bailiff, where an initial solidarity of
malaise masks the speaker's ploys to legitimate his social standing, *Epistles*
1.16 starts from the premise that the poet enjoys greater spiritual well-being
than his addressee. As the epistle progresses, however, the speaker inti-
mates an awareness that his rhetorical constructions of selfhood are as frag-
ile as the status they attempt to secure. Paradoxically, the revelation of such
awareness is just as rhetorical as the vision of selfhood: for by drawing
attention to the problematic ontology of his own epistolary *imago,* the
speaker in fact more closely identifies himself with his addressee, Quinctius,
a man of public stature and visibility, who may trust too much in his rep-
utation. Thus, in this poem an initial differentiation from the addressee
ironically yields to a similarity—that once again shores up the boundaries
of aristocratic affiliation.

Addressing the various forms of external *bona* that a person might over-
value, the letter explores a Stoic paradox: "In whom there is virtue, this
man lacks nothing for a happy life."[67] Much of the epistle is devoted to a
sober, impersonal, and dialectically reasoned definition of the good man.
Nonetheless, the beginning presents a lavish description of Horace's estate:

> Ne perconteris fundus meus, optime Quincti,
> arvo pascat erum an bacis opulentet olivae,
> pomisne an pratis an amicta vitibus ulmo,
> scribetur tibi forma loquaciter et situs agri.
> Continui montes, ni dissocientur opaca   5
> valle, sed ut veniens dextrum latus aspiciat sol,
> laevum discedens curru fugiente vaporet.[68]
> temperiem laudes. quid si rubicunda benigni
> corna vepres et pruna ferant? si quercus et ilex
> multa fruge pecus, multa dominum iuvet umbra?   10

---

67. Cicero, *Paradoxa Stoicorum* 16: *in quo sit virtus, ei nihil deesse ad beate vivendum.* See
Kilpatrick 1986, 96–102, for a full discussion of the epistle's exploration of the Stoic paradoxes.

68. With the manuscripts I read *discedens* in line 7 rather than Bentley's emendation,
decedens.

dicas adductum propius frondere Tarentum.
fons etiam rivo dare nomen idoneus, ut nec
frigidior Thracam nec purior ambiat Hebrus,
infirmo capiti fluit utilis, utilis alvo.
hae latebrae dulces, etiam, si credis, amoenae,   15
incolumem tibi me praestant Septembribus horis.

Lest you should ask, most noble Quinctius, whether my estate feeds its
master with farmland or enriches him with olives, or with apples or
meadows or the elm entwined in vines, let me describe in a chatty letter
its appearance and basic layout. Hills would reach indefinitely, except
they are interrupted by a shady valley, yet one whose right side the rising
sun gazes upon, and, as it departs in its fleeing chariot, warms on the
left. You would praise the climate. What if the generous thornbushes
bore red cornel berries and plums, if the oak and holm oak keep the
cattle happy with many acorns, and the master with much shade? You
would say that Tarentum was nearby, thick with its green leafage. A
spring, also, strong enough to give its name to a river, so that neither
more cold, nor more pure, does the Hebrus flow around Thrace, ren-
ders useful cures for the ailing head and stomach. This agreeable hide-
away, even, if you believe me, charming and delightful, keeps me healthy—
you should know—in September's hot season. (1.16.1–16)

Though the epistle is marked by consistently rhetorical argumentation, this
opening vignette strikes a markedly different note: it is personal, sensory,
and descriptive. The pretext for the description is Quinctius's anticipated
inquiry about the estate's material capacity to enrich Horace. Once again
the speaker invokes a Hesiodic vision of the agriculture associated with the
farm: grain, fruit of trees and vines, and cattle are mentioned as organic
goods that the estate might produce as it participates in a market economy.
As Richard Thomas points out, these goods constitute the three major di-
visions of agronomy and suggest large-scale agricultural activity (1982, 13).
But instead of answering the question that Quinctius is imagined as posing,
the poet sketches a pleasing picture of the farm as sensuous refuge in whose
pastoral lushness the body, and implicitly the soul, are nourished. And to
emphasize this distinction between a statistical analysis of produce and his
rendering of a sensuous ambience, Horace claims that it is the beauty
(*forma*) of the place, its topography (*situs agri*), that will be described.

What follows includes many of the conventional appurtenances of pas-
toral: the sun's warmth, the shelter of shade, a herd of animals, fruit, foli-
age, and water.[69] At the end of this programmatic description, the poet

69. Leach (1993b, 281) claims that the acorns, "as the food of anthropological 'hard
primitivism,'" signify a different view of the Sabine farm than that presented by *Odes* 1.17,

invokes the concept of "charm" or "loveliness" (*amoenitas*) when he tentatively calls his Sabine retreat *amoenae*, should Quinctius "believe" him (*si credis*). The note of hesitation introduced by *si credis* suggests how *amoenus* conjures up a vision of natural beauty so ideal that one is unlikely to find it anywhere but on the written page. Idealization shades into the wonderful or fantastic—the far end of the pastoral spectrum, where the extremes of the golden age are manifest in organic excess: the spontaneous production of fruit from brambles suggests the *thaumasia* in a tradition of Utopian ethnography,[70] and the oak's produce of acorns is associated with Dodona and human origins in Arcadia (Voit 1975, 414). Moreover, although the speaker presumes to convey the "actuality" of the estate, the invocation of idealized conventions of representation looks back to the original promise of a "discursive" description: not only will the form and layout be described to Quinctius (*scribetur tibi*), but they will be written into existence as a pastoral or golden age topos.[71]

This conception of the estate as a written image—as a linguistic construction—is a crucial part of the poet's philosophic process, his means to attaining equanimity. As the last sentence of the description claims, it is "this lovely retreat" that keeps the speaker safe from harm and "intact" (*incolumem tibi me praestant*). The phrase looks back to the line introducing the sketch of the farm, the promise of a discursive description. In both lines the second-person dative pronoun, *tibi* (to you, as you should know), occupies the same metrical position: the unstressed syllables in a dactylic second foot. Thus the words that precede it, *scribetur* and *incolumem*, are brought into a closer relation by being metrically parallel. Such identification, coupled with the many words that emphasize the aesthetic and literary quality of the farm's image (*utilis, dulcis,* and *amoenus*), suggests, once again, that Horace's well-being here, his health and integrity,

---

where the goats eat arbutus and thyme, "the herbage of Vergilian pastoral." Nonetheless, as Coleman (1977) notes in his commentary on *Ecl.* 10.20, where Menalcas, *uvidus . . . de glande,* attends Gallus's mourning, acorns are variously associated with the soft primitivism of the golden age described in *Geo.* 1.148, the hard primitivism of Lucr. 5.965, the pastoral myth of Theoc. *Id.* 9.19–20, and the historical Arcadia. In all these representations, therefore, acorns symbolize a pastoral existence inasmuch as they stand for a pre-agricultural society; it is precisely this distinction from agronomy that Horace is making in his response to Quinctius.

70. Discussing the phrase *si credis,* Thomas (1982, 17) claims that it or "some variant . . . is regularly found in the company of ethnographical *thaumasia,* and appears to have been attracted from such passages into straightforward and verifiable ethnography."

71. I note the "signifiers" of pastoral, since I believe that the poet emphasizes these most in drawing the distinction from a Hesiodic vision of the land as a place to make a profit from agriculture. However, many critics also point out the epic tone of the language in this description, esp. lines 6 and 12: see McGann 1960, 206; Mayer 1994, ad loc.

are dependent not so much on the farm per se as on the construction of the farm in language.[72] Indeed, the fountain of pure water, here described as *utilis* for head and stomach, is a conventional symbol of poetic inspiration.[73] But both *latebrae* ("retreat," suggestive of the Epicurean dictum *lathe biōsas*) and *incolumem*, implying the physical well-being that grounds the equanimity of *ataraxia*, specifically connote the poetry of philosophy.[74] By constructing the farm as an idealized *locus amoenus*, here with attributes of the golden age, Horace identifies with a poetic image of plenitude clearly associated with an Epicurean state of health and wholeness, a state in which no basic needs are left unmet.

Scholars have generally recognized the distinction between the question hypothetically posed by Quinctius and the speaker's answer, but they have not been interested in relating the two perspectives on the estate to its original status as a gift. In a way that recalls the double vision of *Epistles* 1.14, the health and "freedom from injury" (*incolumitas*) that the speaker claims to derive from the golden age depiction of his estate safeguards against the poet's enslavement to it as an actual material good. In the letter to Quinctius, the depiction of spiritual freedom is connected, as I suggested in chapter 3, with a subliminal fear (more hypothetical than real) of expropriation, displayed in the didactic exemplum with which the poem ends. In this adaptation of a scene from Euripides' *Bacchae*, Pentheus threatens to seize all of Dionysus's *bona* and to throw him in chains. By taunting Dionysus first with the expropriation of real goods and then with the dispossession of his body, the tyrant supplies the test case for true liberty. Dionysus's calm reply, that the god will free him when he wishes, evinces his disregard for actual property or even freedom of movement. Interpreting Dionysus's statement to mean "I will die" (*moriar*), the speaker suggests that pure freedom can be fully realized only at the price of death, the final renunciation of the external and corporeal world.[75] Most scholars have generally avoided connecting Pentheus, as an image of tyranny, with

72. Cf. Hor. *Ars P.* 343–44: *omne tulit punctum qui miscuit utile dulci, / lectorem delectando pariterque monendo.*

73. Comparing Hor. *Ep.* 1.10 to *Ep.* 1.16, Thomas (1982, 18) notes the affiliation of *aqua purior* with Callimachean aesthetics.

74. *Incolumem* suggests an Epicurean sense of well-being insofar as it implies that nothing is wanting to the poet's feeling of psychological and physical contentment. Cicero (*Fin.* 1.38) refers to Epicureanism's definition of the highest pleasure as a complete lack of pain: *cum omni dolore careret, non modo voluptatem esse, verum etiam summam voluptatem.* Interpreting this passage, Mitsis (1988, 35) writes, "Epicurus thinks that when we have satisfied our necessary and natural desires or needs, we will be in the most pleasant psychological (*ataraxia*) and bodily (*aponia*) conditions. Moreover, we also will have attained a condition that satisfies the formal eudaemonist requirements of completeness, invulnerability, and self-sufficiency."

75. The speaker refers either to Stoic suicide as an acceptable solution to an intolerable situation or simply to death as the phenomenon that provides the ultimate release.

Horace's immediate political context (e.g., McGann 1960, 212); but such connotations are difficult to keep at bay if we consider the epistle's ending to be, as one recent critic suggests, the speaker's answer to "the threat of abundance," the cushioned security provided by the Augustan regime (Johnson 1993, 45–46, 59–61).

This abundance is a threat not only because, as a gift, it initiates a sense of debt and obligation, but also because it symbolizes the potential of the giver *not* to give—and even, in certain circumstances, to remove. As discussed in chapter 3, Pentheus's threats display a capacity for capricious dispossession similar to, though entirely more sinister than, that seen at the end of *Epistles* 1.18, where Jove both gives and takes away.[76] These two figures of arbitrary power anticipate, in turn, the clearly allegorical use of Jupiter at the end of *Epistles* 1.19 to refer to Augustus. In addition to this suggestive sequence of endings, the same allegorical identification is also present in the lines concerning *encomia* (*Ep.* 1.16.25–29). Given this web of associations—purposefully veiled—the scene from the *Bacchae* must be read back against the opening of *Epistles* 1.16. The farm as a material possession, emphasized by the stress on the possessive pronoun in *meus fundus,* falls into the category of *bona* that the good man, as exemplified by Dionysus, would ignore. Similarly, it is the farm as place of agricultural production from which the speaker distinguishes himself in his reply to Quinctius. Thus, short of suicide—the ultimate liberation of the individual from the material world—the speaker's freedom, his invulnerability to spiritual enslavement, depends on his indifference to the estate as a place of real economic productivity.

By making this distinction the speaker initially presents himself as closer to the *vir bonus* than is Quinctius, his addressee. Yet by emphasizing the literary quality of the farm as a *topos,* as an aesthetic image that conduces to the poet's health and "wholeness," the speaker paradoxically displays a dependence similar to Quinctius's reliance on reputation. For the *imago* of reputation constitutes a different form of *bonum,* which can be given and taken away as easily as a lictor's rod: "'Certainly, I enjoy being called a good and wise man just as you do.' Whoever has given this epithet today, tomorrow he will remove it, if he so wishes, just as the same man will take away the lictor's rod from someone unworthy to whom he granted it" (*'nempe / vir bonus et prudens dici delector ego ac tu.' / qui dedit hoc hodie cras, si volet auferet, ut, si / detulerit fascis indigno, detrahet idem,* 1.16.31–34).

When the speaker draws attention to the believability of the image of his farm with the phrase *si credis,* he anticipates his own criticisms of Quinctius. His friend, the speaker fears, may depend too much on—believe too

---

76. *Epistles* 1.18, significantly, is all about the potential compromises of liberty that patronage by—or friendship with—the powerful involves.

much in—the evaluations of others, thereby losing sight of his own sense of his virtue (*sed vereor ne cui de te plus quam tibi credas*, 19). Extreme encomium, as one such example of outside evaluation, is appropriate only to Augustus: "and if [someone] were to charm your open ears with these words, 'Let Jupiter, who looks out for both you and the city, keep it uncertain, whether the people wish more for your well-being or you for that of the people,' you would recognize the praises of Augustus."[77] But the echo of *si credis* (If you believe) in *vereor . . . credas* (I fear lest you believe, 19) suggests that the magnification implicit in the idea of encomium, which Horace implies may distort Quinctius's sense of his own internal worth, may in fact characterize the speaker's own self-presentation to his addressee. The speaker's autobiographical snapshot displays the same vulnerability to the excesses and potential misrepresentations of language as does Quinctius's reliance on the words of others, and the phrase *si credis* has even been identified as a convention of Utopian ethnography (Thomas 1982, 17). The effect of these conventions, as Thomas argues, is rhetorically to magnify the farm and thus, I would add, the speaker's plenitude as identified with his land. We catch a further glimpse of the underlying resemblance between these forms of "magnification" in their similar syntax: the conditional form of the question posed to the addressee about encomium, "If someone should talk about the wars you fought on land and on sea, and charm your ears" (*si quis bella tibi terra pugnata marique / dicat . . . permulceat auris*), echoes the conditional syntax, testing the credulity of the addressee, of the *thaumasia* in lines 8–9 (*quid si . . . vepres et pruna ferant?*). In addition, the encomiastic words that potentially "charm" and "soothe" the addressee's ears recall the "sweet" or "pleasant" and "charming" (*dulces . . . amoenae*) epithets for the estate, the source of the speaker's health. Thus, though the praise of Quinctius emanates from others and the Horatian speaker instead endorses his own well-being, both figures provide examples of the linguistic construction of selfhood and its reliance on belief.[78]

This underlying similarity between Quinctius and the speaker derives in part from the solidarity of status affiliation that the poem establishes between the two. We see this alignment clearly in the unanimity of the statement "all of us in Rome have long vaunted your happiness" (*iactamus iam pridem omnis te Roma beatum*, 18). And when the speaker prefaces his designation of his estate as *amoenus* with the qualifying *si credis*, he inevitably recalls the distinction he had earlier drawn between himself and his bailiff

---

77. Hor. *Ep.* 1.16.26–29: *et his verbis vacuas permulceat auris, / 'tene magis salvum populus velit an populum tu, / servet in ambiguo qui consulit et tibi et urbi / Iuppiter,' Augusti laudes agnoscere possis.*

78. Cf. Leach 1992, 293, on the epistle's exploration of "the rhetorical construction of personality."

(1.14.19–20). Quinctius, despite differing in his civic involvement from the country-loving poet, is one who may very well call Horace's retreat *amoenus*. He is *optime* (1), an epithet that has connotations not only of moral worth but also of high social status; and as we have seen, *amoenitas* is associated with social hierarchy. Moreover, by appealing to Quinctius's knowledge of the conventions of topographical representation, the speaker suggests that he is *mecum qui sentit,* one who agrees with the speaker. In this regard, the distinction between the farm as a place of financial productivity and as a site of aesthetic and philosophical experience also serves to inscribe the speaker in relations of elite *amicitia* rather than in the more openly profit-minded ties of patronage. To be sure, one could object that the golden age produce of the estate is humble, with the cornel berries and acorns signs of "hard primitivism" and thus hardly a mark of high status;[79] and initially Horace imputes to Quinctius an interest in the goods of a luxury estate that he conspicuously sidesteps in his description. The important point, however, is not that Horace dismisses Quinctius's possible questions as misplaced but that the poet chooses to construct his estate as a place that yields aesthetic and philosophical returns. By including these questions the poet both claims an aristocratic status for his villa and then furthers such social identification by distancing himself from the mercantile aspect of his livelihood.[80] Unlike the character of Vulteius Mena in the seventh epistle, the Horatian speaker does not view his Sabine villa as a place from which tirelessly to wrest profits (Voit 1975, 425).

Finally, by invoking images of spontaneous production, the speaker once again aligns himself with an ideology of voluntarism, in which the "free gifts" of nature—sun, shade, and the fantastic fruit from brambles—may very well symbolize an ideal view of *amicitia:* they mark the estate as freely given—a benefaction, as the speaker would wish to construct it, that neither answered to the recipient's desire for profit nor issued from the patron's wish for return. Indeed, the adjective *benignus,* "kind, friendly, beneficent, obliging, bounteous," which modifies the thornbushes, or *vepres,* in their generous provision of fruit, recalls the poet's early (and ideological) description of his patron's generosity in *Epode* 1: *satis superque me benignitas tua ditavit* (Enough and more has your beneficence enriched me, 1.31–32). Furthermore, as seen above, the golden age, as a place where "the earth gave more freely, when no one was asking" (*ipsaque tellus / omnia liberius, nullo poscente, ferebat,* Verg. *Geo.* 127–28), echoes the language of patronal ideology, a point reinforced by the speaker's satiric treatment of

79. For these goods as emblematic of "hard primitivism," see n. 69 above and Voit 1975, 419–20.

80. On the idea that economic self-sufficiency or even profit, if achieved through agriculture, was not incompatible with elite status, see D'Arms 1981, 6–7, 84–86; Leach 1993b, 277.

the subject in the very next epistle: "Those who are quiet about their neediness in front of their patron will carry away more than one who demands" (*Coram rege sua de paupertate tacentes / plus poscente ferent,* 1.17.43–44). But calling for silence about desired profit or silence about the profitability of the gift once received, the decorum of benefaction among the elite eschews a focus on *negotia,* of whatever sort, as too crudely trafficking in human relations.

On the one hand, in keeping with Varro's and Servius's definitions of the *locus a-moenus,* Horace represents his estate as a site of pleasure, not profit (*voluptatis plena, quasi 'amunia'*), a sensuous and libidinized landscape that rhetorically recalls the pastoral ideal of the *Eclogues;* the poet employs this aesthetic image to resist the debts and transactions, the social *officia* and civic office, that the farm initially imposed as a gift. The material benefaction of land may have symbolically expropriated the poet, but as a discursive *topos* it "restores him to himself." But though the idealized conventions of representation initially serve to display the poet's "freedom" from material *bona,* presenting him as an emblem of Epicurean *ataraxia,* they in fact demonstrate that he is entitled to the goods of patronage as one who properly appreciates not the *negotia* (business transactions, commerce) but rather the *otium,* aesthetic and philosophic, of aristocratic villa society. Horace's rhetorical manipulation of an Epicurean discourse to affiliate himself with elite status takes different forms in the letters to his *vilicus* (bailiff) and to *optimus* (best, of highest social status) Quinctius: in *Epistles* 1.14, the speaker rhetorically exploits the bailiff so that the demonstration of his spiritual enslavement, his lack of *ataraxia,* naturalizes the poet's own social (landowning) and political liberties; in *Epistles* 1.16, by anticipating and eluding Quinctius's questions about the economic facts and figures of the estate, Horace in fact acknowledges the farm as a place of revenue, even as, by showing his Epicurean disregard for material wealth, he displays his aristocratic sensitivity to the *amoenitas,* or charm, of elite property.

The Gift and the Reading Community

I began this study with the suggestion that the gladiatorial imagery employed by Horace to introduce *Epistles* 1 conforms to a discourse of patronal expenditure, on a large scale, for the purpose of creating symbolic capital—loyalty on the part of a "viewing" audience, the recipient of such civic *munera*. The preceding chapters have revealed the degree to which such expenditure on the poet's part, as well as his "producer's," participated in a form of exchange whose economic aspects the ideology of patronage often misrepresents or even conceals. The analysis of the Roman Odes, and other thematically connected poems, examined Horace's posture of priest of the Muses as one such manifestation of the ideological veil of voluntarism that marks the discourse of elite benefaction. The trope of poems as a form of sacrificial expenditure obscures the more interested exchange of land for verse, even as it conceals the goal of creating loyalty beneath a discourse of religious expiation. But as we have seen, even as gifts oblige, creating symbolic ties whose effects share ground and possibly origins with the archaic practice of the *nexum,* they also carry a libidinal value, both as extensions of the *favor* of the giver and in their capacity to bring pleasure to the recipient. We remarked earlier that one etymology for *res,* as property whose transference led Marcel Mauss to suggest the origins of contract law in primitive gift exchange, connects it to the Sanskrit word *rah, ratih,* gift or present, something that is pleasurable (1990 [1950], 50). This pleasurable element of the gift, Mauss implies, is similar to the notion of "power inherent in a thing" that causes it to be reciprocated. My discussion of Vergilian pastoral, and Horace's adoption of pastoral motifs, has explored the ways in which the gift of property is represented by these authors not only in terms of obligation but also as a source of aesthetic pleasure, the sine qua non in an economy of *otium*.

The previous three chapters have focused on how Horace makes use of the libidinal, pleasurable excess associated with the gift—an excess figured in terms of aesthetic surplus—as a rhetorical strategy of liberation. The gift of property, as source of aesthetics, liberates the poet from the negative implications of his estate as emblem of debt and symbolic enslavement. This capacity of the aesthetic to provide a utopic freedom from social formations—in this case, the reciprocity ethic and ongoing material debt of patronage—constitutes, as I discussed in chapter 3, a somewhat "idealist" reading indebted to Marxist aesthetics.[1] On the other hand, we have also seen that Horace's "freedom" helps inscribe him in the ranks of the aristocratic elite and justifies his entitlement to the perquisites of the upper classes.

Given this trajectory, and the degree to which the poet's liberation may be construed as a form of self-alignment with those who benefit from—rather than those exploited by—the social formation of patronage, we may well ask whether the Horatian epistle provides any form of resistance or subversion that transcends the author's own ambivalent and problematic form of freedom. Here we might return to the gladiatorial image, which, as a metaphor for aristocratic expenditure, also suggests the *recitatio*. Recall the image at the end of *Epistles* 1.19: Horace, refusing to give more public readings and saving his poems for the "ears of Jove," figures a public, poetic competition as a form of gladiatorial combat in which the poet seeks a *diludia*, or "time-out," from the game. Similarly, in *Epistles* 2.2 to Florus, the speaker compares public recitation, and the reciprocal praise demanded by poets of one another, to a fight between Samnite gladiators, in which there is mutual slaughter and destruction of the foe with equivalent blows (*caedimur et totidem plagis consumimus hostem . . . Samnites*, 97–98). Horace's own distaste for the *recitatio* before large audiences, as chapter 4 suggested, arises in part from the political uses to which his patrons put such symbolic gladiatorial expenditure. In a related vein, from the perspective of the writer rather than the patron, such public reading of written texts has recently been analyzed as a means by which authors sought to reclaim the "authoritative presence" that threatened to be undermined by the circulation of writing and literature as a commodity (Habinek 1998, 107). Such readings, depending on the size of the audience, were thus also an assertion of aristocratic and hierarchical power in a face-to-face context of performance. The epistolary form, by contrast, presumes the absence of the author; and although Horace, in *Epistles* 1.19 and 1.20, suggests that individ-

---

1. Kristeva (1975, 19) notes that poetic language "is necessarily the place of inscription of the pleasure elements left unsatisfied by the relations of production and reproduction, or by the ideologies which claim to represent them" (quoted in P. Miller 1994, 127, who is discussing the "libidinal subject" of lyric in relation to poets of late Republican Rome).

ual letters were recited for private audiences, he also makes clear his sense of the text's ultimate "commodification" and liberation from its author when he addresses his book as a freed slave in the *sphragis* poem.

Thus, when we consider anew Horace's "autobiographical" snapshots in *Epistles* 1, they appear, on one reading, to be just another method of claiming authorial presence in a genre predicated on the writer's absence. But because these images also display pastoral motifs and their Epicurean associations as a means of liberating the author (however problematic that liberation may be), we must examine the effect of these cameos of the self on readers other than the specific addressees.

These images are forms of ecphrasis, precisely what Ernst Robert Curtius suggests that the *locus amoenus* had become even as early as Horace's time (1973 [1953], 192–94). Though Curtius is referring to the looser, more generalized understanding of the term in epideictic rhetoric, its specific application to a literary rendering of a work of art suggests the way in which the poet's imaging of himself possesses the visual quality of a cameo: writing for his friends, the speaker objectifies himself in such a way that his *imago* in the setting of his estate becomes easily accessible. This visual image rendered in language recalls the inclusion of the *locus amoenus* in the list of activities or objects that Cicero challenges Torquatus to relate to the body. Moreover, the ecphrastic quality of the self as objectified in the context of the *locus amoenus* has as its counterpart the grammatical objects of the phrases addressing the speaker's equanimity or return to himself: *aequum mi animum ipse parabo* (I will furnish a balanced mind for myself, 1.18.112); *mihi me reddentis agelli* (the farm that returns me to myself, 1.14.1). As I have argued, Horace's association of Epicurean *ataraxia* with the pastoral genre makes the ecphrasis of his estate instrumental to the speaker's own attainment of spiritual health. But the wholeness implied by *incolumem* in *Epistles* 1.16.16 is brought up by the speaker in relation to his addressee: *hae latebrae dulces . . . amoenae / incolumem tibi me praestant* (this delightful, pleasurable retreat keeps me—I would have you know—sound and healthy, 1.16.15–16).

One reading of *tibi* here is simply as an ethical dative or a dative of advantage—making Quinctius a person interested in the speaker's health.[2] However, the syntax of gift relations in the previous phrases suggests that the image of the speaker made whole, or in this case preserved by the farm, passes in turn to the addressee. The Horatian corpus offers further evidence for reading the phrase *incolumem tibi me praestant* in conjunction with the phrase *mihi me reddentis agelli:* in *Odes* 1.3, Horace's propemptikon for

---

2. This is how Wilkins (1955, ad loc.) reads *tibi;* Dilke (1965, ad loc.) reads it as advantage; Mayer (1994, ad loc.) interprets it as either an ethical dative or one of advantage. Kiessling and Heinze (1961a) have no comment.

Vergil's trip to the East, the speaker asks the boat, to which his friend has been entrusted or "loaned" (*creditum*), to "return Vergil whole to him and protect the half of his soul" (*navis, quae tibi creditum / debes Vergilium; finibus Atticis / reddas incolumem, precor, et serves animae dimidium meae*, 5–8). Here, we have the diction of accounting (*creditum, debes, reddas*) applied to the person of Vergil as "sound," "uninjured," "whole" (*incolumem*), suggesting the same metaphor of debt-bondage that *reddere* draws on in *Epistles* 1.[3] Just as the boat is imagined as releasing Vergil, intact and unharmed, to the speaker in *Odes* 1.3, so the estate may be seen as not only returning Horace to himself but also passing him along to his reader. And though in its immediate context *tibi* refers to Quinctius, the impersonal and general tone of so many of the epistles in the first book, and their eventual commodification as a single text, implies a wider readership as well—anyone who might profit from the philosophic lessons of Horace, the *praeceptor*. Their content often rhetorically explores issues of virtue and the good life, thereby making the posture overtly didactic; but the cameo glimpses and, in the case of the sixteenth epistle, the ecphrasis of the poet on his farm teach philosophy in a different way. What I would like to claim is that the places where Horace represents himself in a state of plenitude on his estate serve the same function as images of the Epicurean godhead: that is, they impress the reader so pleasurably that he or she desires to become similar to Horace as an embodiment of the "wise man."

In *The Sculpted Word,* Bernard Frischer addresses this issue of conversion in Epicureanism. He begins by posing the inherent doctrinal paradox: "How did the Epicurean school overcome in a philosophically consistent way the contradiction latent in its philosophical system between its basic mission of bringing salvation to mankind and its basic existential method of withdrawal from the world?" (1982, 5). He goes on to argue that recruitment of the uninitiated must have taken place passively, with the recruit drawn to the philosophy on his or her own initiative (70–71). That those in the Garden were entirely passive and self-involved in their pursuit of the goals of Epicureanism might seem to be contradicted by Epicurus's own letters. By its very nature correspondence reaches beyond the immediate time and place to speak to those who are absent. But the evidence suggests that Epicurus's writings in fact circulated only among members of the group and thus were not readily available to the uninitiated (Frischer 1982, 50). Rather, the average person's first encounter with the philosophy would have been visual and random:

3. See chapter 4, n. 62: one of the distinctions between slavery and debt-bondage was that the latter did not claim full ownership and thus lacked the right to injure the body of the person held in servitude.

Applying the general Epicurean theory of motivation, we should expect the Epicureans to have had the following theory to explain how new initiates could be attracted to the school: by chance exposure to the images continuously emitted by the gods or the godlike sage, the sensory system of the uninitiated—if his mind is so disposed—comes to be impressed with their forms for an instant. This experience is so pleasant that the uninitiated viewer begins to desire to resemble the images permanently so that he can internalize them and become a source of pleasure to himself. This desire to give up an old personality and become similar to the Epicurean gods is precisely that simultaneously self-critical and self-renewing act which can be called the crucial first step of conversion. (82–83)

Though Horace by no means displays an exclusively Epicurean orientation, the self-representation that is such a strong feature of *Epistles* 1 creates a dynamic with his readership similar to the process by which Epicurean visual images of the godlike sage (in painting, sculpture, and on rings) may have been received by uninitiated viewers. That is, not only does the Horatian speaker create for himself an image that he can internalize and draw on for his own state of equanimity, but he also emits this image to the reader during his or her engagement with the overtly argued philosophical issues of *Epistles* 1. To be sure, the population in Rome that was literate and thus capable of being influenced by these verse letters was just a fraction of those who, in Epicurus's time or later, might be exposed to random visual images of the godhead. Nonetheless, the dynamic by which the recipient of an image is pleasurably impressed to the point of motivation is parallel. Indeed, Frischer first speculated about this theory of conversion in his analysis of the function of the *locus amoenus* and other pleasurable images related to *ataraxia* in *Eclogue* 7. In addition to initiating Thyrsis's self-awareness and first steps toward Epicurean wisdom, Corydon's images and the *locus amoenus* in which Daphnis reposes in the prelude engage and motivate the receptive reader to the threshold of conversion (Frischer 1975, 258–60).

The pleasurable quality of the image that attracts the reader makes relevant Servius's comment that *amoenus* signifies pleasure, or *voluptas*. As rhetorical ecphrasis, the concept of the *locus amoenus* gives pleasure specifically through its aesthetic quality. But as I remarked earlier, Isidore (quoting Varro) connects the *locus amoenus* to *amor*, for such places "furnish only love and, alluring, attract love to themselves" (*amoena loca dicta Varro ait, quod solum amorem praestant, et ad se amanda alliciant*).[4] This capacity to attract—*alliciant*—through the aesthetic pleasure or *voluptas* of the *locus*

---

4. Isid. 14.8.33. These references are drawn from *TLL*, s.v. "amoenus." See chapter 5, n. 48, for the text of Servius.

amoenus thus looks back to the erotic situations of pastoral, the advertisements of the shepherd to his beloved analyzed at the beginning of chapter 5. The relationship of *voluptas* to *amoenus*, and hence to *amor*, underscores the libidinal element of the pastoral landscape and its particular crystallization in the topos of golden age excess. In keeping with the nature of the gift, the libidinal excess that accompanies the farm, analyzed in chapter 3, conditions both its figuration as a *locus amoenus* and the ecphrastic image of the poet that the letter transmits. Having received the material farm, the poet transforms it into an aesthetic image whose golden age properties, in *Epistles* 1, give the speaker back to himself. And just as the symbol of the *cornucopia* implicates an audience in *Odes* 1.17, a poem in which the libidinal character of aesthetic excess passes to an addressee, Tyndaris, who becomes a singer in her own right, so the aestheticized image of the speaker in *Epistles* 1 is given, in turn, to his readers as the image of an Epicurean sage in a didactic verse letter.

But we may speculate more broadly about the reception of these poems: just as the process of writing *Epistles* 1 has brought the poet some success in his wish to subordinate his *res* to himself (*mihi res non me rebus subiungere conor*, 1.1.19), so reading these poems may make it possible for an audience to resist full determination by their material conditions. To be sure, such an interpretation must acknowledge that the material conditions of the poems' production originally worked against the resistance encouraged by the aesthetic aspects of their form.[5] The use of the papyrus roll demanded a certain level of affluence from a potential readership, but the letter form itself, in keeping with the Epicurean concept of retreat from the social world, the place of ideological production, encourages a critical view from a distance of the social formations and their material basis that shape individual identity. And as the more easily manipulated and transported parchment codex began to replace the papyrus roll, so the epistolary "fiction" of absence would become a reality for general readers; with reading for oneself beginning to replace the public *recitatio*, there was gradually less face-to-face contact with the elite at performances.[6] As a text released to the literate public these letters would have had an expanding circle of readers, with copies eventually being made for those who were not

5. It is no coincidence that the view of autonomy espoused by Marx in the *Economic and Philosophic Manuscripts of 1844*, an early work, displays an ideal vision of human *sensuous* enrichment and appreciation that is both aesthetic and clearly indebted to Epicurus. See the discussion in Rose 1992, 18.

6. See Habinek 1998, 118–21, for the argument that the use of the papyrus roll, rather than the more convenient and less expensive parchment codex, helped maintain aristocratic hegemony.

necessarily friends or acquaintances of the author.[7] In place of the aristocratic hierarchy of historical Rome, these poems could establish over time an egalitarian, if imaginary, community of readers held together in a form of collective ego, an abstract garden of philosophy cohering in the common cultural possession of the *Epistles*.

7. See Starr 1987 on the "publication" and dissemination of literary texts in ancient Rome.

REFERENCES

Adorno, T. 1974. "Lyric Poetry and Society." *Telos* 20:56–71.

Ahl, F. 1984. "The Rider and the Horse: Politics and Power in Roman Poetry from Horace to Statius." In *Aufstieg und Niedergang der römischen Welt (ARNW)* 2.32.1: 40–110. Berlin.

Allen, W., Jr., et al. 1970. "The Addressees in Horace's First Book of *Epistles.*" *Studies in Philology* 67.3:255–66.

———. 1973. "Horace's First Book of Epistles as Letters." *Classical Journal* 68.2:119–33.

Alpers, P. 1979. *The Singer of the "Eclogues": A Study of Vergilian Pastoral.* Berkeley.

———. 1990. "Schiller's *Naive and Sentimental Poetry* and the Modern Idea of Pastoral." In M. Griffith and D. J. Mastronarde, eds., *Cabinet of the Muses: Essays on Classical and Comparative Literature,* 319–31. Atlanta.

Amundsen, L. 1942. "The 'Roman Odes' of Horace." In *Serta Eitremiana. Symbolae Osloenses,* 1–42. Supplement, no. 11. Oslo.

Ancona, R. 1994. *Time and the Erotic in Horace's Odes.* Durham, N.C.

Anderson, W. S. 1982. *Essays on Roman Satire.* Princeton.

———. 1995. "*Horatius Liber,* Child and Freedman's Free Son." *Arethusa* 28.2–3: 151–64.

André, J. M. 1949. *La vie et l'oeuvre d'Asinius Pollion.* Paris.

———. 1966. *L'otium dans la vie morale et intellectuelle romaine.* Paris.

———. 1969. "Les Odes Romaines." In *Hommages à Marcel Renard,* 31–46. Collection Latomus, no. 101. Brussels.

Appadurai, A. 1988. *The Social Life of Things: Commodities in Cultural Perspective.* Cambridge.

Arac, J. 1985. "Afterword: Lyric Poetry and the Bounds of New Criticism." In C. Hošek and P. Parker, eds., *Lyric Poetry: Beyond New Criticism,* 345–55. Ithaca.

Armstrong, D. 1989. *Horace.* New Haven.

Arnold, B. 1994. "The Literary Experience of Vergil's Fourth Eclogue." *Classical Journal* 90.2:143–60.

Arthur, M., and D. Konstan. 1984. "Marxism and the Study of Classical Antiquity." In B. Ollman and E. Vernoff, eds., *The Left Academy: Marxist Scholarship on American Campuses*, 2:55–77. Praeger Special Studies. New York.

Asmis, E. 1995. "Epicurean Poetics." In D. Obbink, ed., *Philodemus and Poetry: Poetic Theory and Practice in Lucretius, Philodemus, and Horace*, 15–34. Oxford.

Auguet, R. 1994 [1972]. *Cruelty and Civilization: The Roman Games*. New York.

Bailey, C., ed. 1926. *Epicurus: The Extant Remains*. Oxford.

Bailey, S. 1982. *Profile of Horace*. Cambridge, Mass.

Barker, D. 1996. "'The golden age is proclaimed'? The *Carmen Saeculare* and the Renascence of the Golden Race." *Classical Quarterly* 46:434–46.

Barton, C. 1993. *The Sorrows of the Ancient Romans: The Gladiator and the Monster*. Princeton.

Basore, J. W., trans. 1935. *Seneca: Moral Essays*. 3 vols. Loeb Classical Library. Cambridge, Mass.

Bataille, G. 1985. *Visions of Excess. Selected Writings: 1927–1939*. Trans. A. Stoekl, with C. Lovitt and D. Leslie Jr. Minneapolis.

———. 1986. *Erotism: Death and Sensuality*. Trans. M. Dalwood. San Francisco.

Batstone, W. 1993. "Logic, Rhetoric, and Poesis." *Helios* 20:143–72.

Beard, M. 1990. "Priesthood in the Roman Republic." In M. Beard and J. North, eds., *Pagan Priests: Religion and Power in the Ancient World*, 47–48. Ithaca.

Beard, M., and M. Crawford. 1985. *Rome in the Late Republic*. London.

Beard, M., and J. North, eds. 1990. *Pagan Priests: Religion and Power in the Ancient World*. Ithaca.

Beard, M., J. North, and S. Price. 1998. *Religions of Rome*. 2. vols. Cambridge.

Becker, C. 1963. *Das Spätwerk des Horaz*. Göttingen.

Benveniste, E. 1971. *Problems in General Linguistics*. Trans. E. B. Meek. Coral Gables, Fla.

———. 1973. *Indo-European Language and Society*. Trans. E. Palmer. Coral Gables, Fla.

Berres, T. 1992. "'Erlebnis und Kunstgestalt' im 7. Brief des Horaz." *Hermes* 120: 216–37.

Bouché-Leclerq, A. 1892. "Devotio." In C. Daremberg and E. Saglio, *Dictionnaire des antiquités grecques et romaines*, 2.1:113–19. Paris.

Bourdieu, P. 1977. *Outline of a Theory of Practice*. Trans. R. Nice. Cambridge.

Bowditch, L. 1994. "Horace's Poetics of Political Integrity: *Epistle* 1.18." *American Journal of Philology* 115.3:409–26.

———. 1996. "The Horatian Poetics of Ezra Pound and Robert Pinsky." *Classical World* 89.6:451–77.

Bowie, A. M. 1993. *Aristophanes: Myth, Ritual, and Comedy*. Cambridge.

Bradshaw, A. 1989. "Horace *in Sabinis*." *Latomus* 206:160–86.

Brenkman, J. 1985. "The Concrete Utopia of Poetry: Blake's 'A Poison Tree.'" In C. Hosek and P. Parker, eds., *Lyric Poetry: Beyond New Criticism*, 182–93. Ithaca.

Brind'Amour, P. 1972. "*Paulum Silvae Super His Foret*: Horace, Satires, II.6.3." *Revue des Études Anciennes* 74:86–93.

Brink, C. O., ed. 1982. *Horace on Poetry. Epistles Book II*. Cambridge.

Brunt, P. A. 1965. "*Amicitia* in the Late Roman Republic." *Proceedings of the Cambridge Philological Society* 191, n.s. 2:1–20

———. 1971. *Italian Manpower, 225 B.C.–A.D. 14*. Oxford.

———. 1988. *The Fall of the Roman Republic*. Oxford.

Brunt, P. A., and J. Moore, eds. 1967. *Res Gestae Divi Augusti*. Oxford.

Büchner, K. 1962. *Studien zur römischen Literatur*. Vol. 3, *Horaz*. Wiesbaden.

———. 1969. "Horace et Épicure." In *Association Guillaume Budé. Actes du 8ième Congrès (5–10 avril 1968)*, 457–69. Paris.

———. 1972 [1940]. "Der siebente Brief des Horaz." In H. Oppermann, ed., *Wege zu Horaz*, 89–110. Darmstadt.

Burkert, W. 1966. "Greek Tragedy and Sacrificial Ritual." *Greek, Roman, and Byzantine Studies* 7.1:87–121.

———. 1983. *Homo Necans: The Anthropology of Ancient Greek Sacrificial Ritual and Myth*. Trans. P. Bing. Berkeley.

———. 1985. *Greek Religion: Archaic and Classical*. Trans. J. Raffan. Cambridge, Mass.

Cairns, F. 1971. "Five Religious Odes of Horace." *American Journal of Philology* 92: 433–52.

———. 1972. *Generic Composition in Greek and Roman Poetry*. Edinburgh.

———. 1984. "Propertius and the Battle of Actium. (4.6)." In T. Woodman and D. West, eds., *Poetry and Politics in the Age of Augustus*, 129–68. Cambridge.

———. 1992. "The Power of Implication: Horace's Invitation to Maecenas (*Odes* 1.20)." In T. Woodman and A. Powell, eds., *Author and Audience in Latin Literature*. Cambridge.

Calhoon, C. "Lucretia, Savior and Scapegoat: The Dynamics of Sacrifice in Livy 1.57–59." *Helios* 24:151–69.

Carson, A. 1986. *Eros the Bittersweet: An Essay*. Princeton.

Castriota, D. 1995. *The Ara Pacis Augustae and the Imagery of Abundance in Later Greek and Early Roman Imperial Art*. Princeton.

Clausen, W. 1982. "Theocritus and Vergil." In E. J. Kenney and W. V. Clausen, eds., *Cambridge History of Classical Literature*, 84–109. Cambridge.

———, ed. 1994. *A Commentary on Virgil: Eclogues*. Oxford.

Cohen, E. E. 1992. *Athenian Economy and Society: A Banking Perspective*. Princeton.

Coleman, R., ed. 1997. *Vergil: Eclogues*. Cambridge.

Commager, S. 1962. *The Odes of Horace: A Critical Study*. New Haven.

Connolly, C. 1981 [1944]. *The Unquiet Grave: A Word Cycle by Palinurus*. New York.

Connor, P. J. 1972. "The Balance Sheet: Considerations of the Second Roman Ode." *Hermes* 100:241–48.

———. 1987. *Horace's Lyric Poetry: The Force of Humor*. Ramus Monograph. Berwick, Vic.

Conte, G. B. 1994. *Latin Literature: A History*. Trans. J. B. Solodow. Baltimore.

Conway, G. S., and R. Stoneman, trans. 1977 [1972]. *Pindar: The Odes and Selected Fragments*. Ed. R. Stoneman. London.

Cook, A. 1988. *History/Writing*. New York.

Cook, E. 1995. *The Odyssey in Athens*. Ithaca.

Cooper, L., ed. 1916. *A Concordance to the Works of Horace*. Washington, D.C..

Cornell, T. J. 1995. *The Beginnings of Rome*. London.

Cotton, H. 1981. *Documentary Letters of Recommendation in Latin from the Roman Empire*. Beiträge zur klassischen Philologie, vol. 132. Konigstein/Ts.

Courbaud, E. 1914. *Horace: Sa vie et sa pensée à l'épogue des epîtres*. Paris.

Cruttwell, C. T. 1877. *A History of Roman Literature from the Earliest Period to the Death of Marcus Aurelius.* London.

Culler, J. 1978. "On Tropes and Persuasion." *New Literary History* 9:607–18.

Curtius, E. R. 1973 [1953]. *European Literature and the Latin Middle Ages.* Trans. W. R. Trask. Princeton.

D'Arms, J. 1981. *Commerce and Social Standing in Ancient Rome.* Cambridge, Mass.

Davis, G. 1983. "Silence and Decorum: Encomiastic Convention and the Epilogue of Horace *Carm.* 3.2." *Classical Antiquity* 2:9–26.

———. 1991. *Polyhymnia: The Rhetoric of Horatian Lyric Discourse.* Berkeley.

de Man, P. 1979a. *Allegories of Reading.* New Haven.

———. 1979b. "Autobiography as De-facement." *Modern Language Notes* 94:919–30.

Derrida, J. 1976. *Of Grammatology.* Trans. G. Spivak. Baltimore.

———. 1978. "Structure, Sign, and Play in the Discourse of the Human Sciences." In *Writing and Difference,* 278–93. Trans. A. Bass. Chicago.

———. 1992. *Given Time.* Vol. 1, *Counterfeit Money.* Trans. P. Kamuf. Chicago.

de Ste.-Croix, G. E. M. 1981. *The Class Struggle in the Ancient Greek World from the Archaic Age to the Arab Conquests.* London.

Detienne, M. 1979. *Dionysos Slain.* Trans. M. Muellner and L. Muellner. Baltimore.

DeWitt, N. W. 1939. "Epicurean Doctrine in Horace." *Classical Philology* 34:127–34.

———. 1954. *Epicurus and His Philosophy.* Minneapolis.

Diano, C. 1968. "Orazio e l'epicureismo." In *Saggezza e poetiche degli antichi,* 13–30. Venezia.

Dilke, O. A. W., ed. 1965. *Horace: Epistles Book I.* 3rd ed. London.

———. 1981. "The Interpretation of Horace's Epistles." *Aufstieg und Niedergang der römischen Welt (ANRW)* 2.31.3:1837–65. Berlin.

Dixon, S. 1993. "The Meaning of Gift and Debt in the Roman Elite." *Echos du Monde Classique/Classical Views* 37:451–64

Doblhofer, E. 1966. *Die Augustuspanegyrik des Horaz in formalhistorischer Sicht.* Heidelberg.

———. 1981. "Horaz und Augustus." *Aufstieg und Niedergang der römischen Welt (ANRW)* 2.31.3:1922–86. Berlin.

Donlan, W. 1993. "Reciprocities in Homer." *Classical World* 75.3:137–75.

Duncan-Jones, R. 1974. *The Economy of the Roman Empire.* Cambridge.

Dunn, F. 1990. "An Invitation to Tyndaris: Horace, *Ode* 1.17." *Transactions of the American Philological Association* 1990:203–8.

———. 1995. "Rhetorical Approaches to Horace's *Odes.*" *Arethusa* 28.2–3:165–76.

Du Quesnay, I. 1977. "Vergil's Fourth *Eclogue.*" In F. Cairns, ed., *Papers of the Liverpool Latin Seminar 1976,* 25–99. Liverpool.

———. 1979. "From Polyphemus to Corydon." In D. West and T. Woodman, eds., *Creative Imitation and Latin Literature,* 35–69. Cambridge.

———. 1981. "Vergil's First *Eclogue.*" In F. Cairns, ed., *Papers of the Liverpool Latin Seminar,* 29–182. Vol. 3. Liverpool.

———. 1984. "Horace and Maecenas: The Propaganda Value of *Sermones* I." In T. Woodman and D. West, eds., *Poetry and Politics in the Age of Augustus,* 19–58. Cambridge.

Eagleton, T. 1990. *The Ideology of the Aesthetic.* London.

———. 1991. *Ideology: An Introduction.* London.

Eder, W. 1990. "Augustus and the Power of Tradition: The Augustan Principate as Binding Link between Republic and Empire." In K. Raaflaub and M. Toher, eds., *Between Republic and Empire: Interpretations of Augustus and His Principate,* 71–122. Berkeley.

Edmunds, L. 1982. "The Latin Invitation-Poem: What Is It? Where Did It Come From?" *American Journal of Philology* 103:184–88.

———. 1992. *From a Sabine Jar: Reading Horace, "Odes" 1.9.* Chapel Hill, N.C.

Eisenstadt, A. N., and L. Roniger, 1984. *Patrons, Clients, and Friends: Interpersonal Relations and the Structure of Trust in Society.* Cambridge.

Elsner, J. 1991. "Cult and Sculpture: Sacrifice in the Ara Pacis Augustae." *Journal of Roman Studies* 81:50–61.

———. 1996. "Reflections on the Religious Appreciation of Classical Art." *Classical Quarterly* 46:515–31.

Falconer, W. A., trans. 1923. *Cicero: De Senectute, De Amicitia, De Divinatione.* Loeb Classical Library. Cambridge, Mass.

Falter, O. 1934. *Der Dichter und sein Gott bei den Griechen und Römern.* Würzberg.

Feeney, D. C. 1992. "*Si licet et fas est:* Ovid's *Fasti* and the Problem of Free Speech under the Principate." In A. Powell, ed. *Roman Poetry and Propaganda in the Age of Augustus,* 1–25. London.

———. 1998. *Literature and Religion at Rome.* Cambridge.

Feldherr, A. 1998. *Spectacle and Society in Livy's History.* Berkeley.

Finley, M. I. 1973. *The Ancient Economy.* Berkeley.

———. 1974. "Aristotle and Economic Analysis." In *Studies in Ancient Society,* 26–52. London.

———. 1976. "Private Farm Tenancy in Italy Before Diocletian." In M. I. Finley, ed., *Studies in Roman Property,* 103–18. Cambridge.

———. 1979 [1954]. *The World of Odysseus.* London.

———. 1982 [1955]. "Marriage, Sale, and Gift in the Homeric World." In *Economy and Society in Ancient Greece,* 233–45. New York.

Fitzgerald, W. 1995. *Catullan Provocations: Lyric Poetry and the Drama of Position.* Berkeley.

Foster, B. O., ed. 1919. *Livy: Books I and II.* Loeb Classical Library. Cambridge, Mass.

Foucault, M. 1970. *The Order of Things: An Archaeology of the Human Sciences.* New York.

Fowler, D. 1995. "Horace and the Aesthetics of Politics." In S. J. Harrison, ed., *Homage to Horace: A Bimillenary Celebration,* 248–66. Oxford.

Foxhall, L. 1990. "The Dependent Tenant: Land Leasing and Labour in Italy and Greece." *Journal of Roman Studies* 80:97–114.

Fraenkel, E. 1957. *Horace.* London.

Freudenburg, K. 1993. *The Walking Muse.* Princeton.

Friedländer, L. 1908–13. *Roman Life and Manners under the Early Empire.* Trans. L. A. Magnus, from the 7th ed. 4 vols. London.

Frischer, B. 1975. *At Tu Aureus Esto: Eine Interpretation Von Vergils 7. Ekloge.* Bonn.

———. 1982. *The Sculpted Word: Epicureanism and Philosophical Recruitment in Ancient Greece.* Berkeley.

Frye, N. 1957. *Anatomy of Criticism.* Princeton.

Fumerton, P. 1991. *Cultural Aesthetics: Renaissance Literature and the Practice of Social Ornament.* Chicago.

Galinsky, K. 1992a. *Classical and Modern Interactions.* Austin, Tex.

———, ed. 1992b. *The Interpretation of Roman Poetry: Empiricism or Hermeneutics?* Frankfurt.

———. 1996. *Augustan Culture: An Interpretive Introduction.* Princeton.

Gantar, K. 1972. "Horaz zwischen Akademie und Epikur." *Živa Antika* 22:5–24.

Garnsey, P., K. Hopkins, and C. R. Whittaker, eds. 1983. *Trade in the Ancient Economy.* Berkeley.

Gatz, B. 1967. *Weltalter, goldene Zeit und sinnverwandte Vorstellungen.* Spudasmata 16. Hildesheim.

Geertz, C. 1973. *The Interpretation of Cultures.* New York.

Gellrich, M. 1988. *Tragedy and Theory: The Problem of Conflict Since Aristotle.* Princeton.

Girard, R. 1977. *Violence and the Sacred.* Trans. P. Gregory. Baltimore.

———. 1986. *The Scapegoat.* Trans. Y. Freccero. Baltimore.

Goff, B., ed. 1995a. *History, Tragedy, Theory: Dialogues on Athenian Drama.* Austin. Tex.

———. 1995b. Introduction. In B. Goff, ed., *History, Tragedy, Theory: Dialogues on Athenian Drama,* 1–37. Austin. Tex.

Gold, B. K., ed. 1982. *Literary and Artistic Patronage in Ancient Rome.* Austin, Tex.

———. 1987. *Literary Patronage in Greece and Rome.* Chapel Hill, N.C.

———. 1992. "Openings in Horace's *Satires* and *Odes:* Poet, Patron, and Audience." In F. M. Dunn and T. Cole, eds., *Beginnings in Classical Literature. Yale Classical Studies* 29:161–86.

Goldhill, S. 1986. *Reading Greek Tragedy.* Cambridge.

———. 1990. "The Great Dionysia and Civic Ideology." In J. Winkler and F. Zeitlin, eds., *Nothing to Do with Dionysus? Athenian Drama in Its Social Context,* 97–129. Princeton.

Gordon, R. 1990a. "From Republic to Principate: Priesthood, Religion, and Ideology." In M. Beard and J. North, eds., *Pagan Priests: Religion and Power in the Ancient World,* 177–98. Ithaca.

———. 1990b. "Religion in the Roman Empire: The Civic Compromise and Its Limits." In M. Beard and J. North, eds., *Pagan Priests: Religion and Power in the Ancient World,* 233–55. Ithaca.

———. 1990c. "The Veil of Power: Emperors, Sacrificers, and Benefactors." In M. Beard and J. North, eds., *Pagan Priests: Religion and Power in the Ancient World,* 199–231. Ithaca.

Goux, J-J. 1990. *Symbolic Economies: After Marx and Freud.* Trans. J. Gage. Ithaca.

Greenblatt, S. 1980. *Renaissance Self-Fashioning.* Chicago.

Gregory, C. A. 1982. *Gifts and Commodities.* London.

Griffin, J. 1984. "Augustus and the Poets: 'Caesar qui cogere posset.'" In F. Millar and E. Segal, eds., *Caesar Augustus: Seven Aspects,* 189–218. Oxford.

Griffin, M. T., and E. M. Atkins, eds. 1991. *Cicero, On Duties.* Trans. M. Atkins. Cambridge.

Grimal, P. 1975. "Les Odes romains d'Horace et les causes de la guerre civile." *Revues des Études Latines* 53:135–56.

Gummere, R. M., trans. 1920. *Seneca: Ad Lucilium Epistulae Morales*. 3 vols. Loeb Classical Library. Cambridge, Mass.

Gunning, J. H. 1960. "Der siebente Brief des Horaz und sein Verhältnis zu Maecenas." *Mnemosyne* 10:289–320.

Habinek, T. 1990a. "Sacrifice, Society, and Vergil's Ox-born Bees." In M. Griffith and D. J. Mastronarde, eds., *Cabinet of the Muses: Essays on Classical and Comparative Literature*, 209–23. Atlanta.

————. 1990b. "Towards a History of Friendly Advice: The Politics of Candor in Cicero's *De Amicitia*." *Apeiron* 23:165–85.

————. 1994. "Ideology for an Empire in the Prefaces to Cicero's Dialogues." *Ramus* 23:55–67.

————. 1998. *The Politics of Latin Literature*. Princeton.

Hadas, M. 1952. *A History of Latin Literature*. New York.

Hallet, J. 1993. "Feminist Theory, Historical Periods, Literary Canons, and the Study of Greco-Roman Antiquity." In N. S. Rabinowitz and A. Richlin, eds., *Feminist Theory and the Classics*, 44–72. New York.

Halliwell, S. 1986. *Aristotle's Poetics*. Chapel Hill, N.C.

Halperin, D. 1983. *Before Pastoral: Theocritus and the Ancient Tradition of Bucolic Poetry*. New Haven.

Händel, P. 1959. "Prodigium." In A. Pauly, G. Wissowa, and W. Kroll, eds., *Real-Encyclopädie der classischen Altertumswissenshaft*, 23.2:2283–96 (Nachträge). Stuttgart.

Harker, R., C. Mahar, and C. Wilkes, eds. 1990. *An Introduction to the Work of Pierre Bourdieu: The Practice of Theory*. London.

Harl, K. 1996. *Coinage in the Roman Economy: 300 B.C. to A.D. 700*. Baltimore.

Harris, W. V. 1989. *Ancient Literacy*. Cambridge.

Hartman, G. 1978. Preface to *Psychoanalysis and the Question of the Text*, ed. G. Hartman, vii–xix. Baltimore.

Hauthal, F., ed. 1966. *Acronis et Porphyrionis commentarii in Q. Horatium Flaccum*. Amsterdam.

Heath, M. 1987. *The Poetics of Greek Tragedy*. Stanford.

Hegel, G. W. F. 1975. *Aesthetics: Lectures on Fine Art*. Trans. T. M. Knox. 2 vols. Oxford.

Heinze, R. 1919. "Horazens Buch der Briefe." *Neues Jahrbuch* 43:305–16.

————. 1960. *Vom Geist des Römertums*. Darmstadt.

Hellegouarc'h, J. 1963. *Le vocabulaire latin des relations et des partis politiques sous la république*. Paris.

Hicks, R. D., trans. 1925. *Diogenes Laertius: Lives of Eminent Philosophers*. 2 vols. Loeb Classical Library. Cambridge, Mass.

Hiltbrunner, O. 1960. "Volteius Mena: Interpretationen zu Horace *Epist.* 1.7." *Gymnasium* 67:289–320.

————. 1967. "Der Gutsverwalter des Horaz." *Gymnasium* 74:297–314.

Hinds, S. 1998. *Allusion and Intertext: Dynamics of Appropriation in Roman Poetry*. Cambridge.

Hirth, H-J. 1985. *Horaz, der Dichter der Briefe: Rus und urbs—die Valenz der Briefform am Beispiel der ersten Epistel an Maecenas*. Hildesheim.

Hopkins, K. 1980. "Taxes and Trade in the Roman Empire." *Journal of Roman Studies* 70:101–25.

———. 1983a. *Death and Renewal.* Cambridge.

———. 1983b. Introduction to P. Garnsey, K. Hopkins, and C. R. Whittaker, eds., *Trade in the Ancient Economy,* viii–xxv. Berkeley.

Horsfall, N. 1981. "Poets and Patron: Maecenas, Horace, and the *Georgics,* Once More." *Publications of the Maquaries Ancient History Association* 1981.3:1–24.

Hubbard, T. K. 1995. "Intertextual Hermeneutics in Vergil's Fourth and Fifth Eclogues." *Classical Journal* 91.1:11–23.

Humphrey, J. H., ed. 1991. *Literacy in the Roman World.* Journal of Roman Archaeology Supplementary Series, no. 3. Ann Arbor, Mich.

Hyde, L. 1979. *The Gift: Imagination and the Erotic Life of Property.* New York.

Jameson, F. 1971. *Marxism and Form: Twentieth-Century Dialectical Theories of Literature.* Princeton.

———. 1981. *The Political Unconscious.* Ithaca.

Jocelyn, D. 1980. "The Fate of Varius' *Thyestes.*" *Classical Quarterly* 30:387–400.

Johnson, W. R. 1982. *The Idea of Lyric.* Berkeley.

———. 1993. *Horace and the Dialectic of Freedom: Readings in "Epistles" I.* Cornell.

Joplin, P. K. 1990. "Ritual Work on Human Flesh: Livy's Lucretia and the Rape of the Body Politic." *Helios* 17:51–70.

Kavanagh, J., and F. Jameson. 1984. "The Weakest Link: Marxism in Literary Studies." In B. Ollman and E. Vernoff, eds., *The Left Academy: Marxist Scholarship on American Campuses,* 2:1–23. Praeger Special Studies. New York.

Kennedy, D. 1992. "'Augustan' and 'Anti-Augustan'" Reflections on Terms of Reference." In A. Powell, ed., *Roman Poetry and Propaganda in the Age of Augustus,* 26–58. London.

Kennedy, G. 1972. *The Art of Rhetoric in the Roman World.* Princeton.

Kenner, H. 1971. *The Pound Era.* Berkeley.

Kenney, E. J. 1977. "A Question of Taste: Horace, *Epistles* 1.14.6–9." *Illinois Classical Studies* 2:229–39.

———. 1983. "Virgil and the Elegiac Sensibility." *Illinois Classical Studies* 8:49–52.

Kenney, E. J., and W. V. Clausen, eds. 1982. *The Cambridge History of Classical Literature.* Vol. 2, *Latin Literature.* Cambridge.

Keppie, L. 1983. *Colonisation and Veteran Settlement in Italy.* London.

Keyes, C. W., trans. 1928. *Cicero: De Legibus.* Loeb Classical Library. Cambridge, Mass.

Kiessling, A., and R. Heinze, eds. 1960. *Q. Horatius Flaccus: Oden und Epoden.* 10th ed. Berlin.

———, eds. 1961a. *Q Horatius Flaccus, Briefe.* 7th ed. Berlin.

———, eds. 1961b. *Q. Horatius Flaccus, Satiren.* 8th ed. Berlin.

Kilpatrick, R. 1986. *The Poetry of Friendship.* Edmonton.

———. 1990. *The Poetry of Criticism.* Edmonton.

Klingner, F. 1964a. "Horazens Römeroden." In *Studien zur griechischen und römischen Literatur,* 333–52. Zurich.

———. 1964b [1952]. "Ohnmacht und Macht des musischen Menschen, Horazens Ode Ille et nefasto (II, 13)." In *Studien zur griechischen und römischen Literatur,* 325–33. Zurich.

Konstan, D. 1975. "Marxism and Roman Slavery." *Arethusa* 8.1:145–69.

———. 1979. "A Comment on Class and Labor in Ancient Society." *Marxist Perspectives* 7:124–31.

———. 1995. "Patrons and Friends." *Classical Philology* 90:328–42.

———. 1997. *Friendship in the Classical World*. Cambridge.

Kornemann. 1903. "Pollios Geschichtswerk und Horaz, carm. 2,1." *Klio* 3:550–51.

Kurke, L. 1991. *The Traffic in Praise: Pindar and the Poetics of Social Economy*. Ithaca.

———. 1995. "Herodotus and the Language of Metals." *Helios* 22:36–64.

La Penna, A. 1963. *Orazio e l'ideologia del principato*. Turin.

Latte, K. 1960. *Römische Religionsgeschichte*. Munich.

Leach, E. W. 1974. *Vergil's "Eclogues": Landscapes of Experience*. Ithaca.

———. 1993a. "Absence and Desire in Cicero's *De Amicitia*." *Classical World* 87.2:3–20.

———. 1993b. "Horace's Sabine Topography in Lyric and Hexameter Verse." *American Journal of Philology* 114:271–302.

Lentricchia, F. 1989. "Foucault's Legacy: A New Historicism?" In H. A. Veeser, ed., *The New Historicism*, 231–42. New York.

Lévi-Strauss, C. 1987 [1950]. *Introduction to the Work of Marcel Mauss*. Trans. F. Baker. London.

Liebeschuetz, J. H. W. G. 1979. *Continuity and Change in Roman Religion*. Oxford.

Long, A. A., and D. N. Sedley, eds. 1987. *The Hellenistic Philosophers*. Vol. 2. Cambridge.

Lowrie, M. 1997. *Horace's Narrative Odes*. Oxford.

Lucas, D. W., ed. 1968. *Aristotle: Poetics*. Oxford.

Luterbacher, F. 1967 [1904]. *Der Prodigienglaube und Prodigienstil der Römer*. Darmstadt.

Lyne, R. O. A. M. 1995. *Horace: Behind the Public Poetry*. New Haven.

MacBain, B. 1982. *Prodigy and Expiation: A Study in Religion and Politics in Republican Rome*. Collection Latomus, no. 177. Brussels.

Macleod, C. 1983. "The Poetry of Ethics: Horace, *Epistles* I." In *Collected Essays*, 280–91. Oxford.

Malinowski, B. 1961 [1922]. *Argonauts of the Western Pacific*. New York.

Marcuse, H. 1974 [1955]. *Eros and Civilization*. Boston.

———. 1978. *The Aesthetic Dimension*. Boston.

Martindale, C. 1993. *Redeeming the Text*. Cambridge.

Marx, L. 1981 [1964]. *The Machine in the Garden: Technology and the Pastoral Ideal in America*. Oxford.

Maurach, G. 1968. "Der Grundriss von Horazens erstem Epistelbuch." *Acta Classica* 11:73–124.

Mauss, M. 1990 [1950]. *The Gift: The Form and Reason for Exchange in Archaic Societies*. Trans. W. D. Halls. New York.

Mayer, R. 1986. "Horace's *Epistles* 1 and Philosophy." *American Journal of Philology* 107:55–73.

———, ed. 1994. *Horace: Epistles, Book 1*. Cambridge.

———. 1995. "Horace's *Moyen de Parvenir*." In S. J. Harrison, ed., *Homage to Horace: A Bimillenary Celebration*, 279–95. Oxford.

McGann, M. J. 1960. "The Sixteenth Epistle of Horace." *Classical Quarterly* 10:205–12.

————. 1969. *Studies in Horace's First Book of Epistles*. Collection Latomus, no. 100. Brussels.

Merlan, P. 1949. "Epicureanism and Horace." *Journal of the History of Ideas* 10:445–51.

Merquior, J. G. 1979. *The Veil and the Mask: Essays on Culture and Ideology*. London.

Miller, P. 1994. *Lyric Texts and Lyric Consciousness*. London.

Miller, W., trans. 1913. *Cicero: De Officiis*. Loeb Classical Library. Cambridge, Mass.

Mitsis, P. 1988. *Epicurus' Ethical Theory: The Pleasures of Invulnerability*. Ithaca.

Morris, E. P., ed. 1939. *Horace: Satires and Epistles*. Norman, Okla.

Moussy, C. 1966. *Gratia et sa famille*. Paris.

Murray, O. 1990. Introduction to *Bread and Circuses: Historical Sociology and Political Pluralism*, by P. Veyne, vii–xxii. London.

Mynors, R. A. B., ed. 1969. *P. Vergil Maronis Opera*. Oxford.

Nadeau, Y. 1980. "Speaking Structures: Horace, Odes 2.1 to 2.19." In C. Deroux, ed., *Studies in Latin Literature and Roman History*, 2:177–222. Brussels.

Nagy, G. 1990. *Pindar's Homer: The Lyric Possession of an Epic Past*. Baltimore.

Newman, J. K. 1967. *The Concept of Vates in Augustan Poetry*. Collection Latomus, no. 89. Brussels.

Nicolet, C. 1966. *L'Ordre équestre à l'époque républicaine*. Paris.

————. 1984. "Augustus, Government, and the Propertied Classes." In F. Millar and E. Segal, eds., *Caesar Augustus: Seven Aspects*, 89–128. Oxford.

————. 1988. *The World of the Citizen in Republican Rome*. Trans. P. S. Falla. Berkeley.

Nicoll, W. S. M. 1986. "Horace's Judgement on Sappho and Alcaeus." *Latomus* 45: 603–8.

Nicols, J. 1995. "Civic Patronage in Ancient Rome." Department of History, University of Oregon. Typescript.

Nietzsche, F. 1967. *The Birth of Tragedy and the Case of Wagner*. Trans. W. Kauffman. New York.

Nisbet, R. G. M., and M. Hubbard, eds. 1970. *A Commentary on Horace: Odes, Book I*. Oxford.

————, eds. 1991 [1978]. *A Commentary on Horace: Odes, Book II*. Oxford.

Nussbaum, M. C. 1994. *The Therapy of Desire: Theory and Practice in Hellenistic Ethics*. Princeton.

Obbink, D., ed. 1995. *Philodemus and Poetry: Poetic Theory and Practice in Lucretius, Philodemus, and Horace*. Oxford.

Ogilvie, R. M. 1961. "Lustrum Condere." *Journal of Roman Studies* 51:31–39.

Oldfather, W. A., trans. 1952. *Epictetus: The Discourses as Reported by Arrian; the Manual; and Fragments*. Loeb Classical Library. Cambridge, Mass.

Oliensis, E. 1995. "Life After Publication: *Epistles* 1.20." *Arethusa* 28.2–3:209–24.

————. 1997. "*Ut arte emendaturus fortunam:* Horace, Masidienus, and the Art of Satire." In T. Habinek and A. Schiersaro, eds., *The Roman Cultural Revolution*, 90–104. Cambridge.

————. 1998. *Horace and the Rhetoric of Authority*. Cambridge.

Ollman, B., and E. Vernoff, eds. 1984. *The Left Academy: Marxist Scholarship on American Campuses*. Praeger Special Studies. New York.

Packard Humanities Institute Database of Latin Texts. 1991. CD ROM no. 5.3. Los Altos, Calif.

Pascal, C. B. 1982. "Do ut des." *Epigraphica* 14.1–2:7–16.

———. 1990. "The Dubious Devotion of Turnus." *Transactions of the American Philological Association* 120:251–68.

Pasquali, G. 1964 [1920]. *Orazio Lirico Studi.* Firenze.

Patterson, A. 1987. *Pastoral and Ideology: Virgil to Valéry.* Berkeley.

Pavlock, B. 1982. "Horace's Invitation Poems to Maecenas: Gifts to a Patron." *Ramus* 11:70–98.

Penwill, J. L. 1994. "Image, Ideology and Action in Cicero and Lucretius." *Ramus* 23:68–91.

Peradotto, J. 1983. "Texts and Unrefracted Facts: Philology, Hermeneutics, and Semiotics." *Arethusa* 16.1–2:15–34.

Perkell, C. 1990a. "On *Eclogue* 1.79–83." *Transactions of the American Philological Association* 120:171–81.

———. 1990b. "Vergilian Scholarship in the Nineties: A Panel. The *Eclogues.*" *Vergilius* 36:43–55.

———. 1996. "'The Dying Gallus' and the Design of *Eclogue* 10." *Classical Philology* 91:128–40.

Perret, J. 1964. *Horace.* Trans. B. Humez. New York.

Peterson, W., ed. 1891. *M. Fabi Quintiliani Institutionis Oratoriae Liber Decimus.* Oxford.

Polanyi, K. 1968. *Primitive, Archaic, and Modern Economies: Essays of Karl Polanyi.* Ed. G. Dalton. Garden City, N.Y.

Porter, D. H. 1987. *Horace's Poetic Journey: A Reading of Odes 1–3.* Princeton.

Pöschl, V. 1968. "Poetry and Philosophy in Horace." In D. C. Allen and H. T. Rowell, eds., *The Poetic Tradition,* 47–61. Baltimore.

———. 1991. *Horazische Lyrik.* Expanded ed. Heidelberg.

Powell, A. 1992. *Roman Poetry and Propaganda in the Age of Augustus.* London.

Préaux, J. Q., ed 1968. *Horatius Flaccus. Epistulae. Liber Primus.* Paris.

Preminger, A., and T. V. F. Brogan, eds. 1993. *New Princeton Encyclopedia of Poetry and Poetics.* Princeton.

Pucci, P. 1975. "Horace's Banquet in *Odes* 1.17." *Transactions of the American Philological Association* 105:259–81.

———. 1992. "Human Sacrifices in the *Oresteia.*" In R. Hexter and D. Selden, eds., *Innovations in Antiquity,* 513–36. Routledge.

Putnam, M. C. J. 1970. *Vergil's Pastoral Art: Studies in the Eclogues.* Princeton.

———. 1986. *Artifices of Eternity. Horace's Fourth Book of Odes.* Ithaca.

———. 1994. "Structure and Design in Horace *Odes* 1.17." *Classical World* 87.5:357–75.

———. 1995. "From Lyric to Letter: Iccius in Horace *Odes* 1.29 and *Epistles* 1.20." *Arethusa* 28.2–3:193–207.

Quinn, K. 1982. "The Poet and His Audience in the Augustan Age." *Aufstieg und Niedergang der römischen Welt (ANRW)* 2.30.1:76–180. Berlin.

———, ed. 1992 [1980]. *Horace: The Odes.* Edinburgh.

Raaflaub, K., and M. Toher, eds. 1990. *Between Republic and Empire: Interpretations of Augustus and His Principate.* Berkeley.

Rackham, H., trans. 1914. *Cicero: De Finibus.* Loeb Classical Library. Cambridge, Mass.

Rawson, E. 1987. *"Discrimina Ordinum:* The *Lex Julia Theatralis."* *Papers of the British School at Rome* 55:83–114.

Reckford, K. J. 1958. "Some Appearances of the Golden Age." *Classical Journal* 54.2: 79–87.

———. 1959. "Horace and Maecenas." *Transactions of the American Philological Association* 90:195–208.

———. 1969. *Horace.* New York.

Rolfe, J. C., trans. 1914. *Suetonius.* 2 vols. Loeb Classical Library. Cambridge, Mass.

Rose, P. 1992. *Sons of the Gods; Children of Earth: Ideology and Literary Form in Ancient Greece.* Ithaca.

———. 1995. "Historicizing Sophocles' Ajax." In B. Goff, ed. *History, Tragedy, Theory: Dialogues on Athenian Drama,* 59–90. Austin, Tex.

Rosenmeyer, T. 1969. *The Green Cabinet: Theocritus and the European Pastoral Lyric.* Berkeley.

Rudd, N. 1966. *The Satires of Horace: A Study.* Cambridge.

———, ed. 1989. *Horace: Epistles Book II and Epistle to the Pisones.* Cambridge.

Sahlins, M. 1965. "On the Sociology of Primitive Exchange." In M. Banton, ed., *The Relevance of Models for Social Anthropology,* 139–236. New York.

———. 1968. *Tribesmen.* Englewood Cliffs, N.J.

———. 1972. *Stone Age Economics.* New York.

Saller, R. P. 1982. *Personal Patronage under the Early Empire.* Cambridge.

———. 1989. "Patronage and Friendship in Early Imperial Rome: Drawing the Distinction." In A. Wallace-Hadrill, ed., *Patronage in Ancient Society,* 49–62. New York.

Sallman, K. 1987. "Lyrischer Krieg. Die Verschiebung der Genera in der Pollio Ode, 2.1 des Horaz." In *Filologia e forme letterarie. Studi Offerti a Francesco della Corte,* 69–87. Urbino.

Santirocco, M. 1986. *Unity and Design in Horace's Odes.* Chapel Hill, N.C.

———. 1995. "Horace and Augustan Ideology." *Arethusa* 2.3:225–43.

Schiller, F. 1966. *Naive and Sentimental Poetry; On the Sublime.* Trans. J. A. Elias. New York.

———. 1967. *On the Aesthetic Education of Man.* Ed. and trans. E. Wilkinson and L. A. Willoughby. Oxford.

Schmidt, E. A. 1977. "Das horazische Sabinum als Dichterlandschaft." *Antike und Abendland* 23:97–112

Schönbeck, G. 1962. *Der Locus Amoenus Von Homer Bis Horaz.* Diss., Heidelberg.

Scullard, H. H. 1981. *Festivals and Ceremonies of the Roman Republic.* London.

Seaford, R. 1994. *Reciprocity and Ritual: Homer and Tragedy in the Developing City State.* Oxford.

Seeck, O. 1902. "Horaz an Pollio." *Wiener Studien* 24:499–510.

Segal, C. 1981. *Poetry and Myth in Ancient Pastoral. Essays on Theocritus and Vergil.* Princeton.

Shackleton Bailey, D. R., ed. 1977. *Cicero: Epistulae Ad Familiares.* Cambridge.

———, ed. 1985. *Horatius: Opera.* Stuttgart.

Shell, M. 1978. *The Economy of Literature.* Baltimore.

———. 1982. *Money, Language, and Thought: Literary and Philosophical Economics from the Medieval to the Modern Era.* Berkeley.

Sherwin-White, A. N. 1966. *The Letters of Pliny: A Historical and Social Commentary*.

Shorey, P., and G. Laing, eds. 1960. *Horace: Odes and Epodes*. New York.

Silk, E. T. 1973. "Towards a Fresh Interpretation of Horace, Carm. III. 1." *Yale Classical Studies* 23:131–45.

Silverman, K. 1983. *The Subject of Semiotics*. New York.

Smith, B. L. 1968. "Propaganda." In *International Encyclopedia of the Social Sciences*. New York.

Sonnenburg, P. E. 1904. "De Horatio et Pollione." *Rheinisches Museum* 59:506–11.

Starr, R. J. 1987. "The Circulation of Literary Texts in the Roman World." *Classical Quarterly* 37:213–23.

Stowers, S. 1986. *Letter Writing in Greco-Roman Antiquity*. Philadelphia.

Sykutris, J. 1931. *Paulys Realencyclopädie der classischen Altertumswissenschaft*. Supplement 5. Munich.

Syme, R. 1960 [1939]. *The Roman Revolution*. London.

Syndikus, H. P. 1972. *Die Lyrik des Horaz, Eine Interpretation der Oden*. Vol. 1, *Erstes und zweites Buch*. Darmstadt.

———. 1973. *Die Lyrik des Horaz, Eine Interpretation der Oden*. Vol. 2, *Drittes und viertes Buch*. Darmstadt.

Taylor, L. R. 1968. "Republican and Augustan Writers Enrolled in the Equestrian Centuries." *Transactions of the American Philological Association* 99:469–86.

Tchernia, A. 1983. "Italian Wine in Gaul." In P. Garnsey, K. Hopkins, and C. R. Whittaker, eds., *Trade in the Ancient Economy*, 87–104. Berkeley.

Teuffel, W. S. 1870. *Geschichte der römischen Literatur*. Leipzig.

Thilo, G., ed. 1887. *Servii Grammatici Qui Feruntur in Vergilii Bucolica et Georgica Commentarii*. Leipzig.

Thomas, R. F. 1982. *Lands and Peoples in Roman Poetry: The Ethnographical Tradition*. Cambridge.

Thome, G. 1992. "Crime and Punishment, Guilt and Expiation: Roman Thought and Vocabulary." *Acta Classica* 35:73–98.

Treggiari, S. 1969. *Roman Freedmen During the Late Republic*. Oxford.

———. 1979. "Sentiment and Property: Some Roman Attitudes." In A. Parel and T. Flanagan, eds., *Theories of Property: Aristotle to the Present*, 53–85. Waterloo, Ont.

Turner, V. 1974. *Dramas, Fields, and Metaphors: Symbolic Action in Human Society*. Ithaca.

Ullman, B. L. 1942. "History and Tragedy." *Transactions of the American Philological Association* 73:25–53.

Van Sickle, J. 1978. *The Design of Vergil's "Bucolics."* Rome.

Veeser, H. A., ed. 1989. *The New Historicism*. New York.

Vernant, J-P, and P. Vidal-Nacquet. 1988. *Myth and Tragedy in Ancient Greece*. Trans. J. Lloyd. New York.

Veyne, P. 1988. *Roman Erotic Elegy: Love, Poetry, and the West*. Trans. D. Pellauer. Chicago.

———. 1990. *Bread and Circuses: Historical Sociology and Political Pluralism*. Trans. B. Pearce. London.

Ville, G. 1981. *La gladiature en occident des origines à la mort de Domitien*. Rome.

Voit, L. 1975. "Das Sabinum im 16.Brief des Horaz." *Gymnasium* 82:412–26.

Walbank, F. W. 1960. "History and Tragedy." *Historia* 9:216–34.

Wallace-Hadrill, A. 1982. "The Golden Age and Sin in Augustan Ideology." *Past and Present* 95:19–36.

———. 1989. "Patronage in Roman Society: from Republic to Empire." In A. Wallace-Hadrill, ed., *Patronage in Ancient Society,* 63–88. New York.

Walsh, G. 1984. *The Varieties of Enchantment.* Chapel Hill, N.C.

Watson, A. 1968. *The Law of Property in the Later Roman Republic.* Oxford.

———. 1975. *Rome of the XII Tables.* Princeton.

White, K. D. 1970. *Roman Farming.* Ithaca.

White, P. 1978. "Amicitia and the Profession of Poetry in Early Imperial Rome." *Journal of Roman Studies* 68:74–92.

———. 1982. "Positions for Poets in Early Imperial Rome." In B. Gold, ed., *Literary and Artistic Patronage in Ancient Rome,* 50–66. Austin, Tex.

———. 1993. *Promised Verse: Poets in the Society of Augustan Rome.* Harvard.

Wickham, E. C., ed. 1901. *Q. Horati Flacci Opera.* Oxford.

Wili, W. 1948. *Horaz und die Augusteische Kultur.* Basel.

Wilkins, A. S., ed. 1955. *Q. Horati Flacci Epistulae.* London.

Wilkinson, L. P. 1963. *Golden Latin Artistry.* Cambridge.

Williams, G. 1968. *Tradition and Originality.* London.

———, ed. 1969. *The Third Book of Horace's Odes.* Oxford.

———. 1980. *Figures of Thought in Roman Poetry.* New Haven.

———. 1982. "Phases in Political Patronage of Literature in Rome." In B. Gold, ed., *Literary and Artistic Patronage in Ancient Rome,* 3–27. Austin, Tex.

———. 1990. "Did Maecenas 'Fall from Favor'?" In K. A. Raaflaub and M. Toher, eds., *Between Republic and Empire: Interpretations of Augustus and His Principate,* 258–75. Berkeley.

———. 1995. "*Libertino Patre Natus:* True or False?" In S. J. Harrison, ed., *Homage to Horace: A Bimillenary Celebration,* 296–313. Oxford.

Williams, R. D., ed. 1979. *Virgil: The Eclogues and Georgics.* New York.

Williams, W. G., trans. 1929. *Cicero: The Letters to His Friends.* 3 vols. Loeb Classical Library. Cambridge, Mass.

Wimmel, W. 1960. *Kallimachos in Rom.* Wiesbaden.

———. 1969. "Vir bonus et sapiens dignis ait esse paratus. Zur horazischen Epistel 1.7." *Wiener Studien* 82:60–74.

Wirszubski, C. 1968. *Libertas as a Political Idea at Rome during the Late Republic and Early Principate.* London.

Wissowa, G. 1902. *Religion und Kultus der Römer.* Munich.

Witke, C. 1983. *Horace's Roman Odes: A Critical Examination.* Mnemosyne Supplement, no. 77. Leiden.

Wülker, L. 1903. *Die geschichtliche Entwicklung des Prodigienwesens bei den Römern.* Leipzig.

Zanker, P. 1988. *The Power of Images in the Age of Augustus.* Ann Arbor, Mich.

Zeitlin, F. 1990. "Playing the Other: Theater, Theatricality, and the Feminine in Greek Drama." In J. Winkler and F. Zeitlin, eds., *Nothing to Do with Dionysus? Athenian Drama in Its Social Context,* 63–96. Princeton.

Zetzel, J. E. G. 1982. "The Poetics of Patronage in the Late First Century B.C." In B. Gold, ed., *Literary and Artistic Patronage in Ancient Rome,* 87–102. Austin, Tex.

SUBJECT INDEX

INDEX LOCORUM

Text: 10/12 Baskerville
Display: Baskerville
Composition: Binghamton Valley Composition
Printing and binding: Maple-Vail Book Manufacturing Group